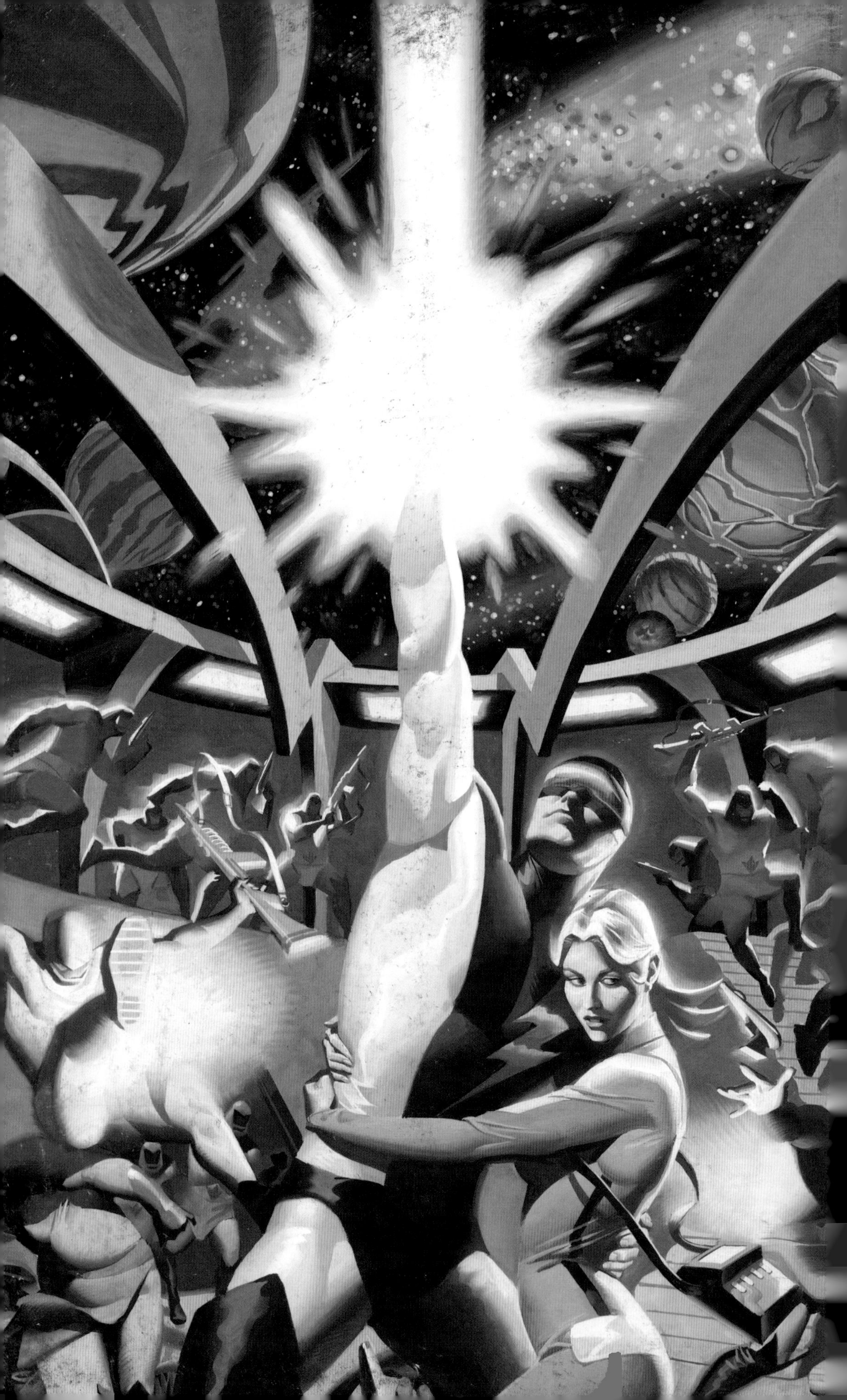

Mike Baron • Steve Rude

NEXUS™

Volume One

NEXUS CREATED BY
Mike Baron
and Steve Rude

FOREWORD BY
Mike Baron

DARK HORSE BOOKS™

PUBLISHER
Mike Richardson

COLLECTION DESIGNER
Heidi Fainza

COLLECTION EDITOR
Dave Land

ART DIRECTOR
Lia Ribacchi

Published by
Dark Horse Books
A division of Dark Horse Comics, Inc.

Dark Horse Comics, Inc.
10956 SE Main Street
Milwaukie, Oregon 97222

darkhorse.com
bloodyredbaron.com
steverude.com

To find a comic shop in your area, call the
Comic Shop Locator Service: (888) 266-4226

First Edition: November 2005
ISBN: 1-59307-398-4

1 3 5 7 9 10 8 6 4 2

Printed in China

NEXUS™ ARCHIVES: VOLUME ONE

This volume collects issues one through three of *Nexus* and issues one through four of *Nexus* Volume Two originally
published by Captial Comics.

TABLE OF CONTENTS
WRITTEN BY MIKE BARON
ART BY STEVE RUDE

FOREWORD
by Mike Baron

I was flipping through an old calendar the other day and came across the first drawing of Nexus, from August 31, 1981. It's obviously the Dude's—I could never draw that lightly or fluidly. The boys at Capital City Distribution wanted to publish a superhero comic. Dude and I hashed it out over bratwurst, lutefisk, and beer. Our hero was a killer of mass murderers, thereby guaranteeing a violent death every issue. He was Russian—my own ancestors were Russian—cursed with a Siberian gloom and a fatalistic outlook, but blessed with a soaring romantic vision. A killer poet.

The twenty-sixth century accrued mass randomly, like a cosmic event. The Dude was enamored of Kirby and Dr. Seuss. I was in thrall to Frank Herbert, Philip Jose Farmer, and film noir. We found common ground in man's inhumanity to man. In *On Moral Fiction*, John Gardner speaks of the need for art to be transformative, not merely entertaining. We must see the triumph of good over evil, eventually, or what's the point? This simple truth is obvious to most comic-book readers, not so obvious to everyone else. When entertainment does not provide uplift, the audience goes elsewhere. The most popular fictions of our time, *Star Wars* and *The Lord of the Rings*, are battles between good and evil. So is it with *Nexus*. We used to rip stories, like steaming entrails, from the daily news, casting human foibles across an alien sky.

Dude still calls, bristling with outrage, at the premature release of a pedophile or the apprehension of a serial killer. He's upset. He wants to do something. I wouldn't put it past him to patrol his neighborhood with a cell phone and a club. More often, that outrage got channeled into our stories. Egotisto Bighair was Radovan Karadzic.

Clayborn contained elements of everyone from Jeffrey Dahmer to the BTK killer. Man cannot live by dread alone. A steady diet of serial killers is worse than a steady diet of cereal. Nexus' expanding universe opened doors to every imaginable type of story. The book frequently trespassed on real science fiction as I tried to ape my idols' moods. The bowl-shaped world was Farmer. I tried to channel Ursula Le Guin in "Killers Unlimited." I thought of Frank Herbert while writing Kreed and Sinclair's berserker days. Not that I consciously tried to emulate their styles, but their moods, their daring, the liberties they took with the laws of physics. Most stories formed around personalities and situations. Precious few formed around ideas.

One idea was that Nexus would trick a group of murderers into murdering one another. "The Experiment" is one of my favorite stories and a fine tribute to Rutger Hauer. Another idea was that enforced conformity inevitably leads to violence, as in "Killers Unlimited."

Dude frequently inserted Egbert, an egg-shaped bird, howler monkeys from the University of Wisconsin Animal Research Lab, and fugitives from Dr. Seuss, Jack Kirby, and Alex Toth. *Nexus* represents a collision of worlds—Dude's and mine. I've always been troubled that we're both human. It's presumptuous of me to create alien species and assign them personalities. If only we had a real alien for input. I could ask any woman, but that's not what I mean. I've come to grips with the fact that everything we write and draw is for consumption by human beings, and it would be pointless and suicidal to attempt a true alien point of view. We could drive ourselves insane. It's always about people. The human however, can twist itself into unrecognizable patterns. Some people go for an alien point of view and it drives them insane.

When *Nexus* #98 came out in 1997, Sundra was pregnant. Time marches on. Nexus and Sundra are now the proud parents of a nine-year-old kid. We have a green light to resume their adventures as soon as Dude finishes with *The Moth*. If you have not seen *The Moth*, every issue is available from Dark Horse. The Moth is Jack Mahoney, circus performer by day, champion of justice by night. Written and inked by Gary Martin, it's a loving tribute to old-time serials and Jack Kirby.

History has left us gasping for breath. When I wrote the Sov stories, I thought the Soviet Union would endure for centuries, a gross, helpless giant, perpetually starved for food, energy, and freedom. How wrong I was. Things only seem like they're forever until suddenly one day they're not. Not even the physical world is secure from rapid change. People thought nothing of living or vacationing on Thailand's golden beaches year after year until one day the sea rose up and slapped civilization in the face. Hard.

I thought the bitter standoffs in Northern Ireland and Israel would last forever. Now even those political Gordian knots are beginning to unravel. Of course they could go south in a hurry. Nothing is as immutable as human nature, and all attempts to breed a better human being (e.g., communism and other wealth redistribution schemes) are doomed to failure. Humanity's a bell curve. Losers on the left, most in the middle, winners on the right. What has changed is mankind's knowledge of what is attainable. The miserable billions born into tyranny need only turn on their televisions (or the village chief's television) to see what's happening in the rest of the world. Not even remotest Tibet is safe from the blandishments of Britney Spears. Political change follows technology. Without advances in telecommunications and electronics, the miserable billions might have remained ignorant of how the rest of the world was doing. Science fiction has always led the way.

I never thought I'd write science fiction. It seemed too daunting. I wouldn't attempt it now except that it's a comic book, and Dude does all the heavy lifting. I have come to grips with the fact that I'm writing for a human audience. There's an alien audience out there—I just know it. If only we could reach them.

—Mike Baron

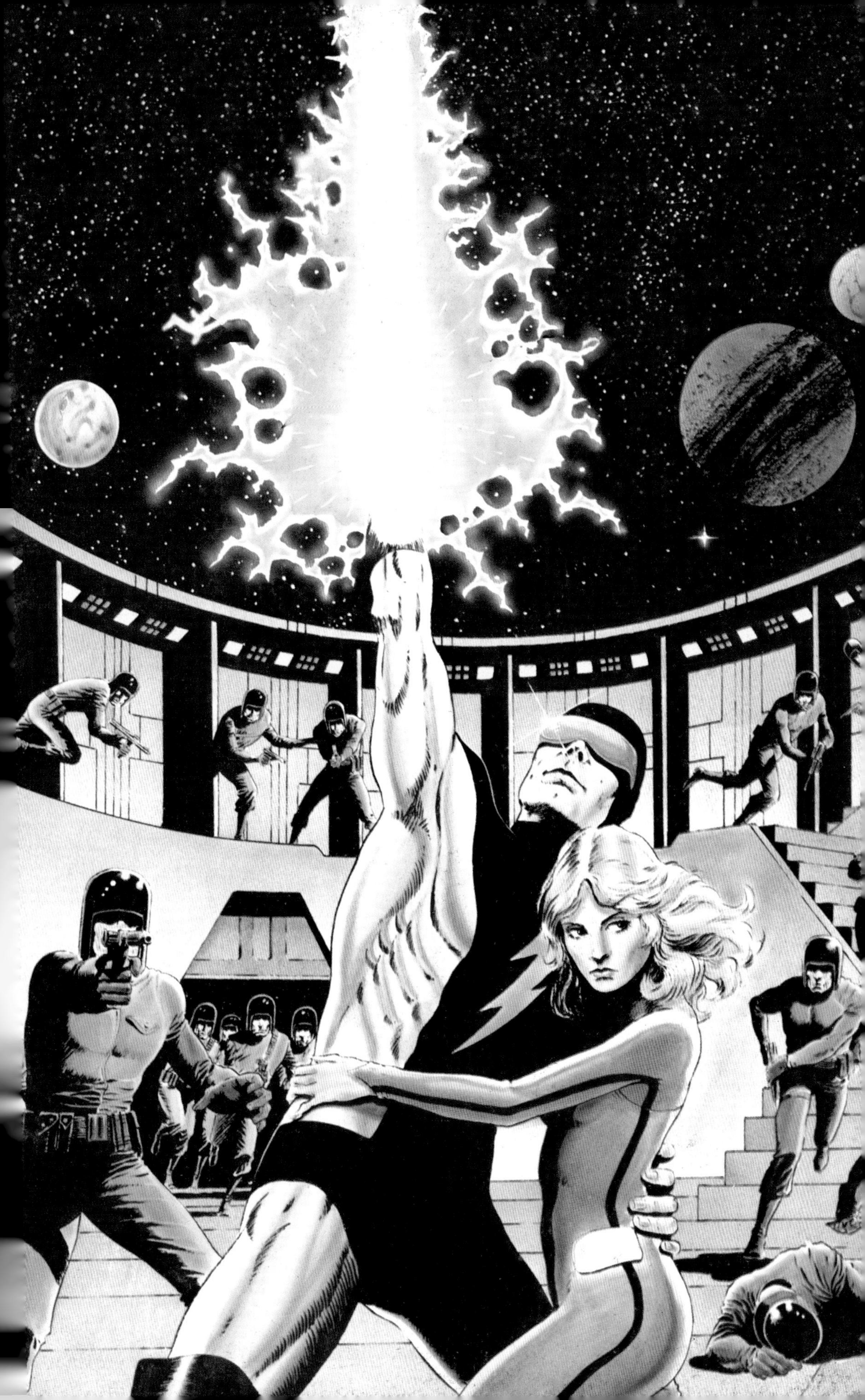

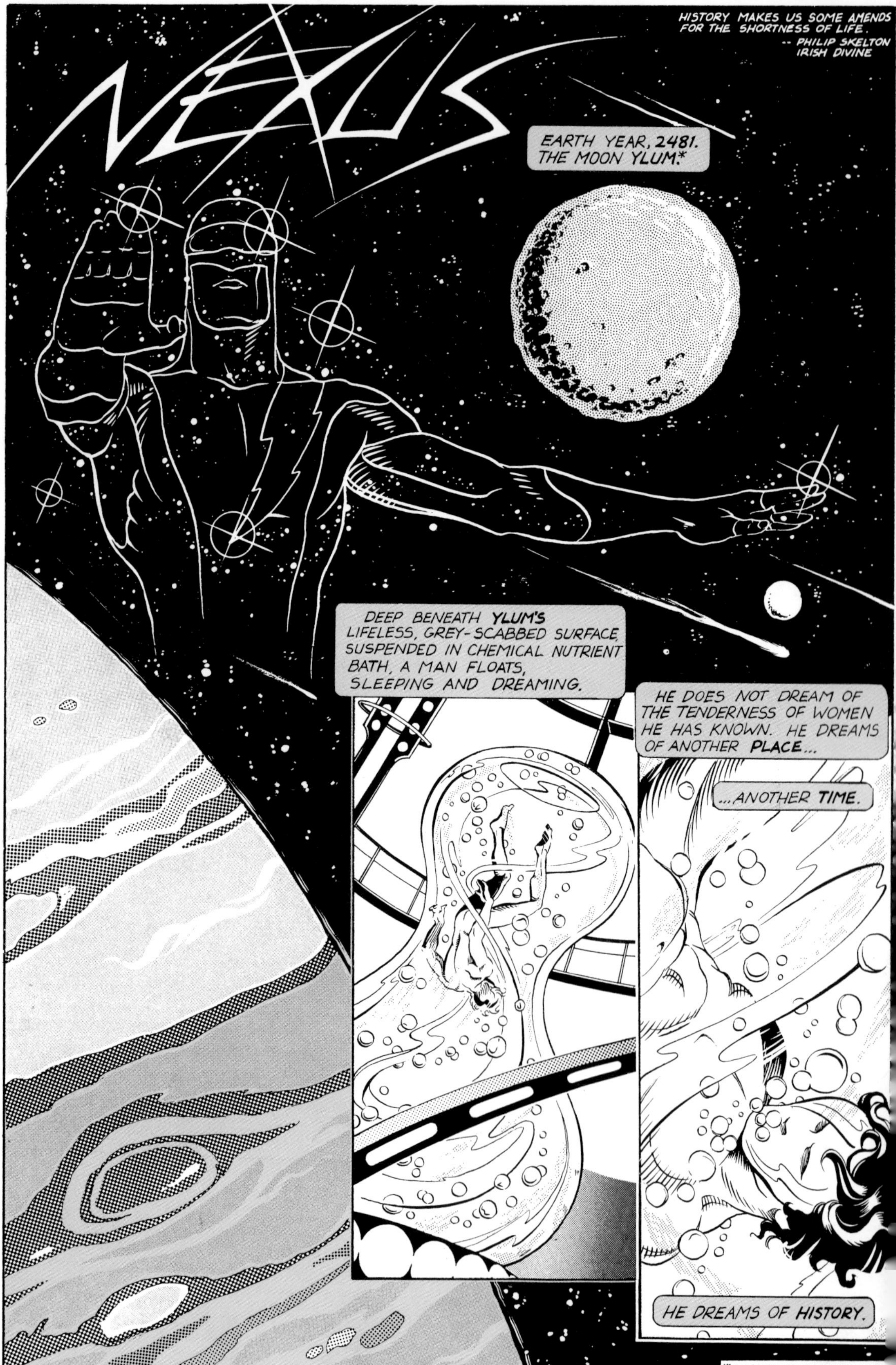
NEXUS
HISTORY MAKES US SOME AMENDS FOR THE SHORTNESS OF LIFE.
-- PHILIP SKELTON IRISH DIVINE
EARTH YEAR, 2481. THE MOON YLUM.*
DEEP BENEATH YLUM'S LIFELESS, GREY-SCABBED SURFACE, SUSPENDED IN CHEMICAL NUTRIENT BATH, A MAN FLOATS, SLEEPING AND DREAMING.
HE DOES NOT DREAM OF THE TENDERNESS OF WOMEN HE HAS KNOWN. HE DREAMS OF ANOTHER PLACE...
...ANOTHER TIME.
HE DREAMS OF HISTORY.
*PRONOUNCED, "EYE-LUM."

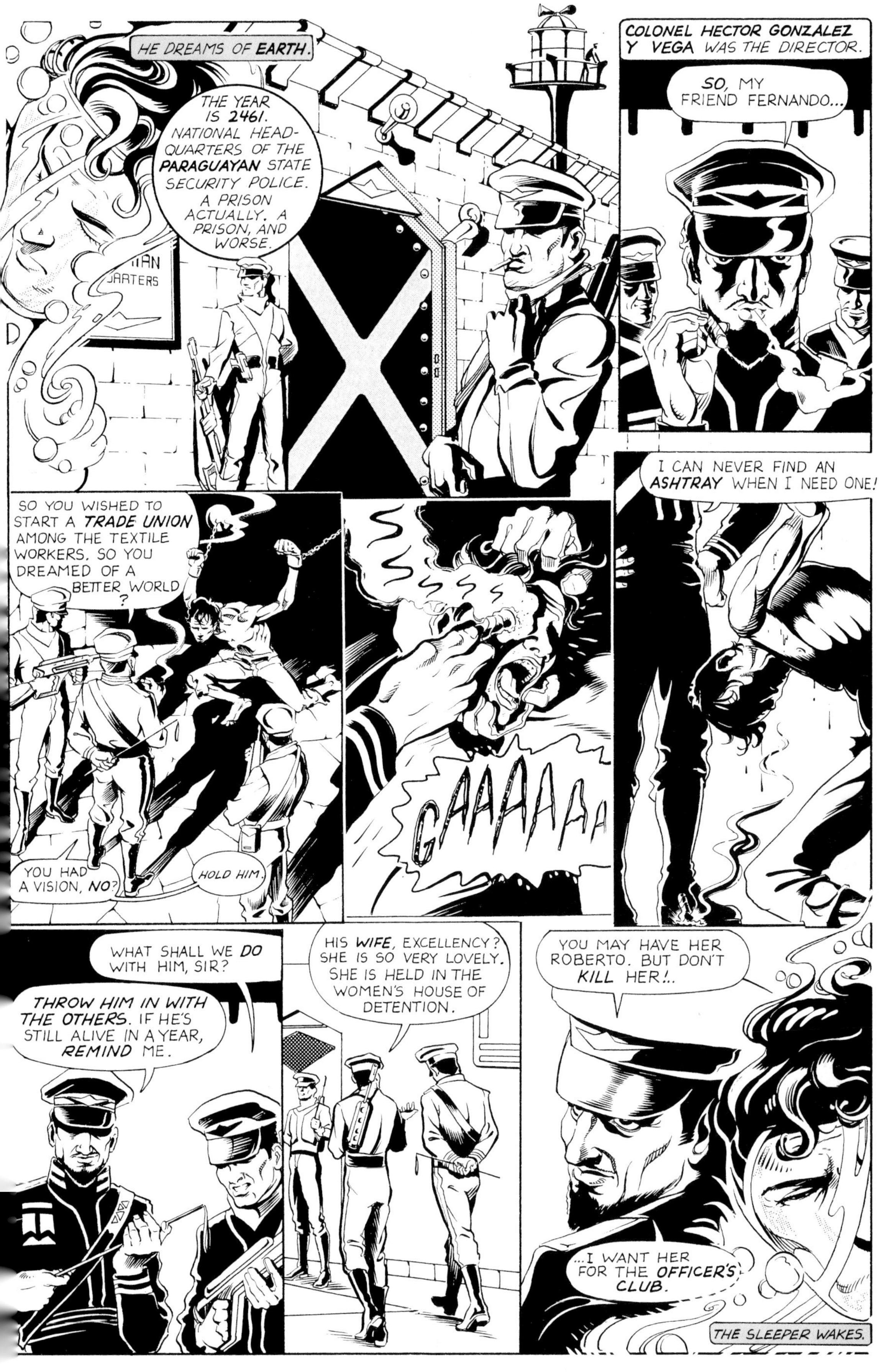

HE DREAMS OF EARTH.
THE YEAR IS 2461. NATIONAL HEAD-QUARTERS OF THE PARAGUAYAN STATE SECURITY POLICE. A PRISON ACTUALLY. A PRISON, AND WORSE.
COLONEL HECTOR GONZALEZ Y VEGA WAS THE DIRECTOR.
SO, MY FRIEND FERNANDO...
SO YOU WISHED TO START A TRADE UNION AMONG THE TEXTILE WORKERS. SO YOU DREAMED OF A BETTER WORLD?
YOU HAD A VISION, NO?
HOLD HIM.
GAAAAAA
I CAN NEVER FIND AN ASHTRAY WHEN I NEED ONE!
WHAT SHALL WE DO WITH HIM, SIR?
THROW HIM IN WITH THE OTHERS. IF HE'S STILL ALIVE IN A YEAR, REMIND ME.
HIS WIFE, EXCELLENCY? SHE IS SO VERY LOVELY. SHE IS HELD IN THE WOMEN'S HOUSE OF DETENTION.
YOU MAY HAVE HER ROBERTO. BUT DON'T KILL HER!..
...I WANT HER FOR THE OFFICER'S CLUB.
THE SLEEPER WAKES.

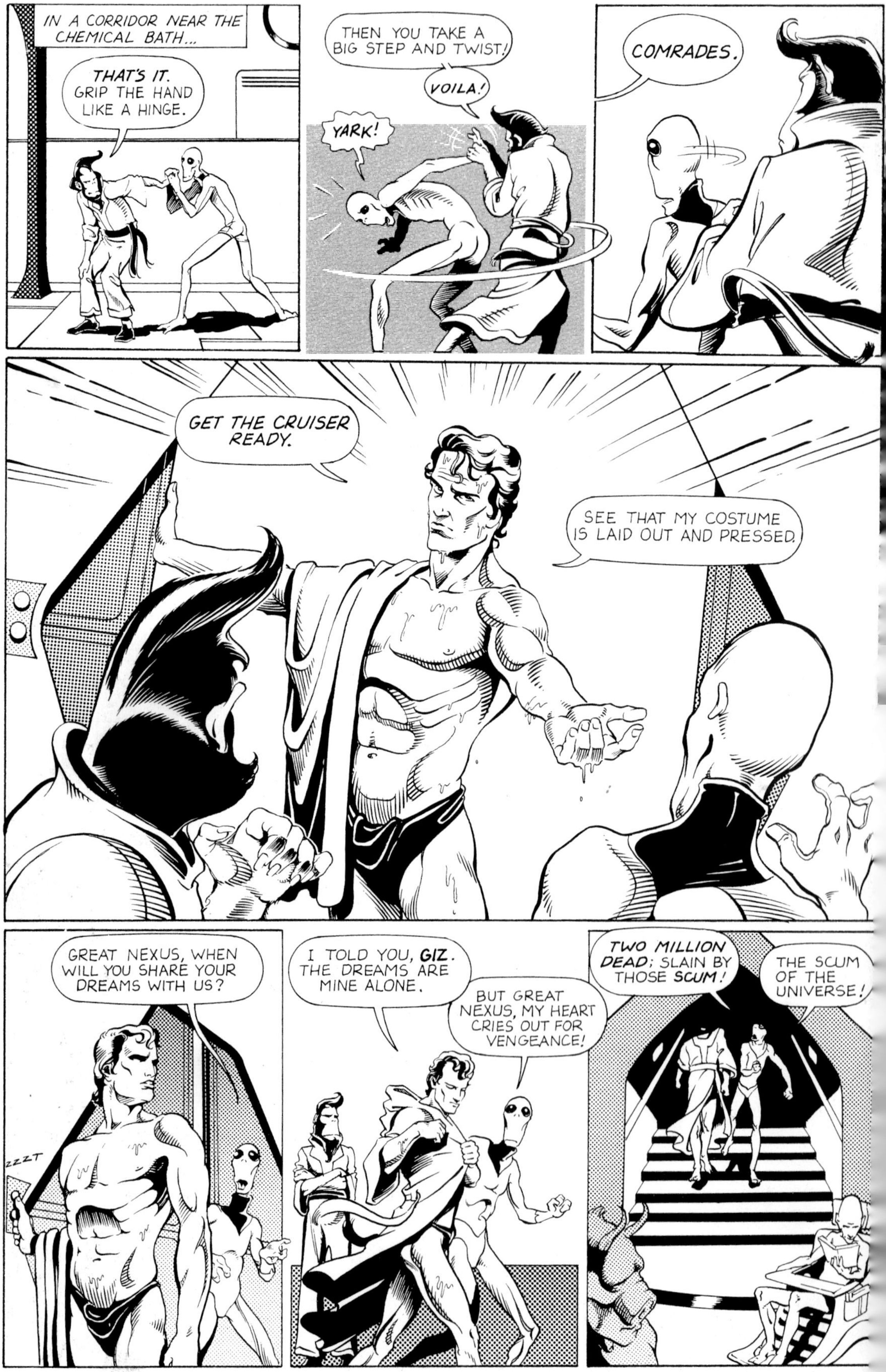
IN A CORRIDOR NEAR THE CHEMICAL BATH...
THAT'S IT. GRIP THE HAND LIKE A HINGE.
THEN YOU TAKE A BIG STEP AND TWIST!
VOILA!
YARK!
COMRADES.
GET THE CRUISER READY.
SEE THAT MY COSTUME IS LAID OUT AND PRESSED.
GREAT NEXUS, WHEN WILL YOU SHARE YOUR DREAMS WITH US?
ZZZT
I TOLD YOU, GIZ. THE DREAMS ARE MINE ALONE.
BUT GREAT NEXUS, MY HEART CRIES OUT FOR VENGEANCE!
TWO MILLION DEAD; SLAIN BY THOSE SCUM!
THE SCUM OF THE UNIVERSE!

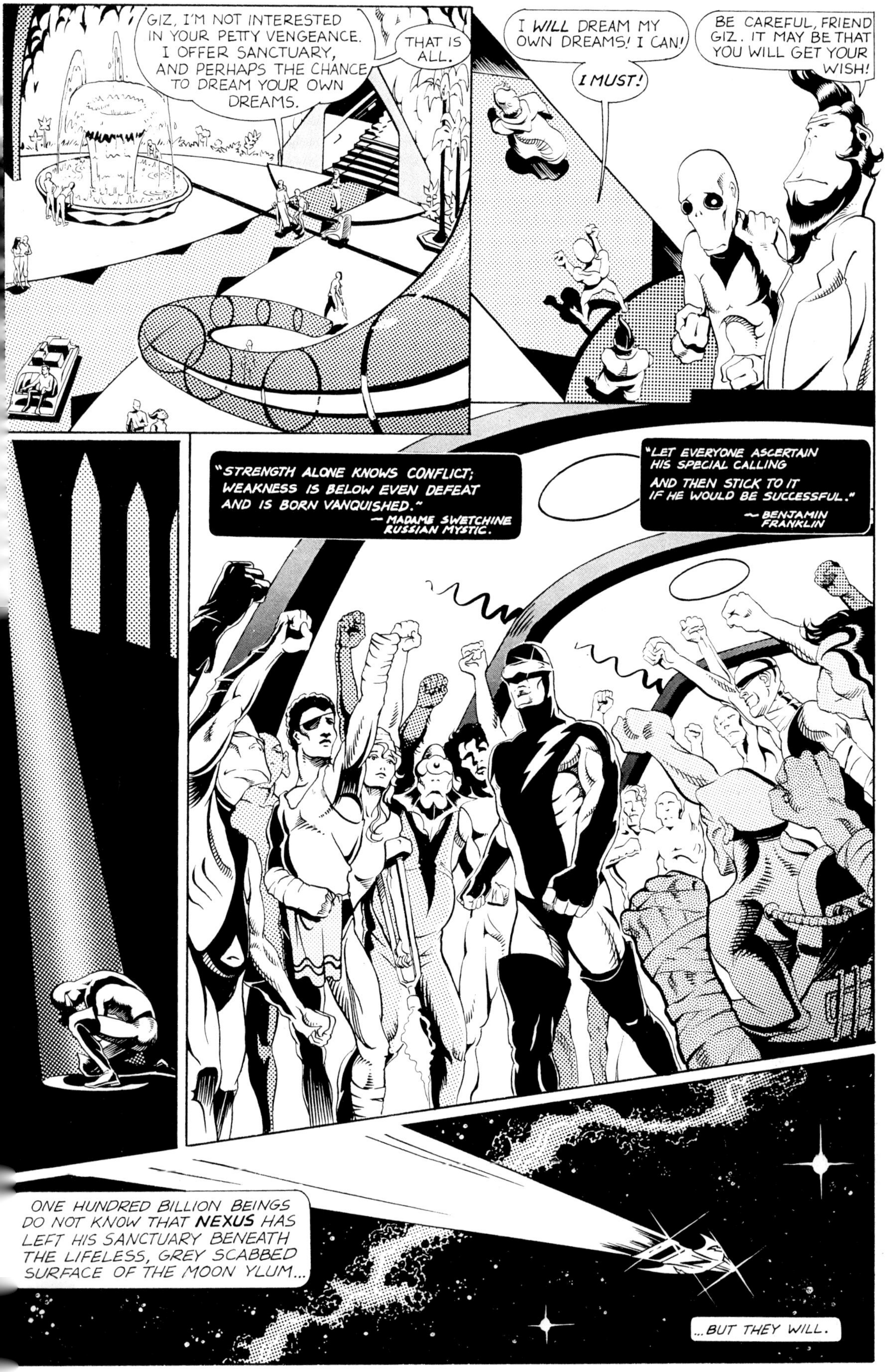
GIZ, I'M NOT INTERESTED IN YOUR PETTY VENGEANCE. I OFFER SANCTUARY, AND PERHAPS THE CHANCE TO DREAM YOUR OWN DREAMS.
THAT IS ALL.
I WILL DREAM MY OWN DREAMS! I CAN!
I MUST!
BE CAREFUL, FRIEND GIZ. IT MAY BE THAT YOU WILL GET YOUR WISH!
"STRENGTH ALONE KNOWS CONFLICT; WEAKNESS IS BELOW EVEN DEFEAT AND IS BORN VANQUISHED."
— MADAME SWETCHINE RUSSIAN MYSTIC.
"LET EVERYONE ASCERTAIN HIS SPECIAL CALLING AND THEN STICK TO IT IF HE WOULD BE SUCCESSFUL."
— BENJAMIN FRANKLIN
ONE HUNDRED BILLION BEINGS DO NOT KNOW THAT NEXUS HAS LEFT HIS SANCTUARY BENEATH THE LIFELESS, GREY SCABBED SURFACE OF THE MOON YLUM...
...BUT THEY WILL.

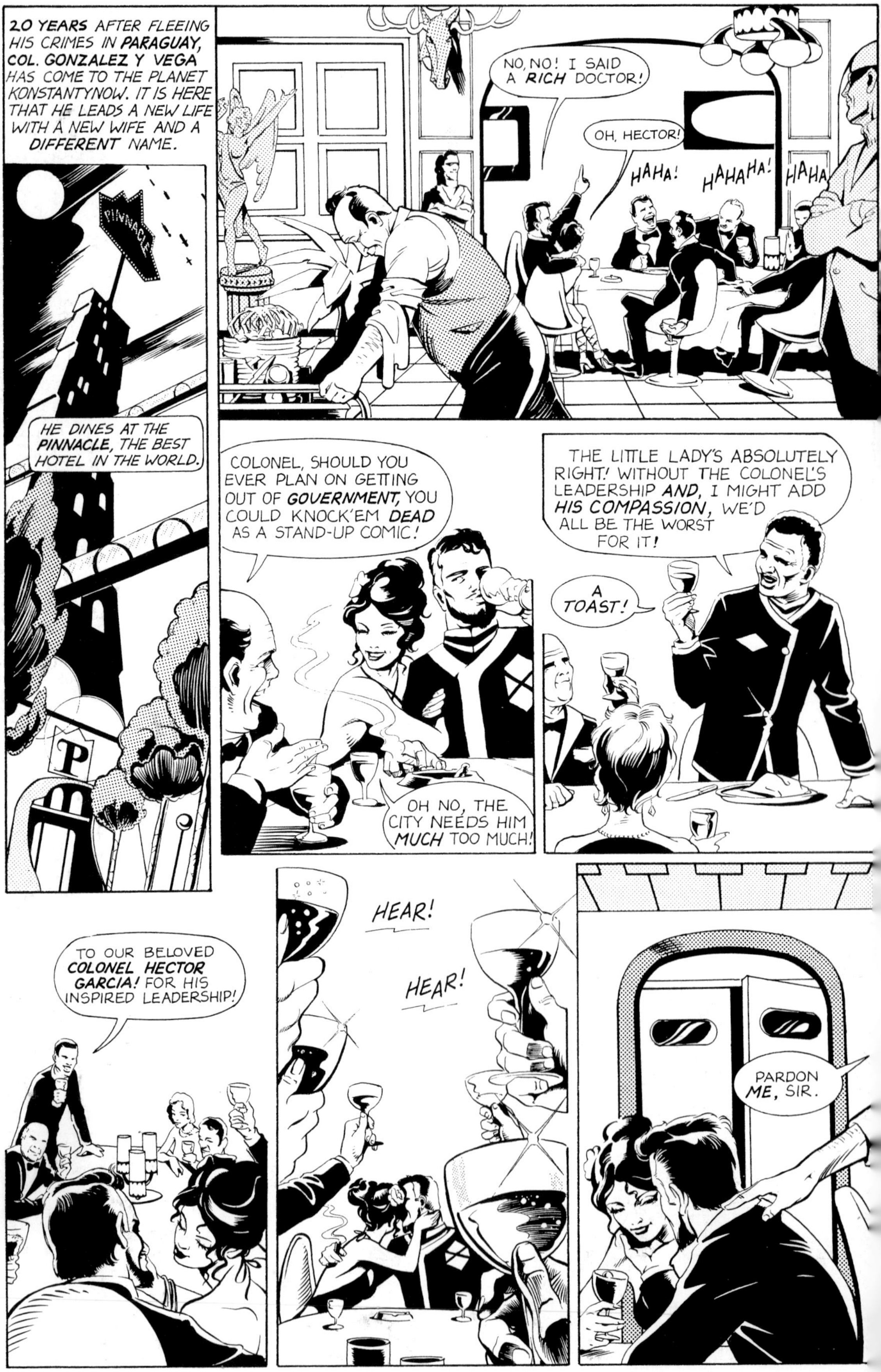
20 YEARS AFTER FLEEING HIS CRIMES IN PARAGUAY, COL. GONZALEZ Y VEGA HAS COME TO THE PLANET KONSTANTYNOW. IT IS HERE THAT HE LEADS A NEW LIFE WITH A NEW WIFE AND A DIFFERENT NAME.
PINNACLE
HE DINES AT THE PINNACLE, THE BEST HOTEL IN THE WORLD.
P
NO, NO! I SAID A RICH DOCTOR!
OH, HECTOR!
HAHA!
HAHAHAHA!
HAHA
COLONEL, SHOULD YOU EVER PLAN ON GETTING OUT OF GOVERNMENT, YOU COULD KNOCK'EM DEAD AS A STAND-UP COMIC!
OH NO, THE CITY NEEDS HIM MUCH TOO MUCH!
THE LITTLE LADY'S ABSOLUTELY RIGHT! WITHOUT THE COLONEL'S LEADERSHIP AND, I MIGHT ADD HIS COMPASSION, WE'D ALL BE THE WORST FOR IT!
A TOAST!
TO OUR BELOVED COLONEL HECTOR GARCIA! FOR HIS INSPIRED LEADERSHIP!
HEAR!
HEAR!
PARDON ME, SIR.

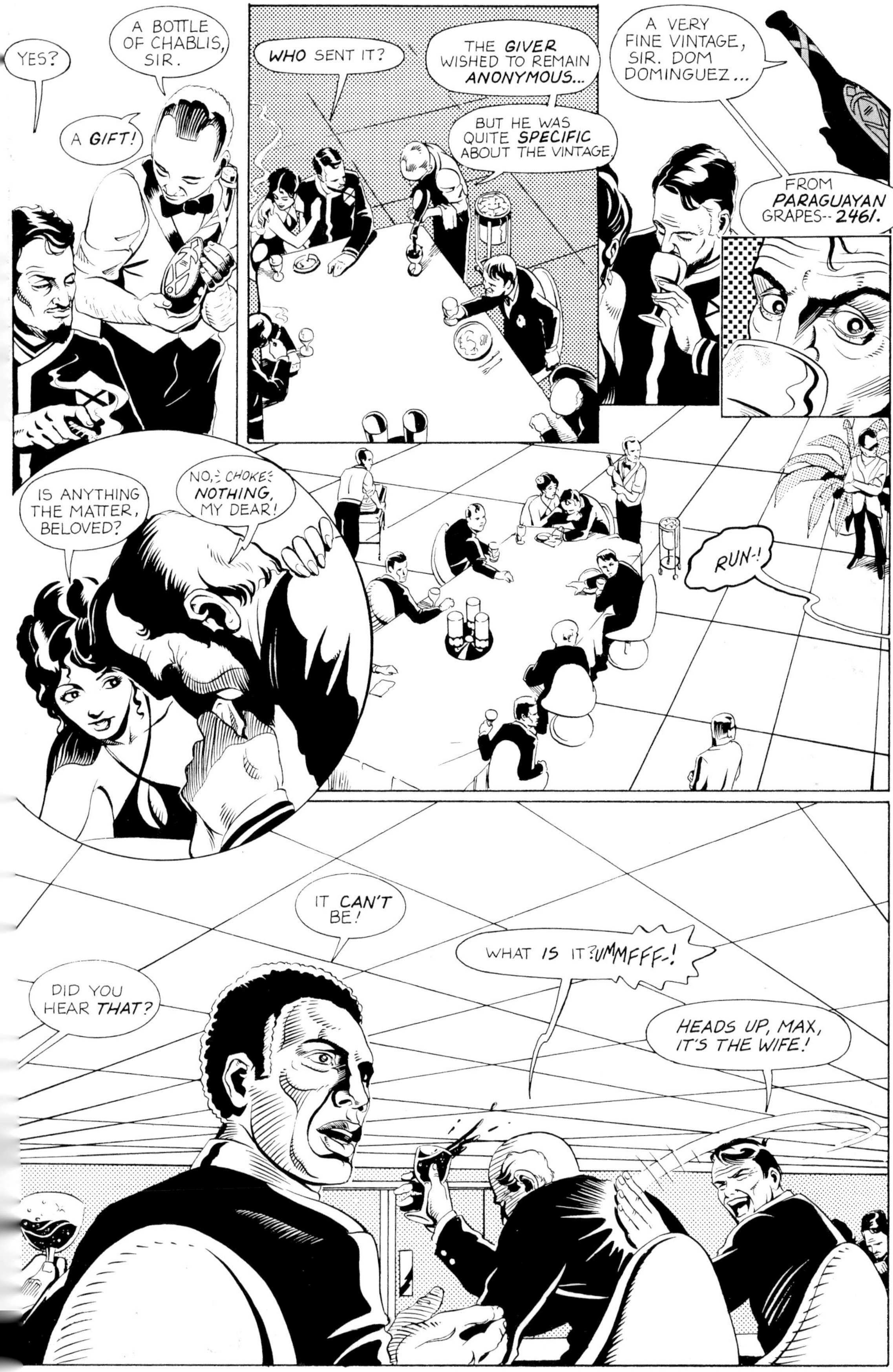

YES?
A BOTTLE OF CHABLIS, SIR.
A GIFT!
WHO SENT IT?
THE GIVER WISHED TO REMAIN ANONYMOUS...
BUT HE WAS QUITE SPECIFIC ABOUT THE VINTAGE.
A VERY FINE VINTAGE, SIR. DOM DOMINGUEZ...
FROM PARAGUAYAN GRAPES-- 2461.
IS ANYTHING THE MATTER, BELOVED?
NO, CHOKE NOTHING, MY DEAR!
RUN-!
DID YOU HEAR THAT?
IT CAN'T BE!
WHAT IS IT? UMMFFF-!
HEADS UP, MAX, IT'S THE WIFE!

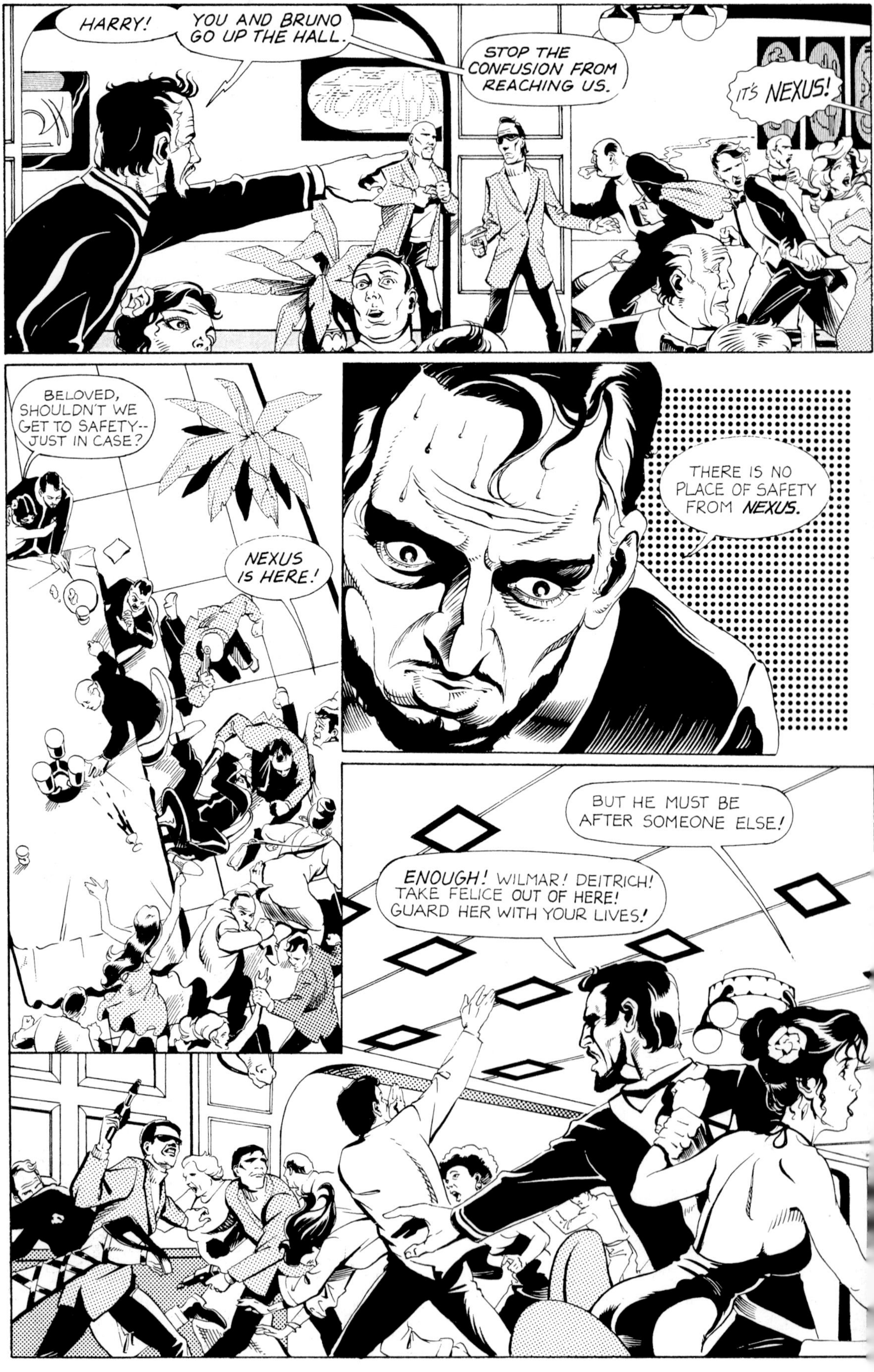
HARRY!
YOU AND BRUNO GO UP THE HALL.
STOP THE CONFUSION FROM REACHING US.
IT'S NEXUS!
BELOVED, SHOULDN'T WE GET TO SAFETY-- JUST IN CASE?
NEXUS IS HERE!
THERE IS NO PLACE OF SAFETY FROM NEXUS.
BUT HE MUST BE AFTER SOMEONE ELSE!
ENOUGH! WILMAR! DEITRICH! TAKE FELICE OUT OF HERE! GUARD HER WITH YOUR LIVES!

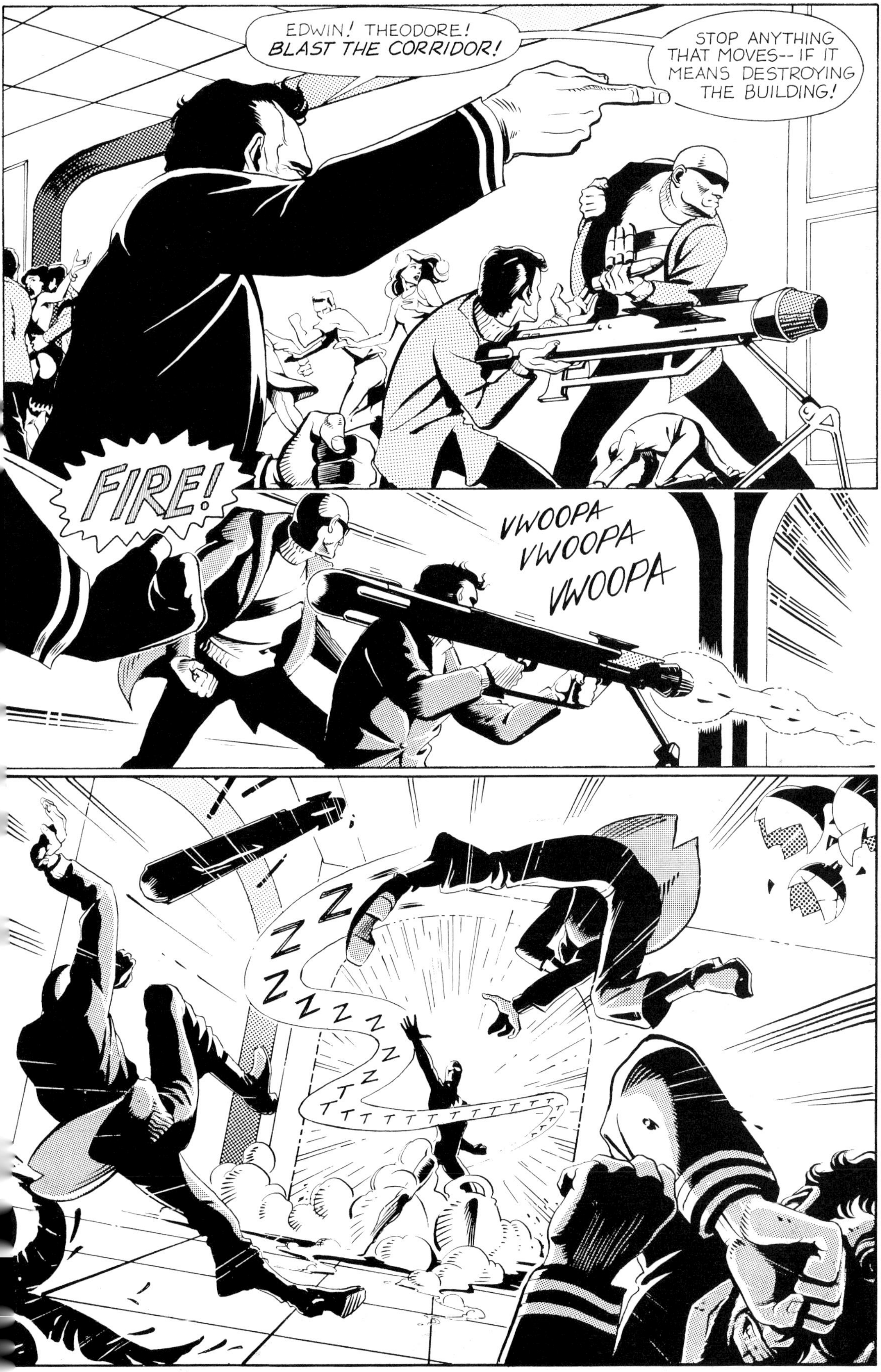
EDWIN! THEODORE! BLAST THE CORRIDOR!
STOP ANYTHING THAT MOVES-- IF IT MEANS DESTROYING THE BUILDING!
FIRE!
VWOOPA VWOOPA VWOOPA
ZZZZZZZZZZZ
TTTTTTTTTTTTTTT

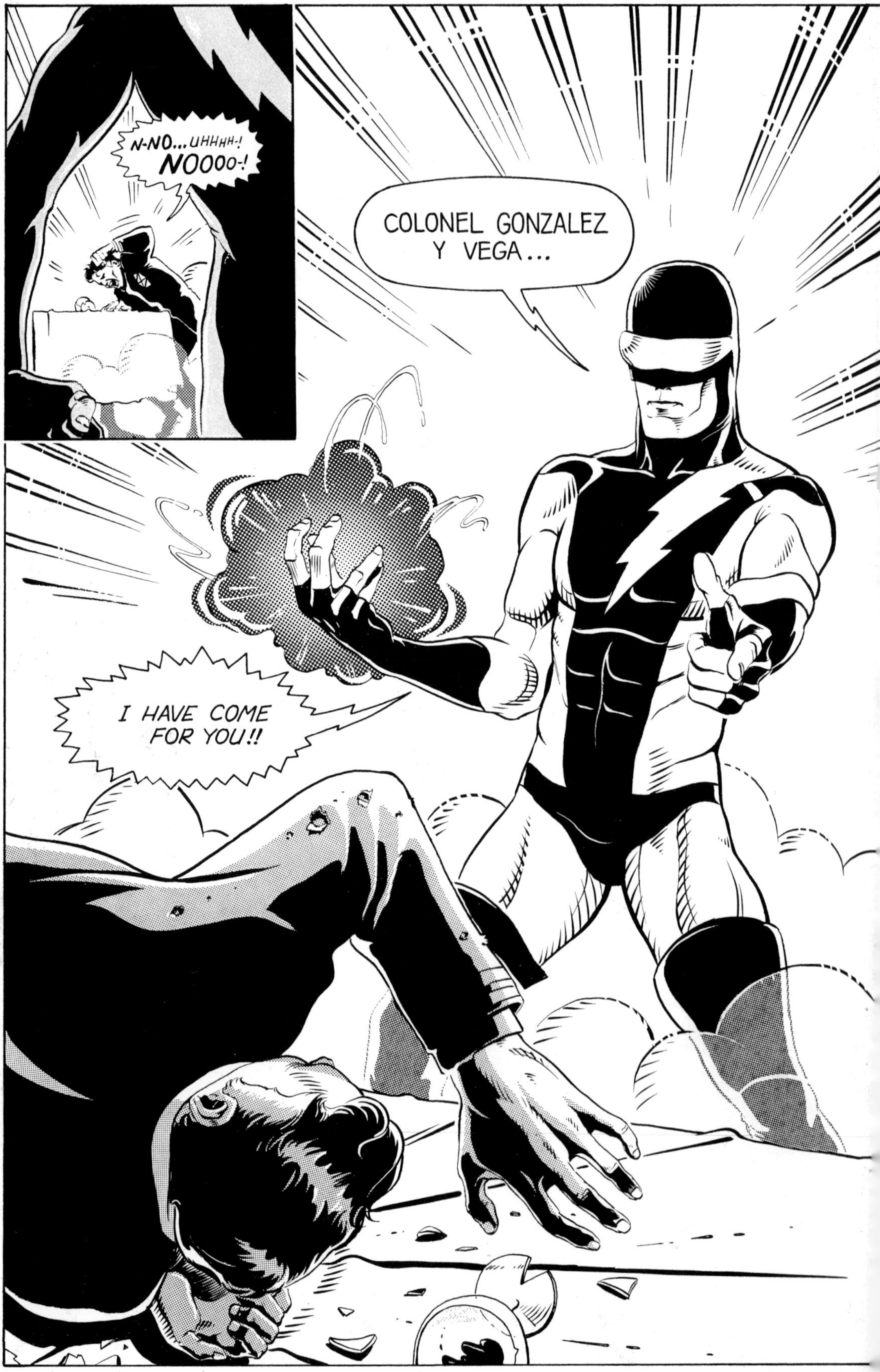
N-NO...UHHHH-! NOOOO-!
COLONEL GONZALEZ Y VEGA...
I HAVE COME FOR YOU!!

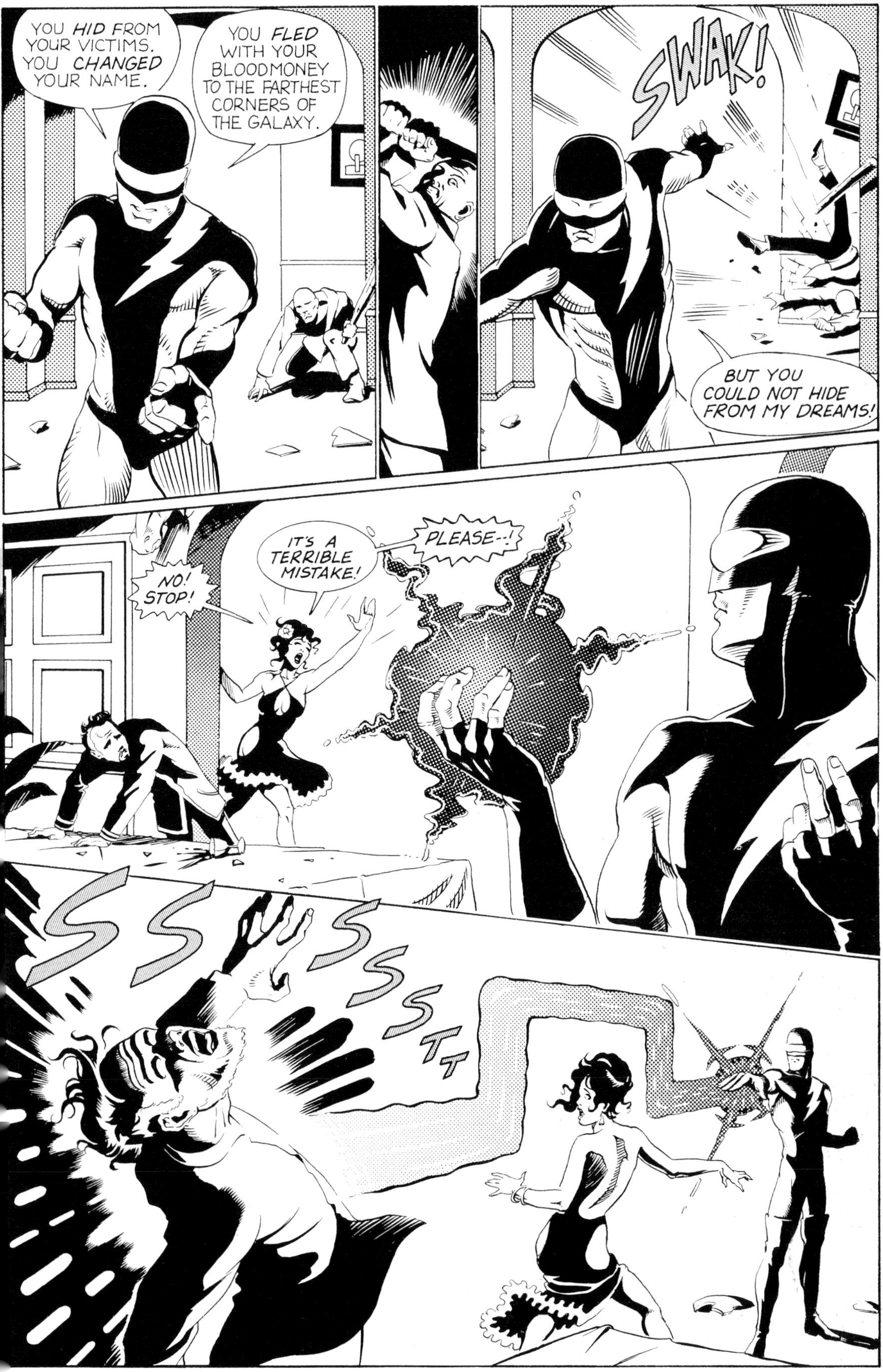
YOU HID FROM YOUR VICTIMS. YOU CHANGED YOUR NAME.
YOU FLED WITH YOUR BLOODMONEY TO THE FARTHEST CORNERS OF THE GALAXY.
SWAK!
BUT YOU COULD NOT HIDE FROM MY DREAMS!
NO! STOP!
IT'S A TERRIBLE MISTAKE!
PLEASE--!
SSSSSSTT

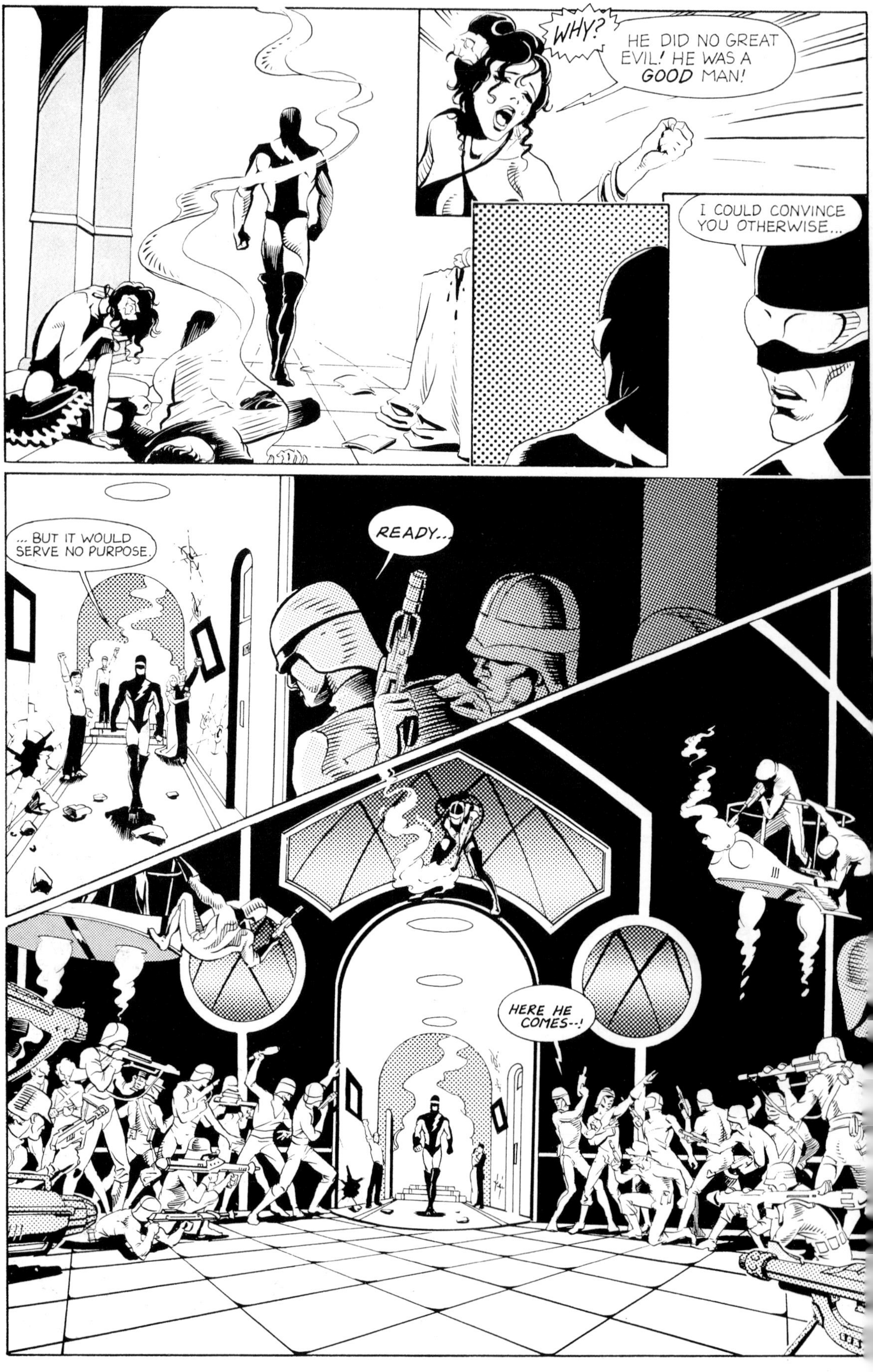
WHY?
HE DID NO GREAT EVIL! HE WAS A GOOD MAN!
I COULD CONVINCE YOU OTHERWISE...
... BUT IT WOULD SERVE NO PURPOSE.
READY...
HERE HE COMES--!

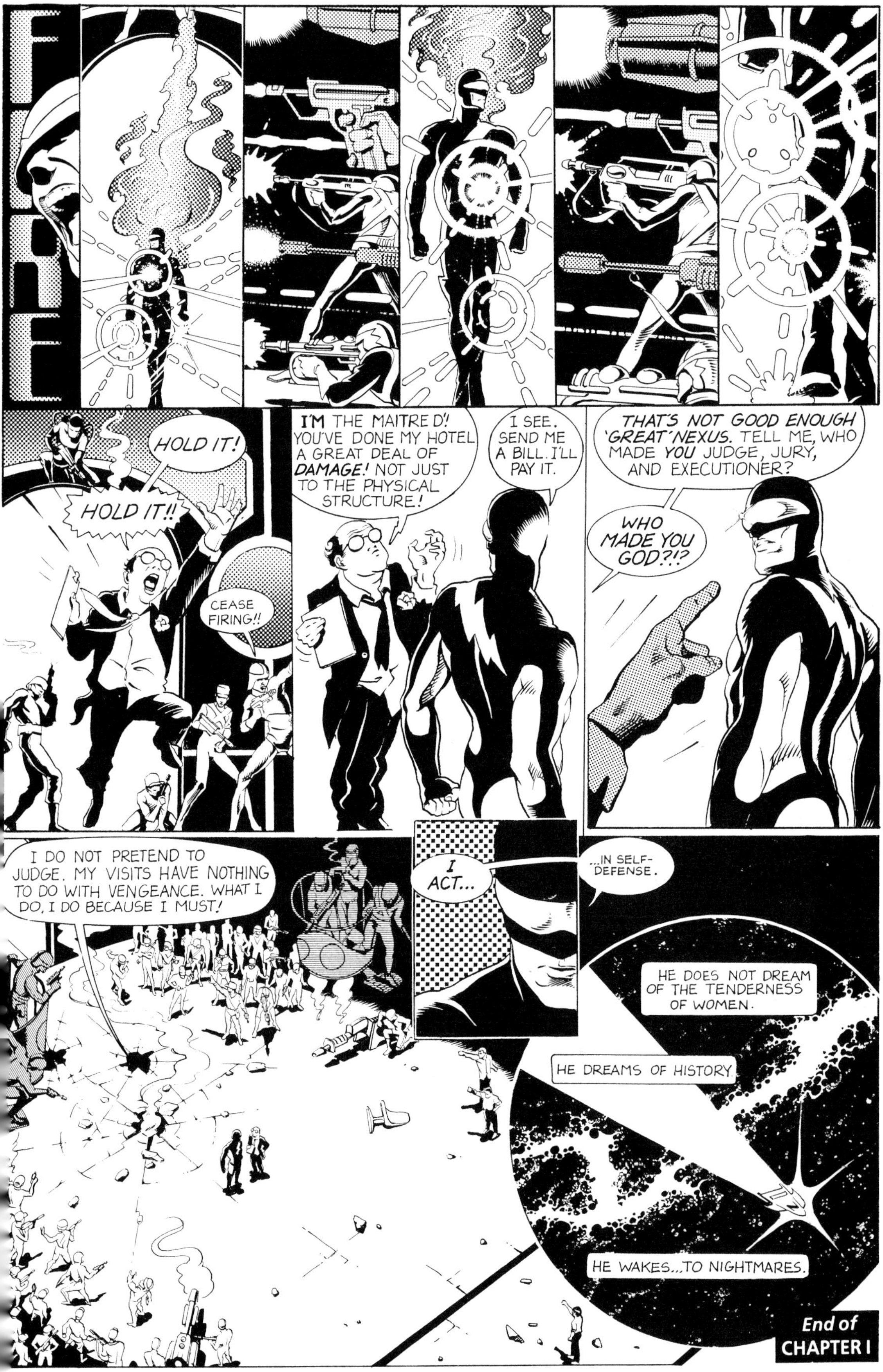
FIRE
HOLD IT!
HOLD IT!!
CEASE FIRING!!
I'M THE MAITRE D'! YOU'VE DONE MY HOTEL A GREAT DEAL OF DAMAGE! NOT JUST TO THE PHYSICAL STRUCTURE!
I SEE. SEND ME A BILL. I'LL PAY IT.
THAT'S NOT GOOD ENOUGH 'GREAT' NEXUS. TELL ME, WHO MADE YOU JUDGE, JURY, AND EXECUTIONER?
WHO MADE YOU GOD?!?
I DO NOT PRETEND TO JUDGE. MY VISITS HAVE NOTHING TO DO WITH VENGEANCE. WHAT I DO, I DO BECAUSE I MUST!
I ACT...
...IN SELF-DEFENSE.
HE DOES NOT DREAM OF THE TENDERNESS OF WOMEN.
HE DREAMS OF HISTORY.
HE WAKES...TO NIGHTMARES.
End of CHAPTER I

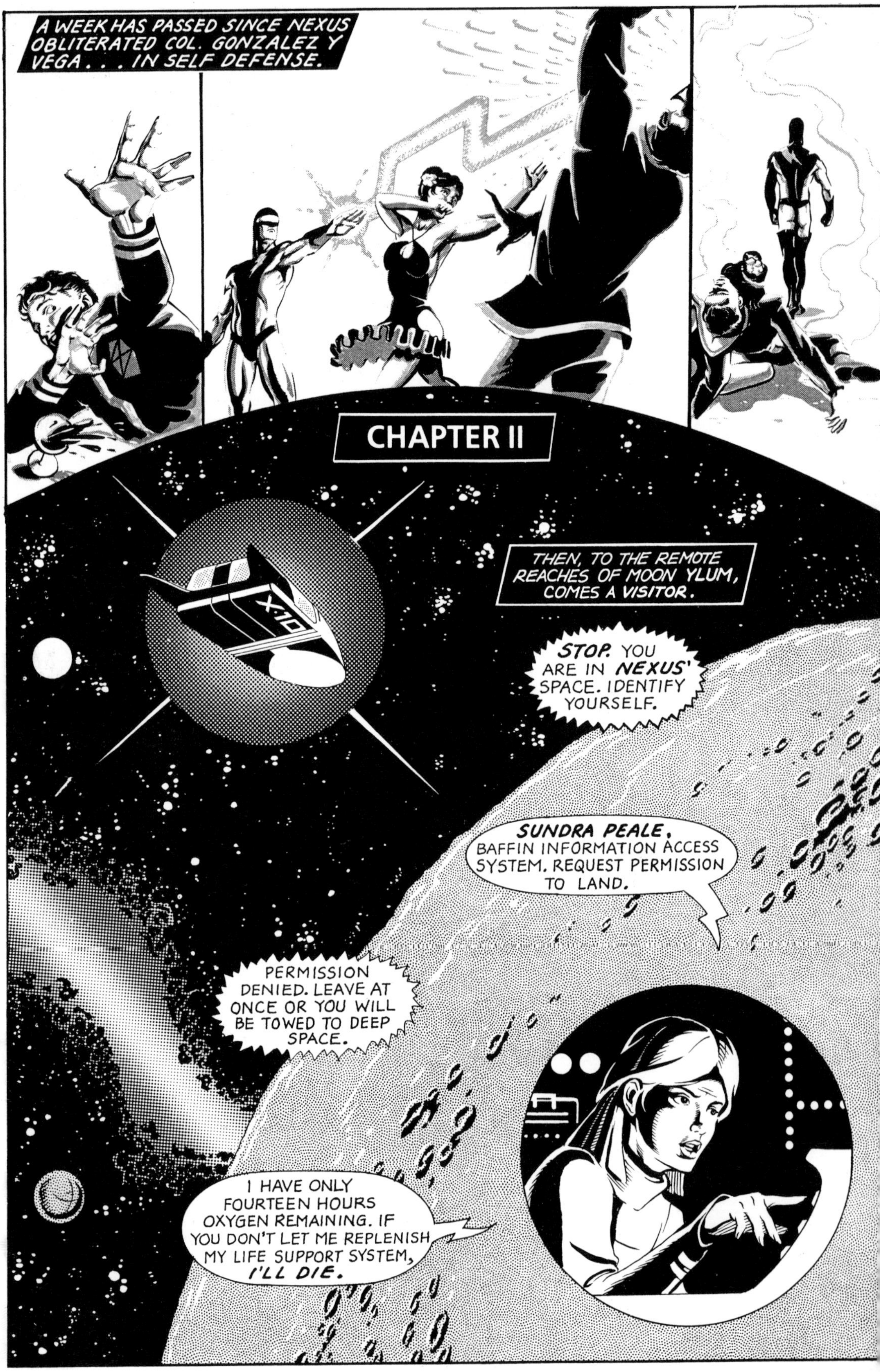
A WEEK HAS PASSED SINCE NEXUS OBLITERATED COL. GONZALEZ Y VEGA . . . IN SELF DEFENSE.
CHAPTER II
THEN, TO THE REMOTE REACHES OF MOON YLUM, COMES A VISITOR.
X-10
STOP. YOU ARE IN NEXUS' SPACE. IDENTIFY YOURSELF.
SUNDRA PEALE. BAFFIN INFORMATION ACCESS SYSTEM. REQUEST PERMISSION TO LAND.
PERMISSION DENIED. LEAVE AT ONCE OR YOU WILL BE TOWED TO DEEP SPACE.
I HAVE ONLY FOURTEEN HOURS OXYGEN REMAINING. IF YOU DON'T LET ME REPLENISH MY LIFE SUPPORT SYSTEM, I'LL DIE.

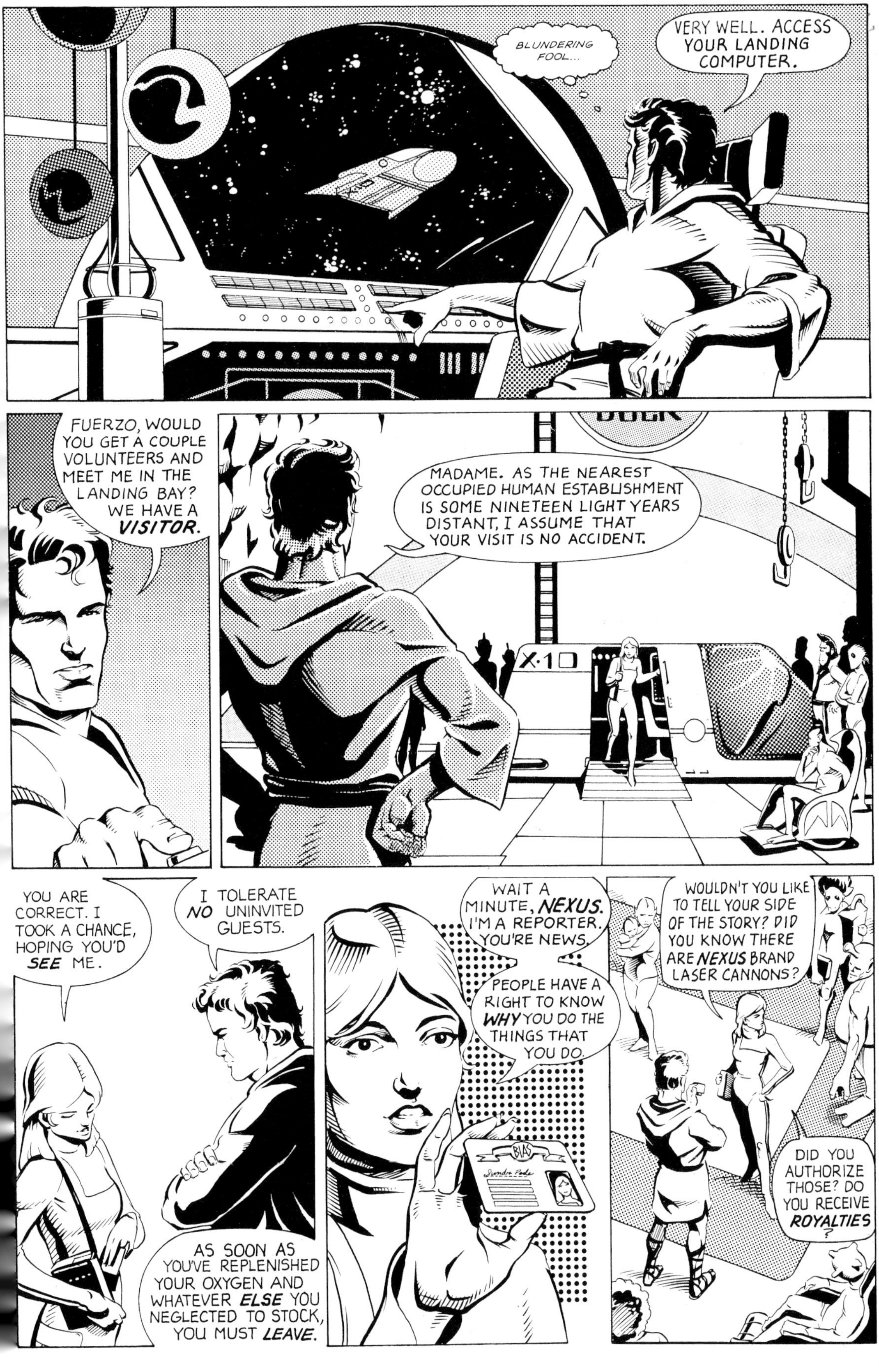

BLUNDERING FOOL...
VERY WELL. ACCESS YOUR LANDING COMPUTER.
FUERZO, WOULD YOU GET A COUPLE VOLUNTEERS AND MEET ME IN THE LANDING BAY? WE HAVE A VISITOR.
MADAME. AS THE NEAREST OCCUPIED HUMAN ESTABLISHMENT IS SOME NINETEEN LIGHT YEARS DISTANT, I ASSUME THAT YOUR VISIT IS NO ACCIDENT.
X-10
YOU ARE CORRECT. I TOOK A CHANCE, HOPING YOU'D SEE ME.
I TOLERATE NO UNINVITED GUESTS.
AS SOON AS YOU'VE REPLENISHED YOUR OXYGEN AND WHATEVER ELSE YOU NEGLECTED TO STOCK, YOU MUST LEAVE.
WAIT A MINUTE, NEXUS. I'M A REPORTER. YOU'RE NEWS.
PEOPLE HAVE A RIGHT TO KNOW WHY YOU DO THE THINGS THAT YOU DO.
BIAS
WOULDN'T YOU LIKE TO TELL YOUR SIDE OF THE STORY? DID YOU KNOW THERE ARE NEXUS BRAND LASER CANNONS?
DID YOU AUTHORIZE THOSE? DO YOU RECEIVE ROYALTIES?

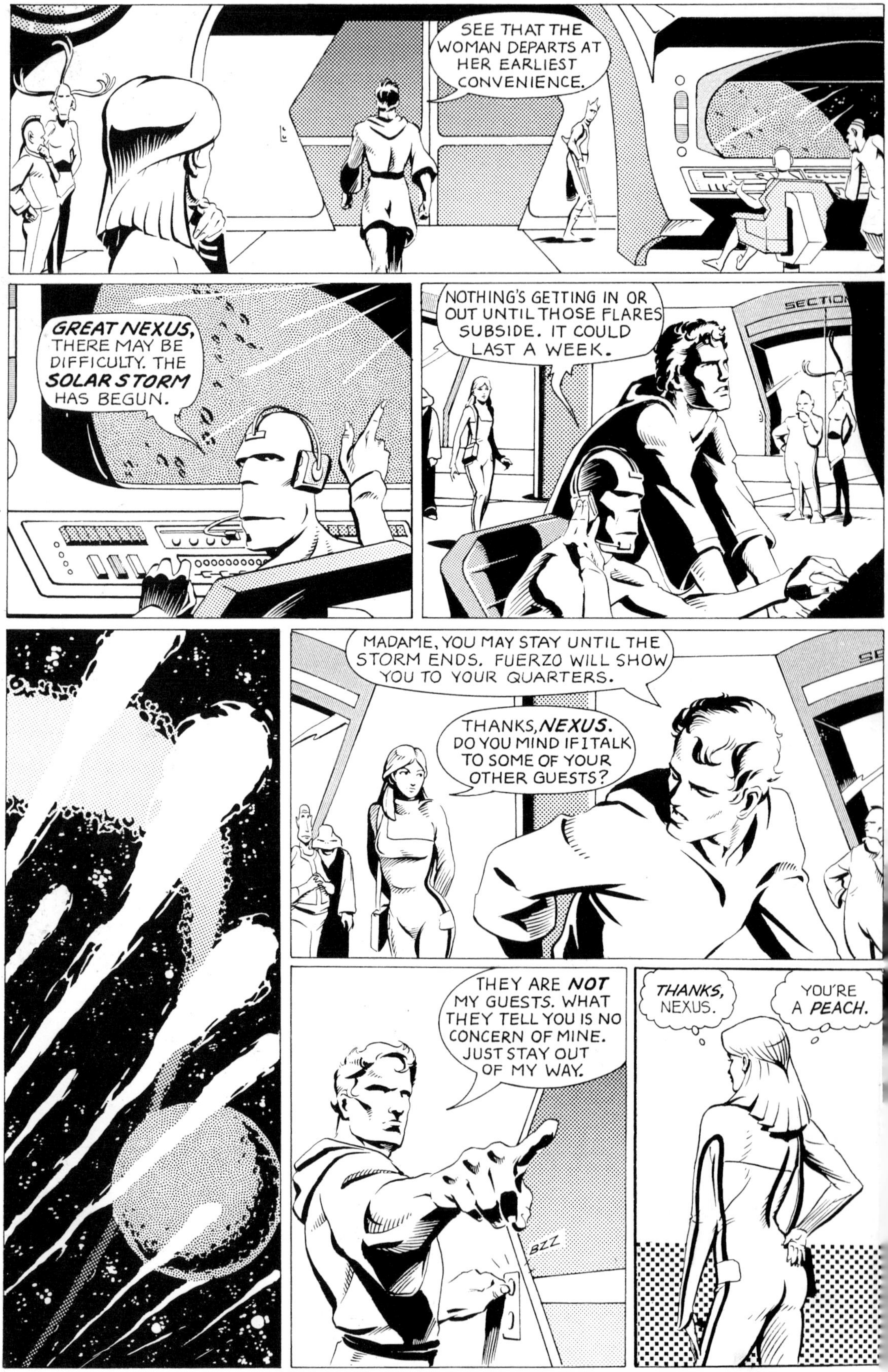
SEE THAT THE WOMAN DEPARTS AT HER EARLIEST CONVENIENCE.
GREAT NEXUS, THERE MAY BE DIFFICULTY. THE SOLAR STORM HAS BEGUN.
NOTHING'S GETTING IN OR OUT UNTIL THOSE FLARES SUBSIDE. IT COULD LAST A WEEK.
SECTION
MADAME, YOU MAY STAY UNTIL THE STORM ENDS. FUERZO WILL SHOW YOU TO YOUR QUARTERS.
THANKS, NEXUS. DO YOU MIND IF I TALK TO SOME OF YOUR OTHER GUESTS?
THEY ARE NOT MY GUESTS. WHAT THEY TELL YOU IS NO CONCERN OF MINE. JUST STAY OUT OF MY WAY.
BZZ
THANKS, NEXUS.
YOU'RE A PEACH.

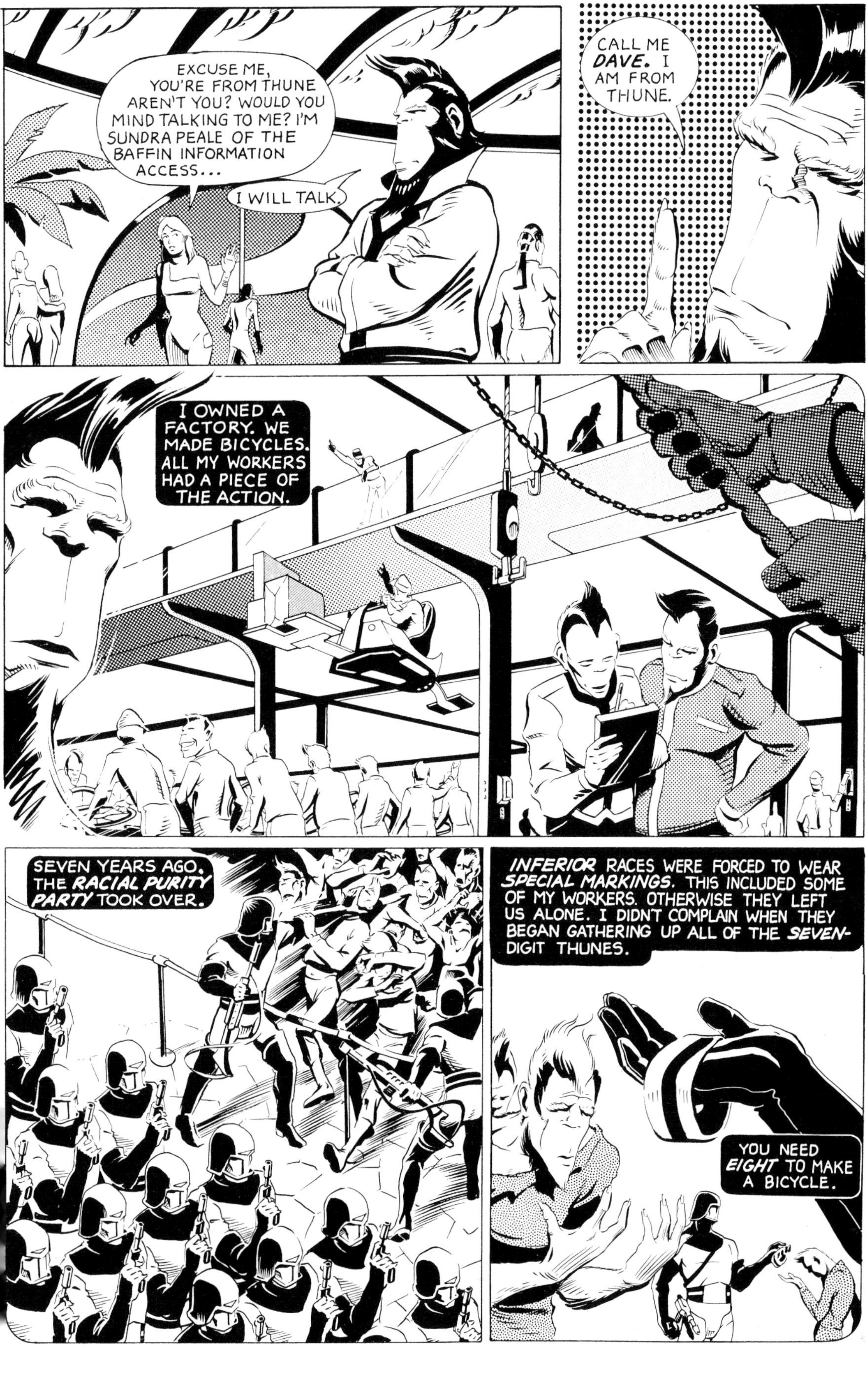
EXCUSE ME, YOU'RE FROM THUNE AREN'T YOU? WOULD YOU MIND TALKING TO ME? I'M SUNDRA PEALE OF THE BAFFIN INFORMATION ACCESS...
I WILL TALK.
CALL ME DAVE. I AM FROM THUNE.
I OWNED A FACTORY. WE MADE BICYCLES. ALL MY WORKERS HAD A PIECE OF THE ACTION.
SEVEN YEARS AGO, THE RACIAL PURITY PARTY TOOK OVER.
INFERIOR RACES WERE FORCED TO WEAR SPECIAL MARKINGS. THIS INCLUDED SOME OF MY WORKERS. OTHERWISE THEY LEFT US ALONE. I DIDN'T COMPLAIN WHEN THEY BEGAN GATHERING UP ALL OF THE SEVEN-DIGIT THUNES.
YOU NEED EIGHT TO MAKE A BICYCLE.

NOT LONG AFTER THAT, THE PARTY CAME TO MY OFFICE. THEY TOLD ME THAT WE WOULD NO LONGER MAKE BICYCLES. WE WOULD BECOME AN ORE REFINERY. THEY TOLD ME WE WOULD NO LONGER EMPLOY WORKERS OF "INFERIOR" RACES...

GET OUT!

THEY **CAME** FOR ME AT MIDNIGHT.

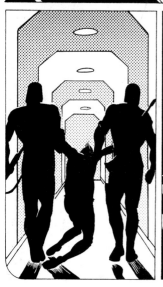

I WAS THROWN INTO A CELL IN MY OWN FACTORY. THEY HAD TURNED PARTS OF THE WAREHOUSE INTO A *PRISON*.

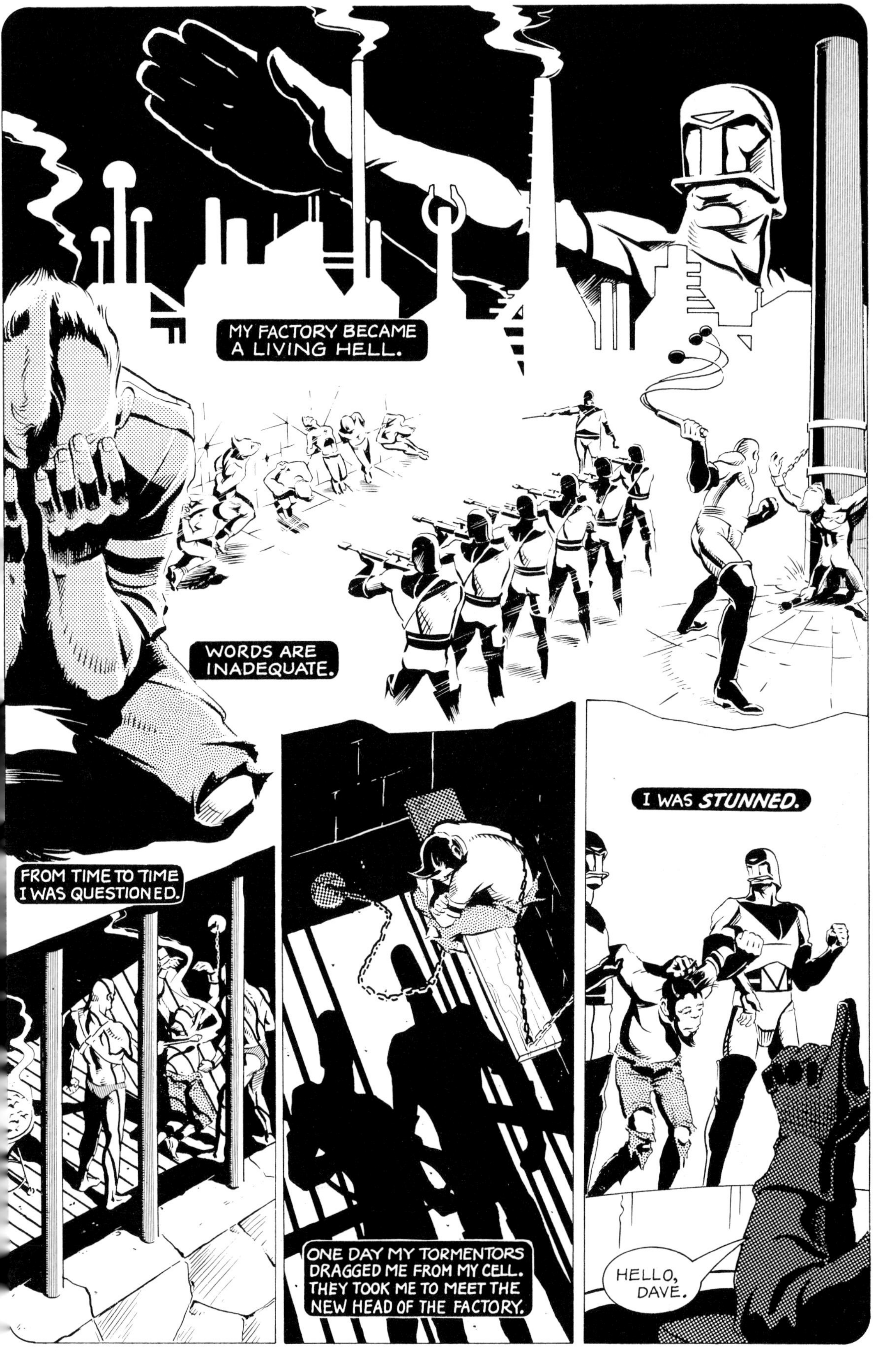
MY FACTORY BECAME A LIVING HELL.
WORDS ARE INADEQUATE.
FROM TIME TO TIME I WAS QUESTIONED.
ONE DAY MY TORMENTORS DRAGGED ME FROM MY CELL. THEY TOOK ME TO MEET THE NEW HEAD OF THE FACTORY.
I WAS STUNNED.
HELLO, DAVE.

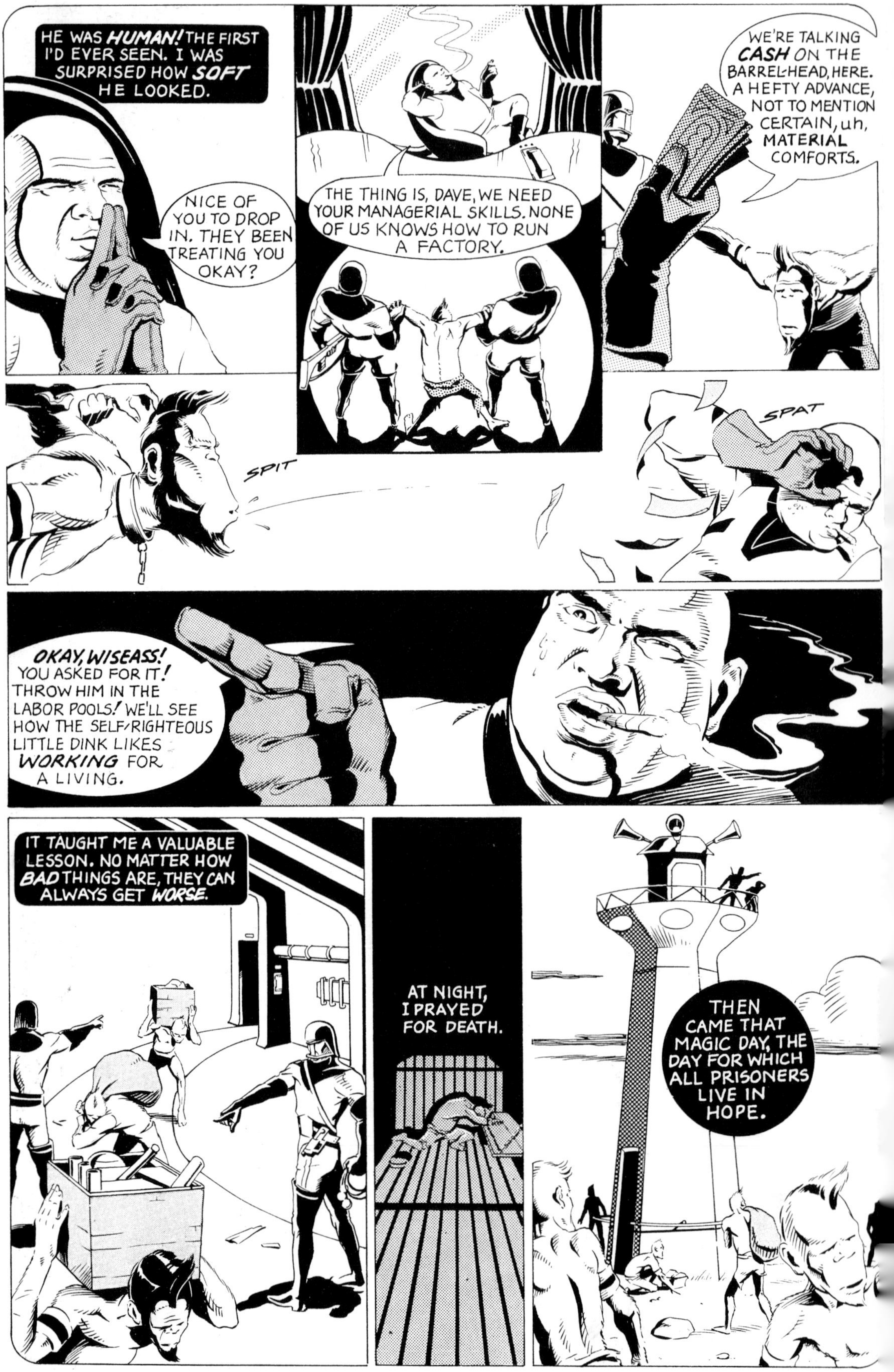
HE WAS HUMAN! THE FIRST I'D EVER SEEN. I WAS SURPRISED HOW SOFT HE LOOKED.
NICE OF YOU TO DROP IN. THEY BEEN TREATING YOU OKAY?
THE THING IS, DAVE, WE NEED YOUR MANAGERIAL SKILLS. NONE OF US KNOWS HOW TO RUN A FACTORY.
WE'RE TALKING CASH ON THE BARREL-HEAD, HERE. A HEFTY ADVANCE, NOT TO MENTION CERTAIN, uh, MATERIAL COMFORTS.
SPIT
SPAT
OKAY, WISEASS! YOU ASKED FOR IT! THROW HIM IN THE LABOR POOLS! WE'LL SEE HOW THE SELF-RIGHTEOUS LITTLE DINK LIKES WORKING FOR A LIVING.
IT TAUGHT ME A VALUABLE LESSON. NO MATTER HOW BAD THINGS ARE, THEY CAN ALWAYS GET WORSE.
AT NIGHT, I PRAYED FOR DEATH.
THEN CAME THAT MAGIC DAY, THE DAY FOR WHICH ALL PRISONERS LIVE IN HOPE.

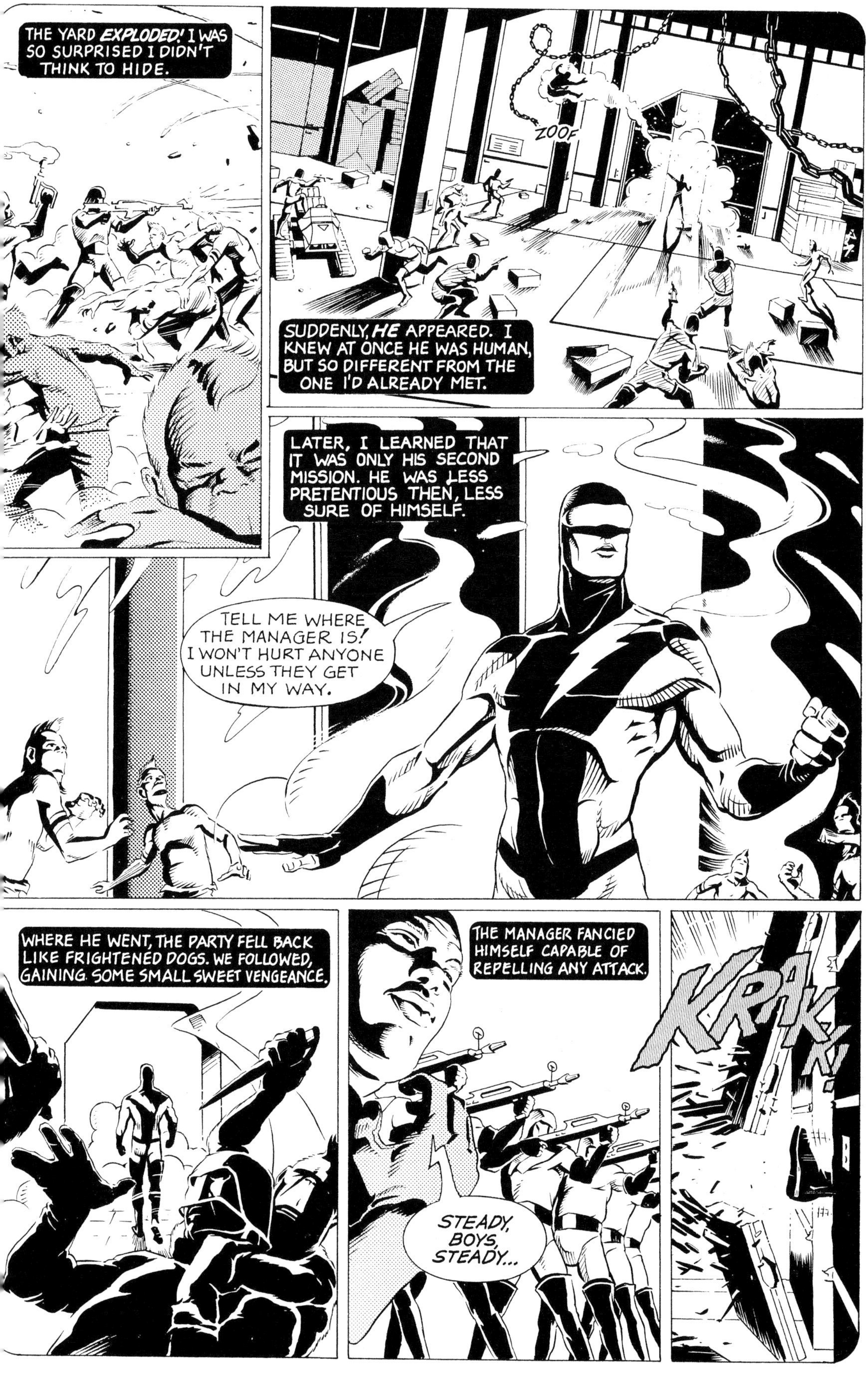
THE YARD EXPLODED! I WAS SO SURPRISED I DIDN'T THINK TO HIDE.
ZOOF
SUDDENLY, HE APPEARED. I KNEW AT ONCE HE WAS HUMAN, BUT SO DIFFERENT FROM THE ONE I'D ALREADY MET.
LATER, I LEARNED THAT IT WAS ONLY HIS SECOND MISSION. HE WAS LESS PRETENTIOUS THEN, LESS SURE OF HIMSELF.
TELL ME WHERE THE MANAGER IS! I WON'T HURT ANYONE UNLESS THEY GET IN MY WAY.
WHERE HE WENT, THE PARTY FELL BACK LIKE FRIGHTENED DOGS. WE FOLLOWED, GAINING SOME SMALL SWEET VENGEANCE.
THE MANAGER FANCIED HIMSELF CAPABLE OF REPELLING ANY ATTACK.
STEADY, BOYS, STEADY...

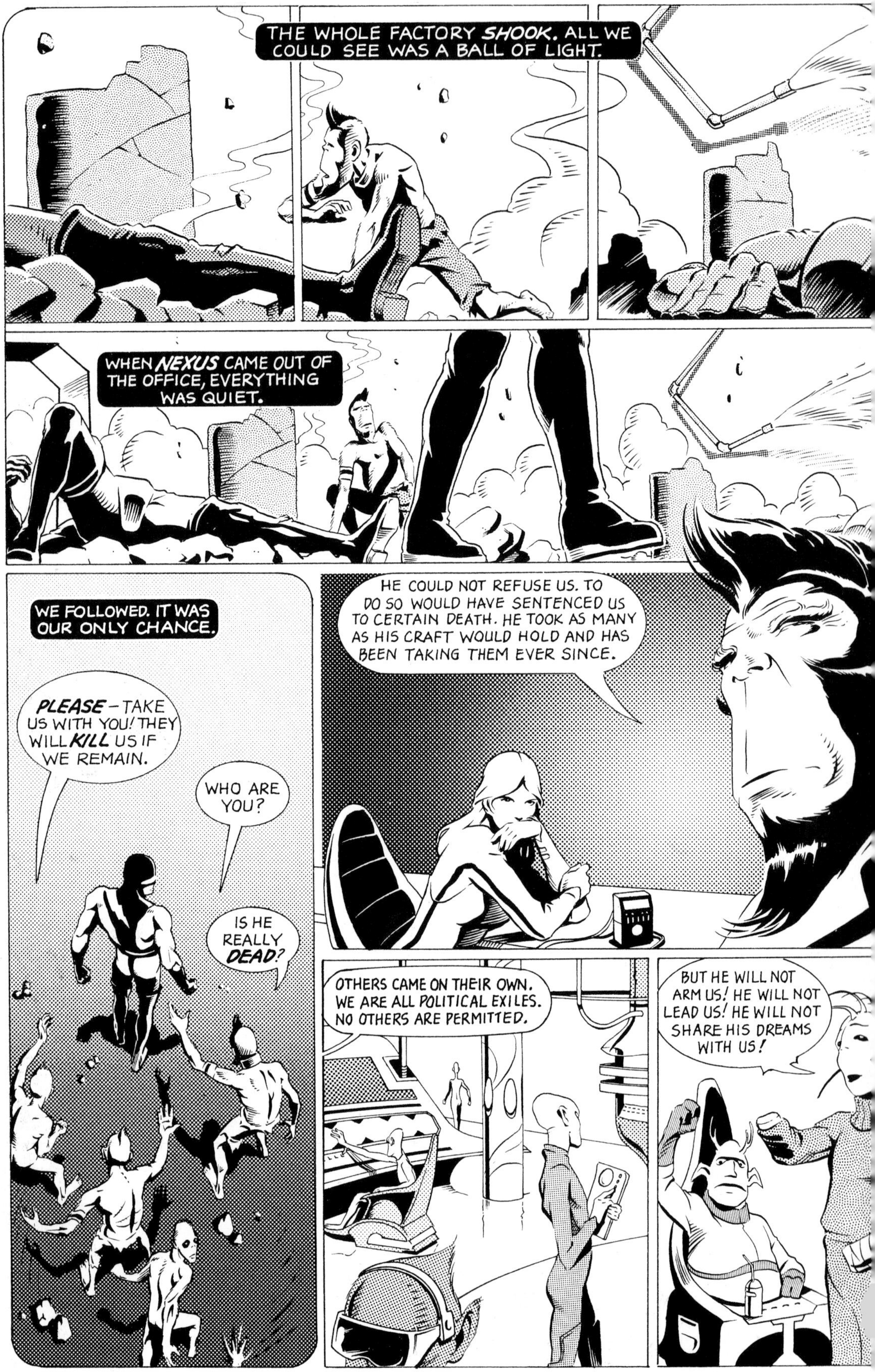

THE WHOLE FACTORY SHOOK. ALL WE COULD SEE WAS A BALL OF LIGHT.
WHEN NEXUS CAME OUT OF THE OFFICE, EVERYTHING WAS QUIET.
WE FOLLOWED. IT WAS OUR ONLY CHANCE.
PLEASE—TAKE US WITH YOU! THEY WILL KILL US IF WE REMAIN.
WHO ARE YOU?
IS HE REALLY DEAD?
HE COULD NOT REFUSE US. TO DO SO WOULD HAVE SENTENCED US TO CERTAIN DEATH. HE TOOK AS MANY AS HIS CRAFT WOULD HOLD AND HAS BEEN TAKING THEM EVER SINCE.
OTHERS CAME ON THEIR OWN. WE ARE ALL POLITICAL EXILES. NO OTHERS ARE PERMITTED.
BUT HE WILL NOT ARM US! HE WILL NOT LEAD US! HE WILL NOT SHARE HIS DREAMS WITH US!

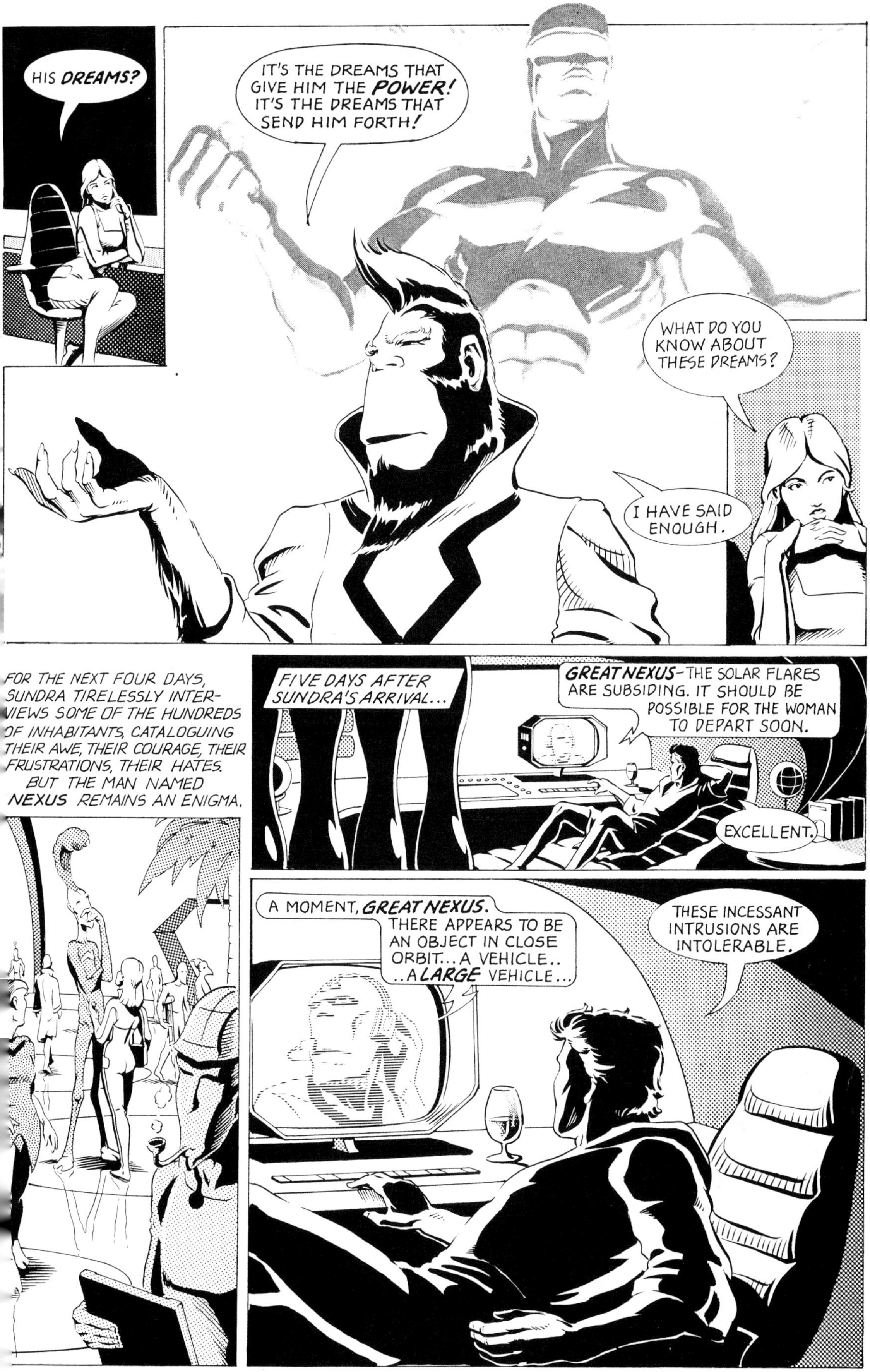
HIS DREAMS?
IT'S THE DREAMS THAT GIVE HIM THE POWER! IT'S THE DREAMS THAT SEND HIM FORTH!
WHAT DO YOU KNOW ABOUT THESE DREAMS?
I HAVE SAID ENOUGH.
FOR THE NEXT FOUR DAYS, SUNDRA TIRELESSLY INTERVIEWS SOME OF THE HUNDREDS OF INHABITANTS, CATALOGUING THEIR AWE, THEIR COURAGE, THEIR FRUSTRATIONS, THEIR HATES. BUT THE MAN NAMED NEXUS REMAINS AN ENIGMA.
FIVE DAYS AFTER SUNDRA'S ARRIVAL...
GREAT NEXUS- THE SOLAR FLARES ARE SUBSIDING. IT SHOULD BE POSSIBLE FOR THE WOMAN TO DEPART SOON.
EXCELLENT.
A MOMENT, GREAT NEXUS.
THERE APPEARS TO BE AN OBJECT IN CLOSE ORBIT... A VEHICLE.. ..A LARGE VEHICLE...
THESE INCESSANT INTRUSIONS ARE INTOLERABLE.

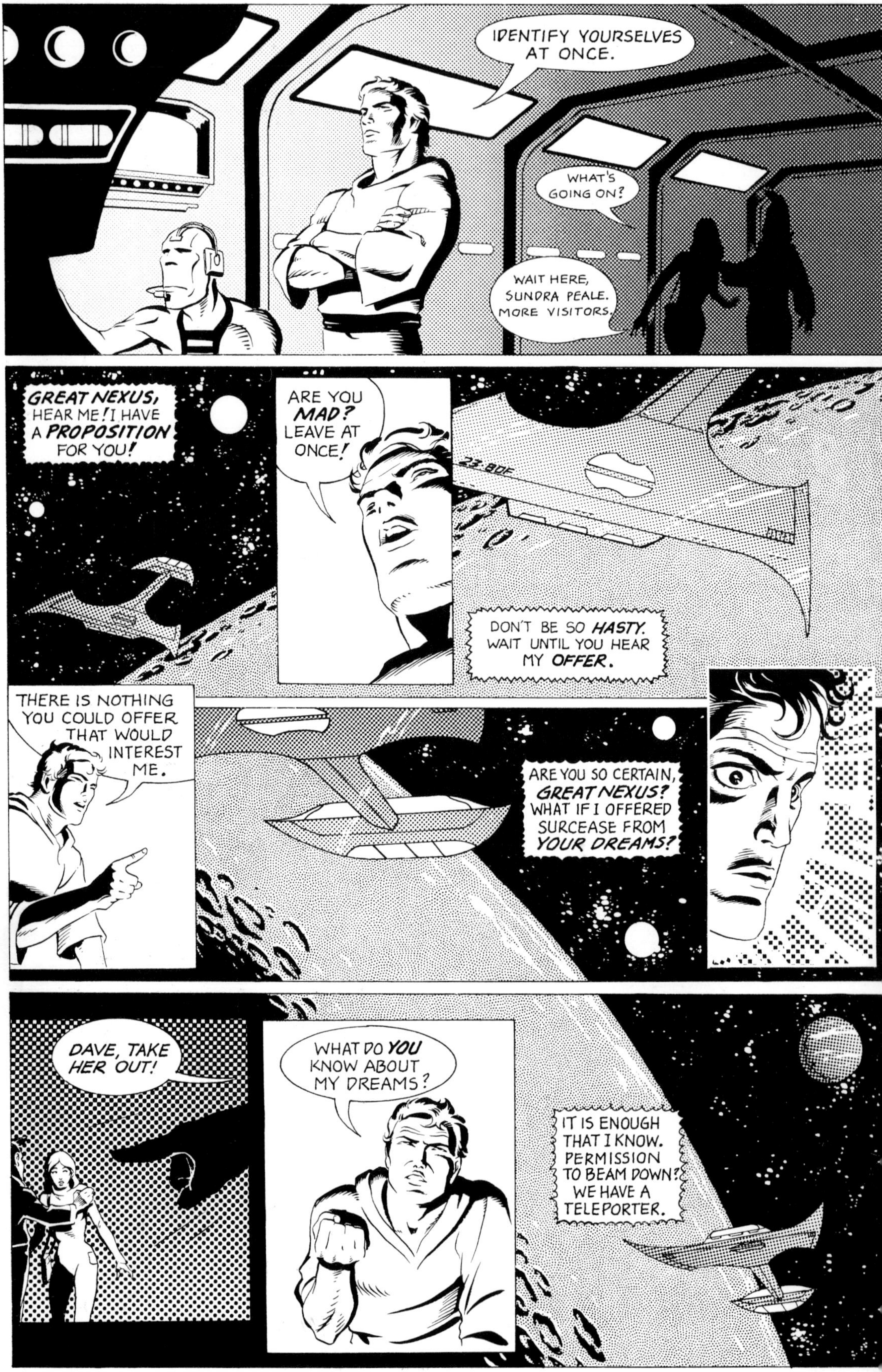
IDENTIFY YOURSELVES AT ONCE.
WHAT'S GOING ON?
WAIT HERE, SUNDRA PEALE. MORE VISITORS.
GREAT NEXUS, HEAR ME! I HAVE A PROPOSITION FOR YOU!
ARE YOU MAD? LEAVE AT ONCE!
23-BDF
DON'T BE SO HASTY. WAIT UNTIL YOU HEAR MY OFFER.
THERE IS NOTHING YOU COULD OFFER THAT WOULD INTEREST ME.
ARE YOU SO CERTAIN, GREAT NEXUS? WHAT IF I OFFERED SURCEASE FROM YOUR DREAMS?
DAVE, TAKE HER OUT!
WHAT DO YOU KNOW ABOUT MY DREAMS?
IT IS ENOUGH THAT I KNOW. PERMISSION TO BEAM DOWN? WE HAVE A TELEPORTER.

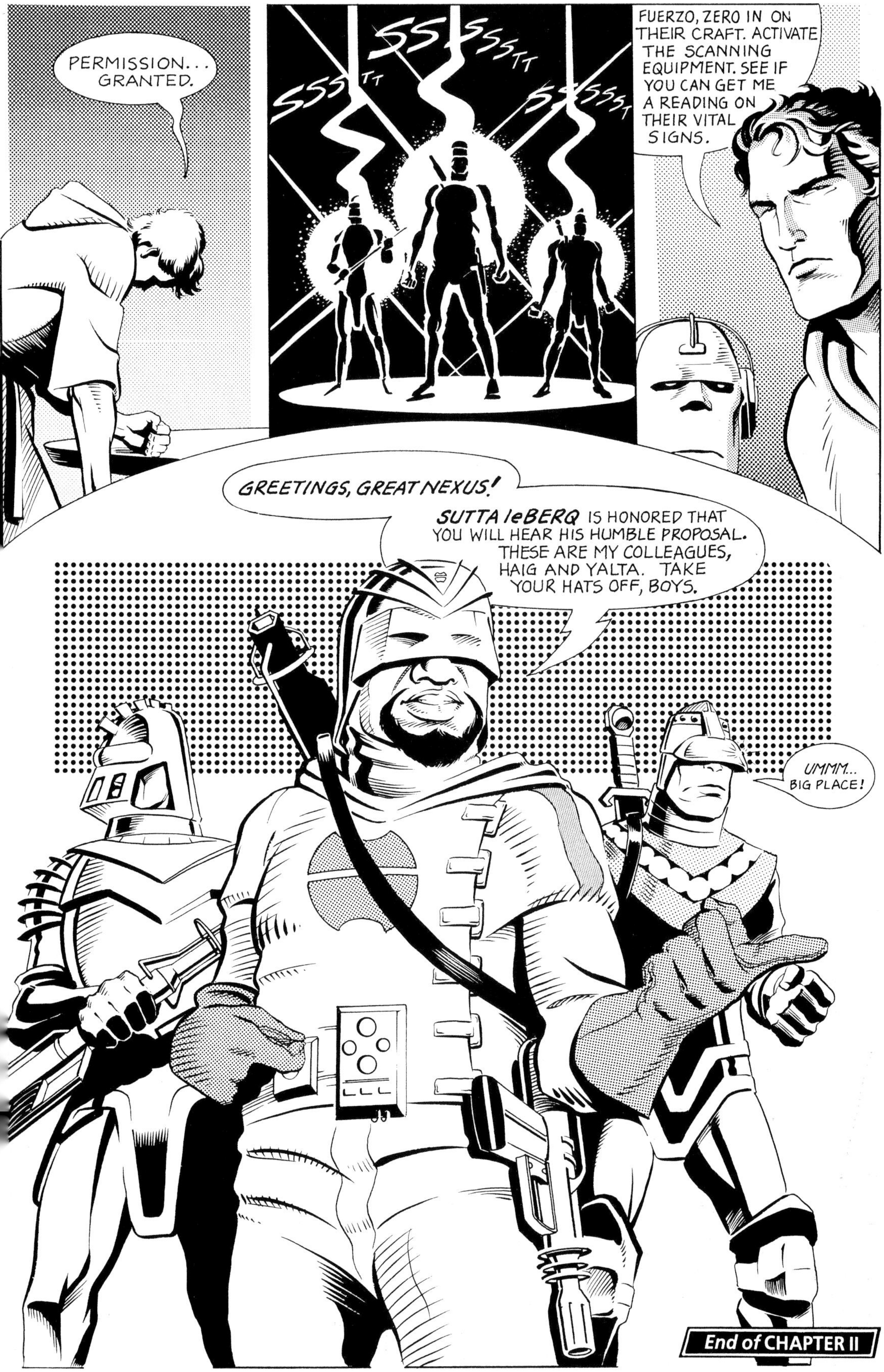

PERMISSION... GRANTED.
SSSSSTT SSSTT SSSSST
FUERZO, ZERO IN ON THEIR CRAFT. ACTIVATE THE SCANNING EQUIPMENT. SEE IF YOU CAN GET ME A READING ON THEIR VITAL SIGNS.
GREETINGS, GREAT NEXUS!
SUTTA leBERQ IS HONORED THAT YOU WILL HEAR HIS HUMBLE PROPOSAL. THESE ARE MY COLLEAGUES, HAIG AND YALTA. TAKE YOUR HATS OFF, BOYS.
UMMM... BIG PLACE!
End of CHAPTER II

CHAPTER III

THIS IS AN *HONOR*, NEXUS.

YOUR FAME HAS SPREAD THROUGHOUT CIVILIZATION. ALL MORAL SENTIENTS KNOW AND APPROVE OF YOUR MISSION.

STATE YOUR PROPOSITION.

WE WILL HIRE YOU TO *KILL* A SENTIENT.

PRESUMPTIOUS MAN.

WHY SHOULD I NOT KILL *YOU*?

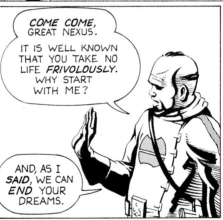

COME COME, GREAT NEXUS.

IT IS WELL KNOWN THAT YOU TAKE NO LIFE *FRIVOLOUSLY*. WHY START WITH ME?

AND, AS I *SAID*, WE CAN *END* YOUR DREAMS.

THIS WAY, GENTLEMEN.

GREAT NEXUS...

MIGHT IT NOT PROVE *WISE* TO HAVE AN *IMPARTIAL OBSERVER*? A *HUMAN* OBSERVER? FOR POSTERITY'S SAKE.

BRING THE *PEALE* WOMAN.

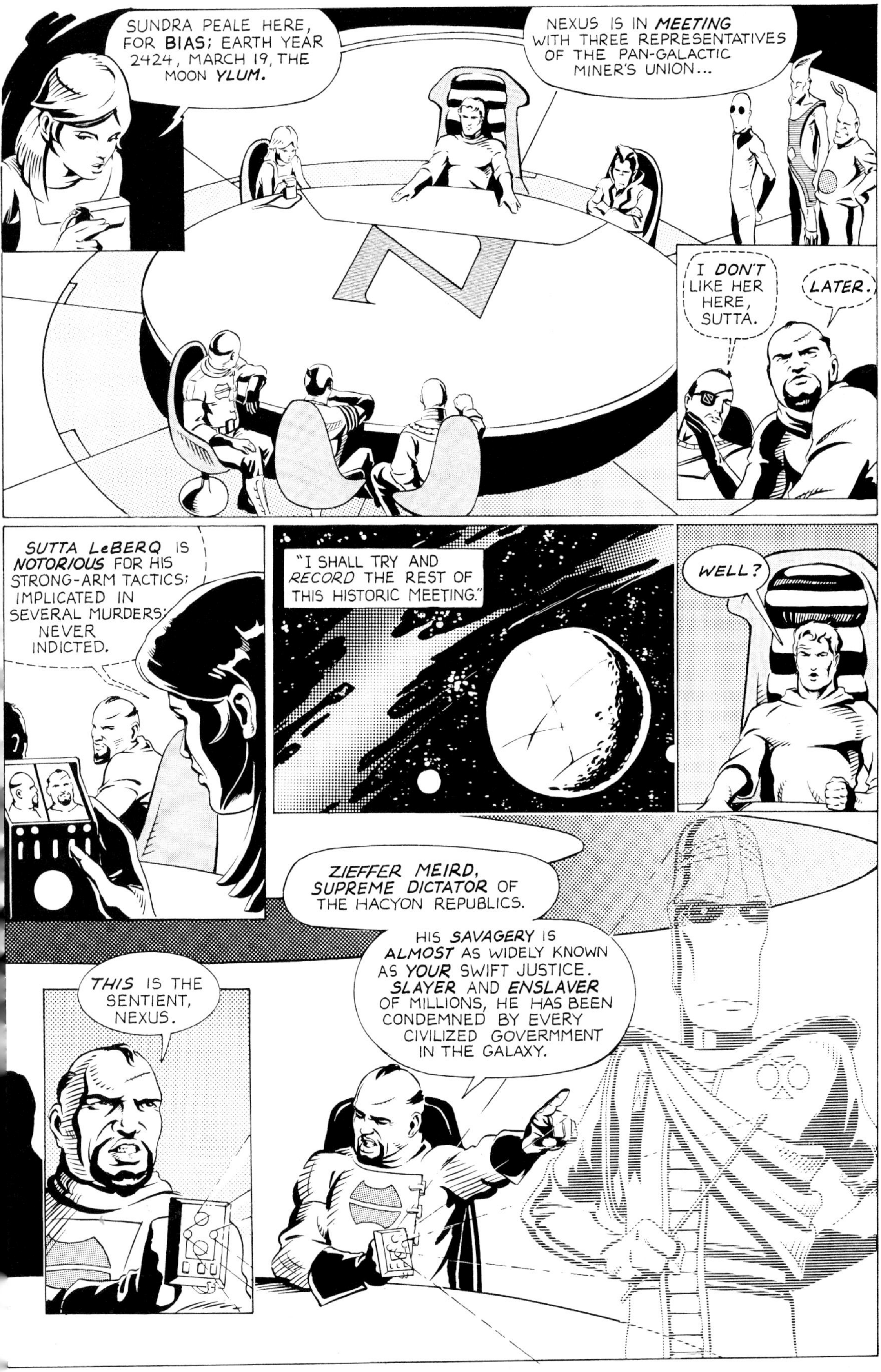
SUNDRA PEALE HERE, FOR BIAS; EARTH YEAR 2424, MARCH 19, THE MOON YLUM.
NEXUS IS IN MEETING WITH THREE REPRESENTATIVES OF THE PAN-GALACTIC MINER'S UNION...
I DON'T LIKE HER HERE, SUTTA.
LATER.
SUTTA LeBERQ IS NOTORIOUS FOR HIS STRONG-ARM TACTICS; IMPLICATED IN SEVERAL MURDERS; NEVER INDICTED.
"I SHALL TRY AND RECORD THE REST OF THIS HISTORIC MEETING."
WELL?
THIS IS THE SENTIENT, NEXUS.
ZIEFFER MEIRD, SUPREME DICTATOR OF THE HACYON REPUBLICS.
HIS SAVAGERY IS ALMOST AS WIDELY KNOWN AS YOUR SWIFT JUSTICE. SLAYER AND ENSLAVER OF MILLIONS, HE HAS BEEN CONDEMNED BY EVERY CIVILIZED GOVERMMENT IN THE GALAXY.

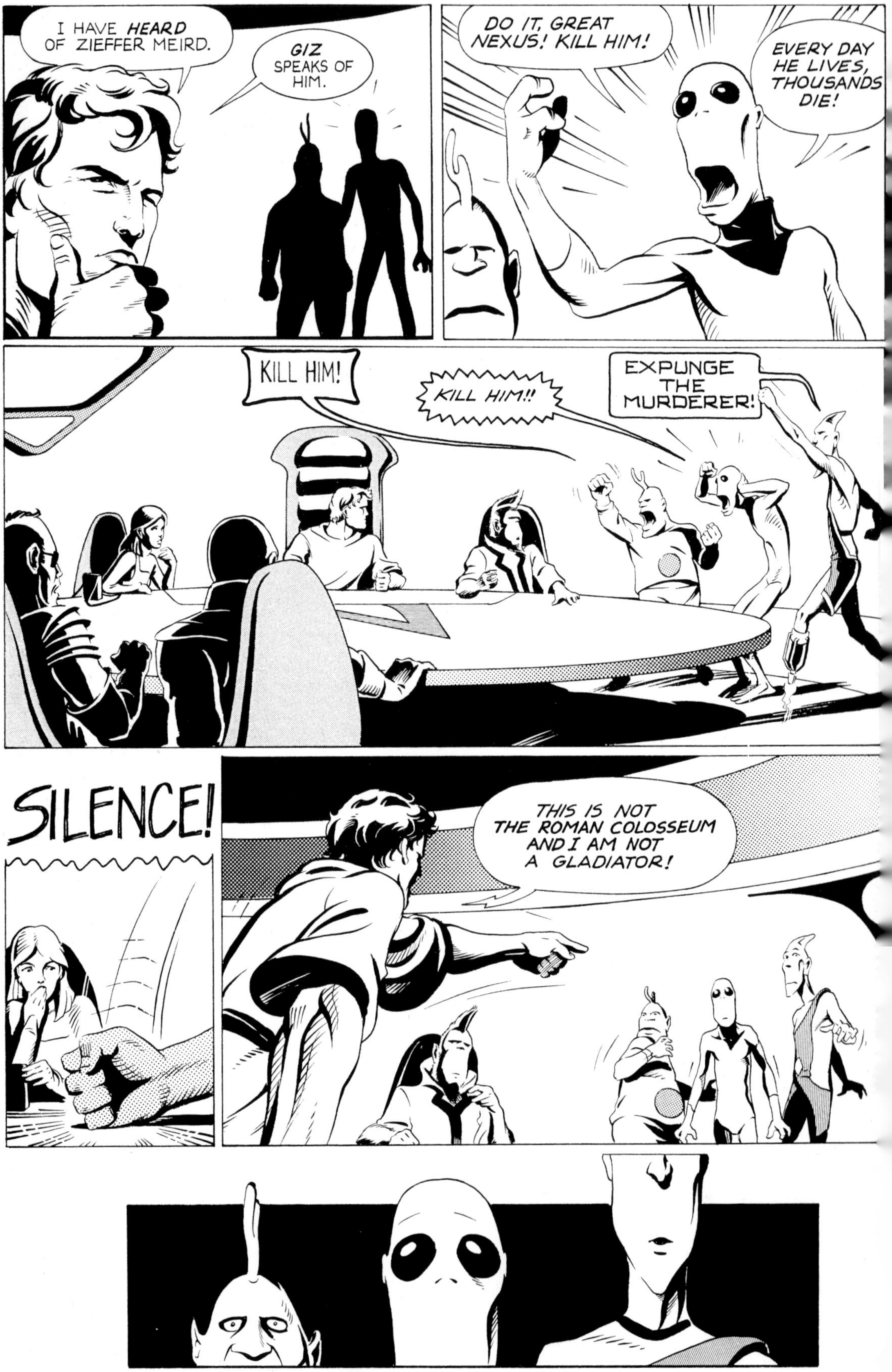
I HAVE HEARD OF ZIEFFER MEIRD.
GIZ SPEAKS OF HIM.
DO IT, GREAT NEXUS! KILL HIM!
EVERY DAY HE LIVES, THOUSANDS DIE!
KILL HIM!
KILL HIM!!
EXPUNGE THE MURDERER!
SILENCE!
THIS IS NOT THE ROMAN COLOSSEUM AND I AM NOT A GLADIATOR!

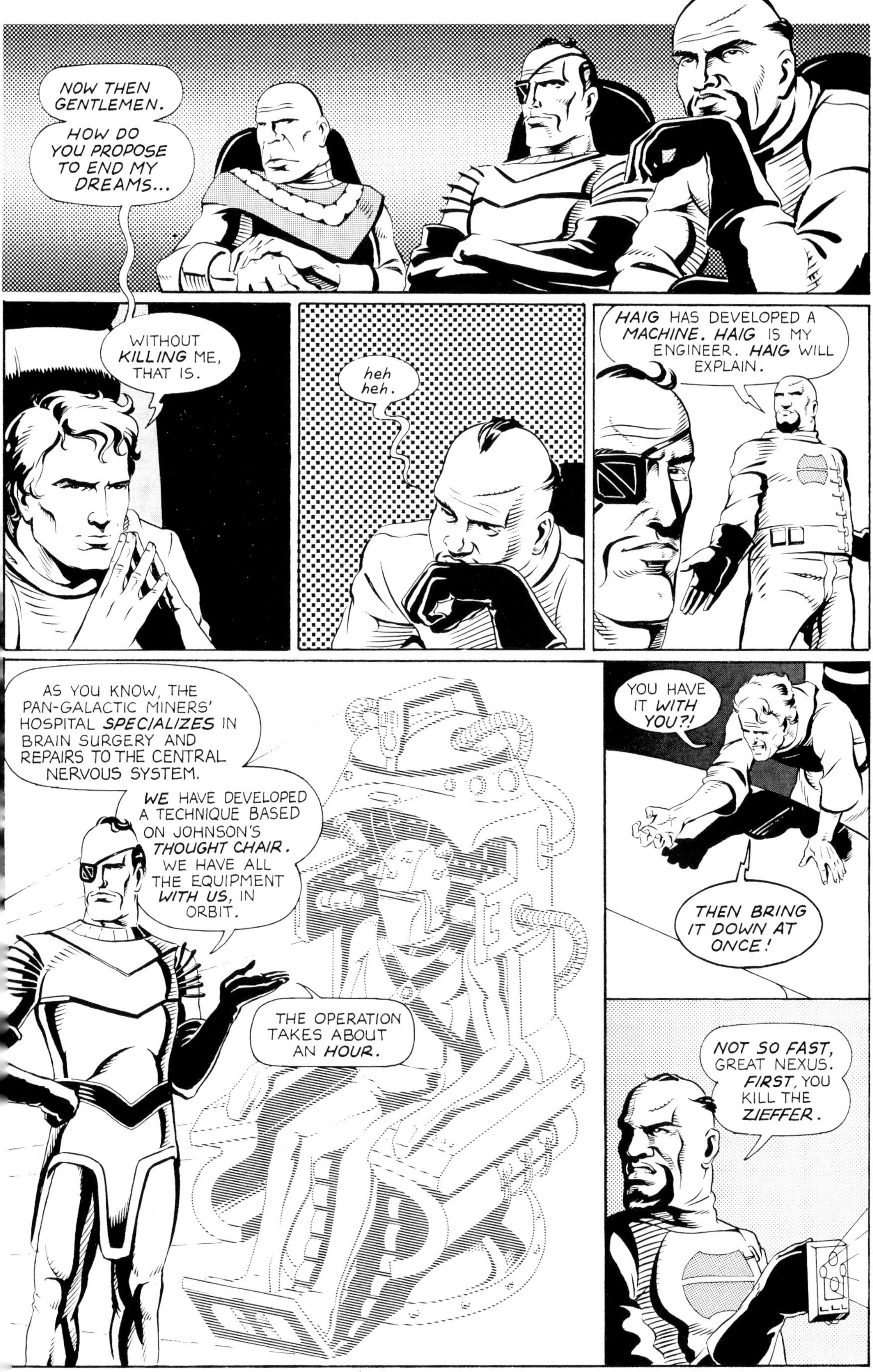
NOW THEN GENTLEMEN.
HOW DO YOU PROPOSE TO END MY DREAMS...
WITHOUT KILLING ME, THAT IS.
heh heh.
HAIG HAS DEVELOPED A MACHINE. HAIG IS MY ENGINEER. HAIG WILL EXPLAIN.
AS YOU KNOW, THE PAN-GALACTIC MINERS' HOSPITAL SPECIALIZES IN BRAIN SURGERY AND REPAIRS TO THE CENTRAL NERVOUS SYSTEM.
WE HAVE DEVELOPED A TECHNIQUE BASED ON JOHNSON'S THOUGHT CHAIR. WE HAVE ALL THE EQUIPMENT WITH US, IN ORBIT.
THE OPERATION TAKES ABOUT AN HOUR.
YOU HAVE IT WITH YOU?!
THEN BRING IT DOWN AT ONCE!
NOT SO FAST, GREAT NEXUS. FIRST, YOU KILL THE ZIEFFER.

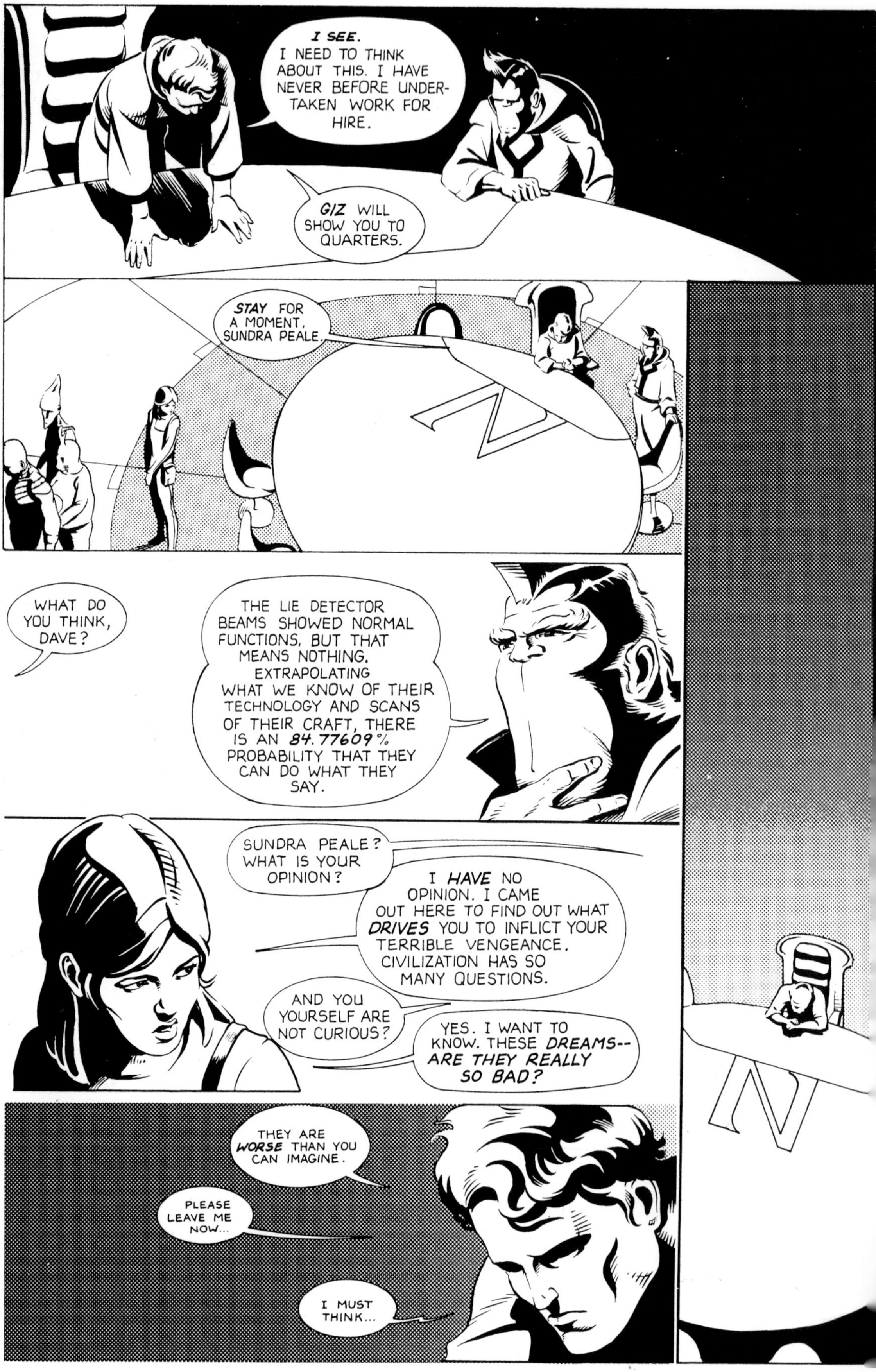
I SEE. I NEED TO THINK ABOUT THIS. I HAVE NEVER BEFORE UNDERTAKEN WORK FOR HIRE.
GIZ WILL SHOW YOU TO QUARTERS.
STAY FOR A MOMENT, SUNDRA PEALE.
WHAT DO YOU THINK, DAVE?
THE LIE DETECTOR BEAMS SHOWED NORMAL FUNCTIONS, BUT THAT MEANS NOTHING. EXTRAPOLATING WHAT WE KNOW OF THEIR TECHNOLOGY AND SCANS OF THEIR CRAFT, THERE IS AN 84.77609% PROBABILITY THAT THEY CAN DO WHAT THEY SAY.
SUNDRA PEALE? WHAT IS YOUR OPINION?
I HAVE NO OPINION. I CAME OUT HERE TO FIND OUT WHAT DRIVES YOU TO INFLICT YOUR TERRIBLE VENGEANCE. CIVILIZATION HAS SO MANY QUESTIONS.
AND YOU YOURSELF ARE NOT CURIOUS?
YES. I WANT TO KNOW. THESE DREAMS-- ARE THEY REALLY SO BAD?
THEY ARE WORSE THAN YOU CAN IMAGINE.
PLEASE LEAVE ME NOW...
I MUST THINK...

"SUNDRA PEALE, HERE...I HAVE INTERVIEWED MANY OF THE INHABITANTS, INCLUDING SKILLED ARCHITECTS, ARTISTS, AND ENGINEERS. BUT NO ONE KNOWS WHO BUILT THIS INCREDIBLE COMPLEX. *THREE DAYS* HAVE PASSED SINCE *NEXUS'* LAST APPEARANCE."

"I AM NOW INVESTIGATING A GREAT *HALL* FILLED WITH STRANGE AND BEAUTIFUL ARTIFACTS..."

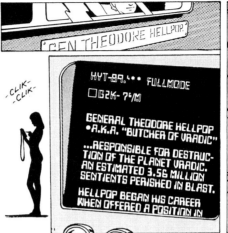

-CLIK-
-CLIK-

"GEN. THEODORE HELLPOP"

HYT-89.** FULLMODE
G2K-7%/M

GENERAL THEODORE HELLPOP
•A.K.A. "BUTCHER OF VRADIC"

...RESPONSIBLE FOR DESTRUC-
TION OF THE PLANET VRADIC.
AN ESTIMATED 3.56 MILLION
SENTIENTS PERISHED IN BLAST.

HELLPOP BEGAN HIS CAREER
WHEN OFFERED A POSITION IN

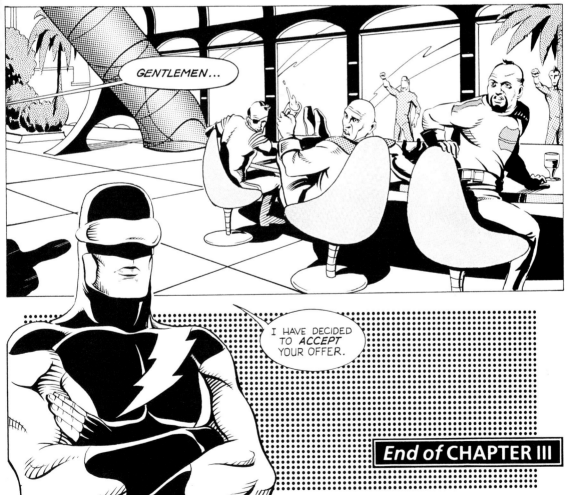

GENTLEMEN...

I HAVE DECIDED TO *ACCEPT* YOUR OFFER.

End of CHAPTER III

39

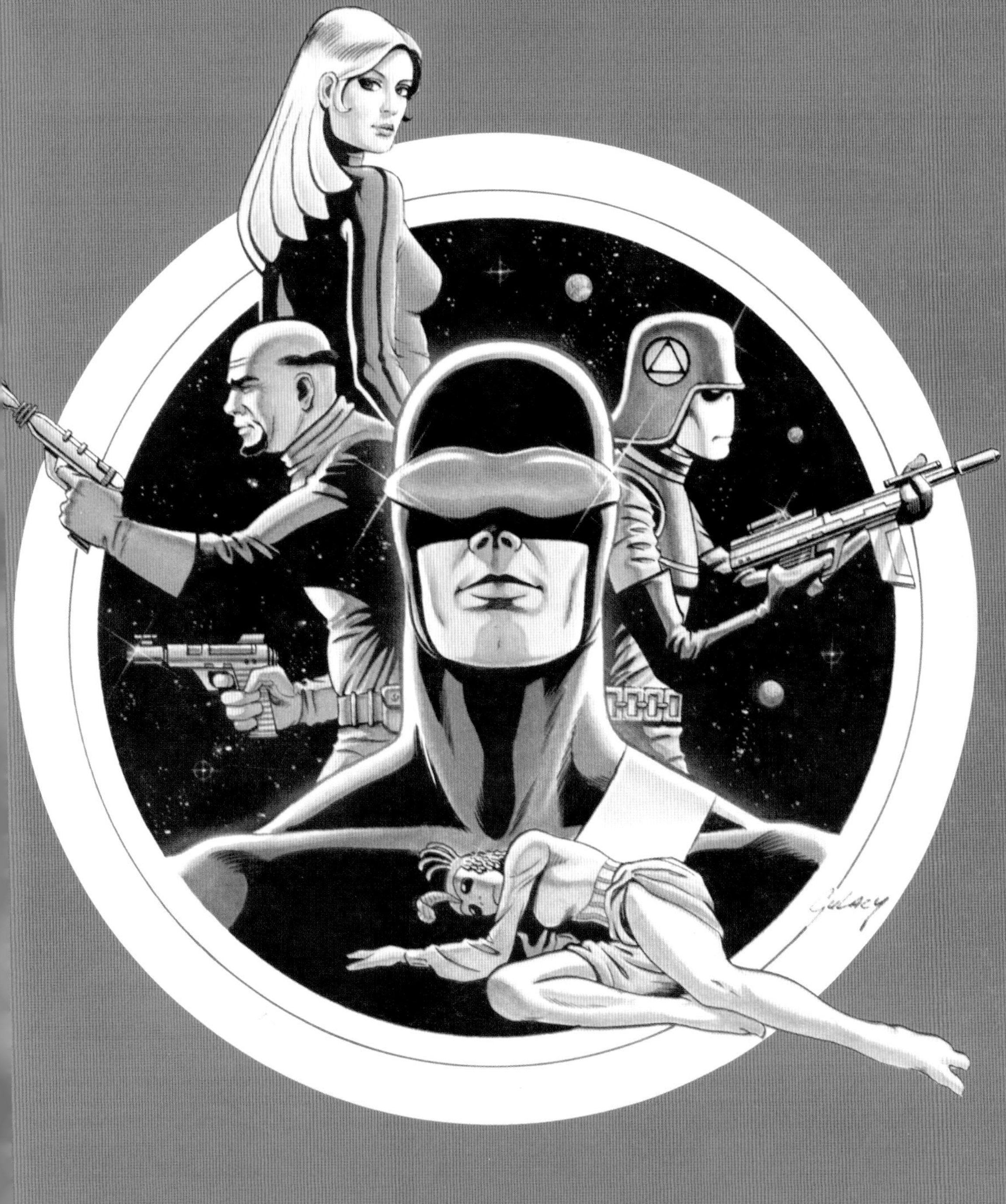

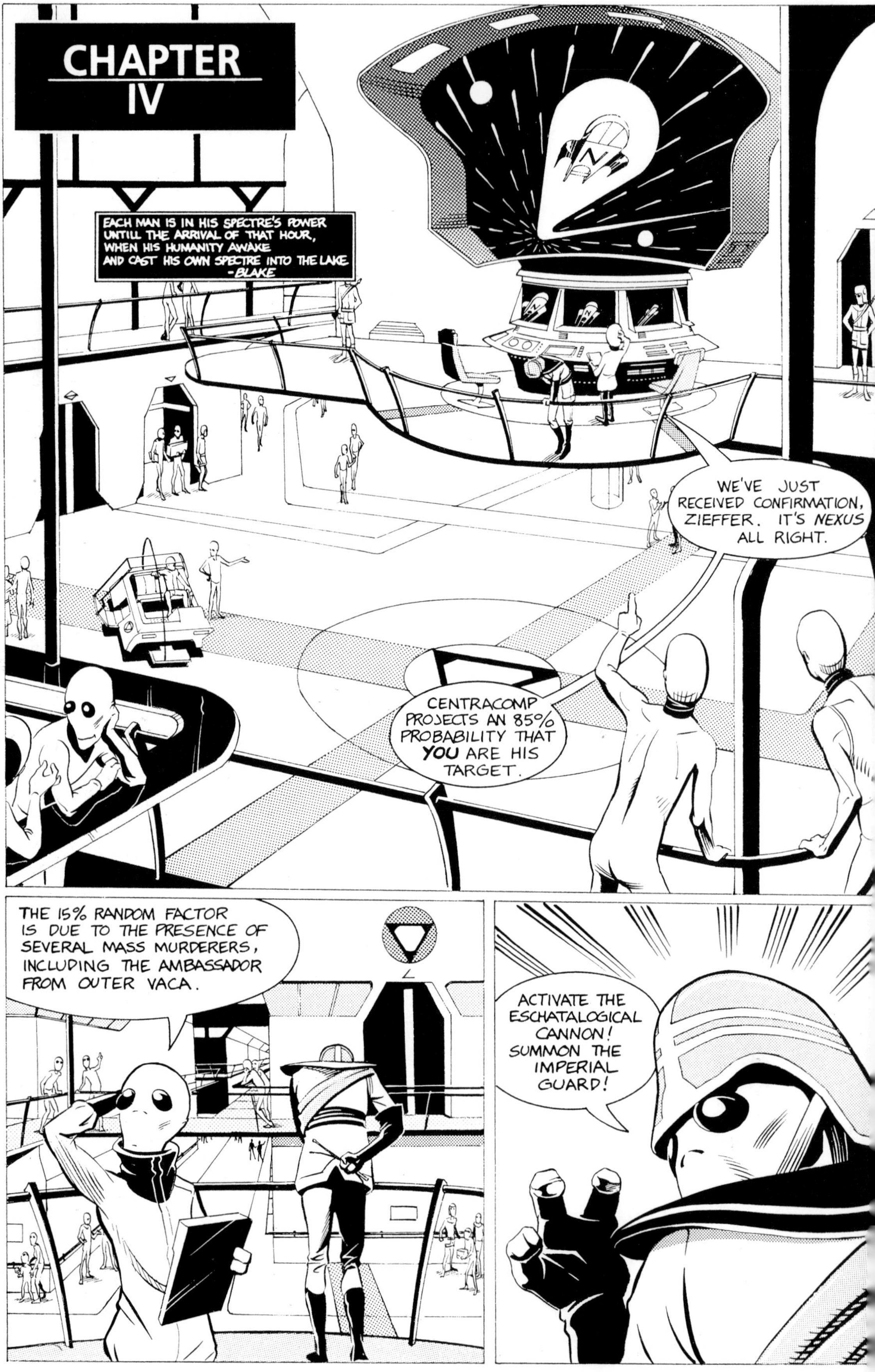
CHAPTER IV
EACH MAN IS IN HIS SPECTRE'S POWER
UNTILL THE ARRIVAL OF THAT HOUR,
WHEN HIS HUMANITY AWAKE
AND CAST HIS OWN SPECTRE INTO THE LAKE
-BLAKE
WE'VE JUST RECEIVED CONFIRMATION, ZIEFFER. IT'S NEXUS ALL RIGHT.
CENTRACOMP PROJECTS AN 85% PROBABILITY THAT YOU ARE HIS TARGET.
THE 15% RANDOM FACTOR IS DUE TO THE PRESENCE OF SEVERAL MASS MURDERERS, INCLUDING THE AMBASSADOR FROM OUTER VACA.
ACTIVATE THE ESCHATALOGICAL CANNON! SUMMON THE IMPERIAL GUARD!

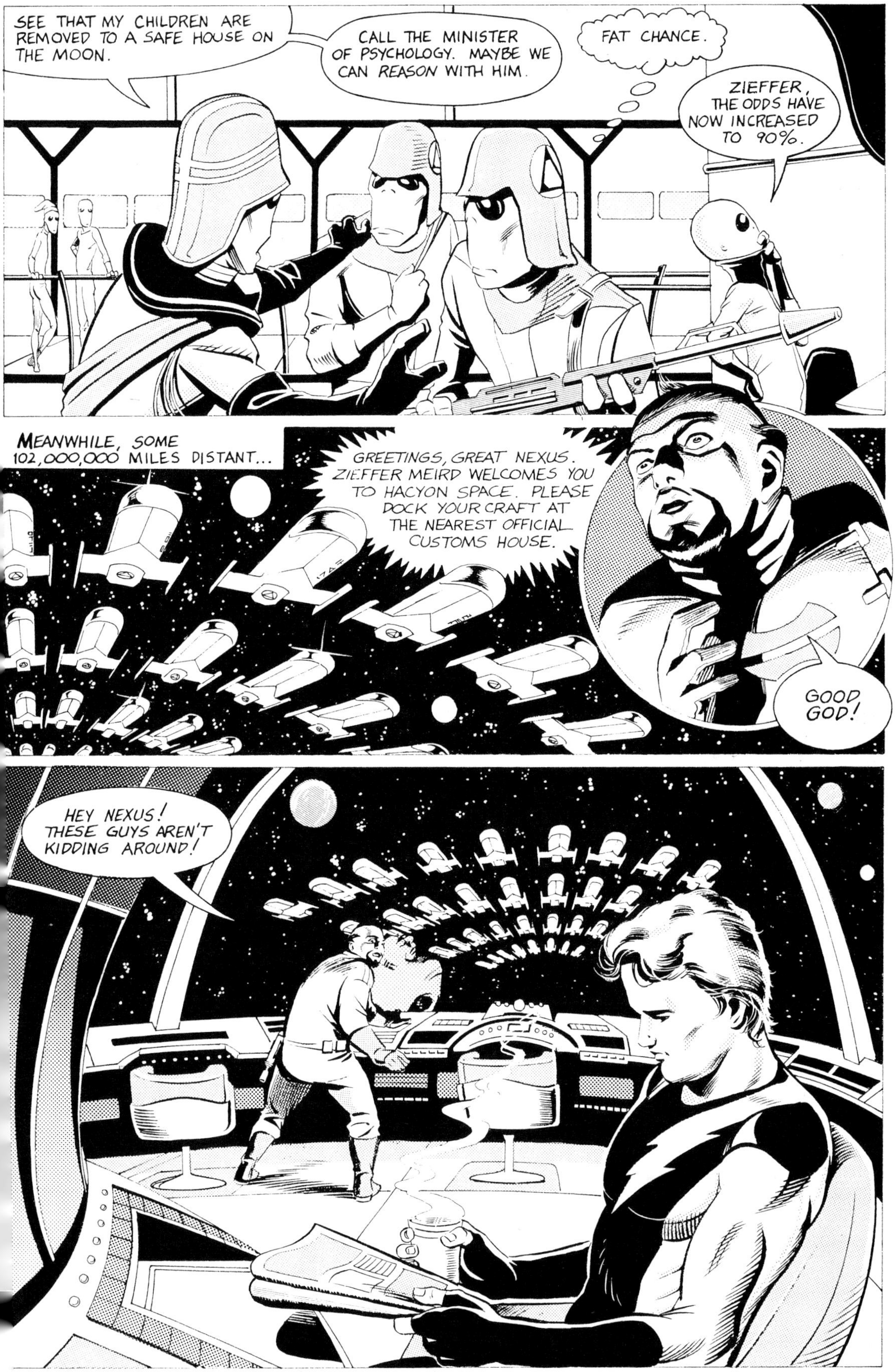
SEE THAT MY CHILDREN ARE REMOVED TO A SAFE HOUSE ON THE MOON.
CALL THE MINISTER OF PSYCHOLOGY. MAYBE WE CAN REASON WITH HIM.
FAT CHANCE.
ZIEFFER, THE ODDS HAVE NOW INCREASED TO 90%.
MEANWHILE, SOME 102,000,000 MILES DISTANT...
GREETINGS, GREAT NEXUS. ZIEFFER MEIRD WELCOMES YOU TO HACYON SPACE. PLEASE DOCK YOUR CRAFT AT THE NEAREST OFFICIAL CUSTOMS HOUSE.
GOOD GOD!
HEY NEXUS! THESE GUYS AREN'T KIDDING AROUND!

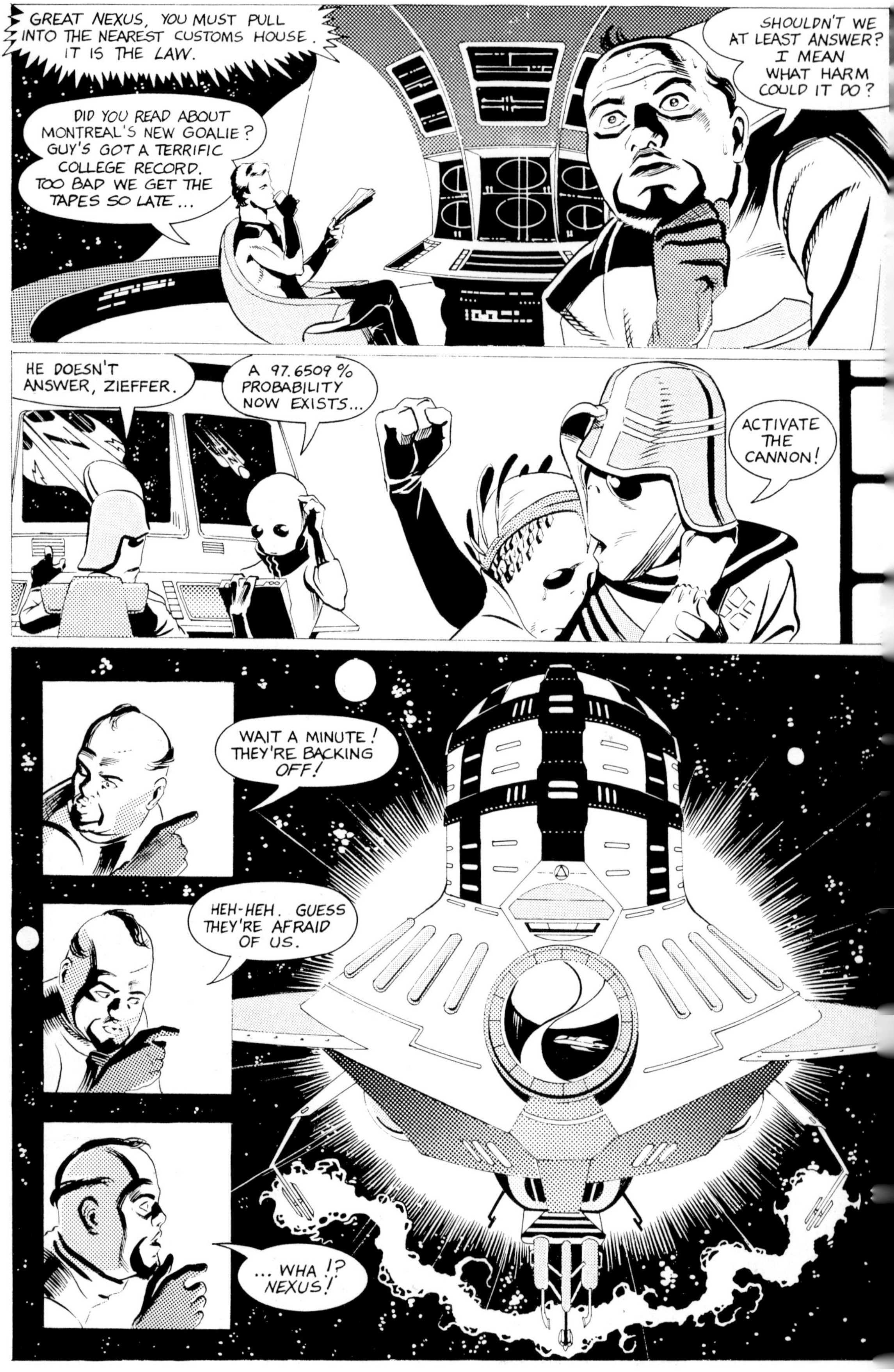
GREAT NEXUS, YOU MUST PULL INTO THE NEAREST CUSTOMS HOUSE. IT IS THE LAW.
DID YOU READ ABOUT MONTREAL'S NEW GOALIE? GUY'S GOT A TERRIFIC COLLEGE RECORD. TOO BAD WE GET THE TAPES SO LATE...
SHOULDN'T WE AT LEAST ANSWER? I MEAN WHAT HARM COULD IT DO?
HE DOESN'T ANSWER, ZIEFFER.
A 97.6509% PROBABILITY NOW EXISTS...
ACTIVATE THE CANNON!
WAIT A MINUTE! THEY'RE BACKING OFF!
HEH-HEH. GUESS THEY'RE AFRAID OF US.
...WHA!? NEXUS!

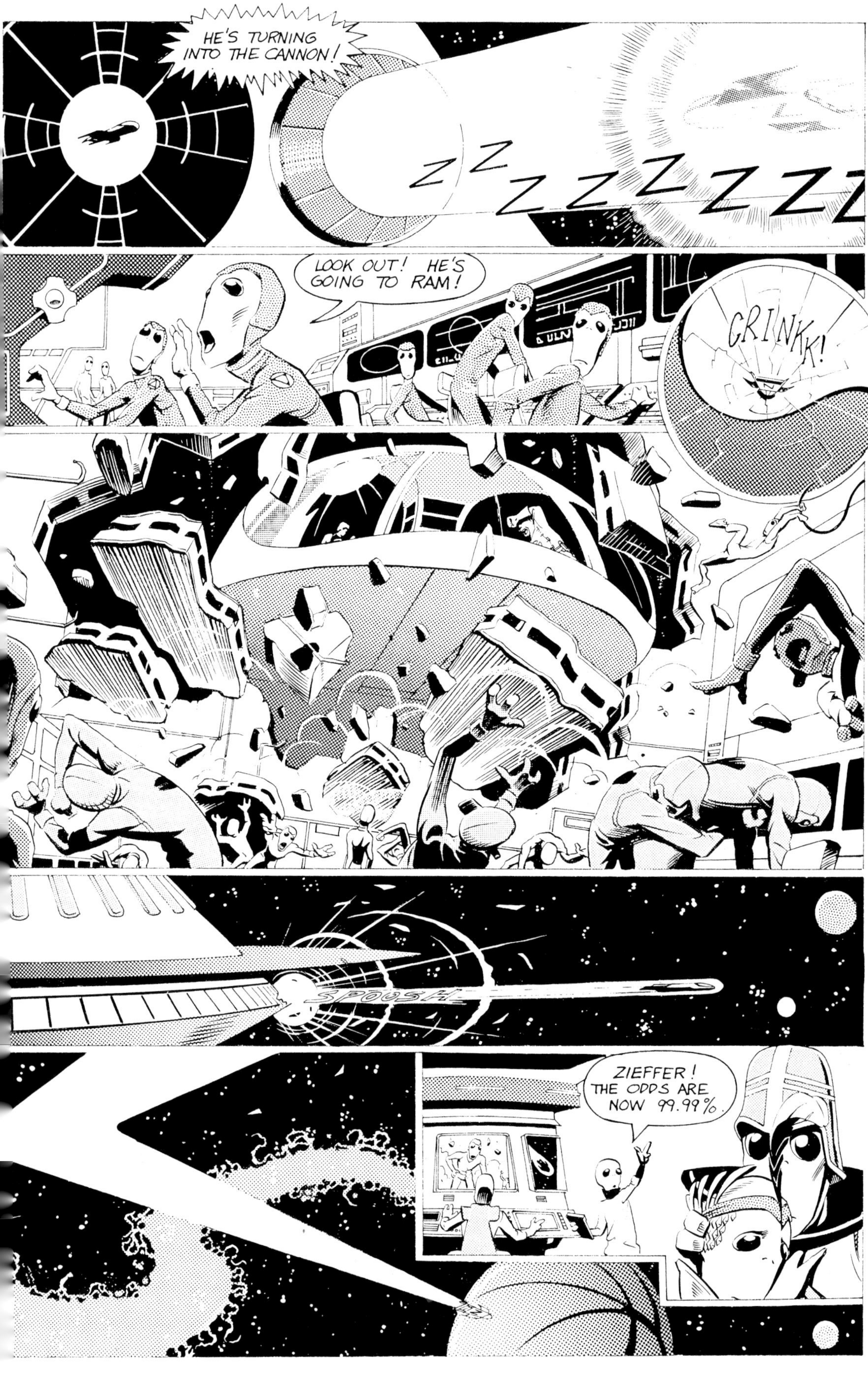
HE'S TURNING INTO THE CANNON!
ZZZZZZZZZ
LOOK OUT! HE'S GOING TO RAM!
CRINKK!
SPOOSH
ZIEFFER! THE ODDS ARE NOW 99.99%.

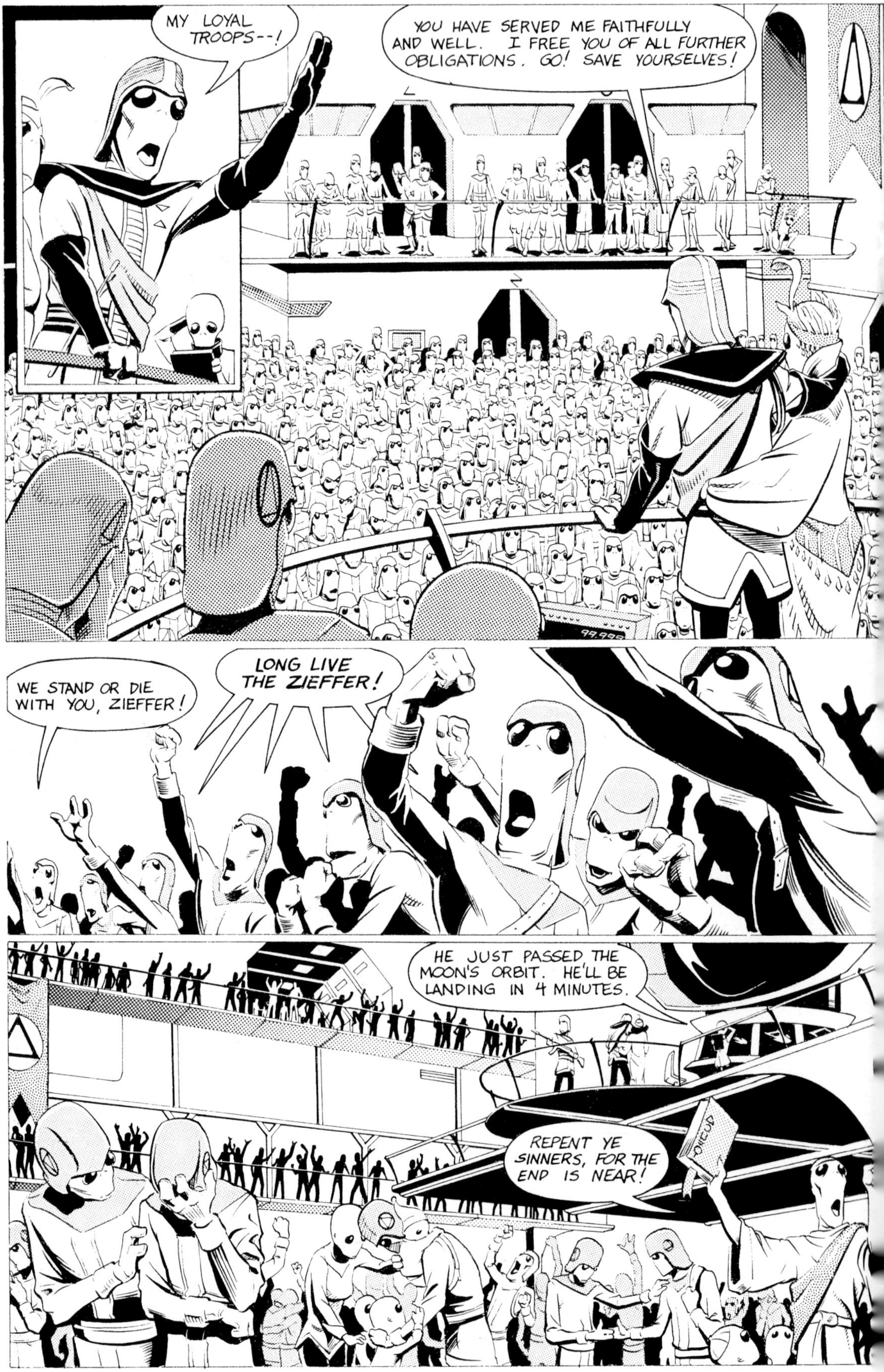
MY LOYAL TROOPS--!
YOU HAVE SERVED ME FAITHFULLY AND WELL. I FREE YOU OF ALL FURTHER OBLIGATIONS. GO! SAVE YOURSELVES!
WE STAND OR DIE WITH YOU, ZIEFFER!
LONG LIVE THE ZIEFFER!
HE JUST PASSED THE MOON'S ORBIT. HE'LL BE LANDING IN 4 MINUTES.
REPENT YE SINNERS, FOR THE END IS NEAR!

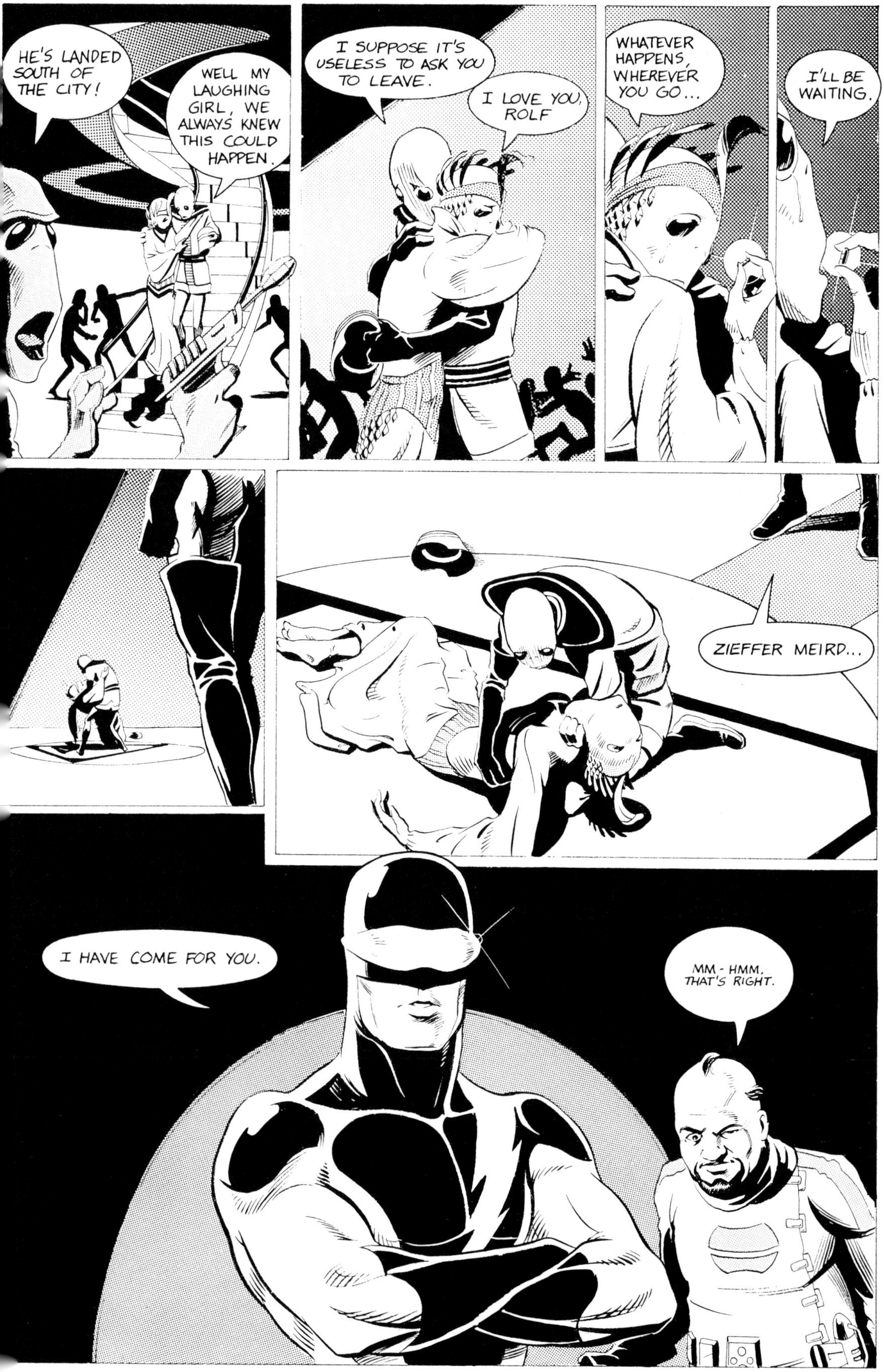
HE'S LANDED SOUTH OF THE CITY!
WELL MY LAUGHING GIRL, WE ALWAYS KNEW THIS COULD HAPPEN.
I SUPPOSE IT'S USELESS TO ASK YOU TO LEAVE.
I LOVE YOU, ROLF
WHATEVER HAPPENS, WHEREVER YOU GO...
I'LL BE WAITING.
ZIEFFER MEIRD...
I HAVE COME FOR YOU.
MM - HMM. THAT'S RIGHT.

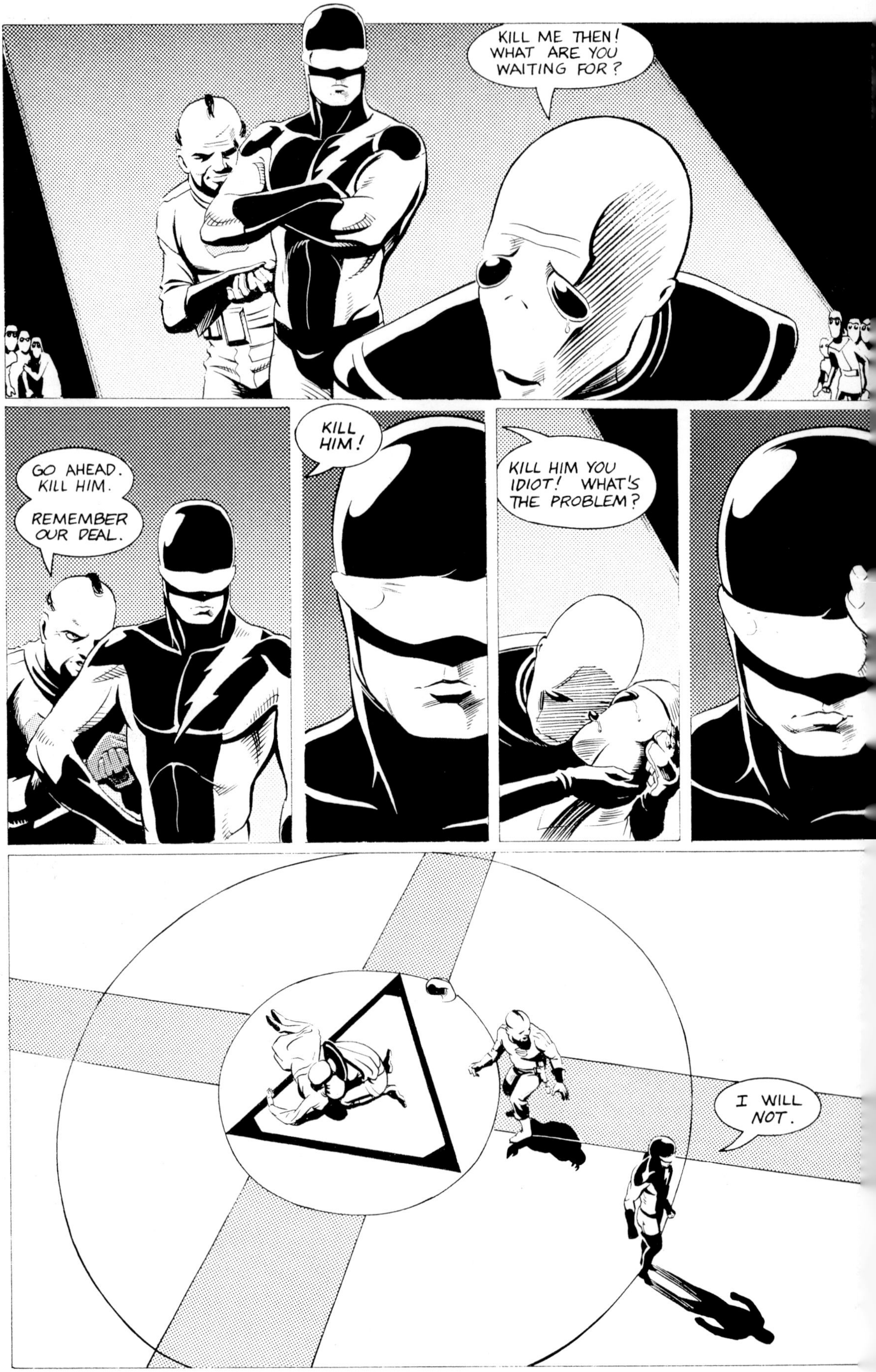
KILL ME THEN! WHAT ARE YOU WAITING FOR?
GO AHEAD. KILL HIM.
REMEMBER OUR DEAL.
KILL HIM!
KILL HIM YOU IDIOT! WHAT'S THE PROBLEM?
I WILL NOT.

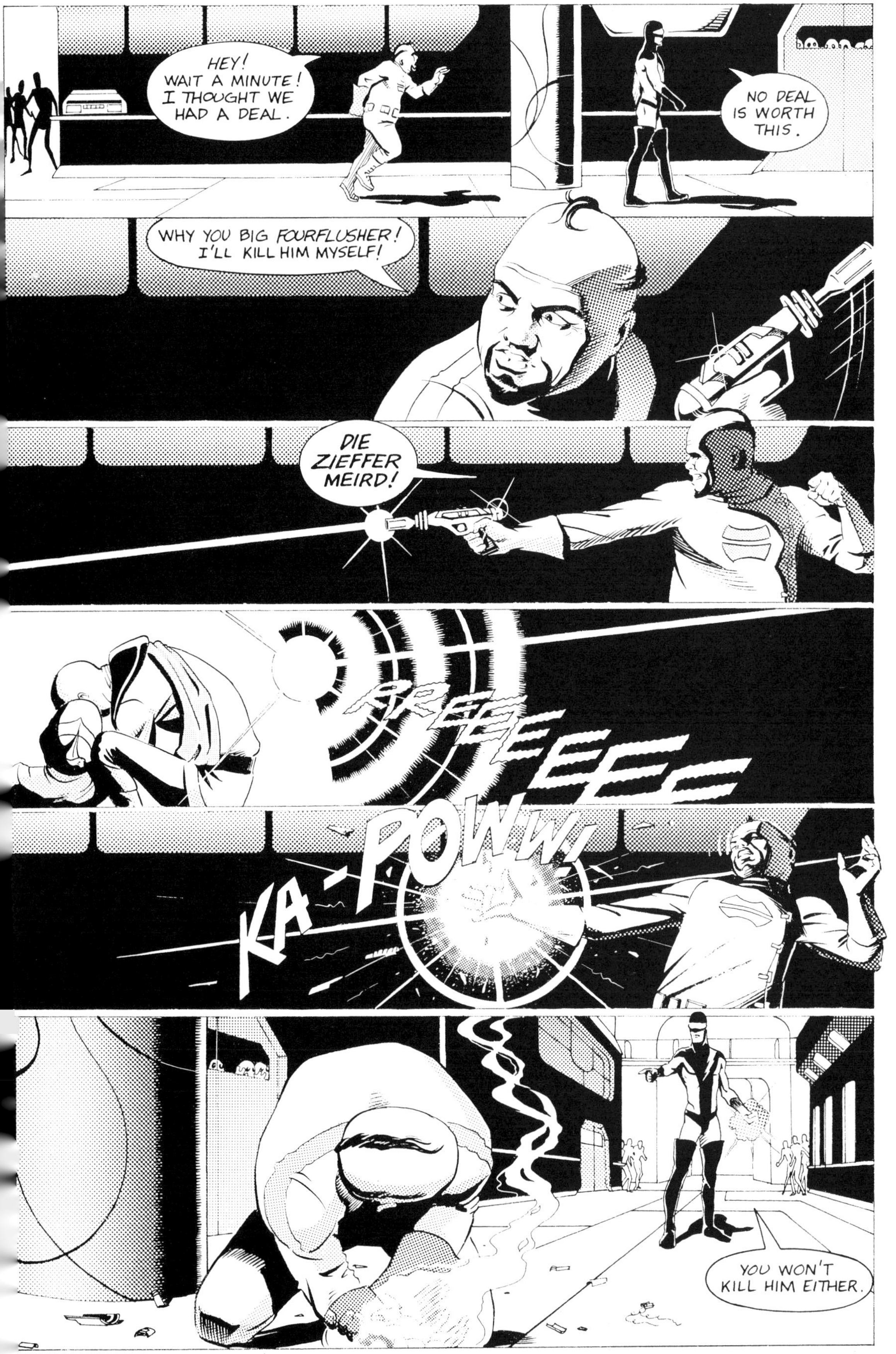
HEY! WAIT A MINUTE! I THOUGHT WE HAD A DEAL.
NO DEAL IS WORTH THIS.
WHY YOU BIG FOURFLUSHER! I'LL KILL HIM MYSELF!
DIE ZIEFFER MEIRD!
RREEEEEEEE
KA-POWW!
YOU WON'T KILL HIM EITHER.

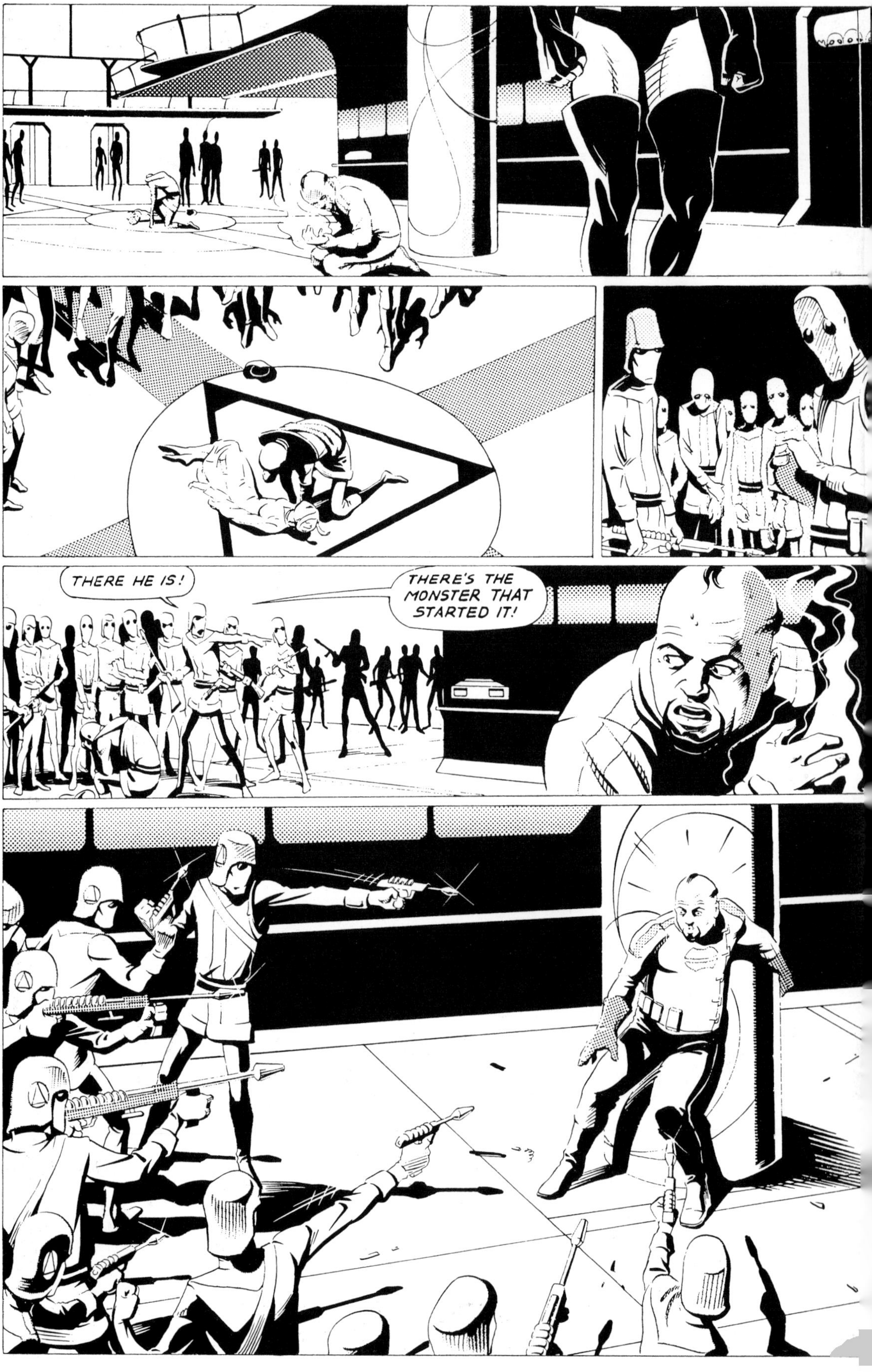
THERE HE IS!
THERE'S THE MONSTER THAT STARTED IT!

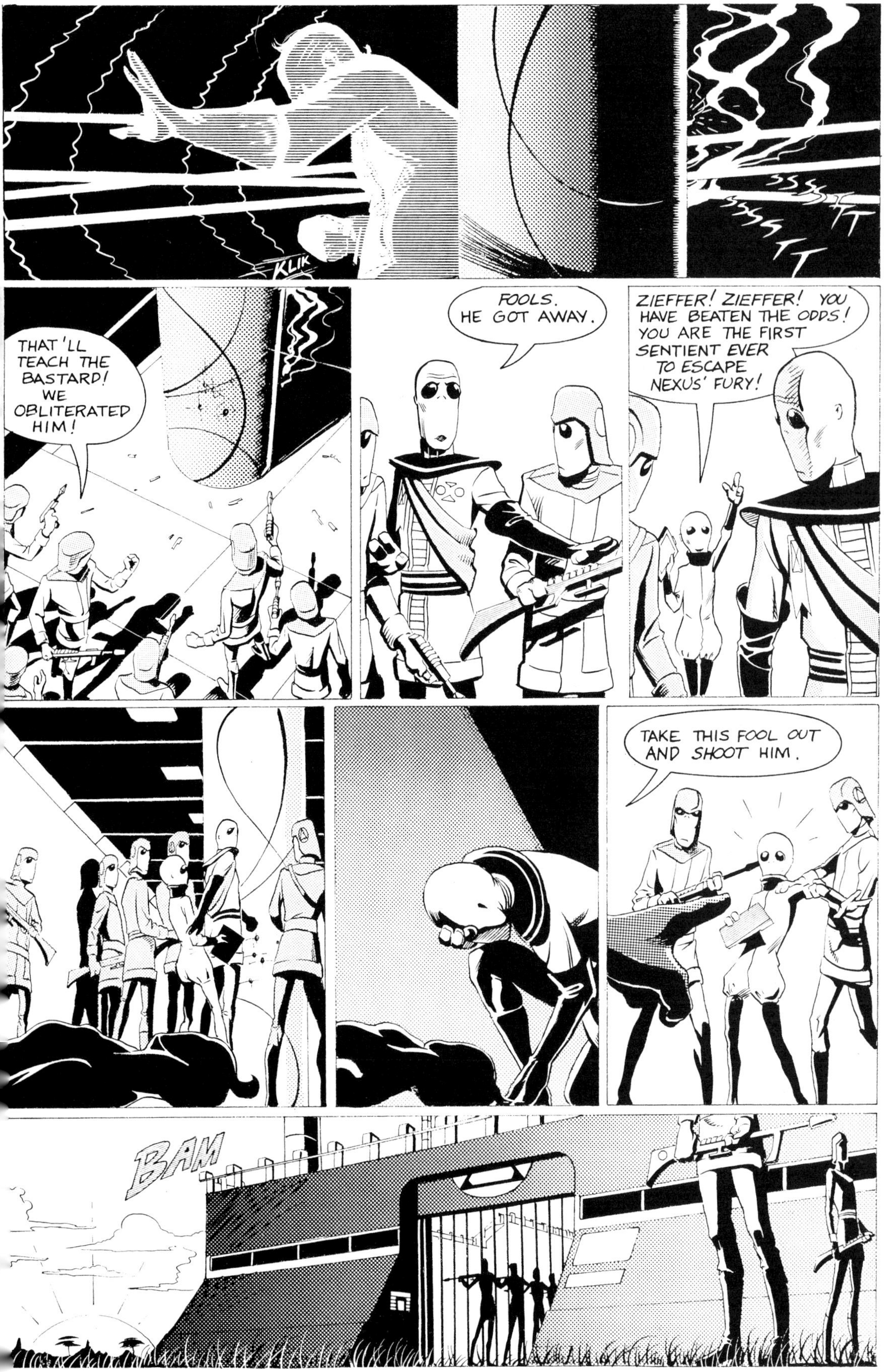
KLIK
SSSSTT
SSSSSTT
THAT'LL TEACH THE BASTARD! WE OBLITERATED HIM!
FOOLS. HE GOT AWAY.
ZIEFFER! ZIEFFER! YOU HAVE BEATEN THE ODDS! YOU ARE THE FIRST SENTIENT EVER TO ESCAPE NEXUS' FURY!
TAKE THIS FOOL OUT AND SHOOT HIM.
BAM

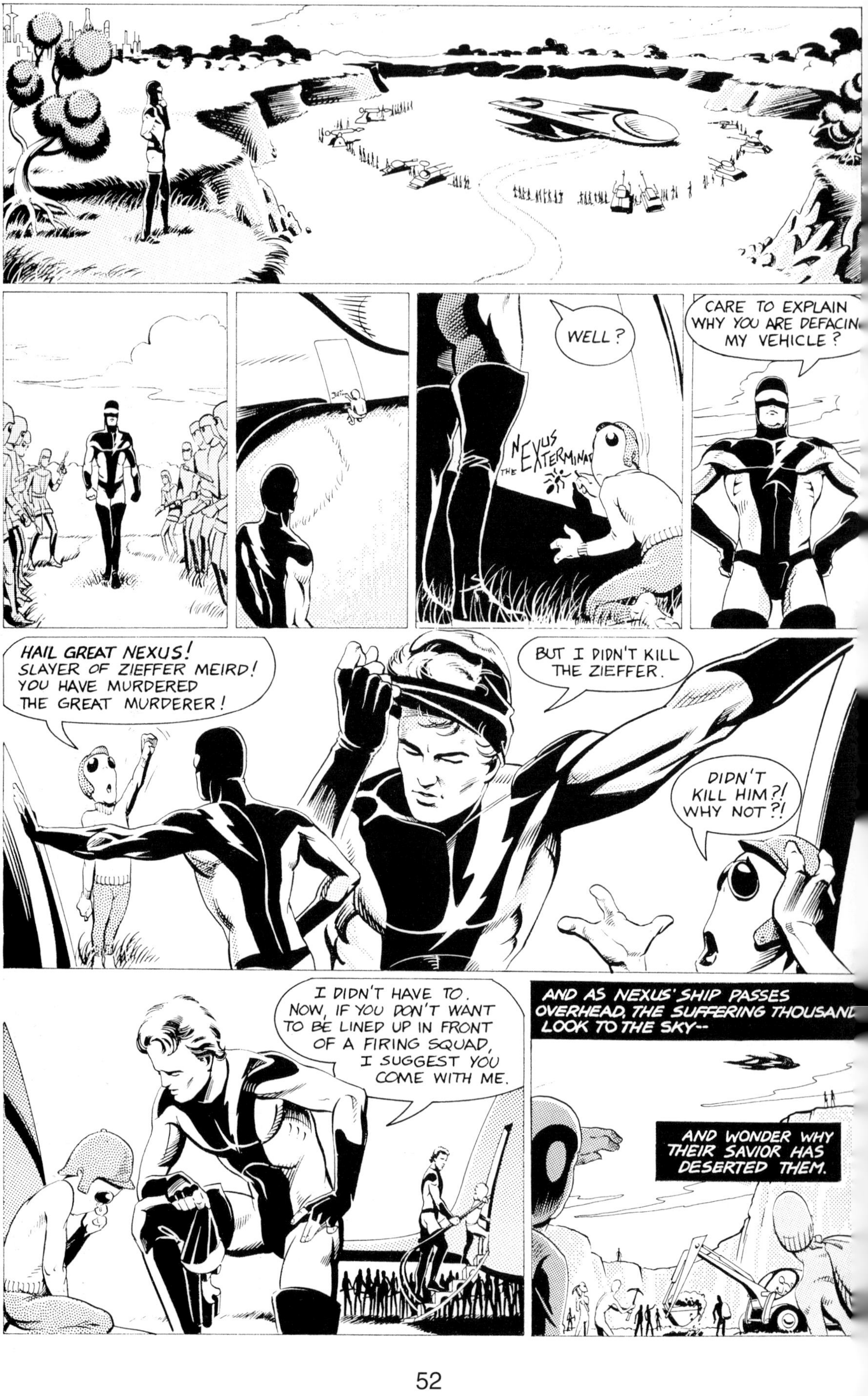
WELL?
CARE TO EXPLAIN WHY YOU ARE DEFACIN MY VEHICLE?
HAIL GREAT NEXUS! SLAYER OF ZIEFFER MEIRD! YOU HAVE MURDERED THE GREAT MURDERER!
BUT I DIDN'T KILL THE ZIEFFER.
DIDN'T KILL HIM?! WHY NOT?!
I DIDN'T HAVE TO. NOW, IF YOU DON'T WANT TO BE LINED UP IN FRONT OF A FIRING SQUAD, I SUGGEST YOU COME WITH ME.
AND AS NEXUS' SHIP PASSES OVERHEAD, THE SUFFERING THOUSAN LOOK TO THE SKY--
AND WONDER WHY THEIR SAVIOR HAS DESERTED THEM.

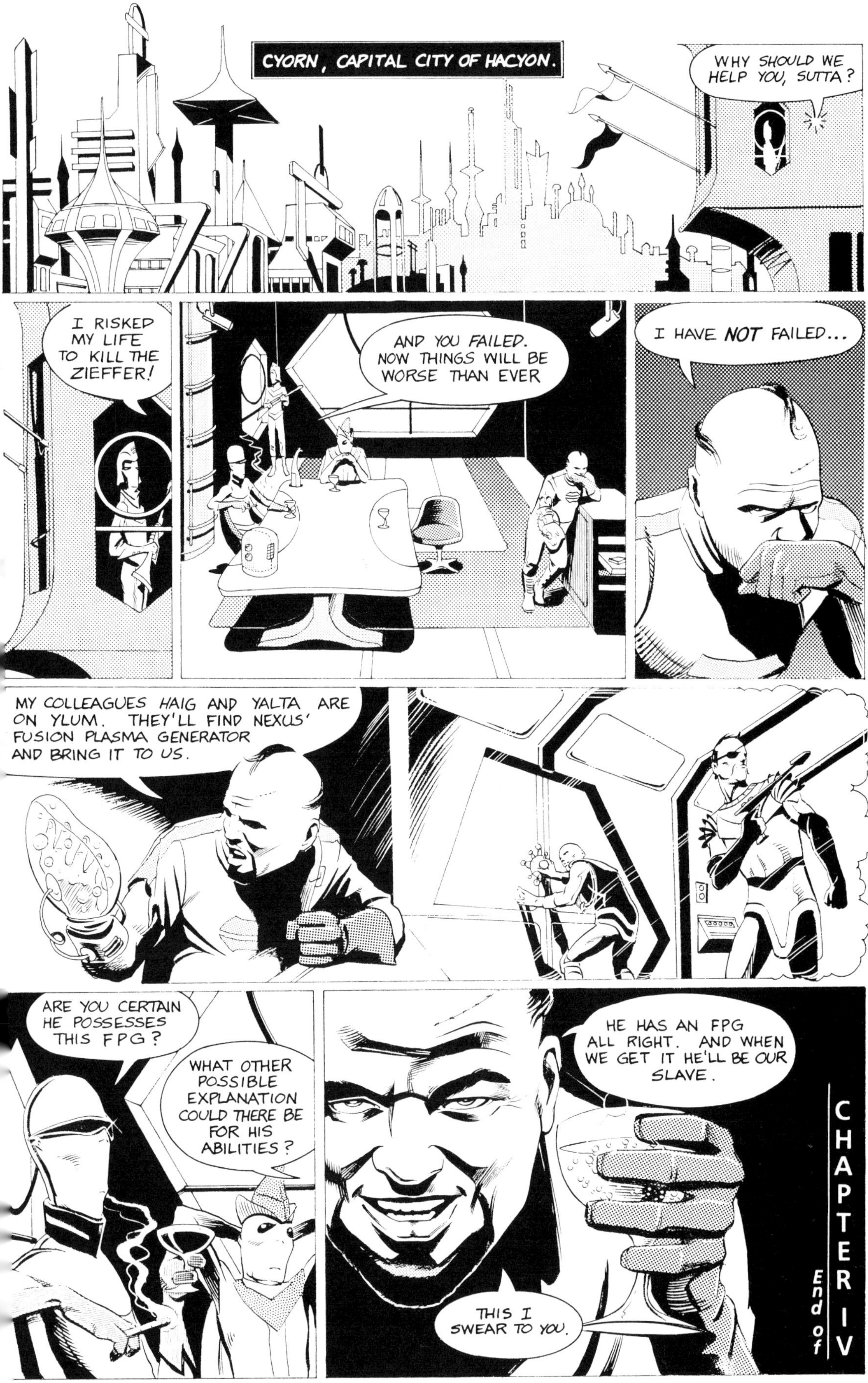
CYORN, CAPITAL CITY OF HACYON.
WHY SHOULD WE HELP YOU, SUTTA?
I RISKED MY LIFE TO KILL THE ZIEFFER!
AND YOU FAILED. NOW THINGS WILL BE WORSE THAN EVER
I HAVE NOT FAILED...
MY COLLEAGUES HAIG AND YALTA ARE ON YLUM. THEY'LL FIND NEXUS' FUSION PLASMA GENERATOR AND BRING IT TO US.
ARE YOU CERTAIN HE POSSESSES THIS FPG?
WHAT OTHER POSSIBLE EXPLANATION COULD THERE BE FOR HIS ABILITIES?
HE HAS AN FPG ALL RIGHT. AND WHEN WE GET IT HE'LL BE OUR SLAVE.
THIS I SWEAR TO YOU.
End of CHAPTER IV

CHAPTER V

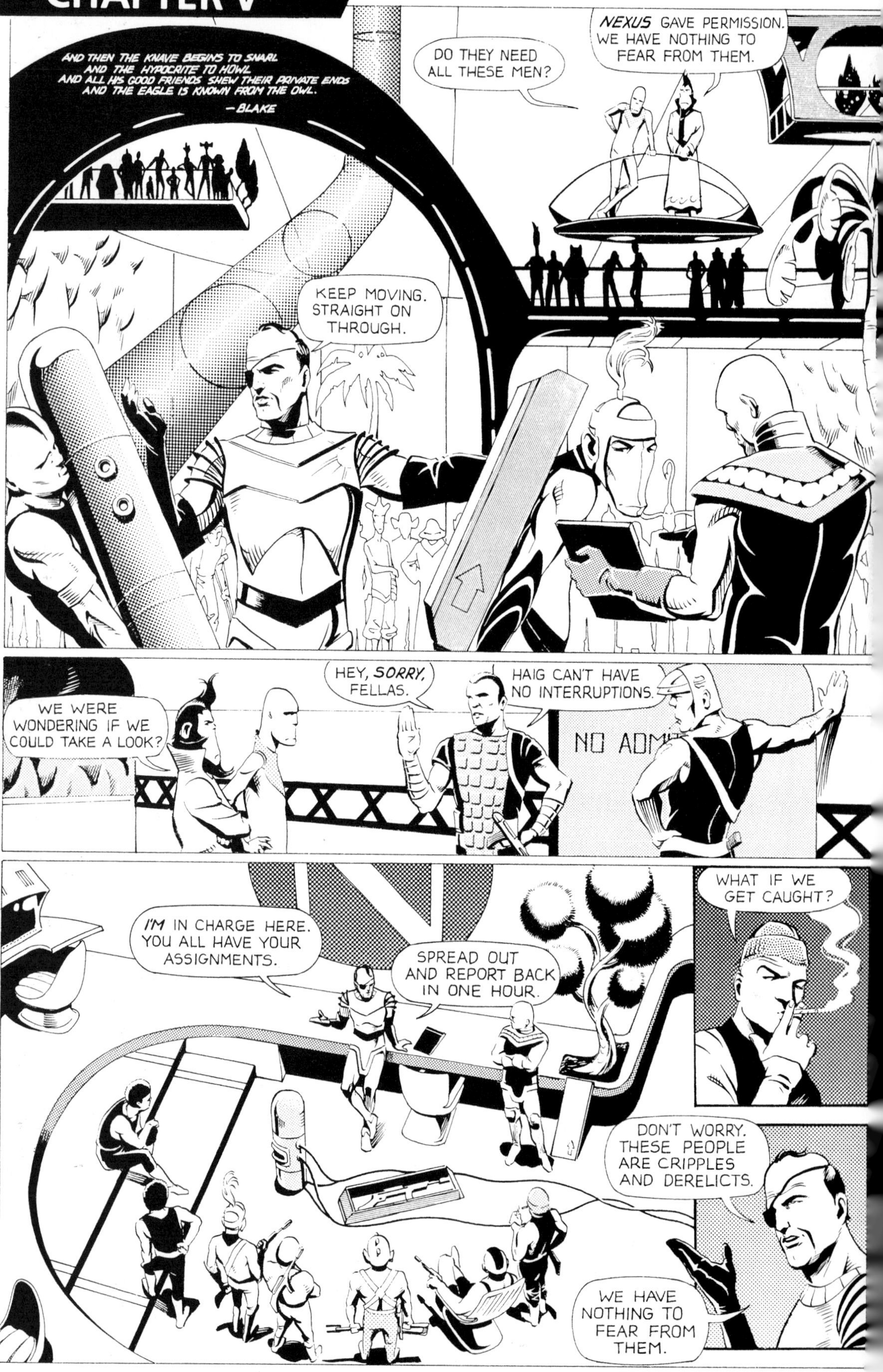
AND THEN THE KNAVE BEGINS TO SNARL
AND THE HYPOCRITE TO HOWL
AND ALL HIS GOOD FRIENDS SHEW THEIR PRIVATE ENDS
AND THE EAGLE IS KNOWN FROM THE OWL.
—BLAKE
DO THEY NEED ALL THESE MEN?
NEXUS GAVE PERMISSION. WE HAVE NOTHING TO FEAR FROM THEM.
KEEP MOVING. STRAIGHT ON THROUGH.
WE WERE WONDERING IF WE COULD TAKE A LOOK?
HEY, *SORRY*, FELLAS.
HAIG CAN'T HAVE NO INTERRUPTIONS.
NO ADM
I'M IN CHARGE HERE. YOU ALL HAVE YOUR ASSIGNMENTS.
SPREAD OUT AND REPORT BACK IN ONE HOUR.
WHAT IF WE GET CAUGHT?
DON'T WORRY. THESE PEOPLE ARE CRIPPLES AND DERELICTS.
WE HAVE NOTHING TO FEAR FROM THEM.

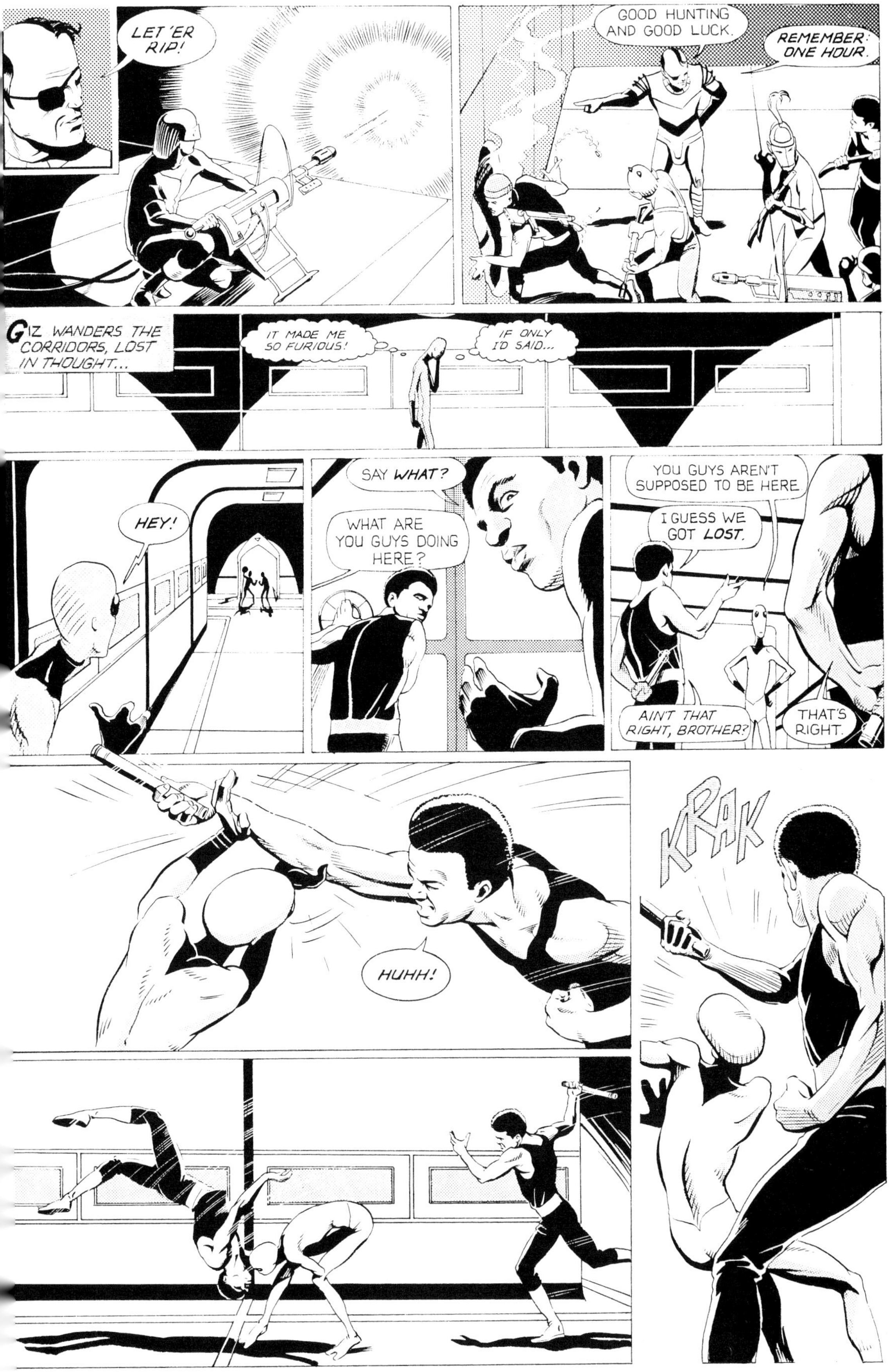
LET'ER RIP!
GOOD HUNTING AND GOOD LUCK.
REMEMBER: ONE HOUR.
GIZ WANDERS THE CORRIDORS, LOST IN THOUGHT...
IT MADE ME SO FURIOUS!
IF ONLY I'D SAID...
HEY!
SAY WHAT?
WHAT ARE YOU GUYS DOING HERE?
YOU GUYS AREN'T SUPPOSED TO BE HERE
I GUESS WE GOT LOST.
AIN'T THAT RIGHT, BROTHER?
THAT'S RIGHT.
HUHH!
KRAK

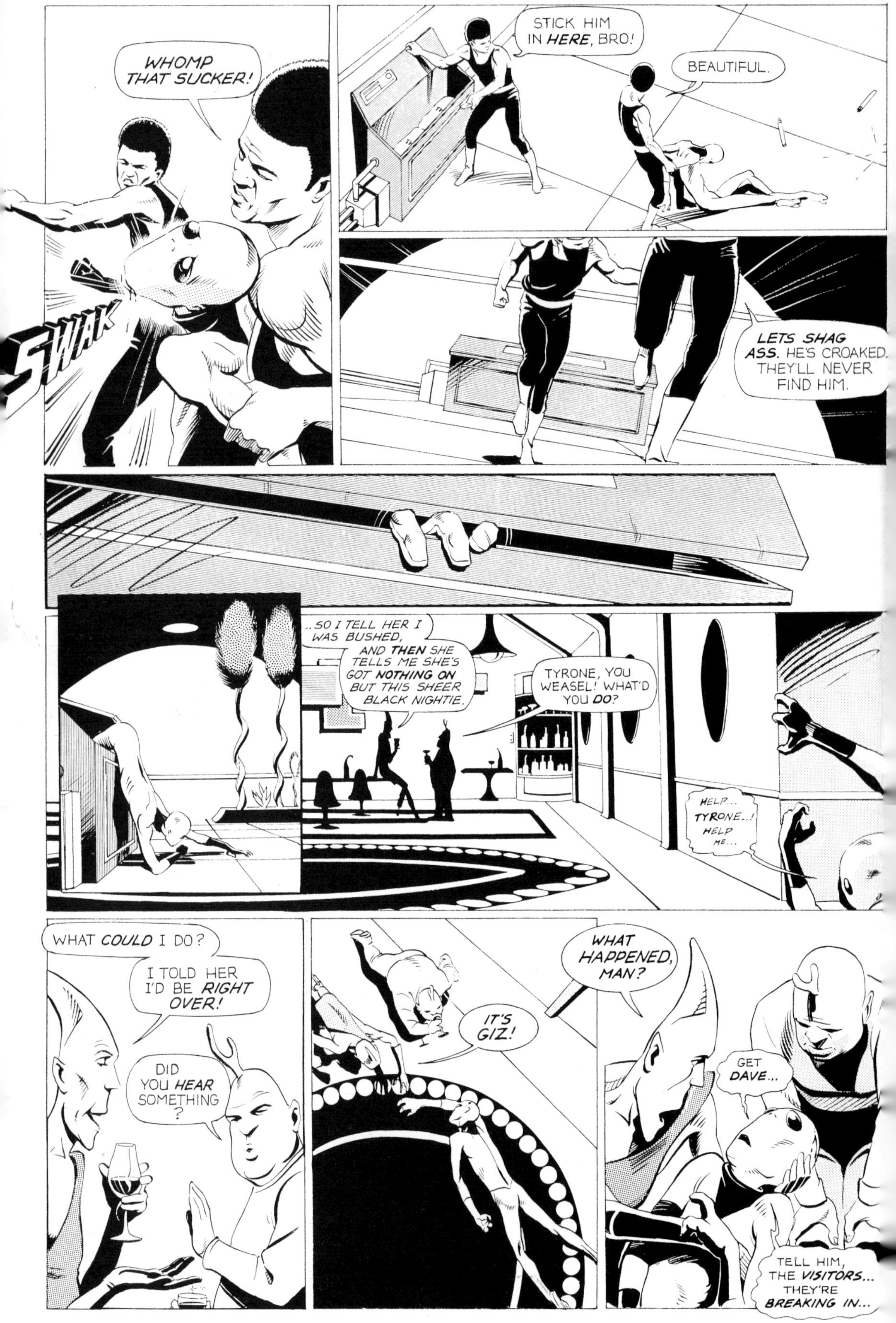
WHOMP THAT SUCKER!
SWAK
STICK HIM IN HERE, BRO!
BEAUTIFUL.
LETS SHAG ASS. HE'S CROAKED. THEY'LL NEVER FIND HIM.
..SO I TELL HER I WAS BUSHED,
AND THEN SHE TELLS ME SHE'S GOT NOTHING ON BUT THIS SHEER BLACK NIGHTIE.
TYRONE, YOU WEASEL! WHAT'D YOU DO?
HELP... TYRONE..! HELP ME...
WHAT COULD I DO?
I TOLD HER I'D BE RIGHT OVER!
DID YOU HEAR SOMETHING?
IT'S GIZ!
WHAT HAPPENED, MAN?
GET DAVE...
TELL HIM, THE VISITORS... THEY'RE BREAKING IN...

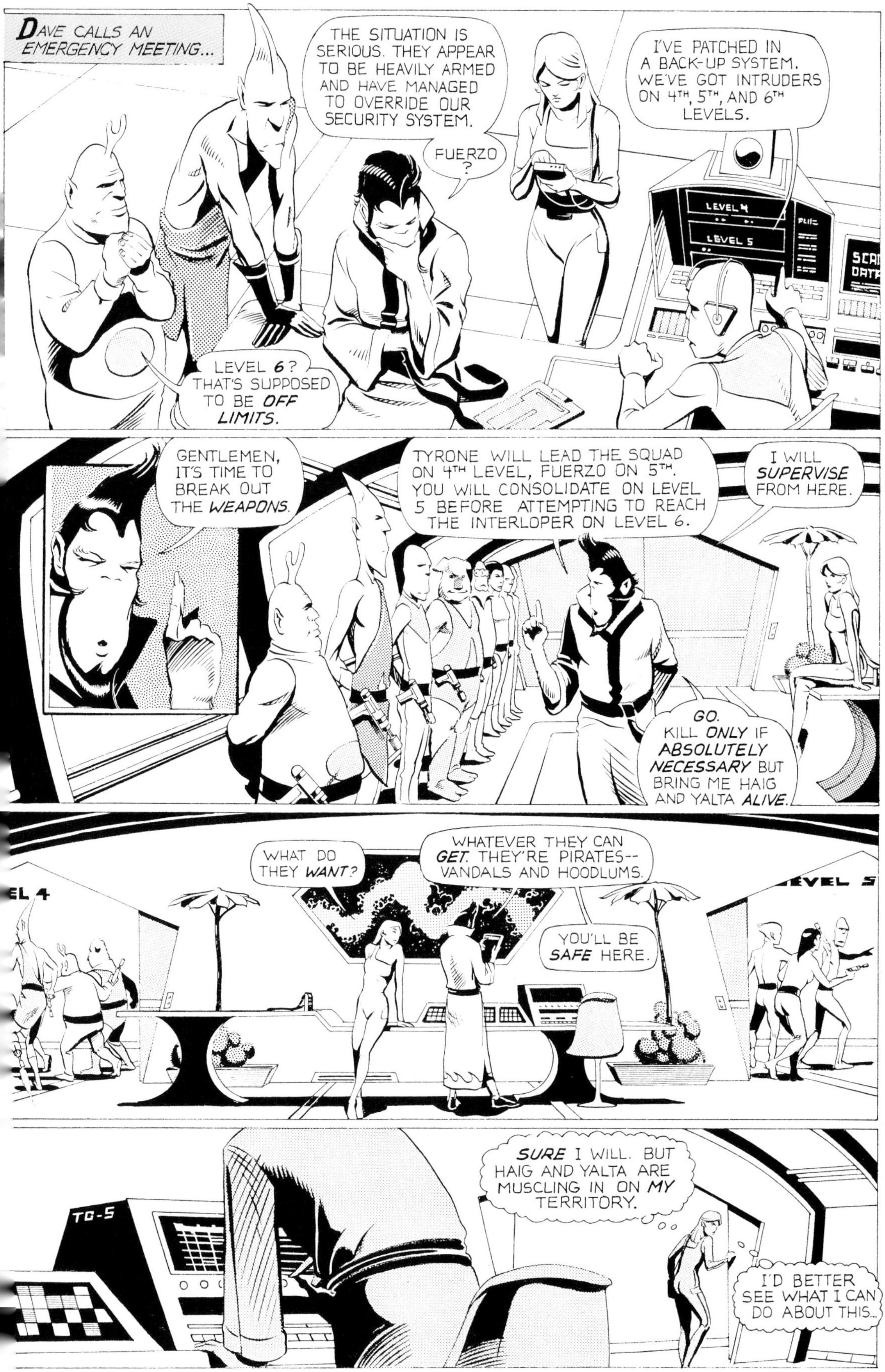
DAVE CALLS AN EMERGENCY MEETING...
THE SITUATION IS SERIOUS. THEY APPEAR TO BE HEAVILY ARMED AND HAVE MANAGED TO OVERRIDE OUR SECURITY SYSTEM.
FUERZO?
I'VE PATCHED IN A BACK-UP SYSTEM. WE'VE GOT INTRUDERS ON 4TH, 5TH, AND 6TH LEVELS.
LEVEL 4
LEVEL 5
LEVEL 6? THAT'S SUPPOSED TO BE OFF LIMITS.
GENTLEMEN, IT'S TIME TO BREAK OUT THE WEAPONS.
TYRONE WILL LEAD THE SQUAD ON 4TH LEVEL, FUERZO ON 5TH. YOU WILL CONSOLIDATE ON LEVEL 5 BEFORE ATTEMPTING TO REACH THE INTERLOPER ON LEVEL 6.
I WILL SUPERVISE FROM HERE.
GO. KILL ONLY IF ABSOLUTELY NECESSARY BUT BRING ME HAIG AND YALTA ALIVE.
WHAT DO THEY WANT?
WHATEVER THEY CAN GET. THEY'RE PIRATES-- VANDALS AND HOODLUMS.
YOU'LL BE SAFE HERE.
SURE I WILL. BUT HAIG AND YALTA ARE MUSCLING IN ON MY TERRITORY.
TC-5
I'D BETTER SEE WHAT I CAN DO ABOUT THIS...

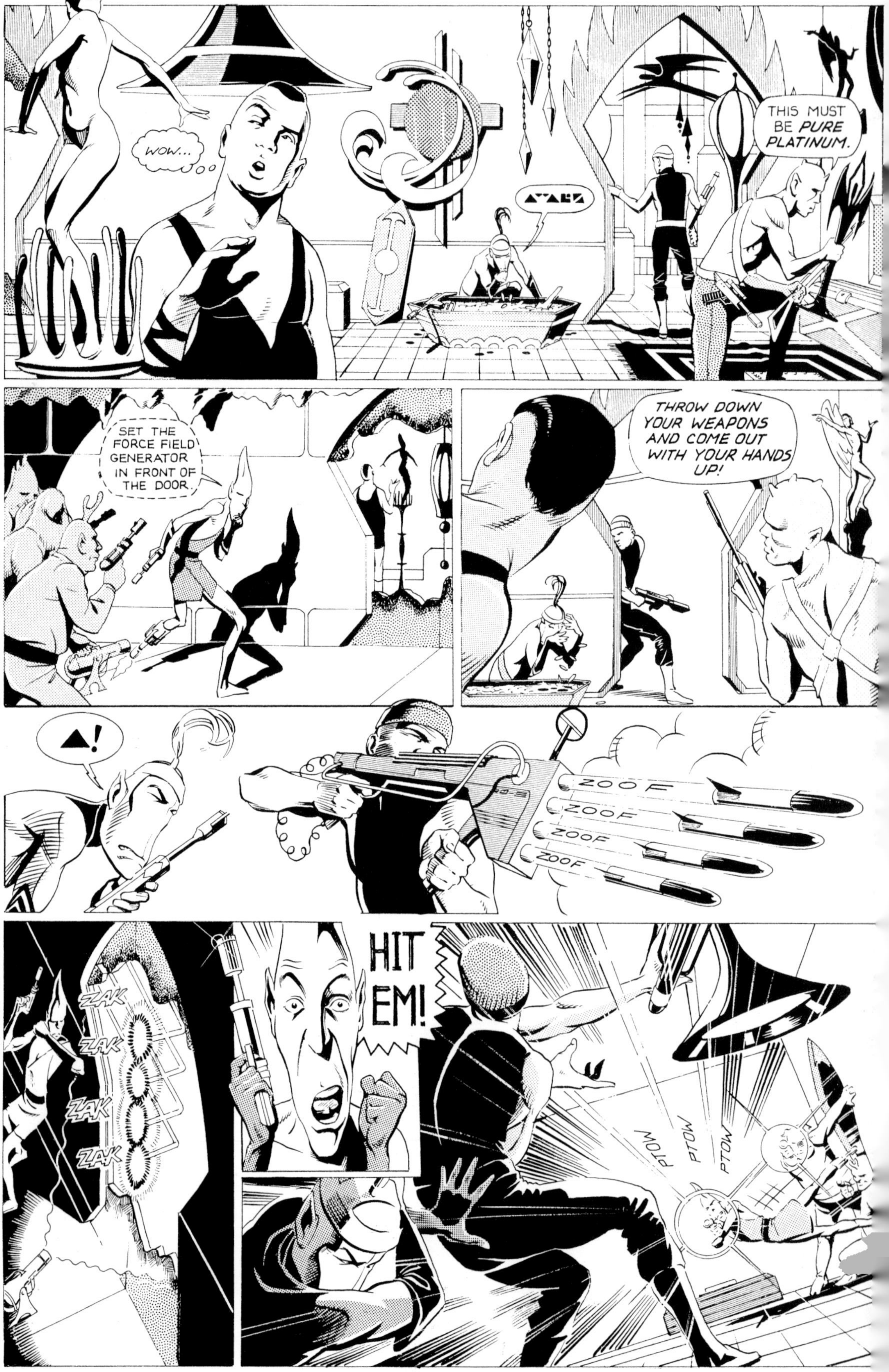
WOW...
THIS MUST BE *PURE PLATINUM*.
SET THE FORCE FIELD GENERATOR IN FRONT OF THE DOOR.
THROW DOWN YOUR WEAPONS AND COME OUT WITH YOUR HANDS UP!
!
ZOOF
ZOOF
ZOOF
ZOOF
HIT EM!
ZAK
ZAK
ZAK
ZAK
PTOW
PTOW
PTOW

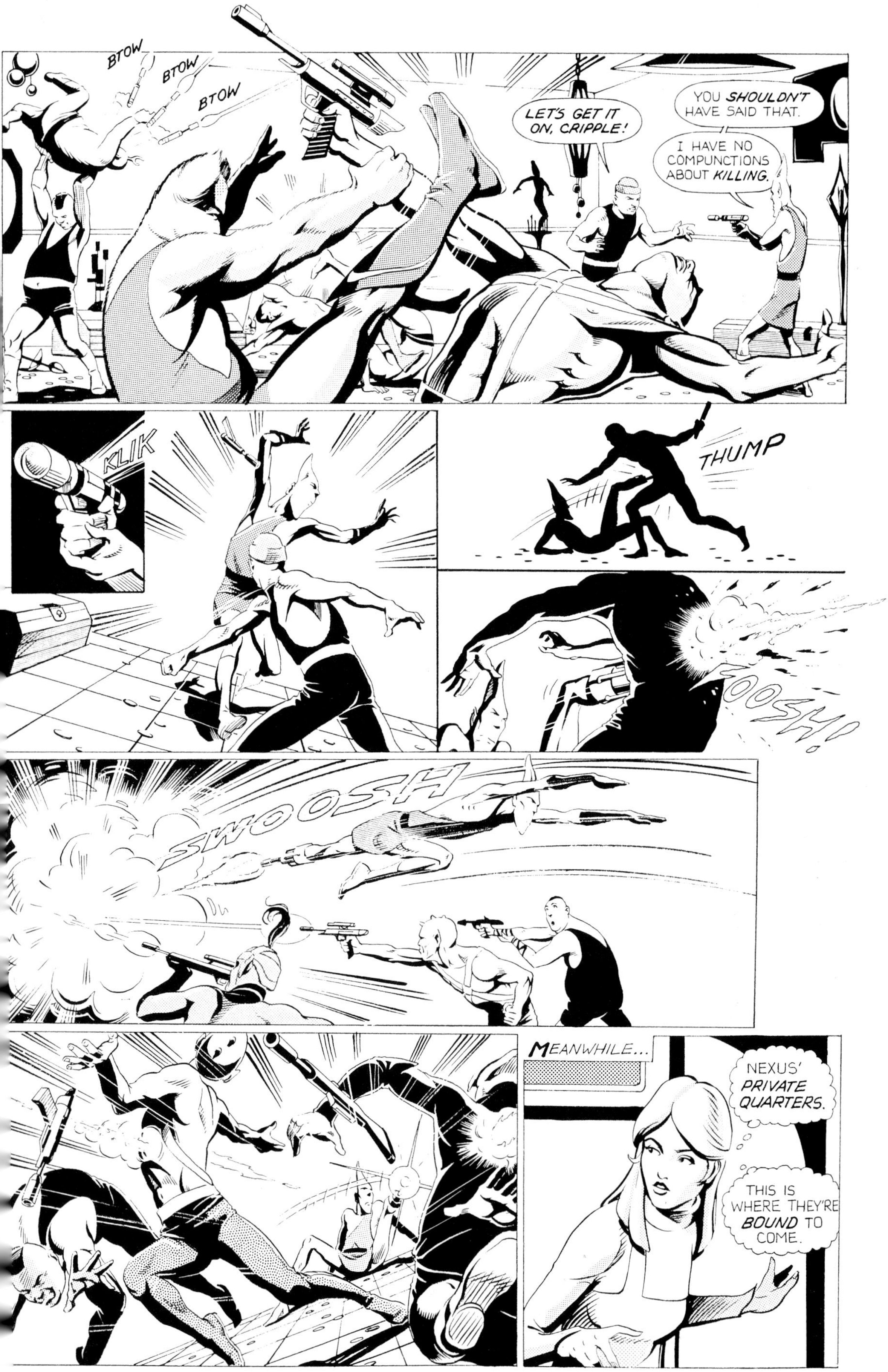
BTOW
BTOW
BTOW
LET'S GET IT ON, CRIPPLE!
YOU SHOULDN'T HAVE SAID THAT.
I HAVE NO COMPUNCTIONS ABOUT KILLING.
KLIK
THUMP
SOOSH!
SWOOSH
MEANWHILE...
NEXUS' PRIVATE QUARTERS.
THIS IS WHERE THEY'RE BOUND TO COME.

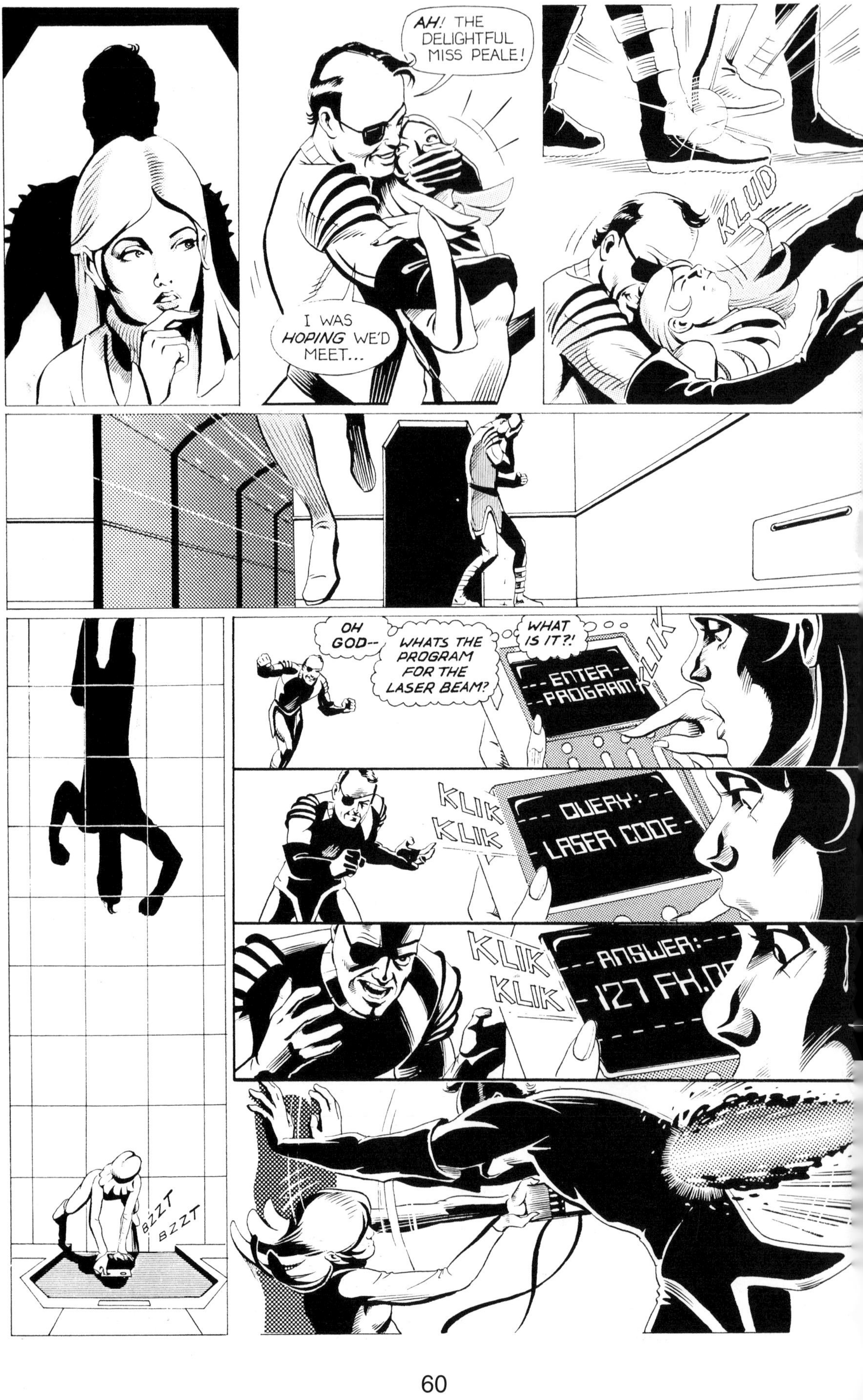
AH! THE DELIGHTFUL MISS PEALE!
I WAS HOPING WE'D MEET...
KLUD
OH GOD--
WHATS THE PROGRAM FOR THE LASER BEAM?
WHAT IS IT?!
--ENTER--
--PROGRAM--
KLIK
KLIK
KLIK
--QUERY:--
-LASER CODE
KLIK
KLIK
--ANSWER:
-127 FH.0
BZZT
BZZT

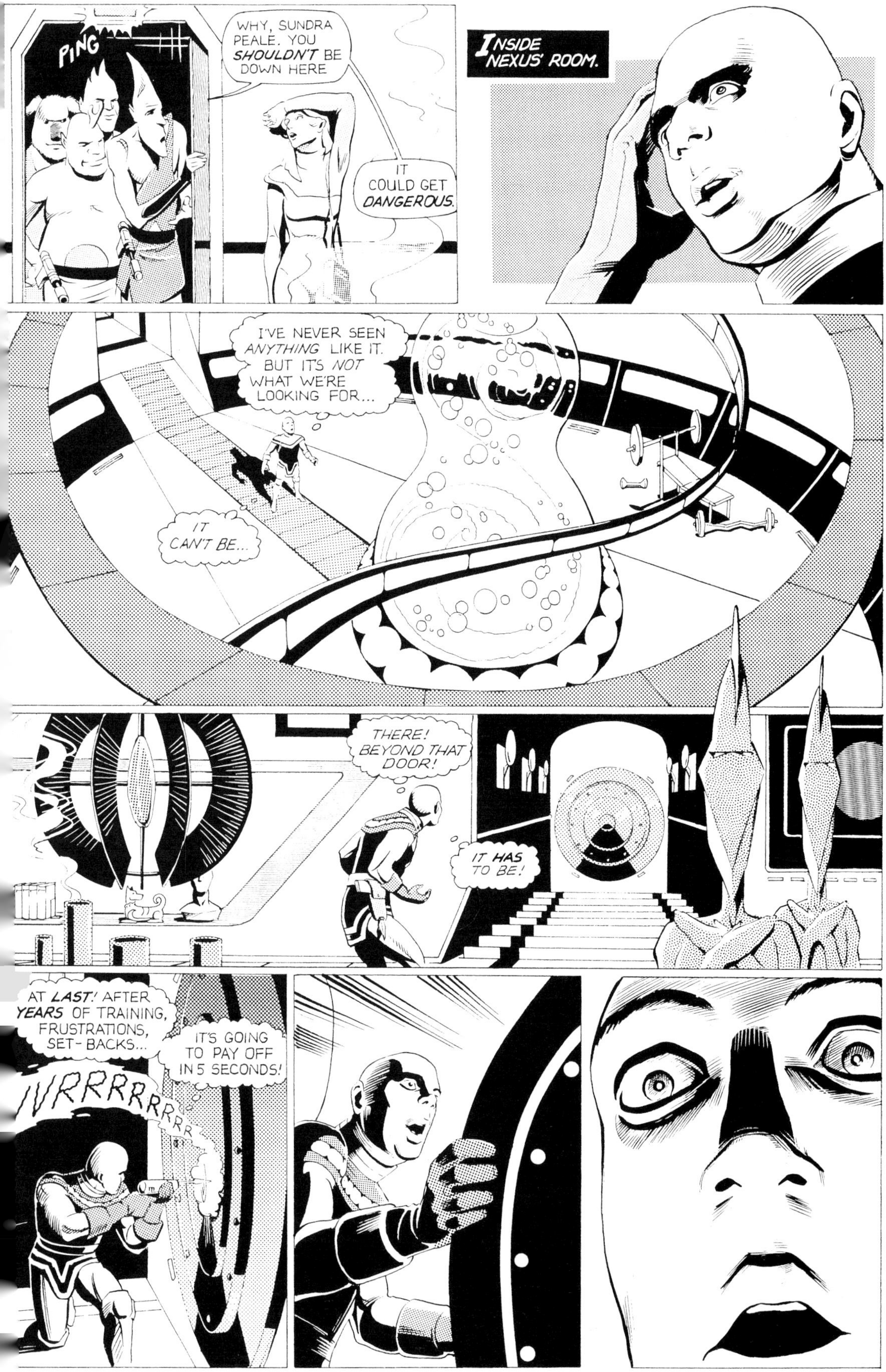
PING
WHY, SUNDRA PEALE. YOU SHOULDN'T BE DOWN HERE
IT COULD GET DANGEROUS.
INSIDE NEXUS' ROOM.
I'VE NEVER SEEN ANYTHING LIKE IT. BUT IT'S NOT WHAT WE'RE LOOKING FOR...
IT CAN'T BE...
THERE! BEYOND THAT DOOR!
IT HAS TO BE!
AT LAST! AFTER YEARS OF TRAINING, FRUSTRATIONS, SET-BACKS...
IT'S GOING TO PAY OFF IN 5 SECONDS!
VRRRRRRRRRR

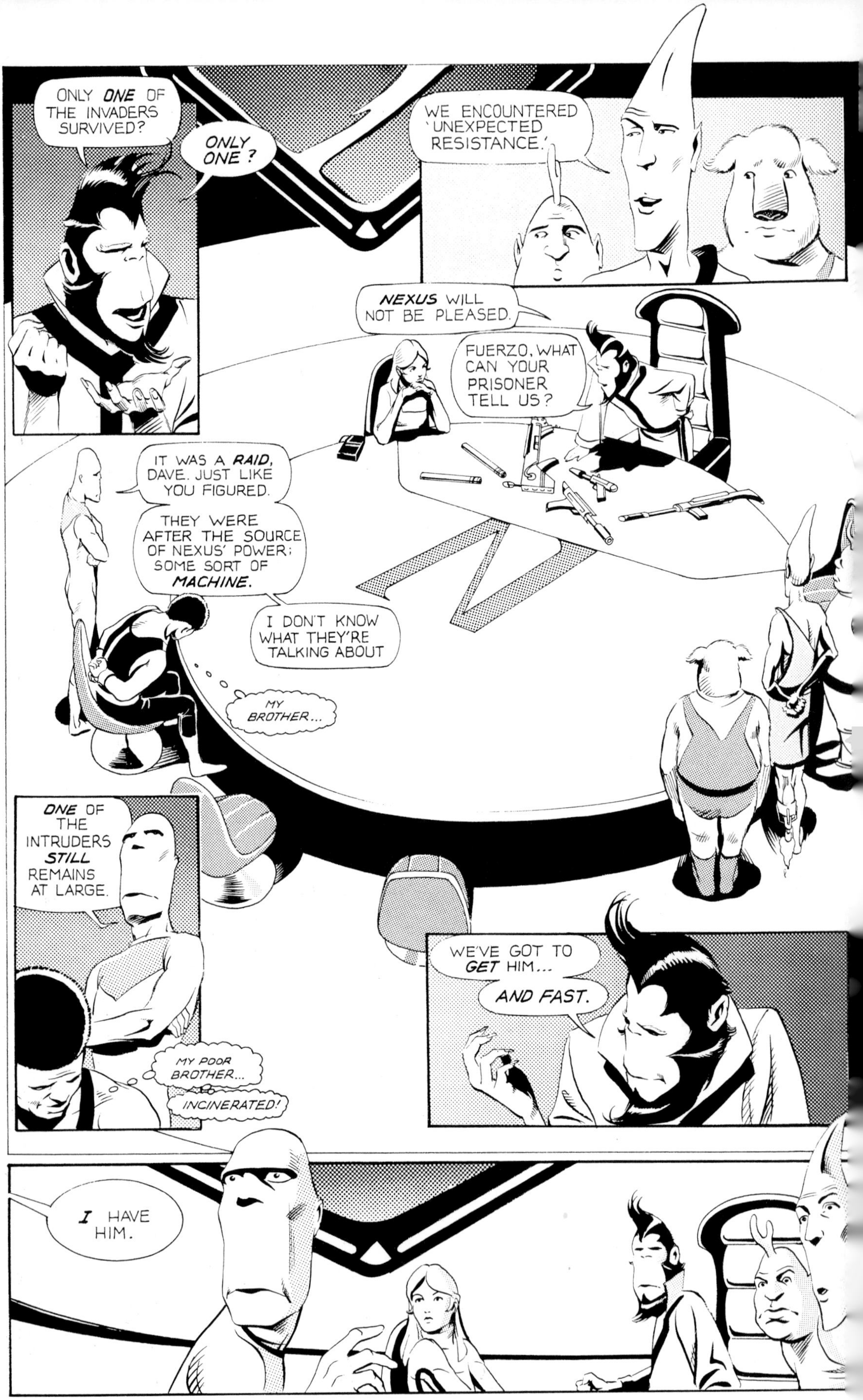
ONLY ONE OF THE INVADERS SURVIVED?
ONLY ONE?
WE ENCOUNTERED 'UNEXPECTED RESISTANCE.'
NEXUS WILL NOT BE PLEASED.
FUERZO, WHAT CAN YOUR PRISONER TELL US?
IT WAS A RAID, DAVE. JUST LIKE YOU FIGURED.
THEY WERE AFTER THE SOURCE OF NEXUS' POWER; SOME SORT OF MACHINE.
I DON'T KNOW WHAT THEY'RE TALKING ABOUT
MY BROTHER...
ONE OF THE INTRUDERS STILL REMAINS AT LARGE.
MY POOR BROTHER...
INCINERATED!
WE'VE GOT TO GET HIM...
AND FAST.
I HAVE HIM.

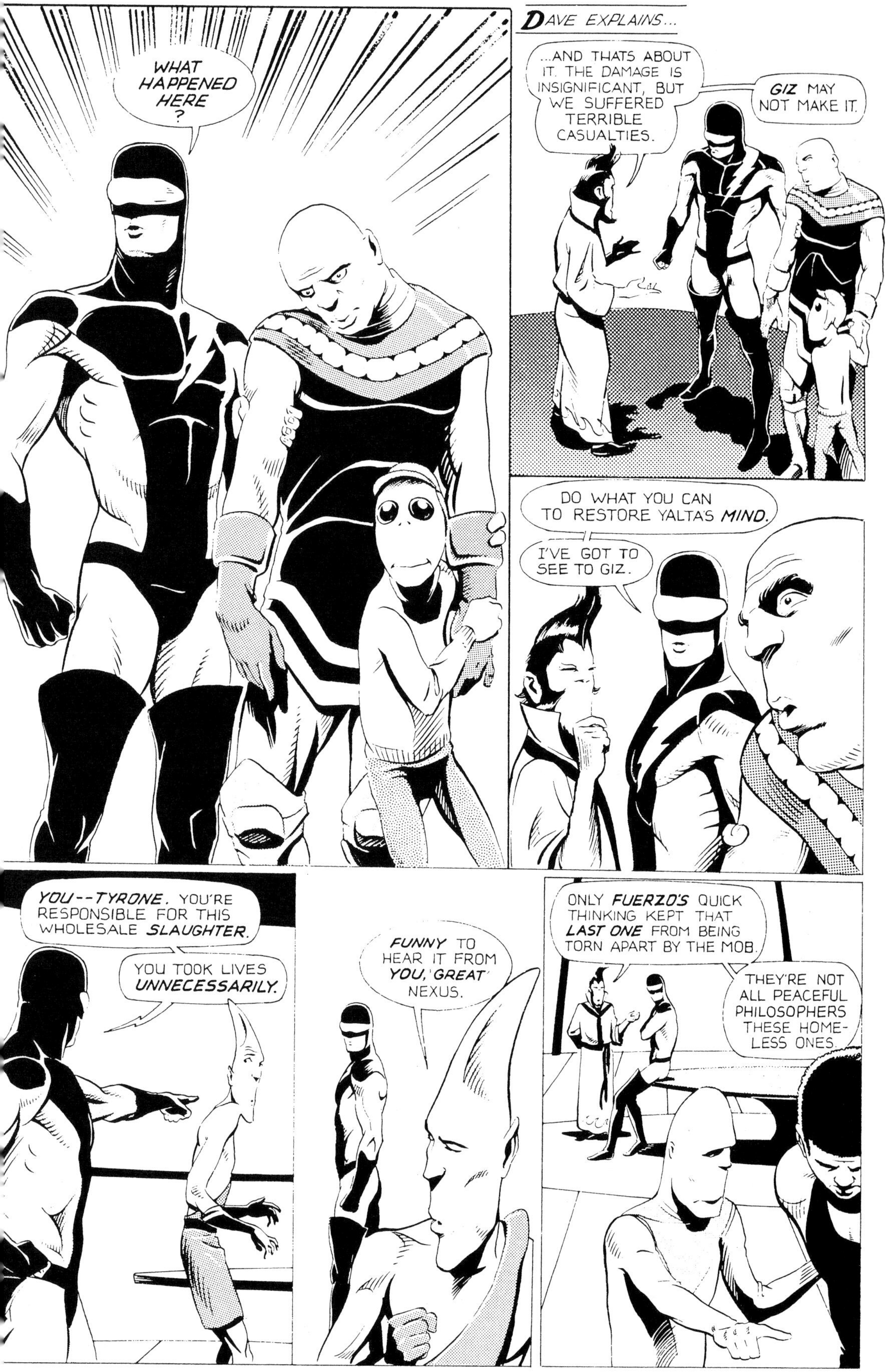
WHAT HAPPENED HERE ?
DAVE EXPLAINS...
...AND THATS ABOUT IT. THE DAMAGE IS INSIGNIFICANT, BUT WE SUFFERED TERRIBLE CASUALTIES.
GIZ MAY NOT MAKE IT.
DO WHAT YOU CAN TO RESTORE YALTA'S MIND.
I'VE GOT TO SEE TO GIZ.
YOU--TYRONE. YOU'RE RESPONSIBLE FOR THIS WHOLESALE SLAUGHTER.
YOU TOOK LIVES UNNECESSARILY.
FUNNY TO HEAR IT FROM YOU, 'GREAT' NEXUS.
ONLY FUERZO'S QUICK THINKING KEPT THAT LAST ONE FROM BEING TORN APART BY THE MOB.
THEY'RE NOT ALL PEACEFUL PHILOSOPHERS THESE HOME-LESS ONES.

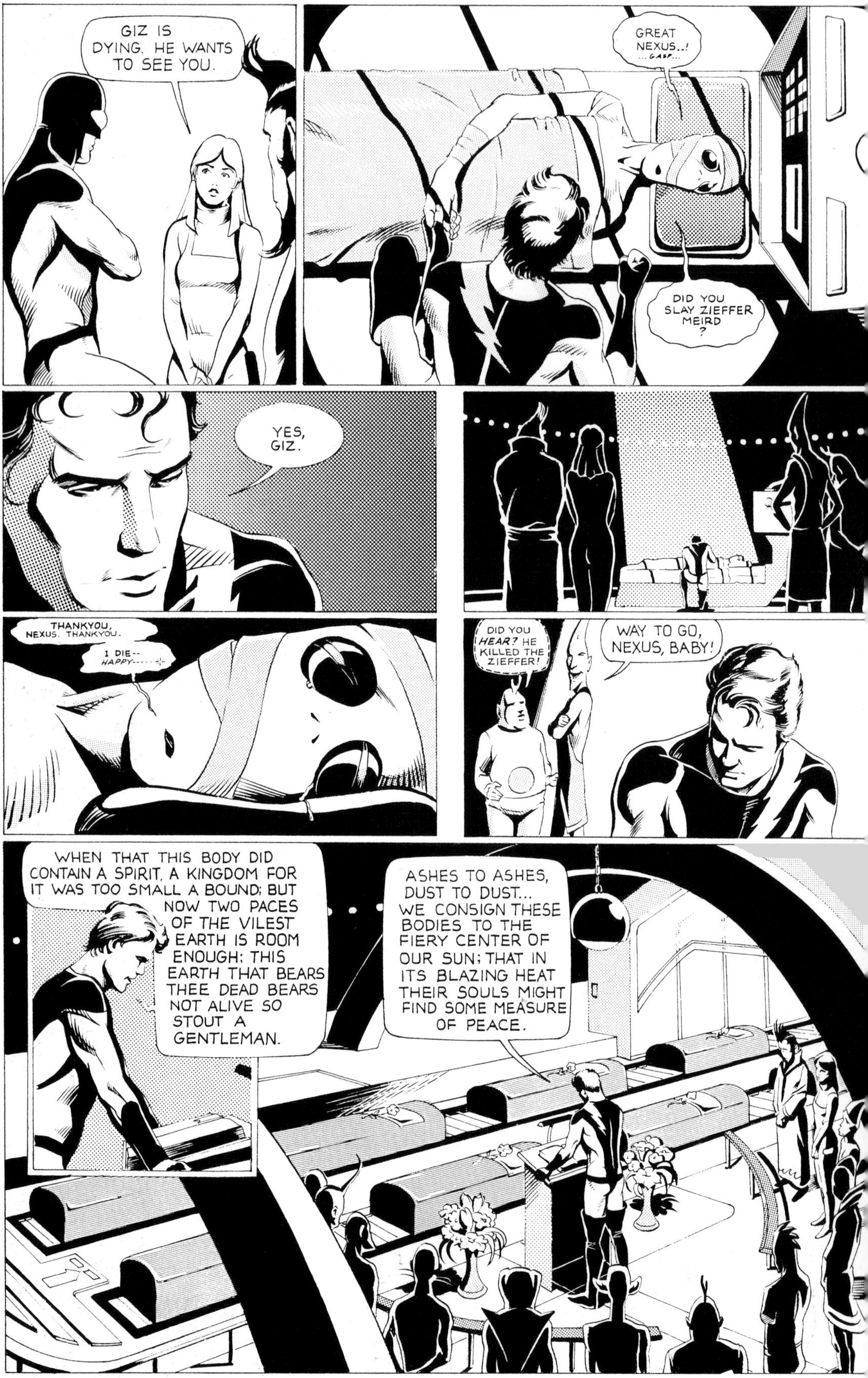
GIZ IS DYING. HE WANTS TO SEE YOU.
GREAT NEXUS..! ...GASP...
DID YOU SLAY ZIEFFER MEIRD ?
YES, GIZ.
THANKYOU, NEXUS. THANKYOU.
I DIE-- HAPPY-----
DID YOU HEAR? HE KILLED THE ZIEFFER!
WAY TO GO, NEXUS, BABY!
WHEN THAT THIS BODY DID CONTAIN A SPIRIT, A KINGDOM FOR IT WAS TOO SMALL A BOUND; BUT NOW TWO PACES OF THE VILEST EARTH IS ROOM ENOUGH; THIS EARTH THAT BEARS THEE DEAD BEARS NOT ALIVE SO STOUT A GENTLEMAN.
ASHES TO ASHES, DUST TO DUST... WE CONSIGN THESE BODIES TO THE FIERY CENTER OF OUR SUN; THAT IN ITS BLAZING HEAT THEIR SOULS MIGHT FIND SOME MEASURE OF PEACE.

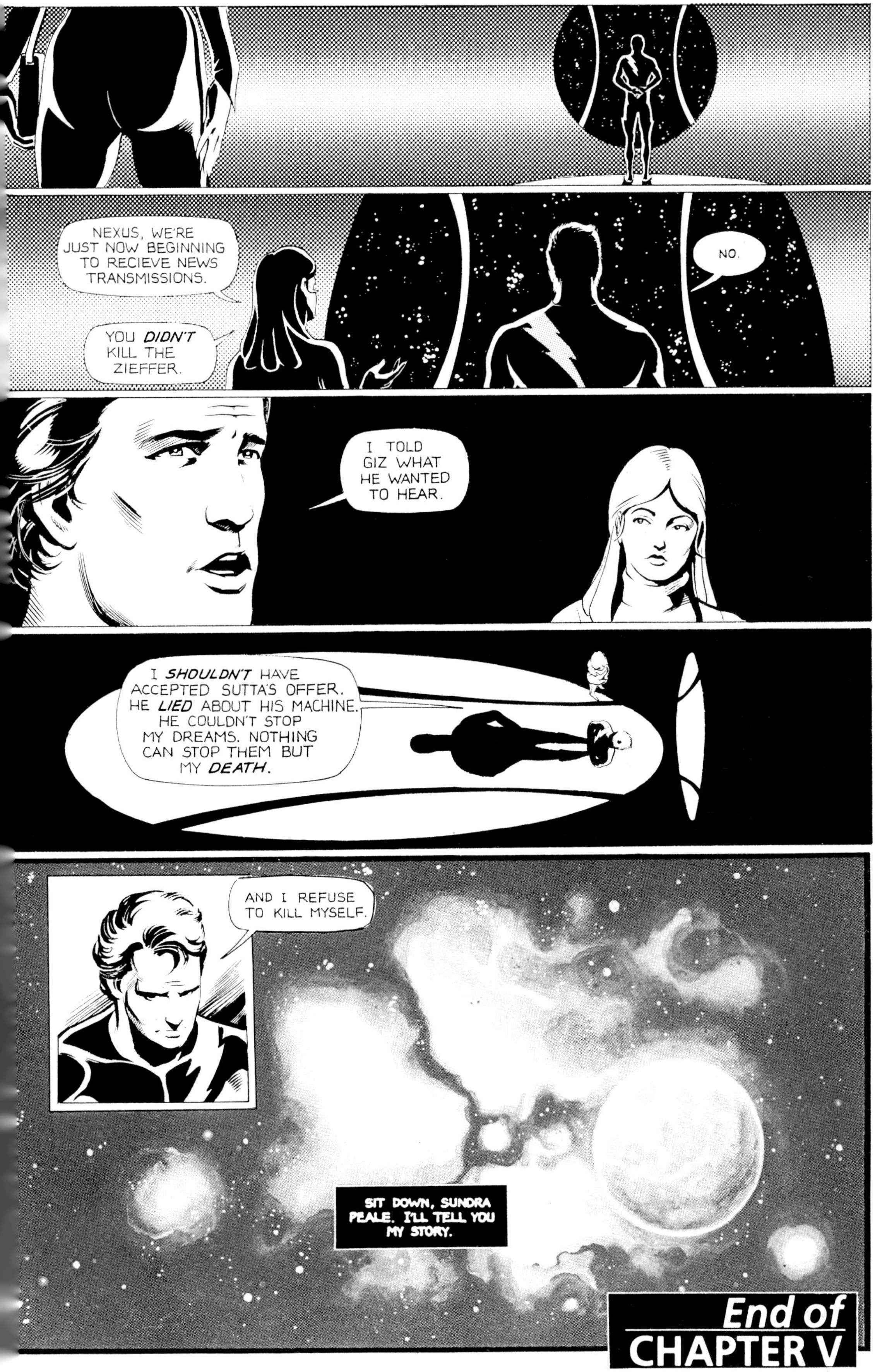
NEXUS, WE'RE JUST NOW BEGINNING TO RECIEVE NEWS TRANSMISSIONS.
YOU DIDN'T KILL THE ZIEFFER.
NO.
I TOLD GIZ WHAT HE WANTED TO HEAR.
I SHOULDN'T HAVE ACCEPTED SUTTA'S OFFER. HE LIED ABOUT HIS MACHINE. HE COULDN'T STOP MY DREAMS. NOTHING CAN STOP THEM BUT MY DEATH.
AND I REFUSE TO KILL MYSELF.
SIT DOWN, SUNDRA PEALE. I'LL TELL YOU MY STORY.
End of CHAPTER V

CHAPTER VI

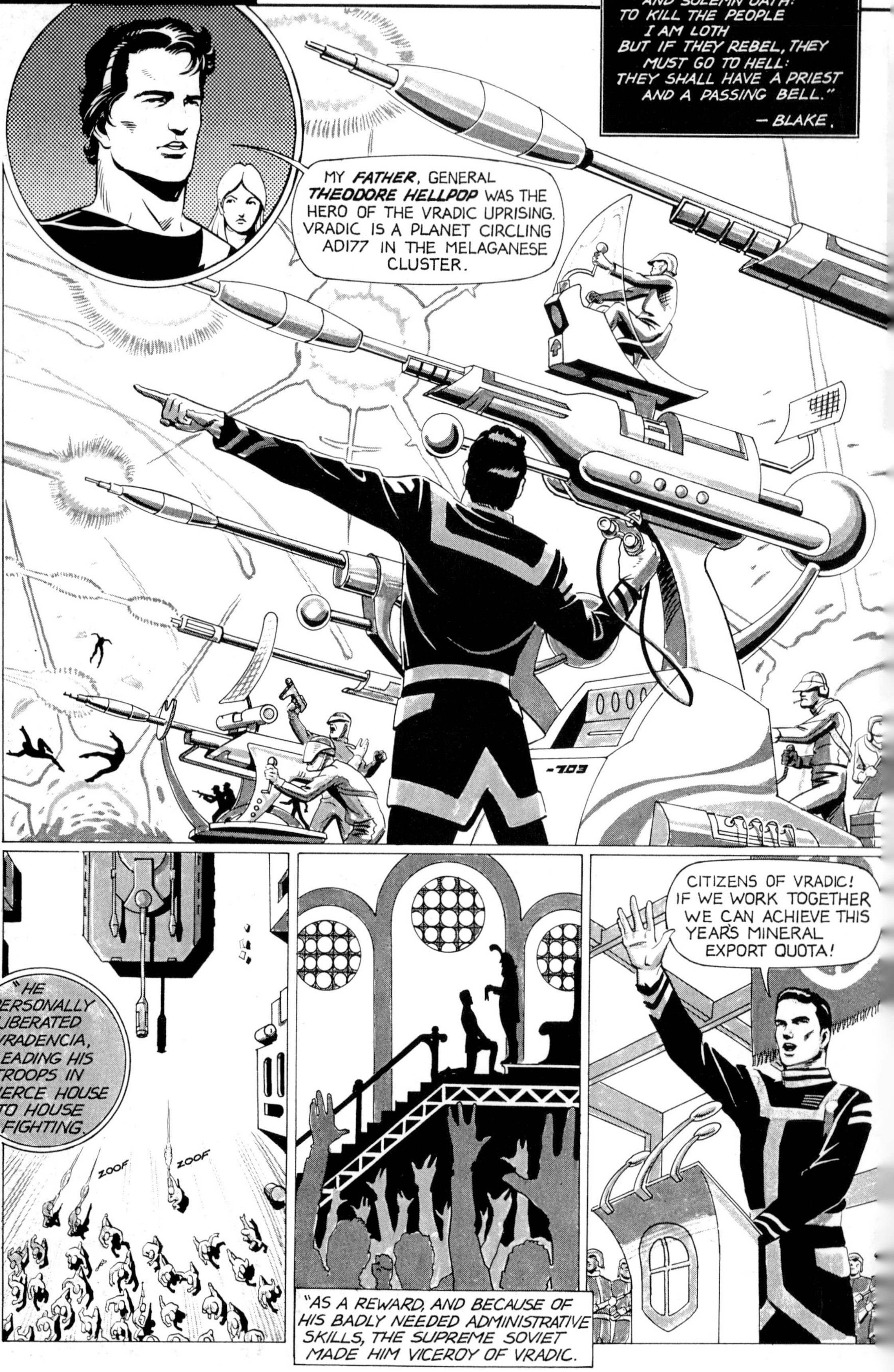
"THEN HE SWORE A GREAT AND SOLEMN OATH: TO KILL THE PEOPLE I AM LOTH BUT IF THEY REBEL, THEY MUST GO TO HELL: THEY SHALL HAVE A PRIEST AND A PASSING BELL."
— BLAKE.
MY FATHER, GENERAL THEODORE HELLPOP WAS THE HERO OF THE VRADIC UPRISING. VRADIC IS A PLANET CIRCLING AD177 IN THE MELAGANESE CLUSTER.
-703
"HE PERSONALLY LIBERATED VRADENCIA, LEADING HIS TROOPS IN FIERCE HOUSE TO HOUSE FIGHTING.
ZOOF
ZOOF
"AS A REWARD, AND BECAUSE OF HIS BADLY NEEDED ADMINISTRATIVE SKILLS, THE SUPREME SOVIET MADE HIM VICEROY OF VRADIC.
CITIZENS OF VRADIC! IF WE WORK TOGETHER WE CAN ACHIEVE THIS YEAR'S MINERAL EXPORT QUOTA!

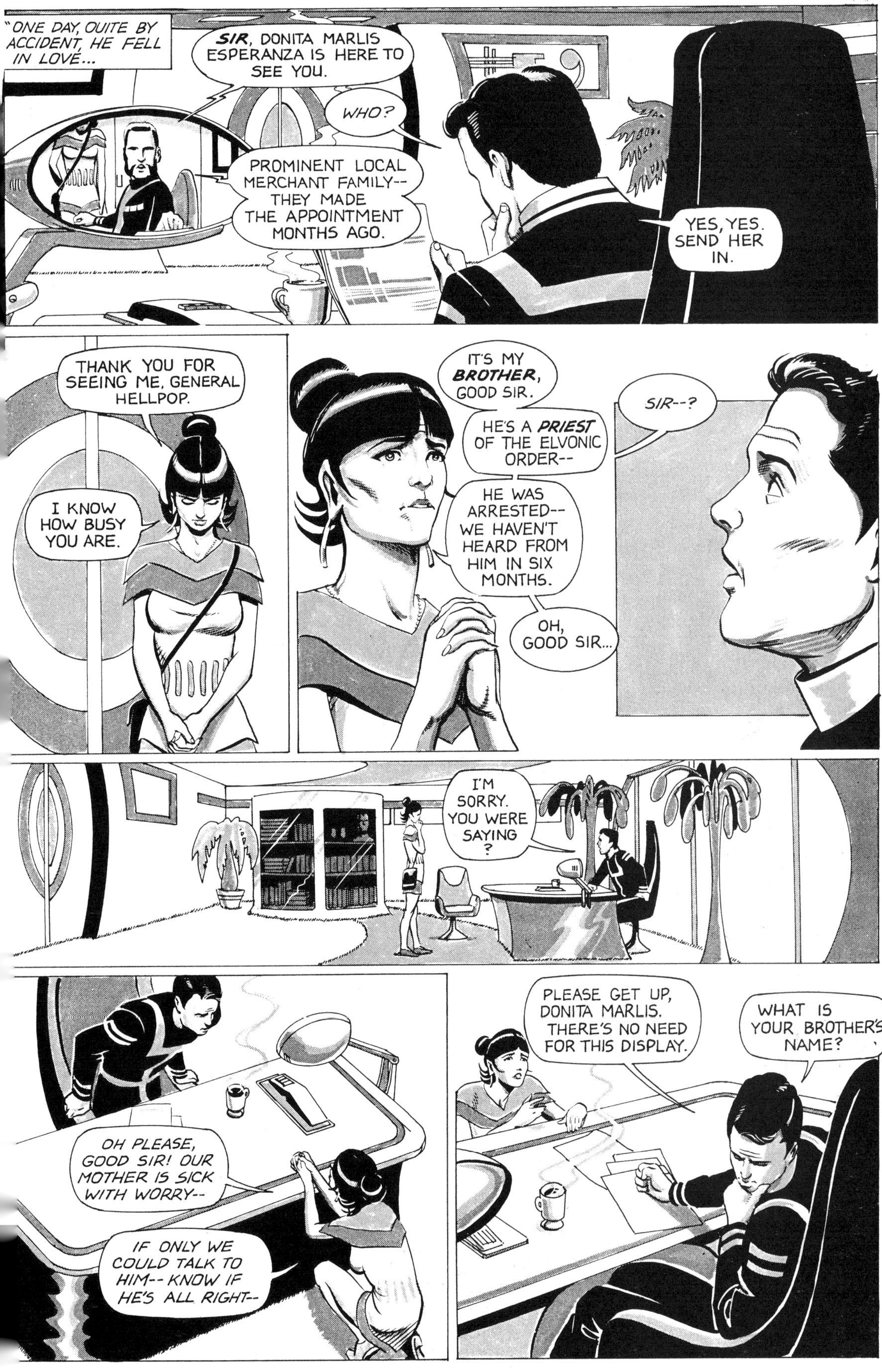
"ONE DAY, QUITE BY ACCIDENT, HE FELL IN LOVE...
SIR, DONITA MARLIS ESPERANZA IS HERE TO SEE YOU.
WHO?
PROMINENT LOCAL MERCHANT FAMILY-- THEY MADE THE APPOINTMENT MONTHS AGO.
YES, YES. SEND HER IN.
THANK YOU FOR SEEING ME, GENERAL HELLPOP.
I KNOW HOW BUSY YOU ARE.
IT'S MY BROTHER, GOOD SIR.
HE'S A PRIEST OF THE ELVONIC ORDER--
HE WAS ARRESTED-- WE HAVEN'T HEARD FROM HIM IN SIX MONTHS.
OH, GOOD SIR...
SIR--?
I'M SORRY. YOU WERE SAYING?
OH PLEASE, GOOD SIR! OUR MOTHER IS SICK WITH WORRY--
IF ONLY WE COULD TALK TO HIM-- KNOW IF HE'S ALL RIGHT--
PLEASE GET UP, DONITA MARLIS. THERE'S NO NEED FOR THIS DISPLAY.
WHAT IS YOUR BROTHER'S NAME?

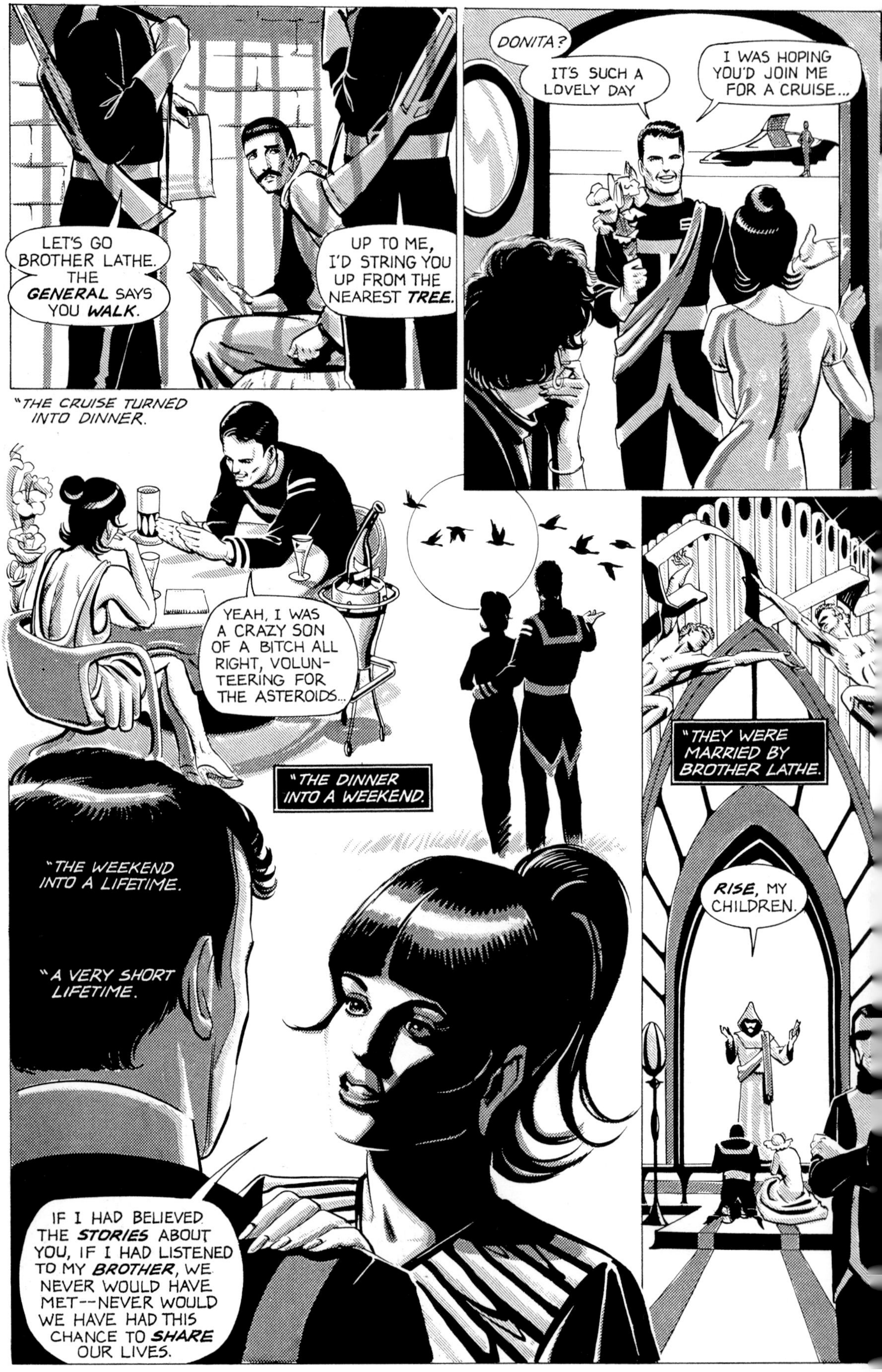
LET'S GO BROTHER LATHE. THE GENERAL SAYS YOU WALK.
UP TO ME, I'D STRING YOU UP FROM THE NEAREST TREE.
DONITA?
IT'S SUCH A LOVELY DAY
I WAS HOPING YOU'D JOIN ME FOR A CRUISE...
"THE CRUISE TURNED INTO DINNER.
YEAH, I WAS A CRAZY SON OF A BITCH ALL RIGHT, VOLUNTEERING FOR THE ASTEROIDS...
"THE DINNER INTO A WEEKEND.
"THEY WERE MARRIED BY BROTHER LATHE.
RISE, MY CHILDREN.
"THE WEEKEND INTO A LIFETIME.
"A VERY SHORT LIFETIME.
IF I HAD BELIEVED THE STORIES ABOUT YOU, IF I HAD LISTENED TO MY BROTHER, WE NEVER WOULD HAVE MET--NEVER WOULD WE HAVE HAD THIS CHANCE TO SHARE OUR LIVES.

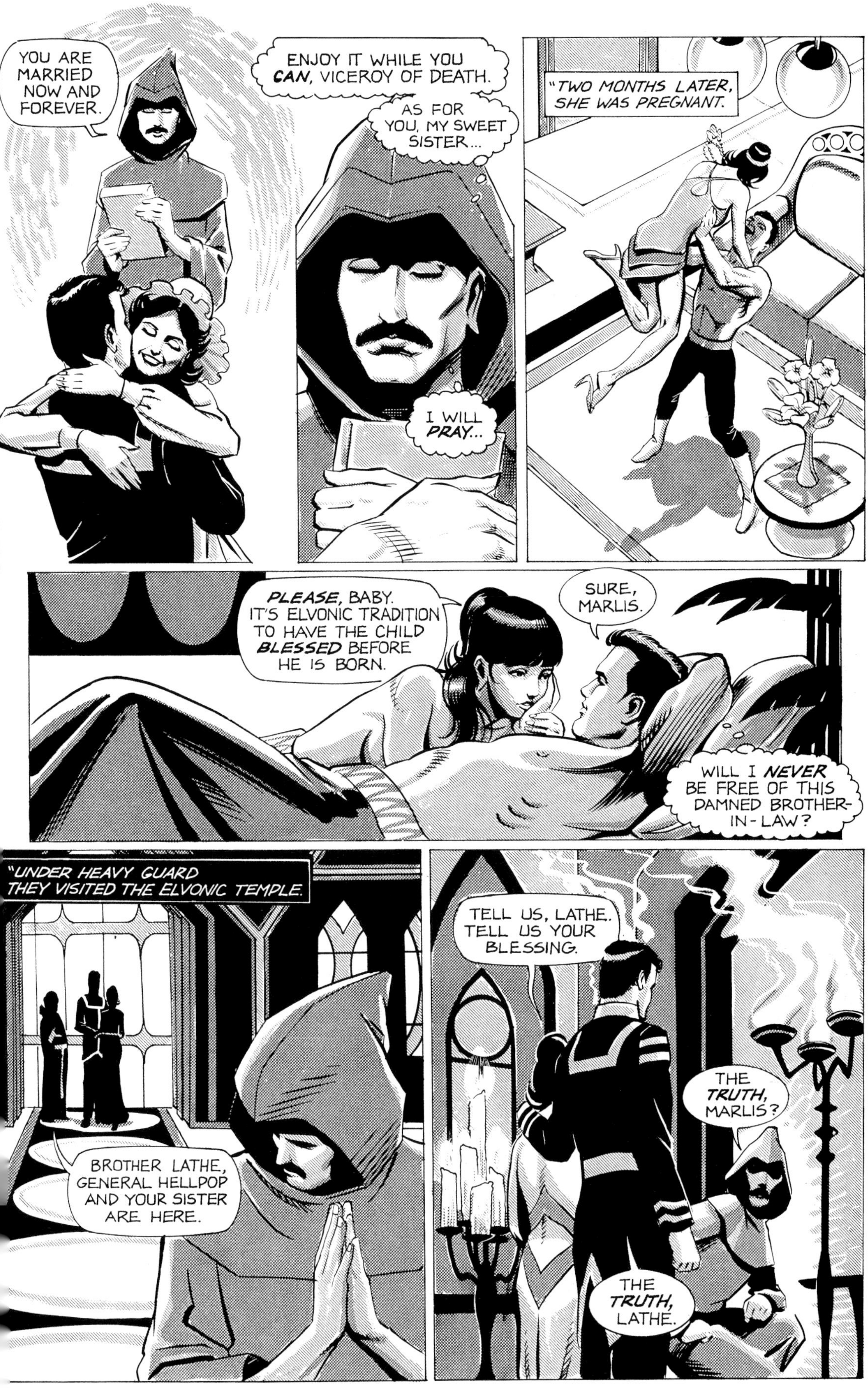
YOU ARE MARRIED NOW AND FOREVER.
ENJOY IT WHILE YOU CAN, VICEROY OF DEATH.
AS FOR YOU, MY SWEET SISTER...
I WILL PRAY...
"TWO MONTHS LATER, SHE WAS PREGNANT.
PLEASE, BABY. IT'S ELVONIC TRADITION TO HAVE THE CHILD BLESSED BEFORE HE IS BORN.
SURE, MARLIS.
WILL I NEVER BE FREE OF THIS DAMNED BROTHER-IN-LAW?
"UNDER HEAVY GUARD THEY VISITED THE ELVONIC TEMPLE.
BROTHER LATHE, GENERAL HELLPOP AND YOUR SISTER ARE HERE.
TELL US, LATHE. TELL US YOUR BLESSING.
THE TRUTH, MARLIS?
THE TRUTH, LATHE.

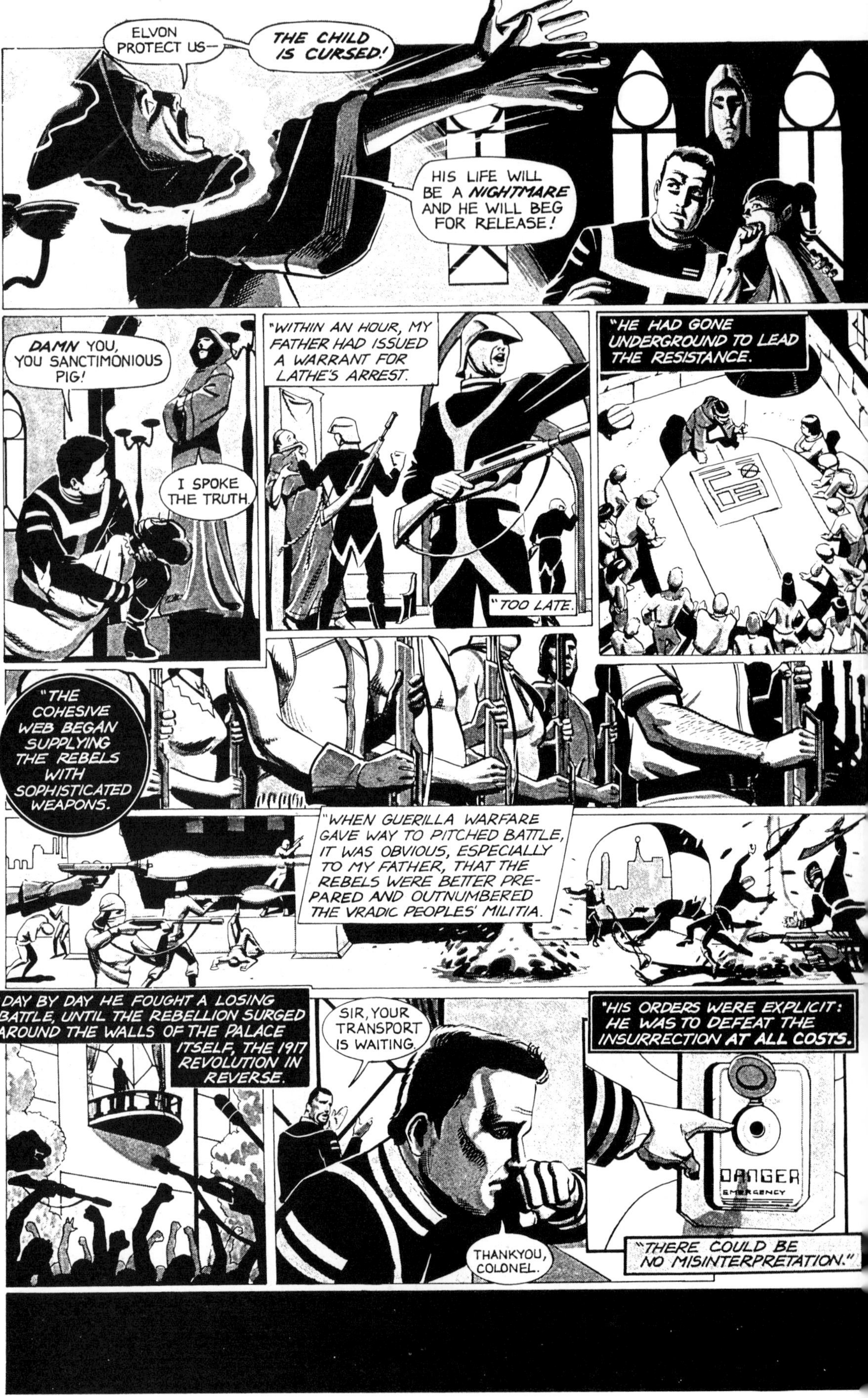

ELVON PROTECT US—
THE CHILD IS CURSED!
HIS LIFE WILL BE A NIGHTMARE AND HE WILL BEG FOR RELEASE!
DAMN YOU, YOU SANCTIMONIOUS PIG!
I SPOKE THE TRUTH.
"WITHIN AN HOUR, MY FATHER HAD ISSUED A WARRANT FOR LATHE'S ARREST.
"TOO LATE.
"HE HAD GONE UNDERGROUND TO LEAD THE RESISTANCE.
"THE COHESIVE WEB BEGAN SUPPLYING THE REBELS WITH SOPHISTICATED WEAPONS.
"WHEN GUERILLA WARFARE GAVE WAY TO PITCHED BATTLE, IT WAS OBVIOUS, ESPECIALLY TO MY FATHER, THAT THE REBELS WERE BETTER PREPARED AND OUTNUMBERED THE VRADIC PEOPLES' MILITIA.
"DAY BY DAY HE FOUGHT A LOSING BATTLE, UNTIL THE REBELLION SURGED AROUND THE WALLS OF THE PALACE ITSELF, THE 1917 REVOLUTION IN REVERSE.
SIR, YOUR TRANSPORT IS WAITING.
THANKYOU, COLONEL.
"HIS ORDERS WERE EXPLICIT: HE WAS TO DEFEAT THE INSURRECTION AT ALL COSTS.
DANGER
EMERGENCY
"THERE COULD BE NO MISINTERPRETATION."

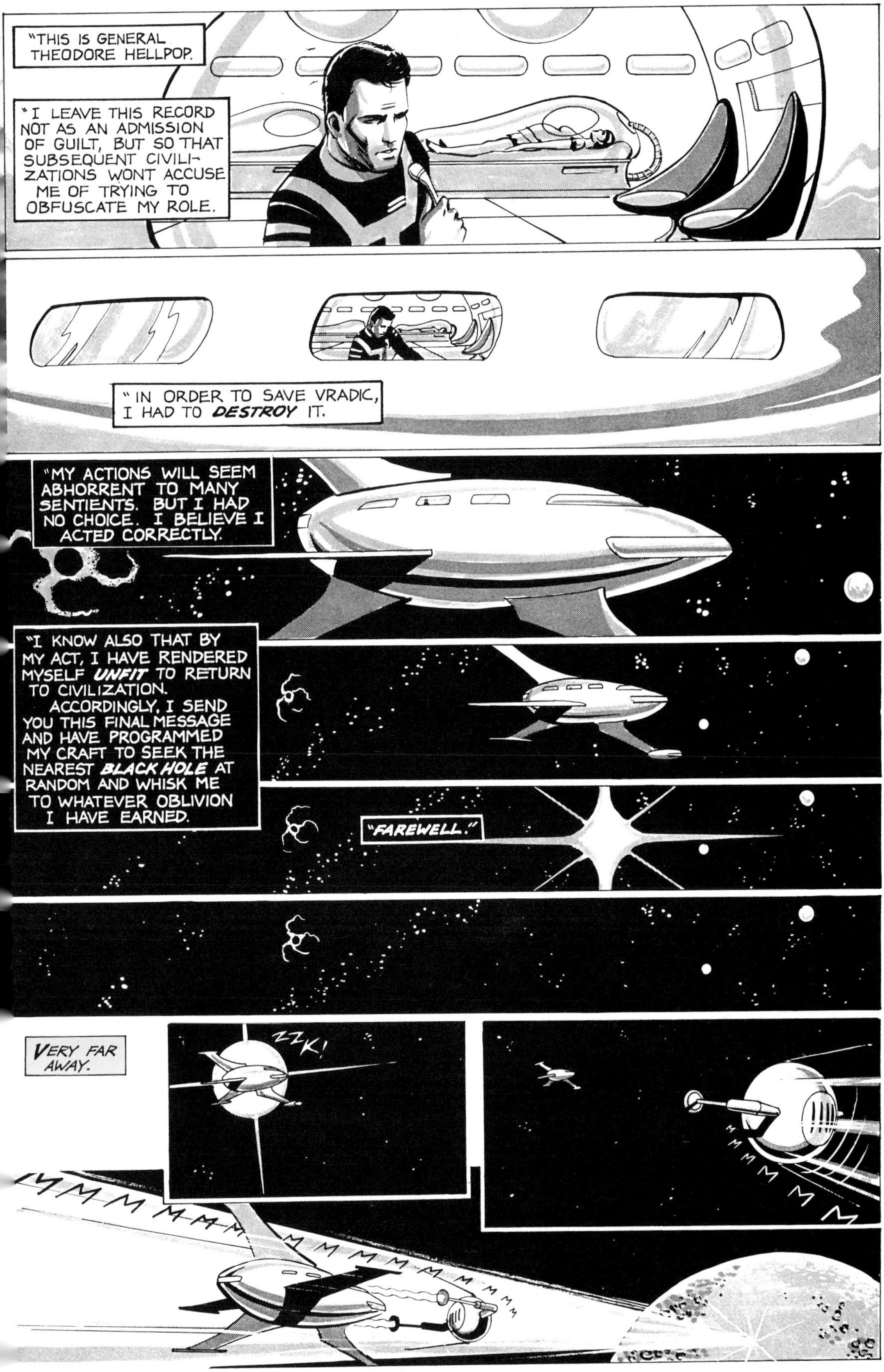
"THIS IS GENERAL THEODORE HELLPOP.
"I LEAVE THIS RECORD NOT AS AN ADMISSION OF GUILT, BUT SO THAT SUBSEQUENT CIVILIZATIONS WONT ACCUSE ME OF TRYING TO OBFUSCATE MY ROLE.
"IN ORDER TO SAVE VRADIC, I HAD TO *DESTROY* IT.
"MY ACTIONS WILL SEEM ABHORRENT TO MANY SENTIENTS. BUT I HAD NO CHOICE. I BELIEVE I ACTED CORRECTLY.
"I KNOW ALSO THAT BY MY ACT, I HAVE RENDERED MYSELF *UNFIT* TO RETURN TO CIVILIZATION. ACCORDINGLY, I SEND YOU THIS FINAL MESSAGE AND HAVE PROGRAMMED MY CRAFT TO SEEK THE NEAREST *BLACK HOLE* AT RANDOM AND WHISK ME TO WHATEVER OBLIVION I HAVE EARNED.
"*FAREWELL.*"
VERY FAR AWAY.
ZZK!
MMMMMMM
MMMMMMMMMMMMMMMMMMMM

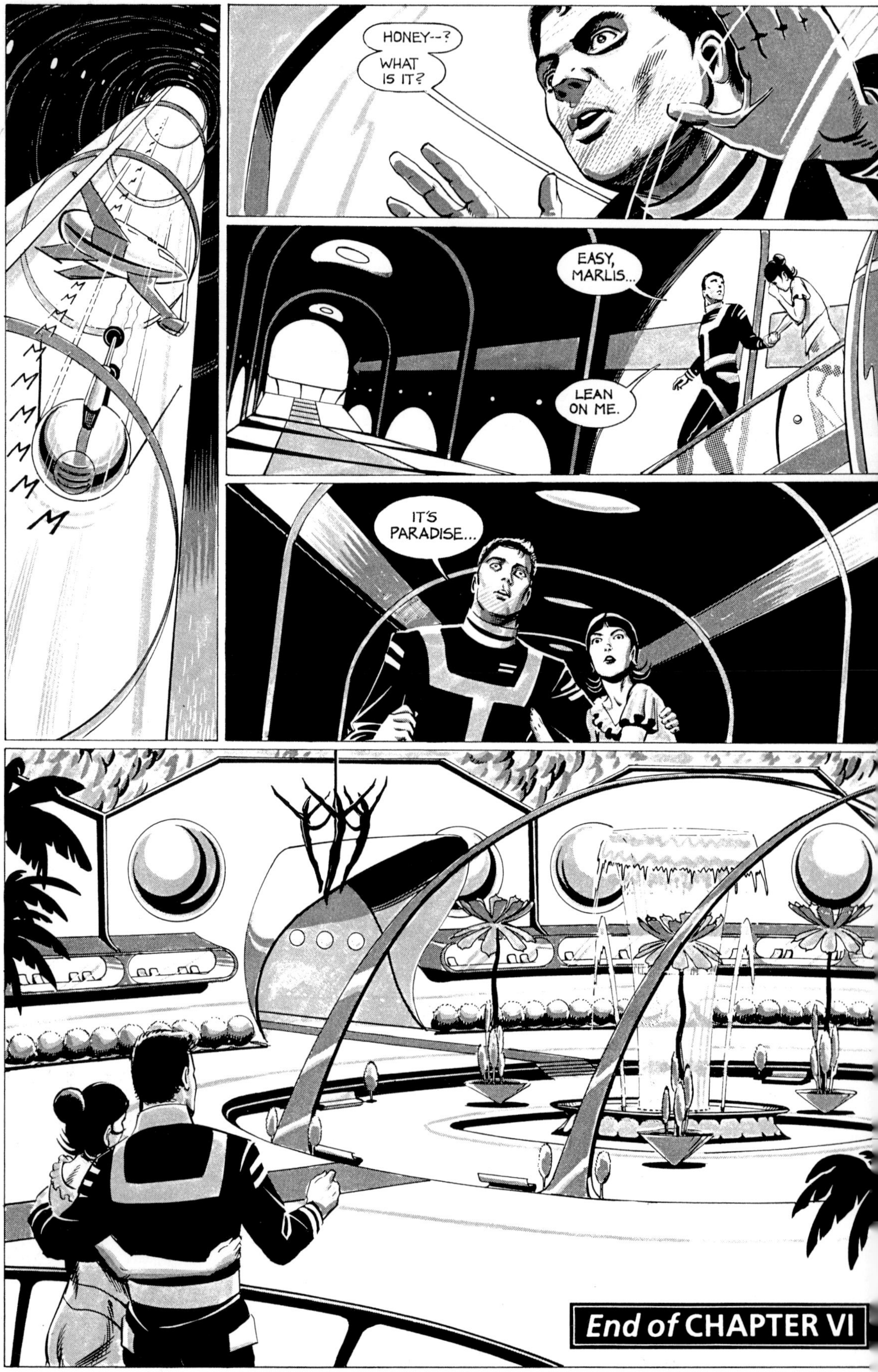
M M M M M M M M
HONEY--?
WHAT IS IT?
EASY, MARLIS...
LEAN ON ME.
IT'S PARADISE...
End of CHAPTER VI

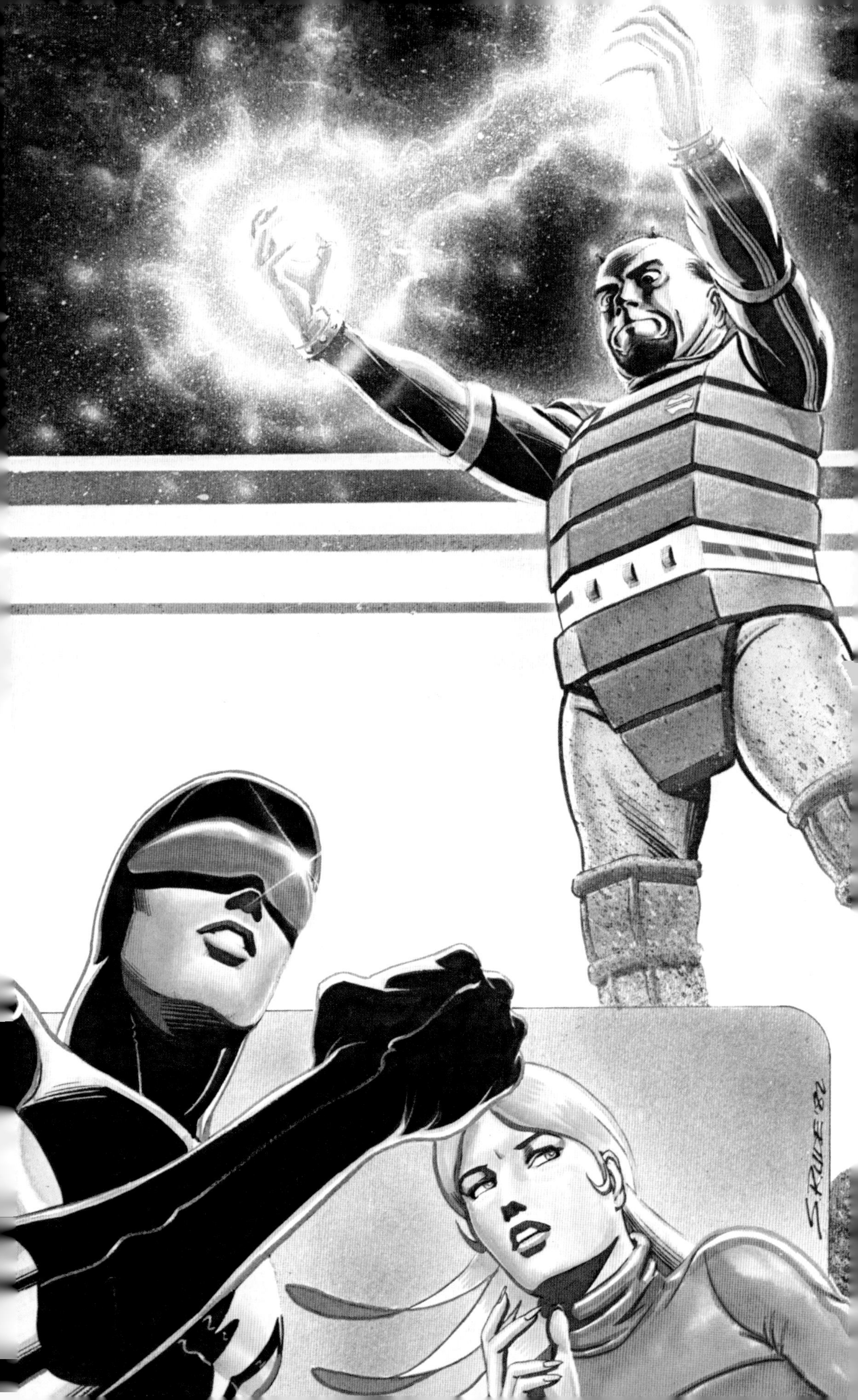
S.RUDE '82

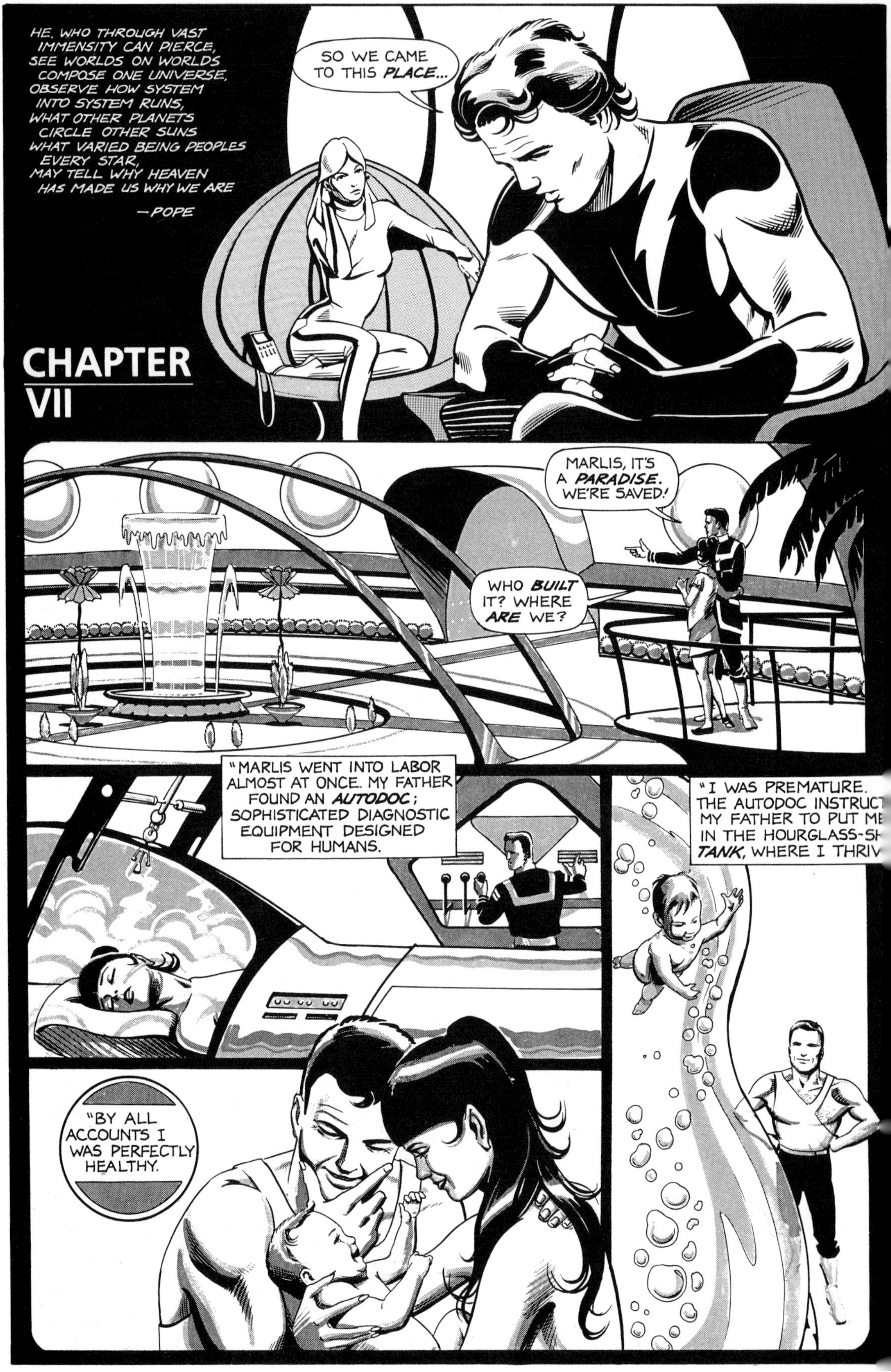
HE, WHO THROUGH VAST IMMENSITY CAN PIERCE, SEE WORLDS ON WORLDS COMPOSE ONE UNIVERSE, OBSERVE HOW SYSTEM INTO SYSTEM RUNS, WHAT OTHER PLANETS CIRCLE OTHER SUNS WHAT VARIED BEING PEOPLES EVERY STAR, MAY TELL WHY HEAVEN HAS MADE US WHY WE ARE
—POPE
SO WE CAME TO THIS PLACE...
CHAPTER VII
MARLIS, IT'S A PARADISE. WE'RE SAVED!
WHO BUILT IT? WHERE ARE WE?
"MARLIS WENT INTO LABOR ALMOST AT ONCE. MY FATHER FOUND AN AUTODOC; SOPHISTICATED DIAGNOSTIC EQUIPMENT DESIGNED FOR HUMANS.
"I WAS PREMATURE. THE AUTODOC INSTRUCT MY FATHER TO PUT ME IN THE HOURGLASS-SH TANK, WHERE I THRIV
"BY ALL ACCOUNTS I WAS PERFECTLY HEALTHY.

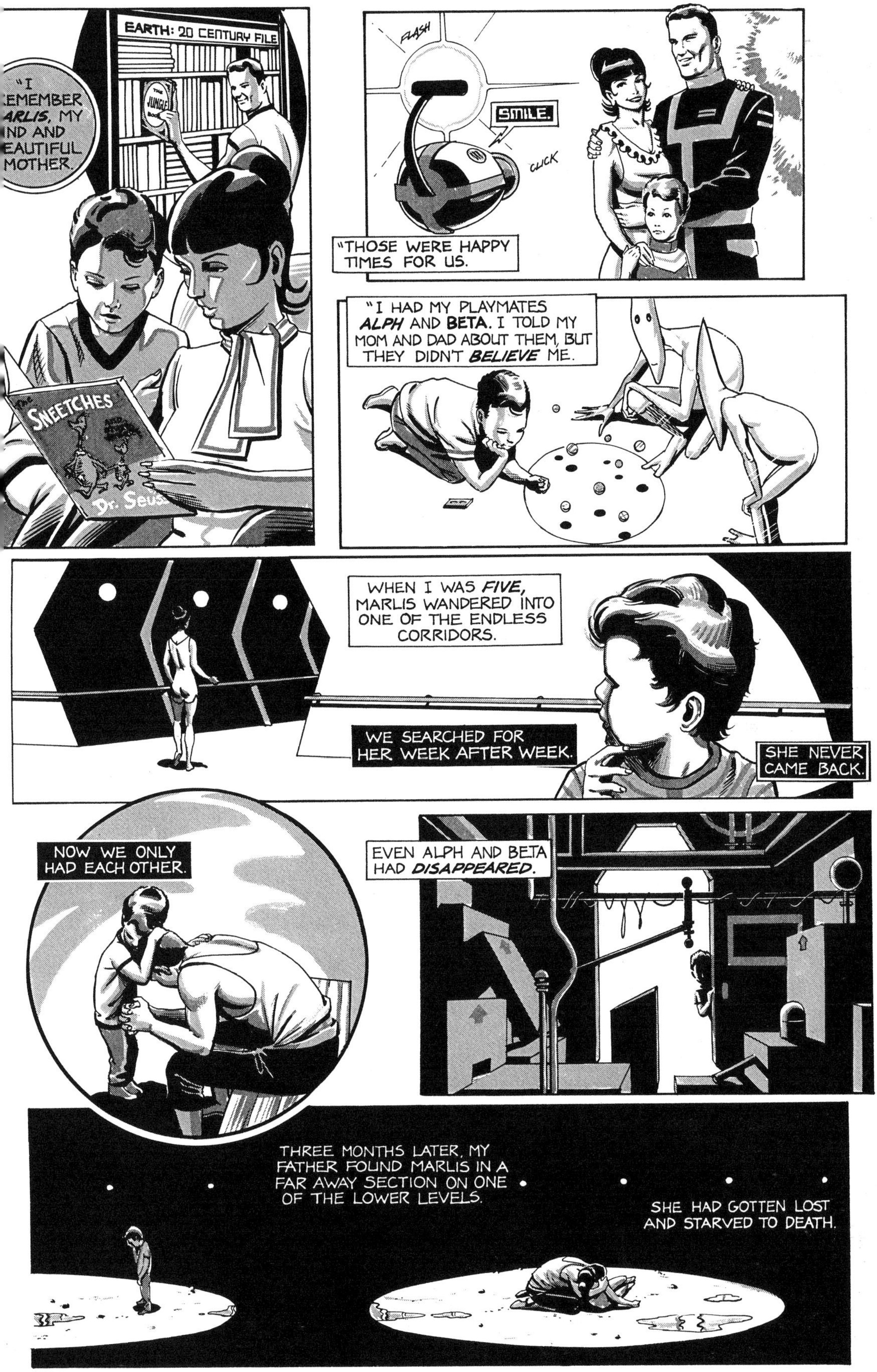
EARTH: 20 CENTURY FILE
"I REMEMBER MARLIS, MY KIND AND BEAUTIFUL MOTHER.
THE JUNGLE BOOK
SNEETCHES
Dr. Seuss
FLASH
SMILE.
CLICK
"THOSE WERE HAPPY TIMES FOR US.
"I HAD MY PLAYMATES ALPH AND BETA. I TOLD MY MOM AND DAD ABOUT THEM, BUT THEY DIDN'T BELIEVE ME.
WHEN I WAS FIVE, MARLIS WANDERED INTO ONE OF THE ENDLESS CORRIDORS.
WE SEARCHED FOR HER WEEK AFTER WEEK.
SHE NEVER CAME BACK.
NOW WE ONLY HAD EACH OTHER.
EVEN ALPH AND BETA HAD DISAPPEARED.
THREE MONTHS LATER, MY FATHER FOUND MARLIS IN A FAR AWAY SECTION ON ONE OF THE LOWER LEVELS.
SHE HAD GOTTEN LOST AND STARVED TO DEATH.

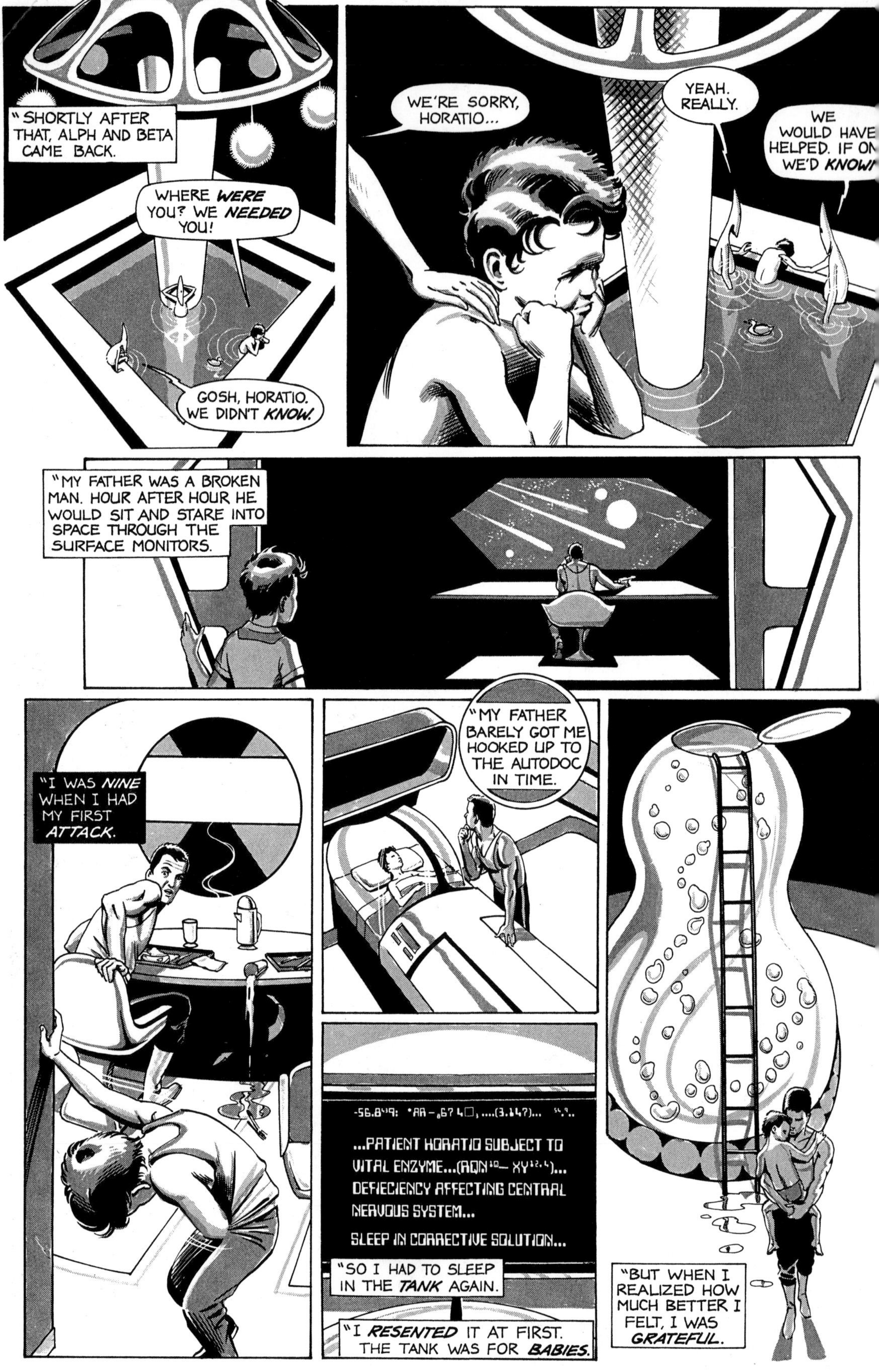
"SHORTLY AFTER THAT, ALPH AND BETA CAME BACK.
WHERE WERE YOU? WE NEEDED YOU!
GOSH, HORATIO. WE DIDN'T KNOW.
WE'RE SORRY, HORATIO...
YEAH. REALLY.
WE WOULD HAVE HELPED. IF ON WE'D KNOW!
"MY FATHER WAS A BROKEN MAN. HOUR AFTER HOUR HE WOULD SIT AND STARE INTO SPACE THROUGH THE SURFACE MONITORS.
"I WAS NINE WHEN I HAD MY FIRST ATTACK.
"MY FATHER BARELY GOT ME HOOKED UP TO THE AUTODOC IN TIME.
...PATIENT HORATIO SUBJECT TO VITAL ENZYME...
DEFIECIENCY AFFECTING CENTRAL NERVOUS SYSTEM...
SLEEP IN CORRECTIVE SOLUTION...
"SO I HAD TO SLEEP IN THE TANK AGAIN.
"I RESENTED IT AT FIRST. THE TANK WAS FOR BABIES.
"BUT WHEN I REALIZED HOW MUCH BETTER I FELT, I WAS GRATEFUL.

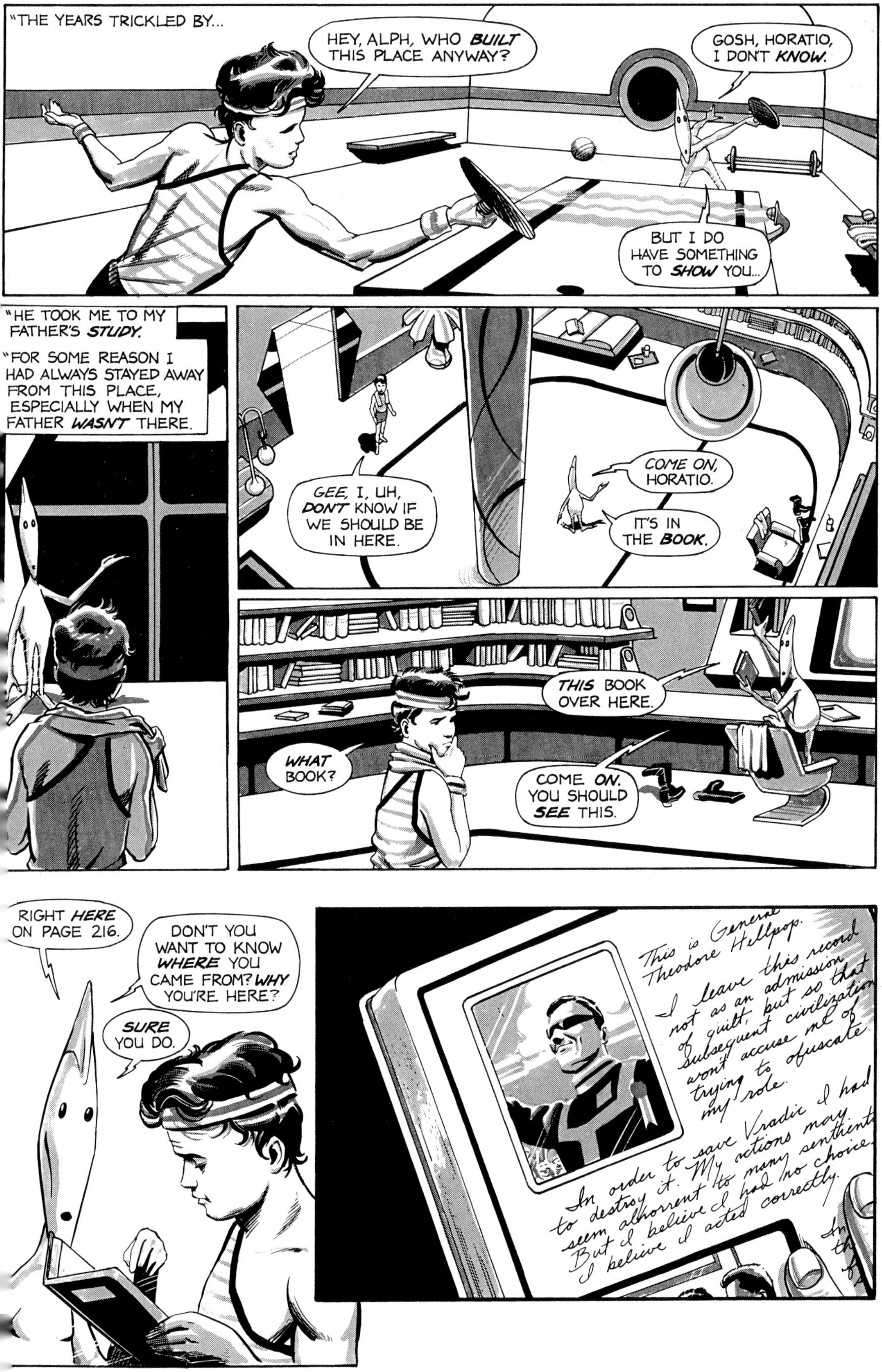

"THE YEARS TRICKLED BY...
HEY, ALPH, WHO *BUILT* THIS PLACE ANYWAY?
GOSH, HORATIO, I DON'T *KNOW*.
BUT I DO HAVE SOMETHING TO *SHOW* YOU...
"HE TOOK ME TO MY FATHER'S *STUDY*.
"FOR SOME REASON I HAD ALWAYS STAYED AWAY FROM THIS PLACE, ESPECIALLY WHEN MY FATHER *WASN'T* THERE.
GEE, I, UH, *DON'T* KNOW IF WE SHOULD BE IN HERE.
COME ON, HORATIO.
IT'S IN THE *BOOK*.
THIS BOOK OVER HERE.
WHAT BOOK?
COME *ON*. YOU SHOULD *SEE* THIS.
RIGHT *HERE* ON PAGE 216.
DON'T YOU WANT TO KNOW *WHERE* YOU CAME FROM? *WHY* YOU'RE HERE?
SURE YOU DO.
This is General Theodore Hellpop.
I leave this record not as an admission of guilt, but so that subsequent civilization won't accuse me of trying to ofuscate my role.
In order to save Vradic I had to destroy it. My actions may seem abhorrent to many sentient. But I believe I had no choice. I believe I acted correctly.

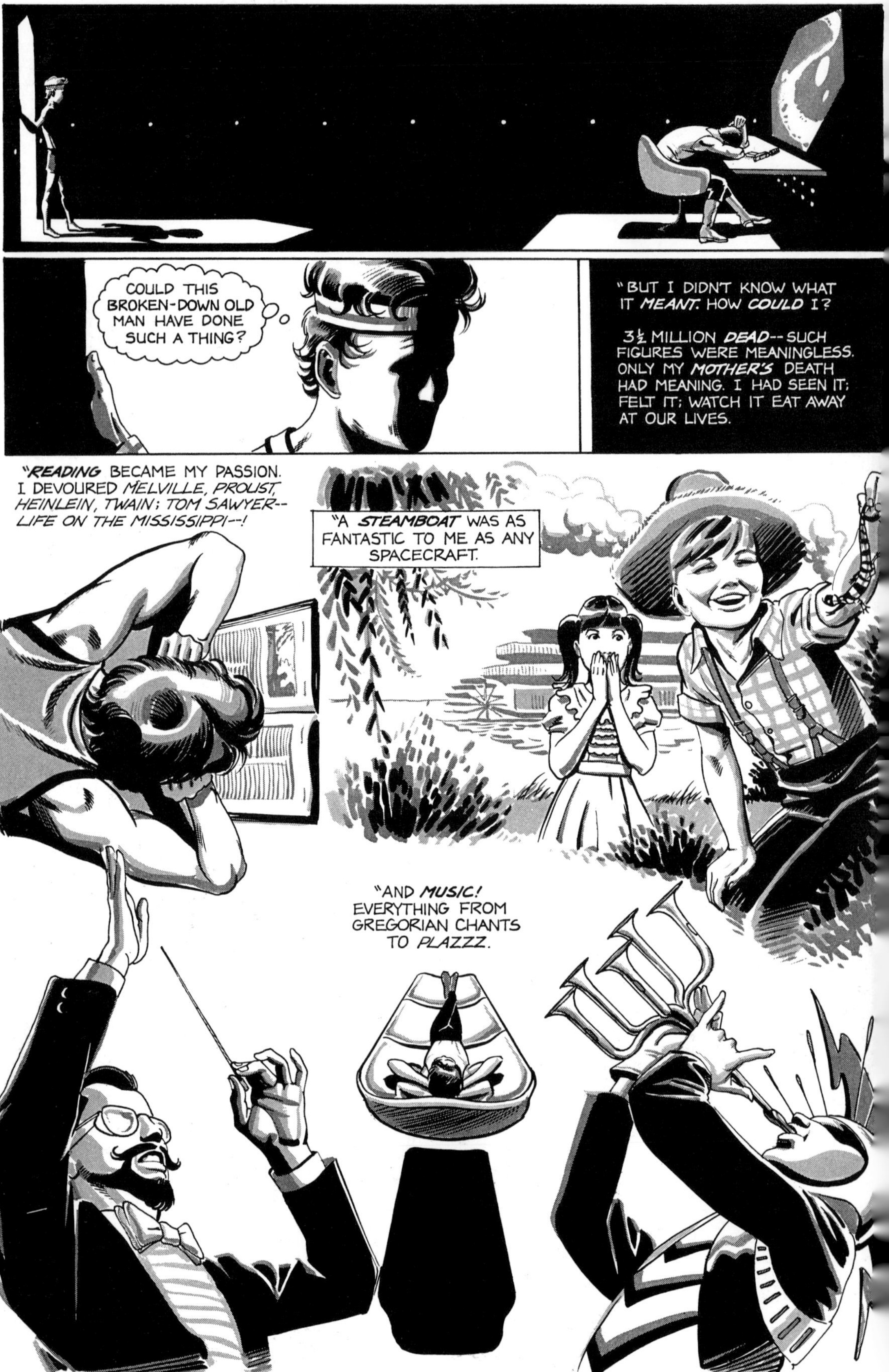
COULD THIS BROKEN-DOWN OLD MAN HAVE DONE SUCH A THING?
"BUT I DIDN'T KNOW WHAT IT *MEANT.* HOW *COULD* I?
3½ MILLION *DEAD*--SUCH FIGURES WERE MEANINGLESS. ONLY MY *MOTHER'S* DEATH HAD MEANING. I HAD SEEN IT; FELT IT; WATCH IT EAT AWAY AT OUR LIVES.
"*READING* BECAME MY PASSION. I DEVOURED *MELVILLE, PROUST, HEINLEIN, TWAIN; TOM SAWYER-- LIFE ON THE MISSISSIPPI*--!
"A *STEAMBOAT* WAS AS FANTASTIC TO ME AS ANY SPACECRAFT.
"AND *MUSIC!* EVERYTHING FROM GREGORIAN CHANTS TO *PLAZZZ.*

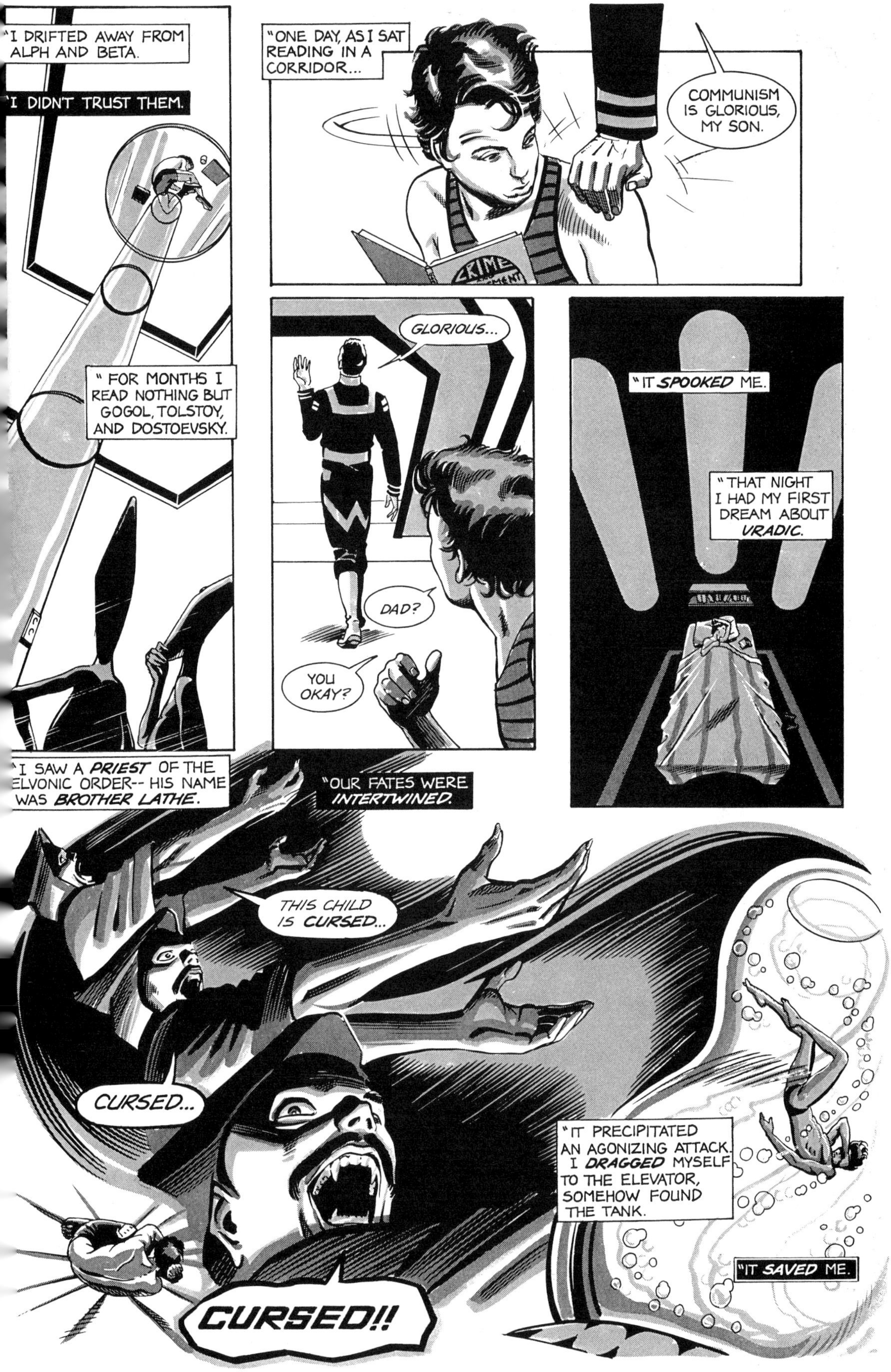
"I DRIFTED AWAY FROM ALPH AND BETA.
"I DIDN'T TRUST THEM.
"FOR MONTHS I READ NOTHING BUT GOGOL, TOLSTOY, AND DOSTOEVSKY.
"ONE DAY, AS I SAT READING IN A CORRIDOR...
COMMUNISM IS GLORIOUS, MY SON.
GLORIOUS...
DAD?
YOU OKAY?
"IT SPOOKED ME.
"THAT NIGHT I HAD MY FIRST DREAM ABOUT VRADIC.
"I SAW A PRIEST OF THE ELVONIC ORDER-- HIS NAME WAS BROTHER LATHE.
"OUR FATES WERE INTERTWINED.
THIS CHILD IS CURSED...
CURSED...
CURSED!!
"IT PRECIPITATED AN AGONIZING ATTACK. I DRAGGED MYSELF TO THE ELEVATOR, SOMEHOW FOUND THE TANK.
"IT SAVED ME.

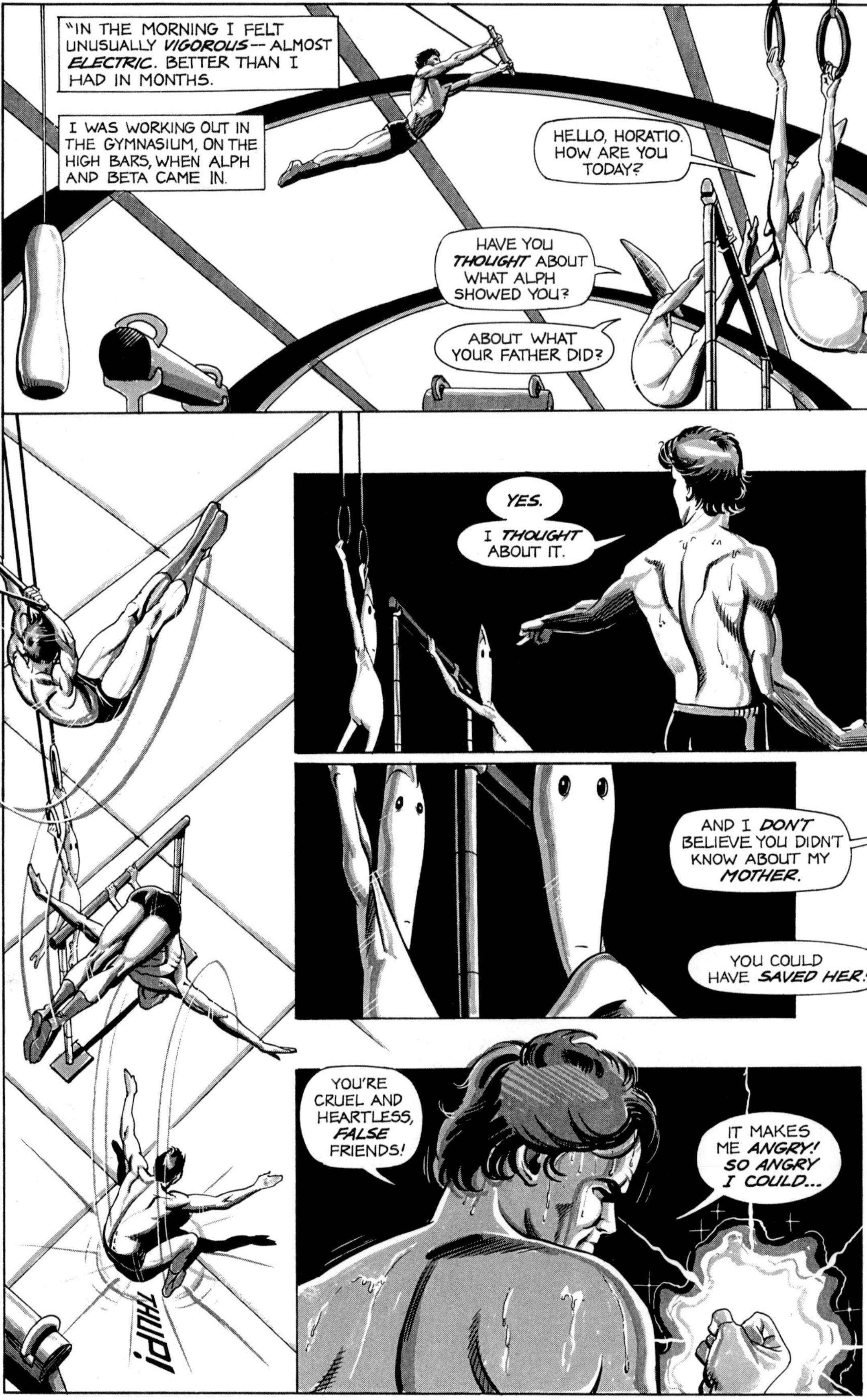
"IN THE MORNING I FELT UNUSUALLY VIGOROUS-- ALMOST ELECTRIC. BETTER THAN I HAD IN MONTHS.
I WAS WORKING OUT IN THE GYMNASIUM, ON THE HIGH BARS, WHEN ALPH AND BETA CAME IN.
HELLO, HORATIO. HOW ARE YOU TODAY?
HAVE YOU THOUGHT ABOUT WHAT ALPH SHOWED YOU?
ABOUT WHAT YOUR FATHER DID?
THUP!
YES.
I THOUGHT ABOUT IT.
AND I DON'T BELIEVE YOU DIDN'T KNOW ABOUT MY MOTHER.
YOU COULD HAVE SAVED HER!
YOU'RE CRUEL AND HEARTLESS, FALSE FRIENDS!
IT MAKES ME ANGRY! SO ANGRY I COULD...

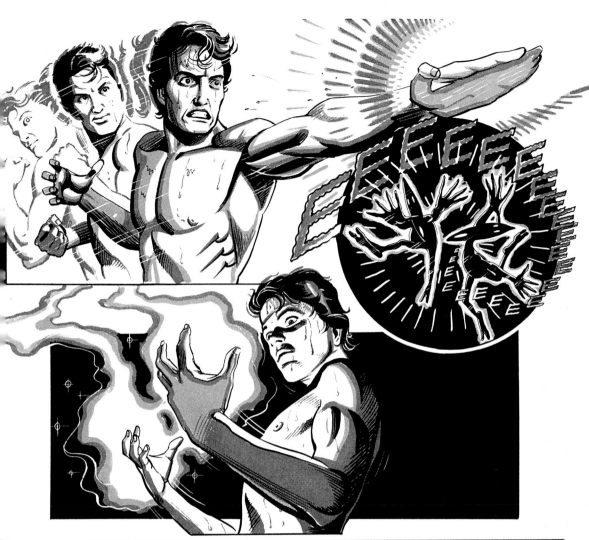

HELLO, SON

HOW ARE YOU?

FINE, DAD.

JUST FINE.

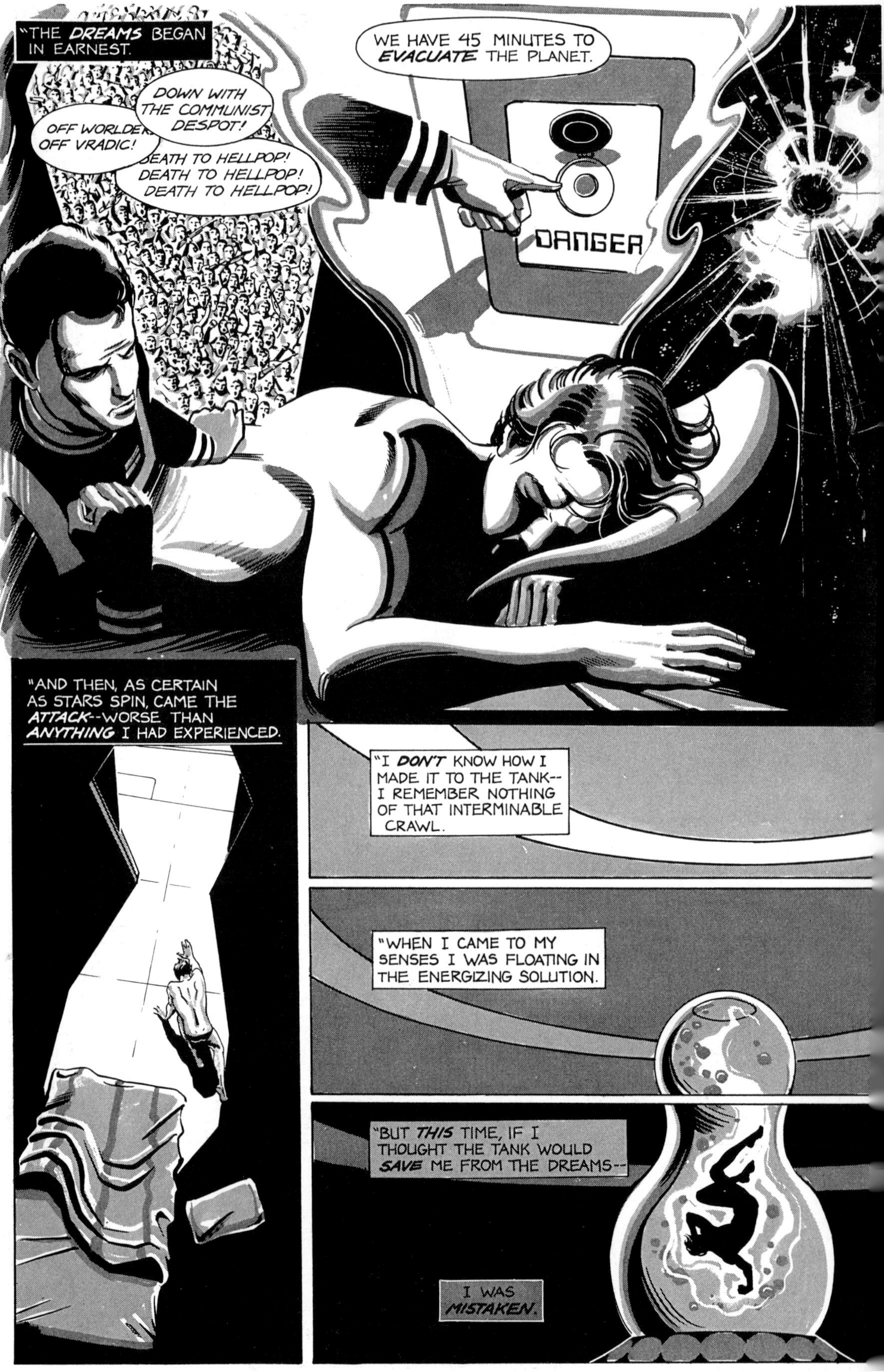
"THE DREAMS BEGAN IN EARNEST.
DOWN WITH THE COMMUNIST DESPOT!
OFF WORLDER! OFF VRADIC!
DEATH TO HELLPOP! DEATH TO HELLPOP! DEATH TO HELLPOP!
WE HAVE 45 MINUTES TO EVACUATE THE PLANET.
DANGER
"AND THEN, AS CERTAIN AS STARS SPIN, CAME THE ATTACK--WORSE THAN ANYTHING I HAD EXPERIENCED.
"I DON'T KNOW HOW I MADE IT TO THE TANK-- I REMEMBER NOTHING OF THAT INTERMINABLE CRAWL.
"WHEN I CAME TO MY SENSES I WAS FLOATING IN THE ENERGIZING SOLUTION.
"BUT THIS TIME, IF I THOUGHT THE TANK WOULD SAVE ME FROM THE DREAMS--
I WAS MISTAKEN.

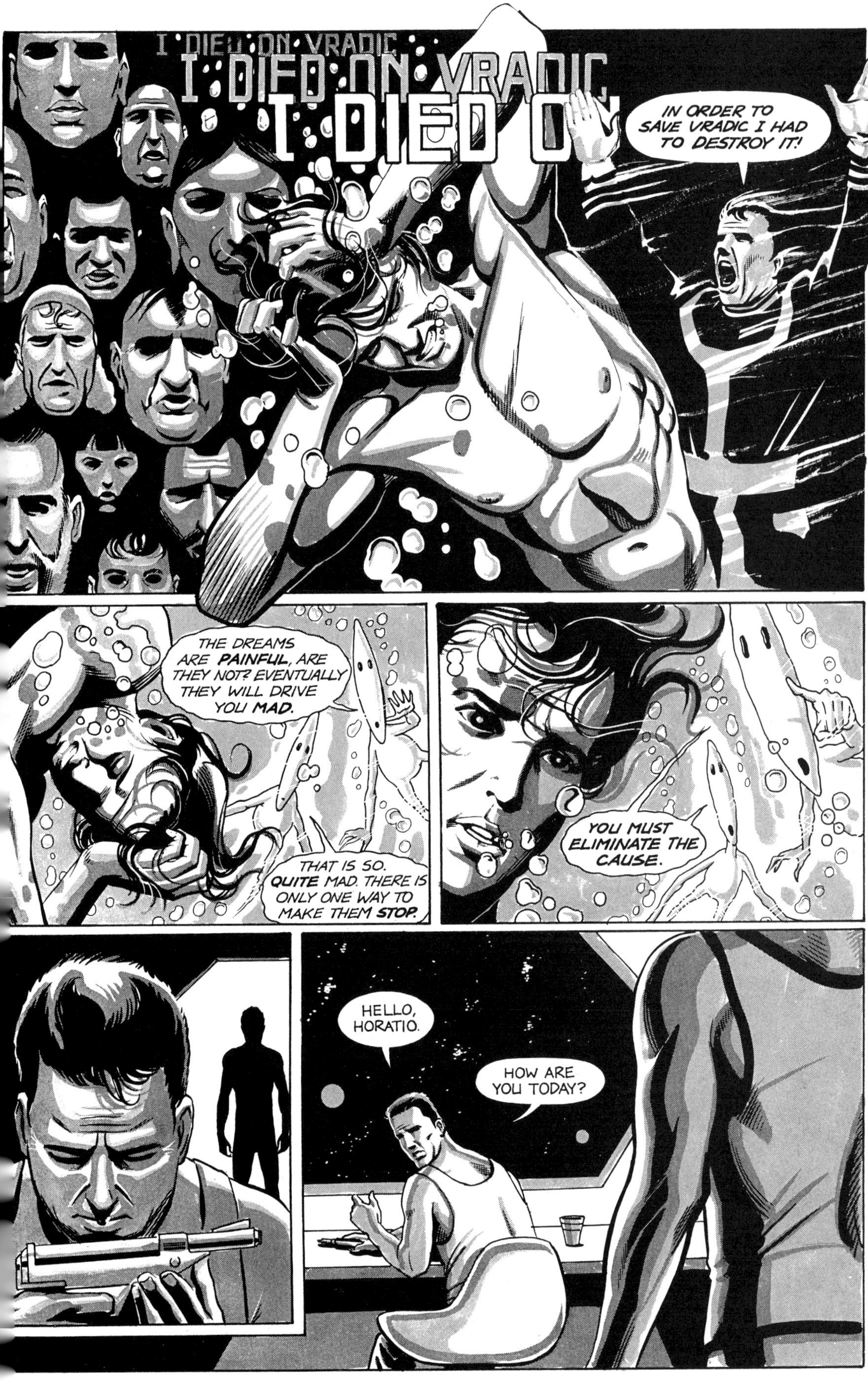

I DIED ON VRADIC
I DIED ON VRADIC
I DIED O
IN ORDER TO SAVE VRADIC I HAD TO DESTROY IT!
THE DREAMS ARE **PAINFUL**, ARE THEY NOT? EVENTUALLY THEY WILL DRIVE YOU **MAD**.
THAT IS SO. **QUITE** MAD. THERE IS ONLY ONE WAY TO MAKE THEM **STOP**.
YOU MUST ELIMINATE THE CAUSE.
HELLO, HORATIO.
HOW ARE YOU TODAY?

FINE, DAD.

I LOVE YOU, DAD.

GEEZZZTT!

DAD, I'M SORRY.

I'M SORRY...

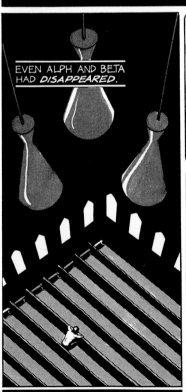

EVEN ALPH AND BETA HAD *DISAPPEARED*.

"I THINK, PERHAPS, THEY WERE THE *GHOSTS* OF THOSE MY FATHER HAD *MURDERED*, WHO HAD SOMEHOW STOWED AWAY ON BOARD HIS SHIP.

"*TWO* YEARS PASSED BEFORE THE ATTACKS AGAIN DROVE ME TO THE TANK. THIS TIME I *ACCEPTED* THE DREAM AS A BIRD ACCEPTS FLIGHT.

"I *EMBRACED* THE DREAM: A MAN CALLED THE *MANAGER*, ON A PLANET CALLED *THUNE*. *DAVE* WAS IN IT. YOU KNOW DAVE.

"AND AS I FLOATED AND SUFFERED, YET I WAS FILLED WITH A STRANGE ECSTACY, FOR THE *UNCERTAINTY* WAS OVER. A *WORD* CAME TO ME-- NO; *MORE* THAN A WORD. IT WAS WHO I *AM*...

NEXUS

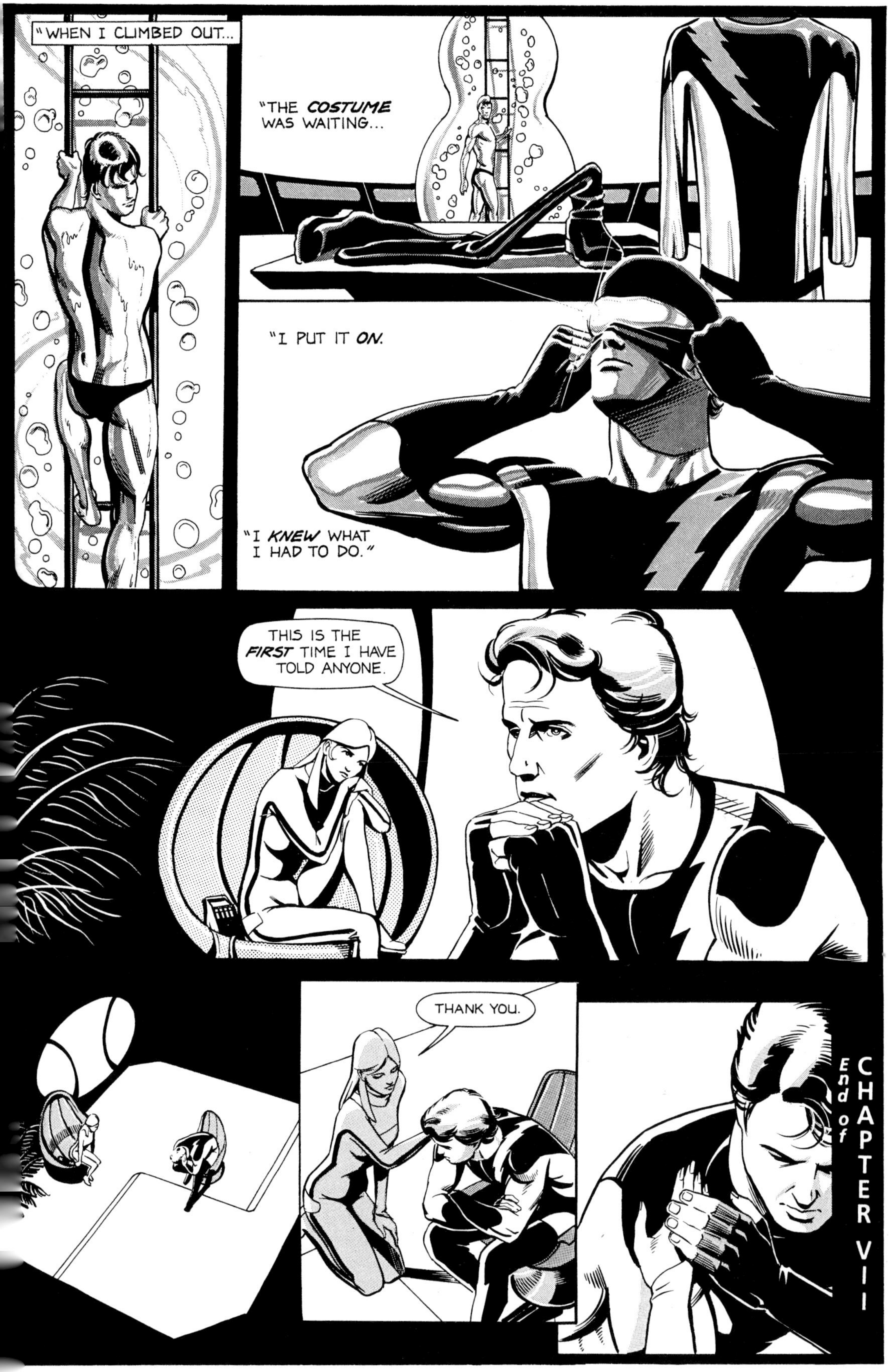
"WHEN I CLIMBED OUT...
"THE COSTUME WAS WAITING...
"I PUT IT ON.
"I KNEW WHAT I HAD TO DO."
THIS IS THE FIRST TIME I HAVE TOLD ANYONE.
THANK YOU.
End of CHAPTER VII

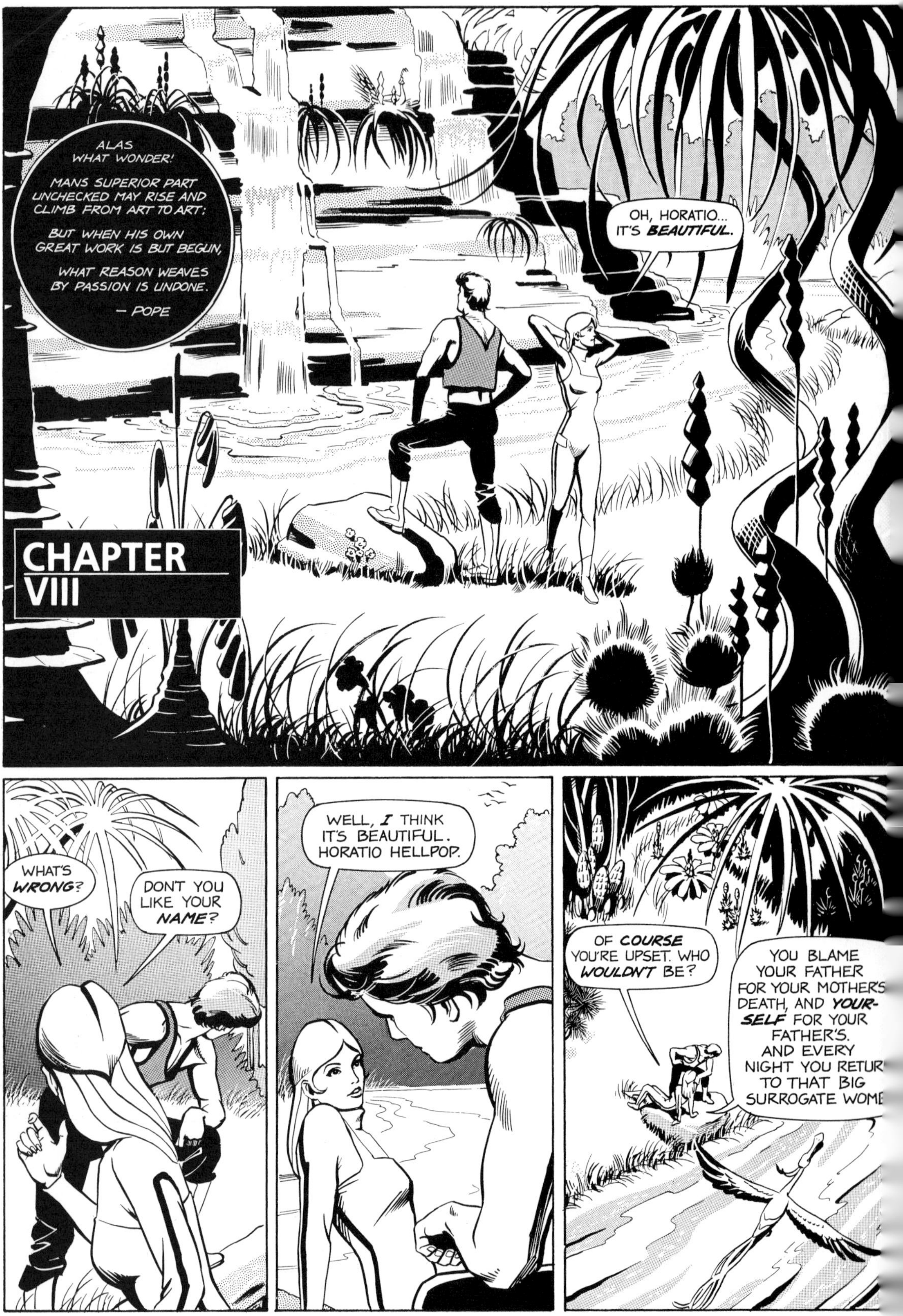
ALAS
WHAT WONDER!
MANS SUPERIOR PART
UNCHECKED MAY RISE AND
CLIMB FROM ART TO ART:
BUT WHEN HIS OWN
GREAT WORK IS BUT BEGUN,
WHAT REASON WEAVES
BY PASSION IS UNDONE.
— POPE
OH, HORATIO... IT'S BEAUTIFUL.
CHAPTER VIII
WHAT'S WRONG?
DON'T YOU LIKE YOUR NAME?
WELL, I THINK IT'S BEAUTIFUL. HORATIO HELLPOP.
OF COURSE YOU'RE UPSET. WHO WOULDN'T BE?
YOU BLAME YOUR FATHER FOR YOUR MOTHER'S DEATH, AND YOURSELF FOR YOUR FATHER'S. AND EVERY NIGHT YOU RETUR TO THAT BIG SURROGATE WOM

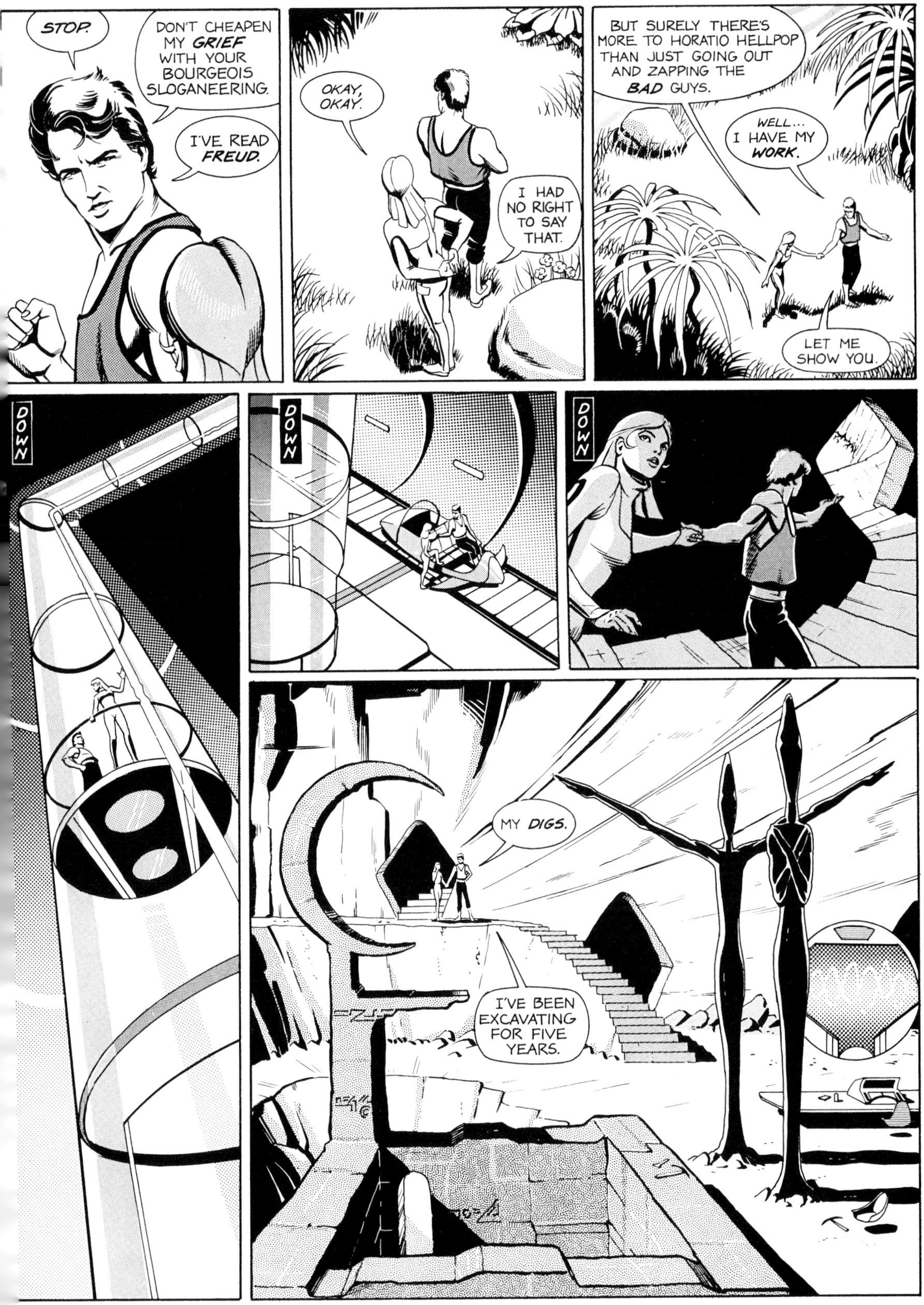
STOP.
DON'T CHEAPEN MY GRIEF WITH YOUR BOURGEOIS SLOGANEERING.
I'VE READ FREUD.
OKAY, OKAY.
I HAD NO RIGHT TO SAY THAT.
BUT SURELY THERE'S MORE TO HORATIO HELLPOP THAN JUST GOING OUT AND ZAPPING THE BAD GUYS.
WELL... I HAVE MY WORK.
LET ME SHOW YOU.
DOWN
DOWN
DOWN
MY DIGS.
I'VE BEEN EXCAVATING FOR FIVE YEARS.

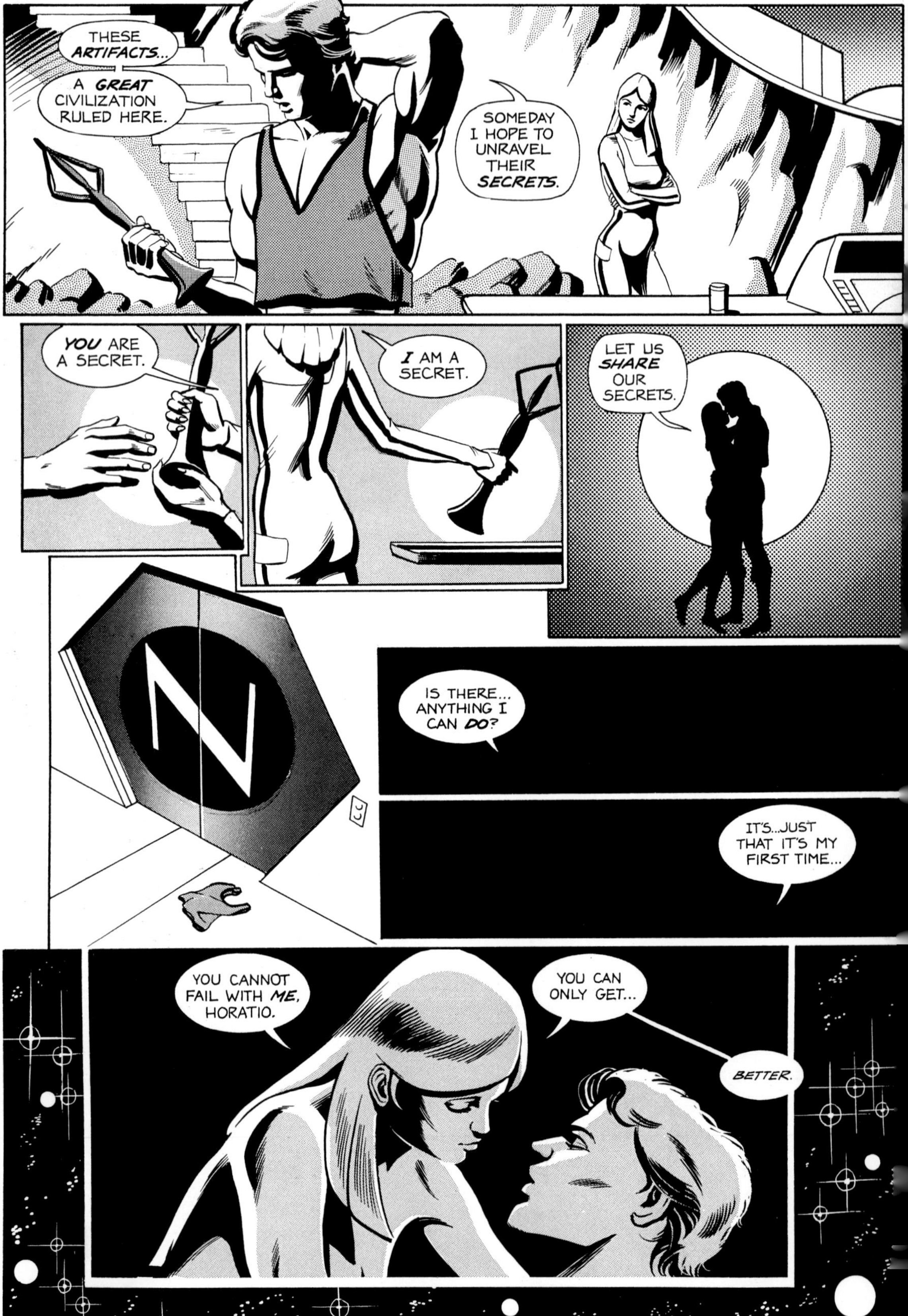
THESE ARTIFACTS...
A GREAT CIVILIZATION RULED HERE.
SOMEDAY I HOPE TO UNRAVEL THEIR SECRETS.
YOU ARE A SECRET.
I AM A SECRET.
LET US SHARE OUR SECRETS.
IS THERE... ANYTHING I CAN DO?
IT'S...JUST THAT IT'S MY FIRST TIME...
YOU CANNOT FAIL WITH ME, HORATIO.
YOU CAN ONLY GET...
BETTER.

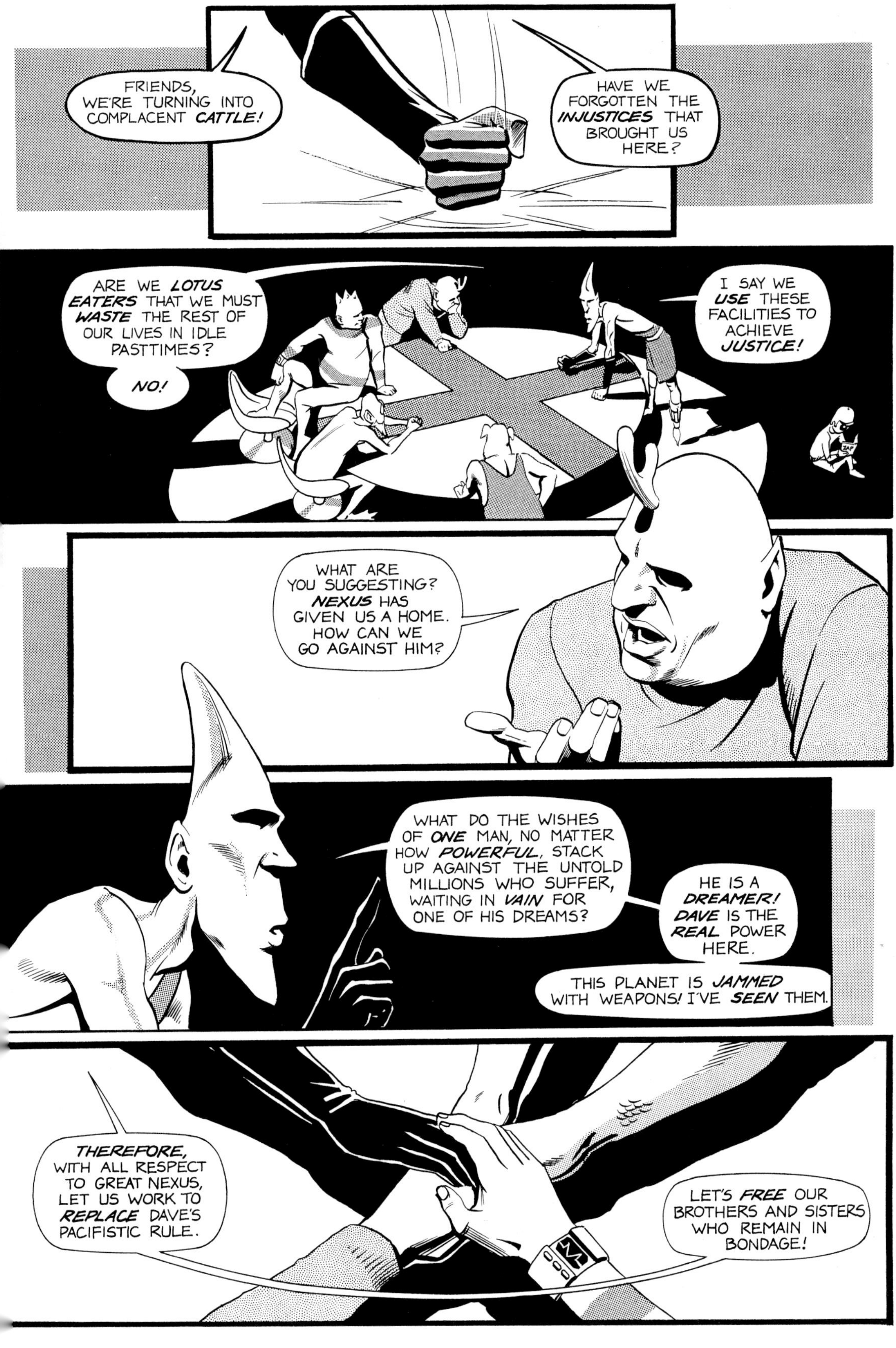
FRIENDS, WE'RE TURNING INTO COMPLACENT CATTLE!
HAVE WE FORGOTTEN THE INJUSTICES THAT BROUGHT US HERE?
ARE WE LOTUS EATERS THAT WE MUST WASTE THE REST OF OUR LIVES IN IDLE PASTTIMES?
NO!
I SAY WE USE THESE FACILITIES TO ACHIEVE JUSTICE!
ZAP
WHAT ARE YOU SUGGESTING? NEXUS HAS GIVEN US A HOME. HOW CAN WE GO AGAINST HIM?
WHAT DO THE WISHES OF ONE MAN, NO MATTER HOW POWERFUL, STACK UP AGAINST THE UNTOLD MILLIONS WHO SUFFER, WAITING IN VAIN FOR ONE OF HIS DREAMS?
HE IS A DREAMER! DAVE IS THE REAL POWER HERE.
THIS PLANET IS JAMMED WITH WEAPONS! I'VE SEEN THEM.
THEREFORE, WITH ALL RESPECT TO GREAT NEXUS, LET US WORK TO REPLACE DAVE'S PACIFISTIC RULE.
LET'S FREE OUR BROTHERS AND SISTERS WHO REMAIN IN BONDAGE!

WHOA--!

IT'S OKAY.

YOU WERE JUST HAVING A NIGHTMARE.

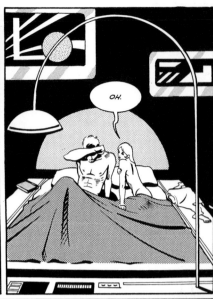

OH.

I'LL HAVE TO GO IN THE *TANK* SOON...

I CAN *FEEL* IT.

HAVE YOU...

HAVE YOU EVER THOUGHT ABOUT USING YOUR POWER TO *CREATE* SOMETHING?

INSTEAD OF YOU KNOW...

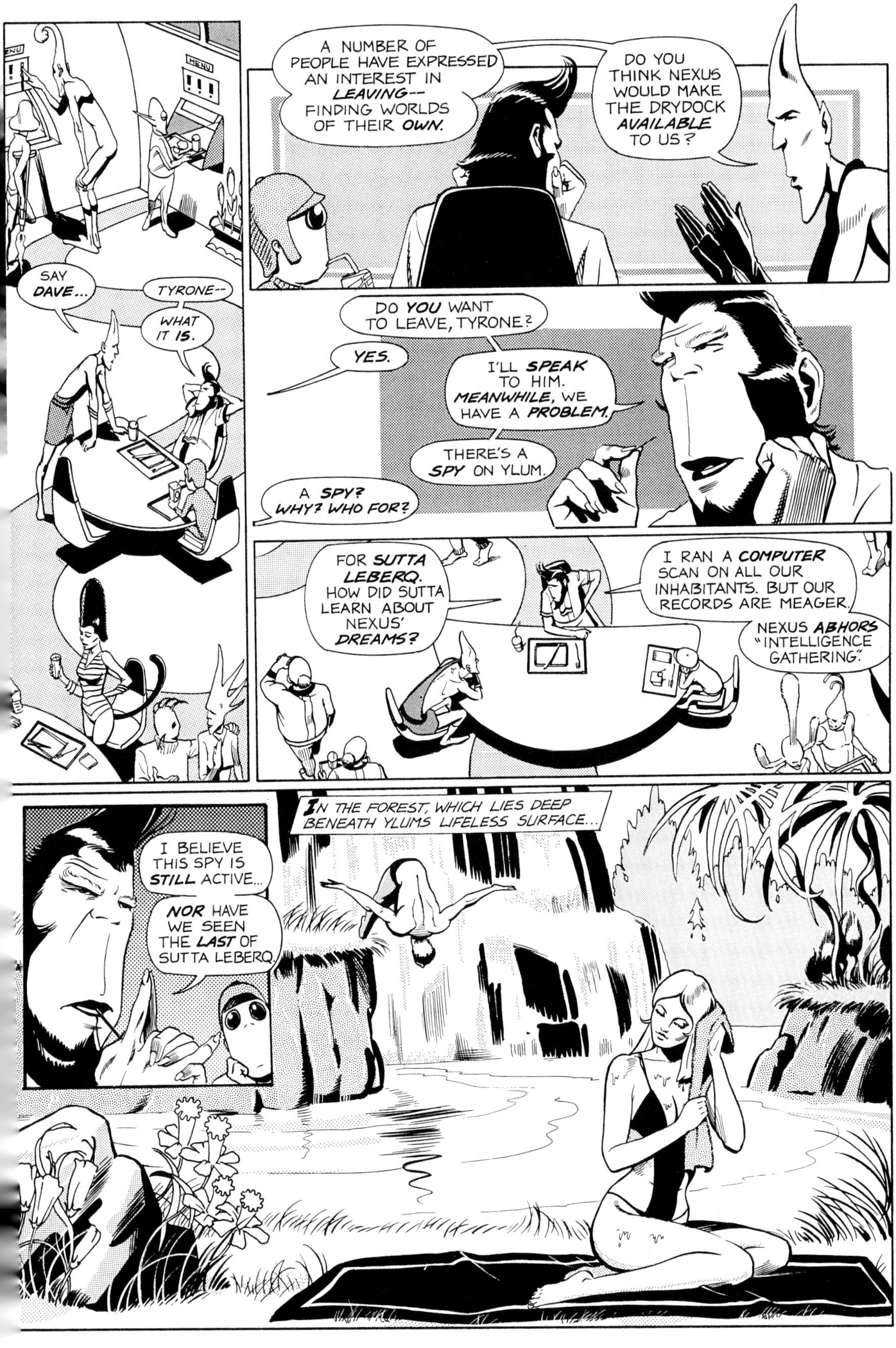
A NUMBER OF PEOPLE HAVE EXPRESSED AN INTEREST IN LEAVING-- FINDING WORLDS OF THEIR OWN.
DO YOU THINK NEXUS WOULD MAKE THE DRYDOCK AVAILABLE TO US?
MENU
MENU
SAY DAVE...
TYRONE--
WHAT IT IS.
DO YOU WANT TO LEAVE, TYRONE?
YES.
I'LL SPEAK TO HIM. MEANWHILE, WE HAVE A PROBLEM.
THERE'S A SPY ON YLUM.
A SPY? WHY? WHO FOR?
FOR SUTTA LEBERQ. HOW DID SUTTA LEARN ABOUT NEXUS' DREAMS?
I RAN A COMPUTER SCAN ON ALL OUR INHABITANTS. BUT OUR RECORDS ARE MEAGER.
NEXUS ABHORS "INTELLIGENCE GATHERING."
I BELIEVE THIS SPY IS STILL ACTIVE...
NOR HAVE WE SEEN THE LAST OF SUTTA LEBERQ.
IN THE FOREST, WHICH LIES DEEP BENEATH YLUMS LIFELESS SURFACE...

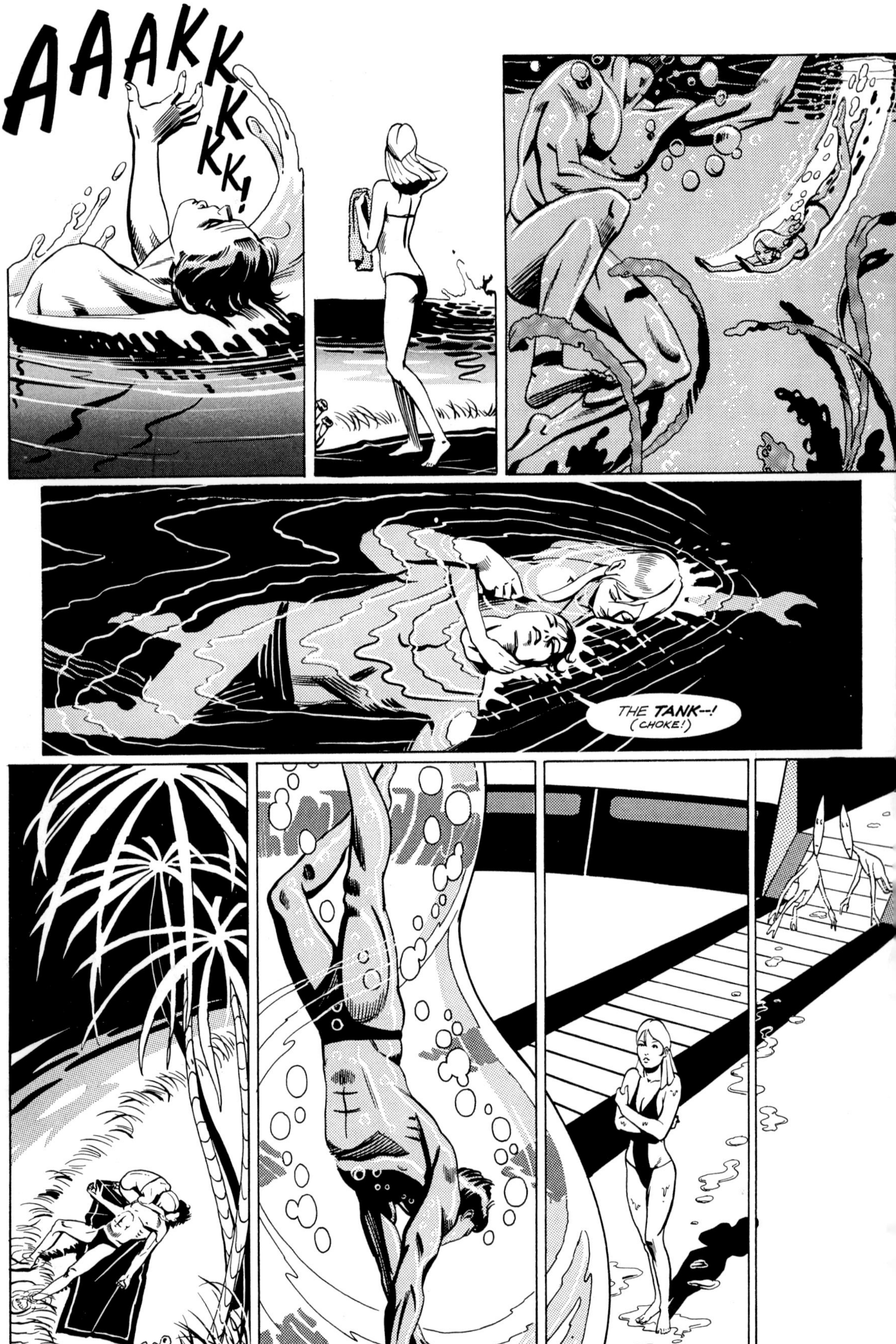
AAAKKKKK!
THE TANK--! (CHOKE!)

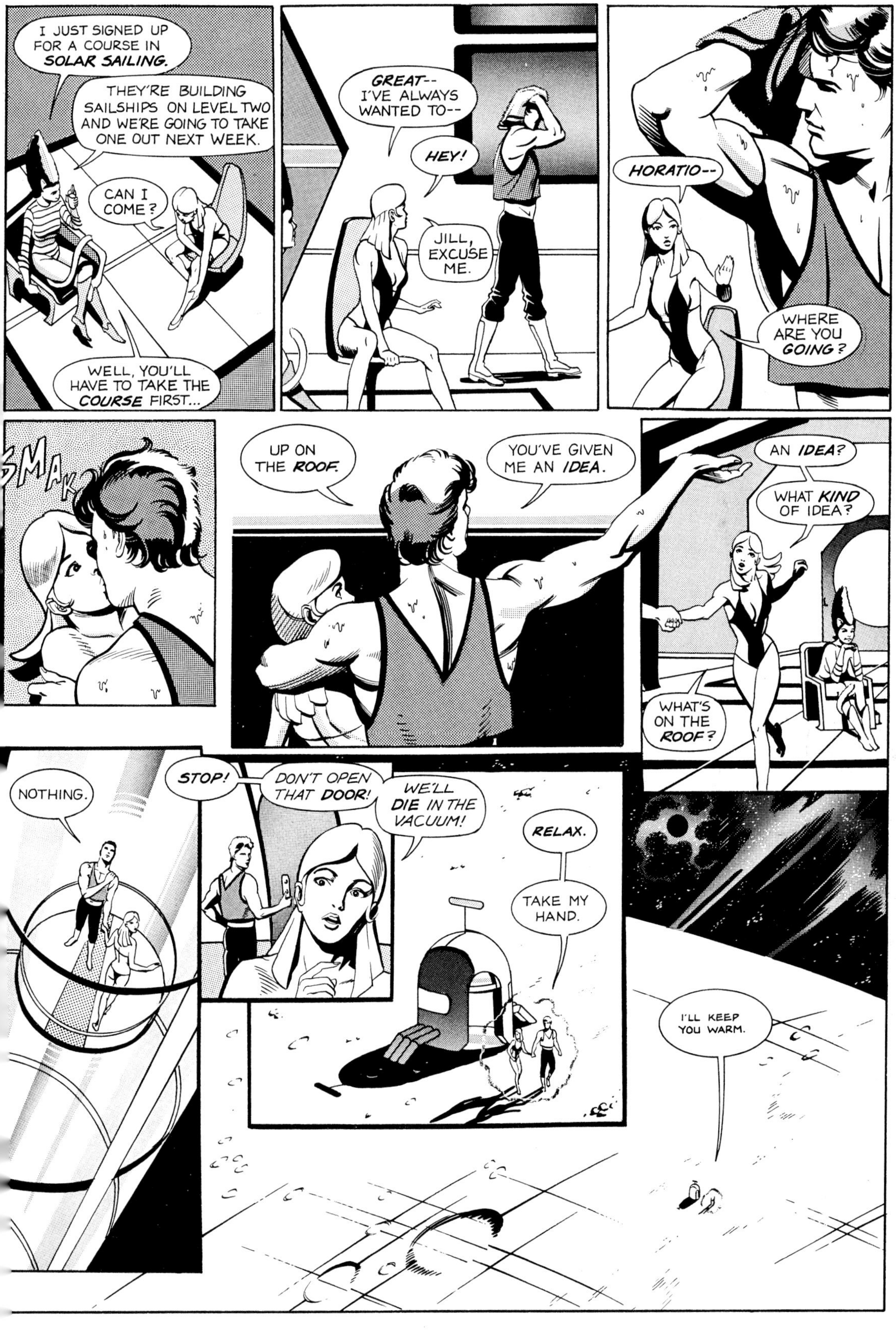
I JUST SIGNED UP FOR A COURSE IN SOLAR SAILING.
THEY'RE BUILDING SAILSHIPS ON LEVEL TWO AND WE'RE GOING TO TAKE ONE OUT NEXT WEEK.
CAN I COME?
WELL, YOU'LL HAVE TO TAKE THE COURSE FIRST...
GREAT-- I'VE ALWAYS WANTED TO--
HEY!
JILL, EXCUSE ME.
HORATIO--
WHERE ARE YOU GOING?
SMAK
UP ON THE ROOF.
YOU'VE GIVEN ME AN IDEA.
AN IDEA?
WHAT KIND OF IDEA?
WHAT'S ON THE ROOF?
NOTHING.
STOP!
DON'T OPEN THAT DOOR!
WE'LL DIE IN THE VACUUM!
RELAX.
TAKE MY HAND.
I'LL KEEP YOU WARM.

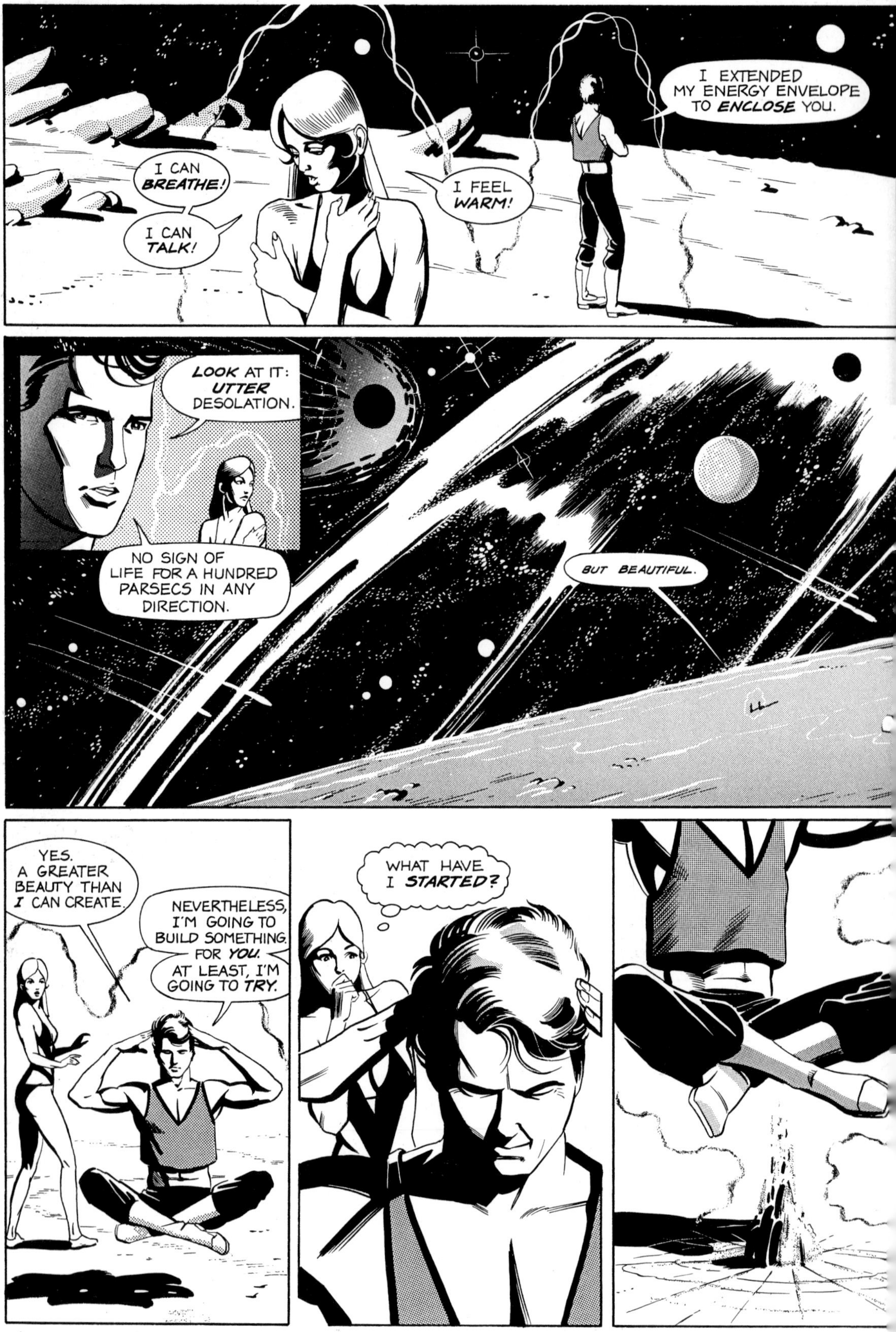
I EXTENDED MY ENERGY ENVELOPE TO ENCLOSE YOU.
I CAN BREATHE!
I CAN TALK!
I FEEL WARM!
LOOK AT IT: UTTER DESOLATION.
NO SIGN OF LIFE FOR A HUNDRED PARSECS IN ANY DIRECTION.
BUT BEAUTIFUL.
YES. A GREATER BEAUTY THAN I CAN CREATE.
NEVERTHELESS, I'M GOING TO BUILD SOMETHING. FOR YOU.
AT LEAST, I'M GOING TO TRY.
WHAT HAVE I STARTED?

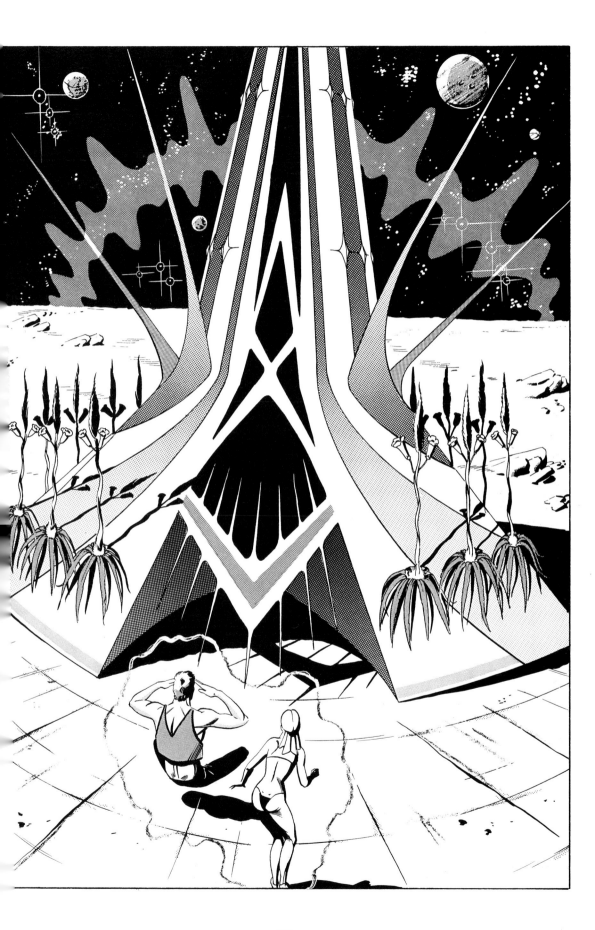

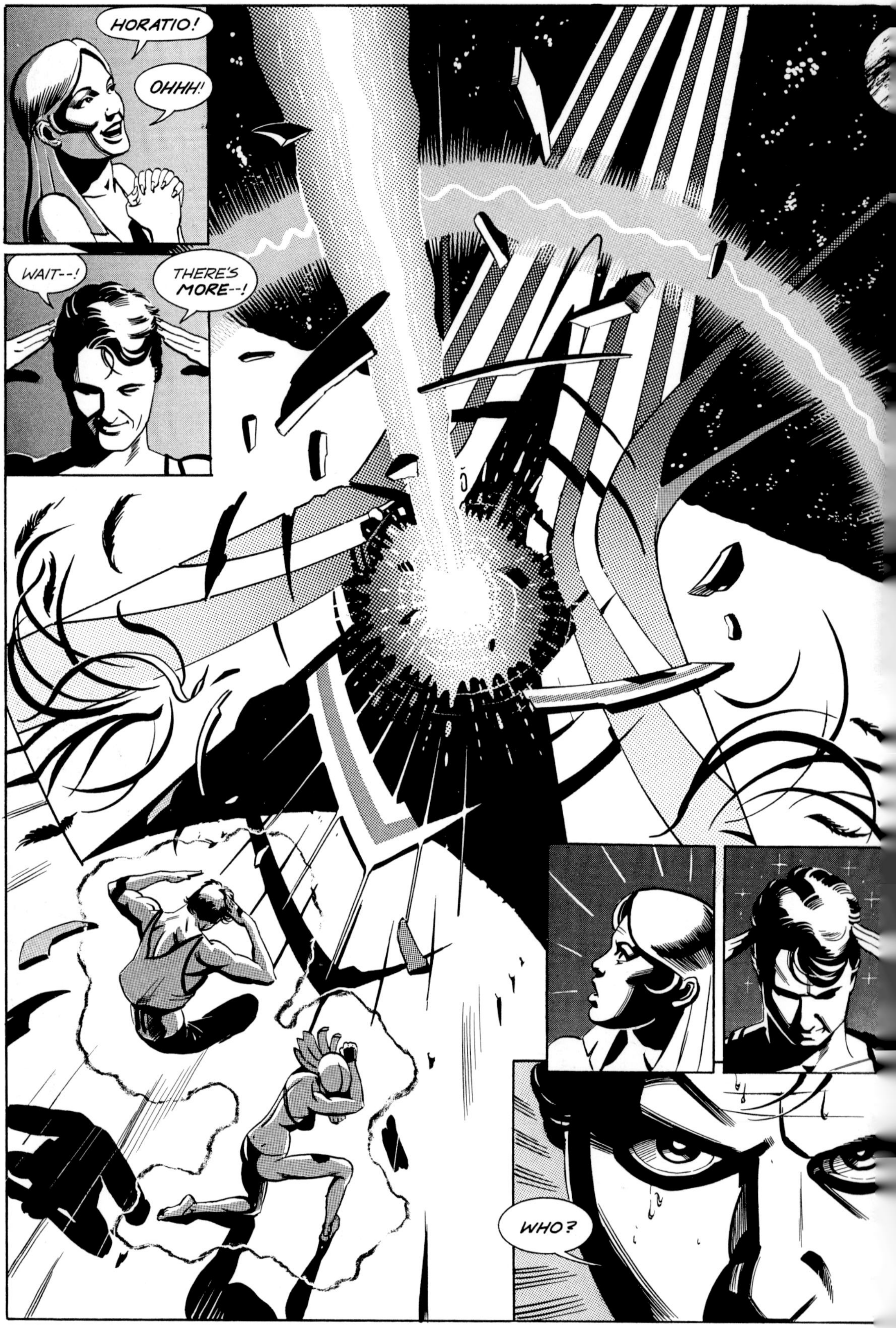
HORATIO!
OHHH!
WAIT--!
THERE'S MORE--!
WHO?

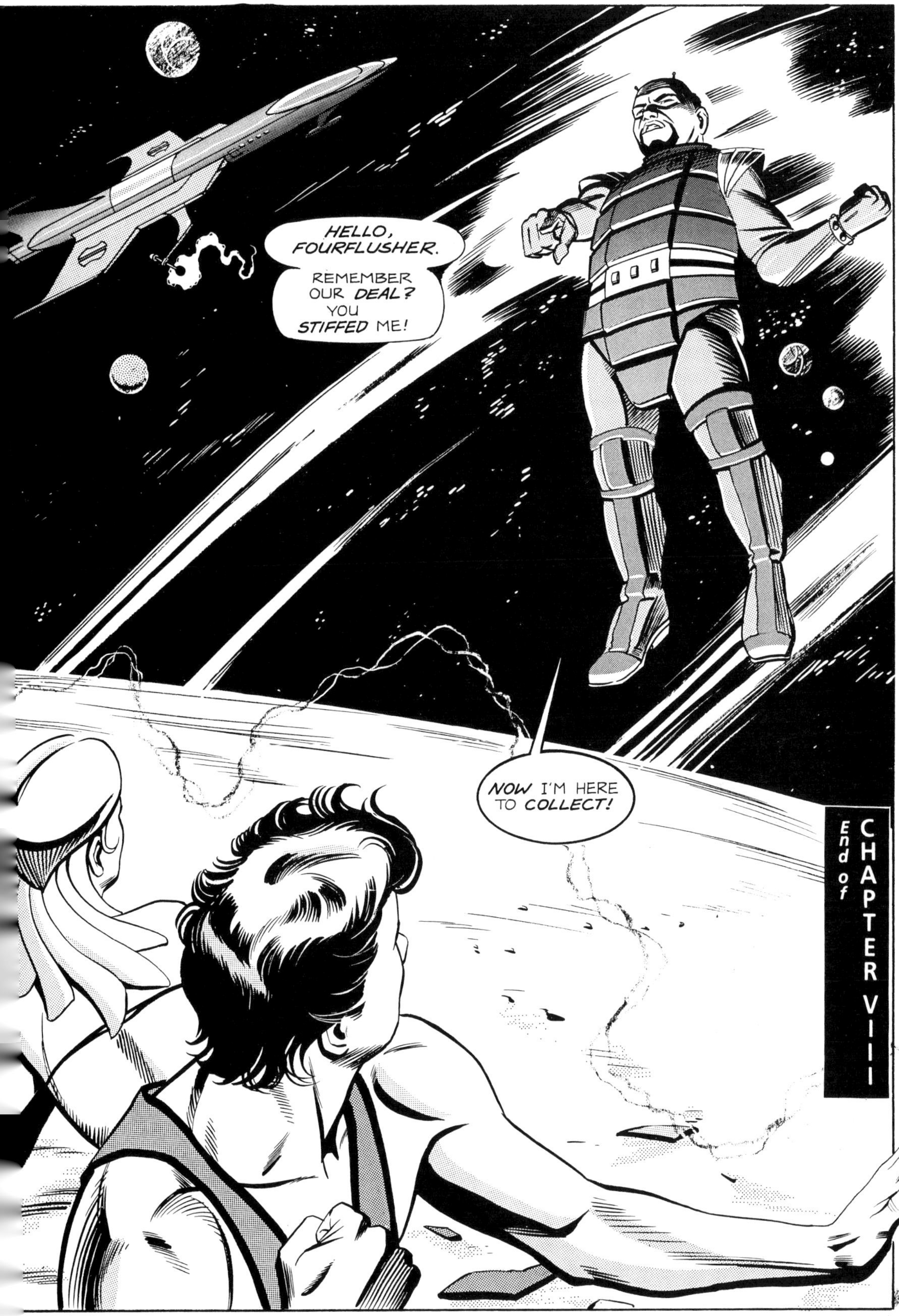
HELLO, FOURFLUSHER.
REMEMBER OUR DEAL? YOU STIFFED ME!
NOW I'M HERE TO COLLECT!
End of CHAPTER VIII

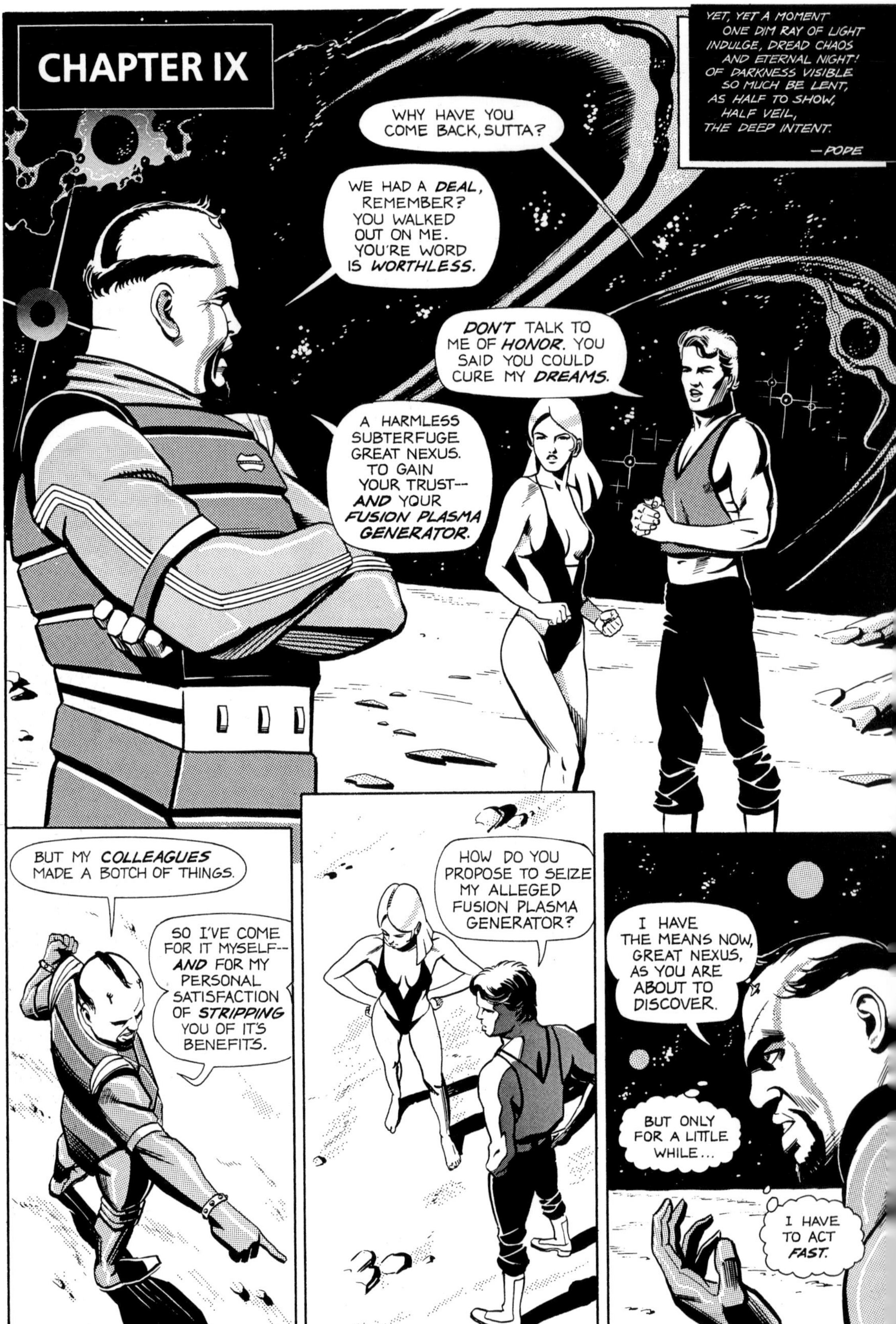
CHAPTER IX
YET, YET A MOMENT
ONE DIM RAY OF LIGHT
INDULGE, DREAD CHAOS
AND ETERNAL NIGHT!
OF DARKNESS VISIBLE
SO MUCH BE LENT,
AS HALF TO SHOW,
HALF VEIL,
THE DEEP INTENT.
—POPE
WHY HAVE YOU COME BACK, SUTTA?
WE HAD A DEAL, REMEMBER? YOU WALKED OUT ON ME. YOU'RE WORD IS WORTHLESS.
DON'T TALK TO ME OF HONOR. YOU SAID YOU COULD CURE MY DREAMS.
A HARMLESS SUBTERFUGE GREAT NEXUS. TO GAIN YOUR TRUST-- AND YOUR FUSION PLASMA GENERATOR.
BUT MY COLLEAGUES MADE A BOTCH OF THINGS.
SO I'VE COME FOR IT MYSELF-- AND FOR MY PERSONAL SATISFACTION OF STRIPPING YOU OF IT'S BENEFITS.
HOW DO YOU PROPOSE TO SEIZE MY ALLEGED FUSION PLASMA GENERATOR?
I HAVE THE MEANS NOW, GREAT NEXUS, AS YOU ARE ABOUT TO DISCOVER.
BUT ONLY FOR A LITTLE WHILE...
I HAVE TO ACT FAST.

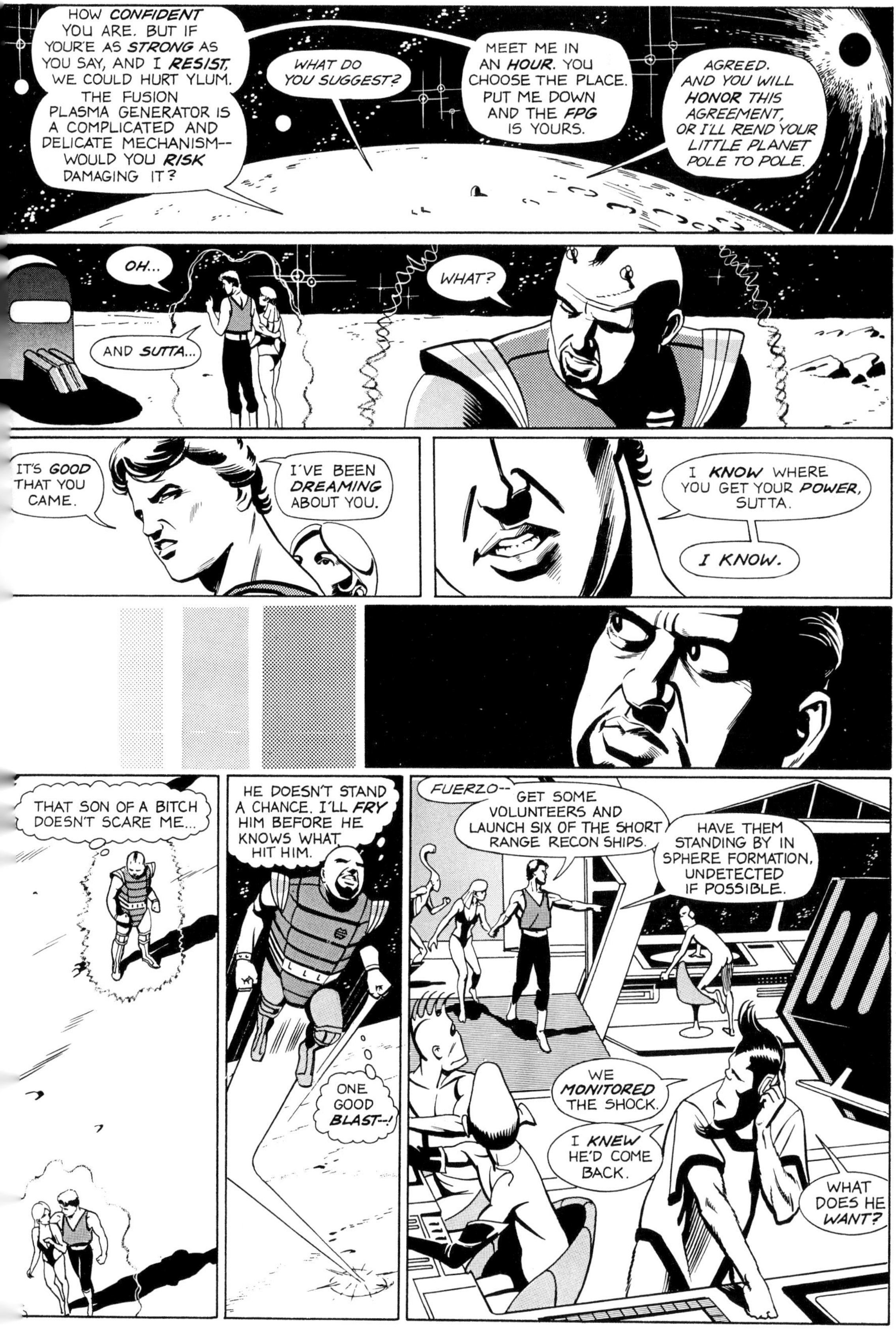
HOW CONFIDENT YOU ARE. BUT IF YOUR'E AS STRONG AS YOU SAY, AND I RESIST, WE COULD HURT YLUM.
THE FUSION PLASMA GENERATOR IS A COMPLICATED AND DELICATE MECHANISM-- WOULD YOU RISK DAMAGING IT?
WHAT DO YOU SUGGEST?
MEET ME IN AN HOUR. YOU CHOOSE THE PLACE. PUT ME DOWN AND THE FPG IS YOURS.
AGREED. AND YOU WILL HONOR THIS AGREEMENT, OR I'LL REND YOUR LITTLE PLANET POLE TO POLE.
OH...
AND SUTTA...
WHAT?
IT'S GOOD THAT YOU CAME.
I'VE BEEN DREAMING ABOUT YOU.
I KNOW WHERE YOU GET YOUR POWER, SUTTA.
I KNOW.
THAT SON OF A BITCH DOESN'T SCARE ME...
HE DOESN'T STAND A CHANCE. I'LL FRY HIM BEFORE HE KNOWS WHAT HIT HIM.
ONE GOOD BLAST--!
FUERZO--
GET SOME VOLUNTEERS AND LAUNCH SIX OF THE SHORT RANGE RECON SHIPS.
HAVE THEM STANDING BY IN SPHERE FORMATION, UNDETECTED IF POSSIBLE.
WE MONITORED THE SHOCK.
I KNEW HE'D COME BACK.
WHAT DOES HE WANT?

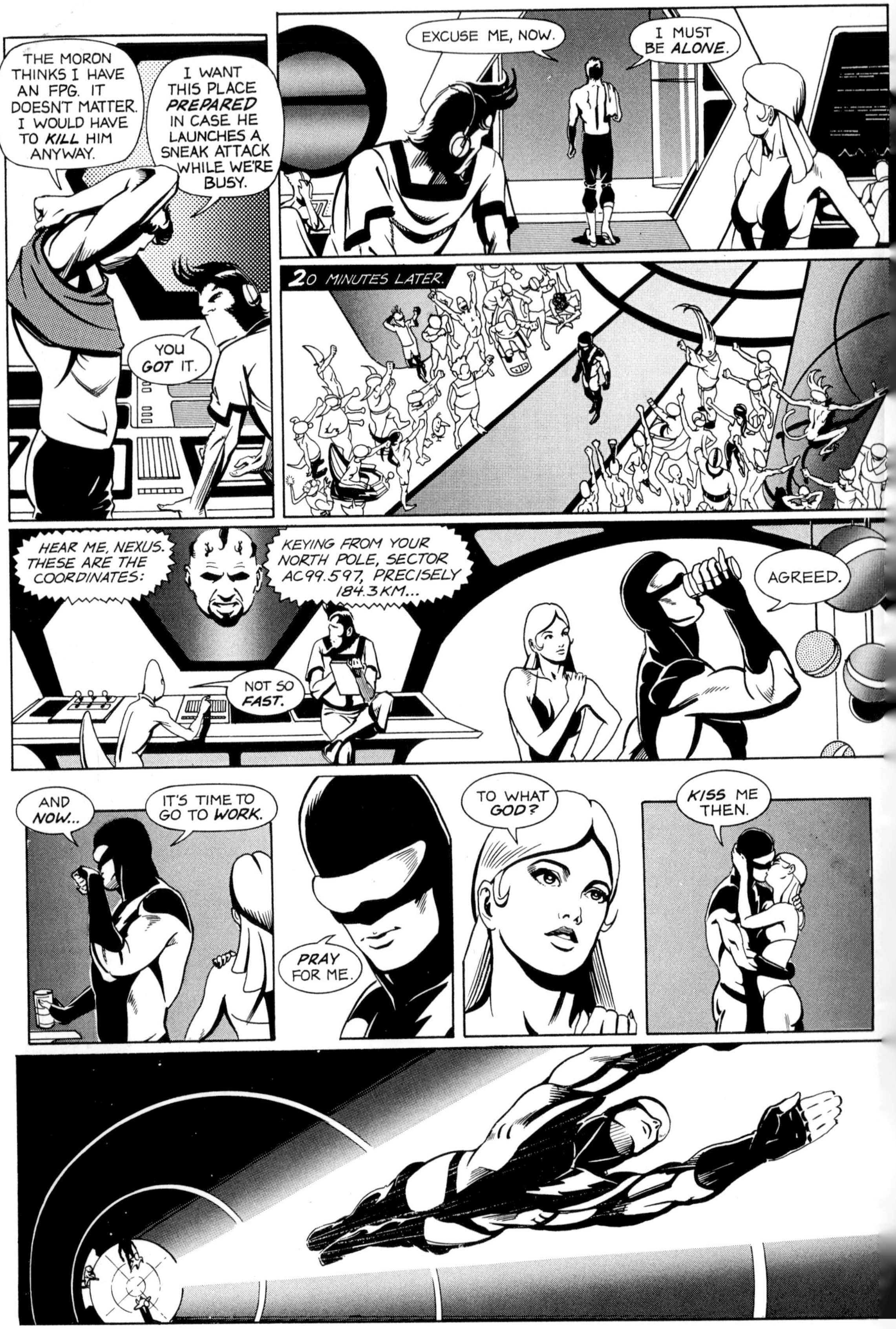
THE MORON THINKS I HAVE AN FPG. IT DOESN'T MATTER. I WOULD HAVE TO KILL HIM ANYWAY.
I WANT THIS PLACE PREPARED IN CASE HE LAUNCHES A SNEAK ATTACK WHILE WE'RE BUSY.
YOU GOT IT.
EXCUSE ME, NOW.
I MUST BE ALONE.
20 MINUTES LATER.
HEAR ME, NEXUS. THESE ARE THE COORDINATES:
KEYING FROM YOUR NORTH POLE, SECTOR AC99.597, PRECISELY 184.3KM...
NOT SO FAST.
AGREED.
AND NOW...
IT'S TIME TO GO TO WORK.
PRAY FOR ME.
TO WHAT GOD?
KISS ME THEN.

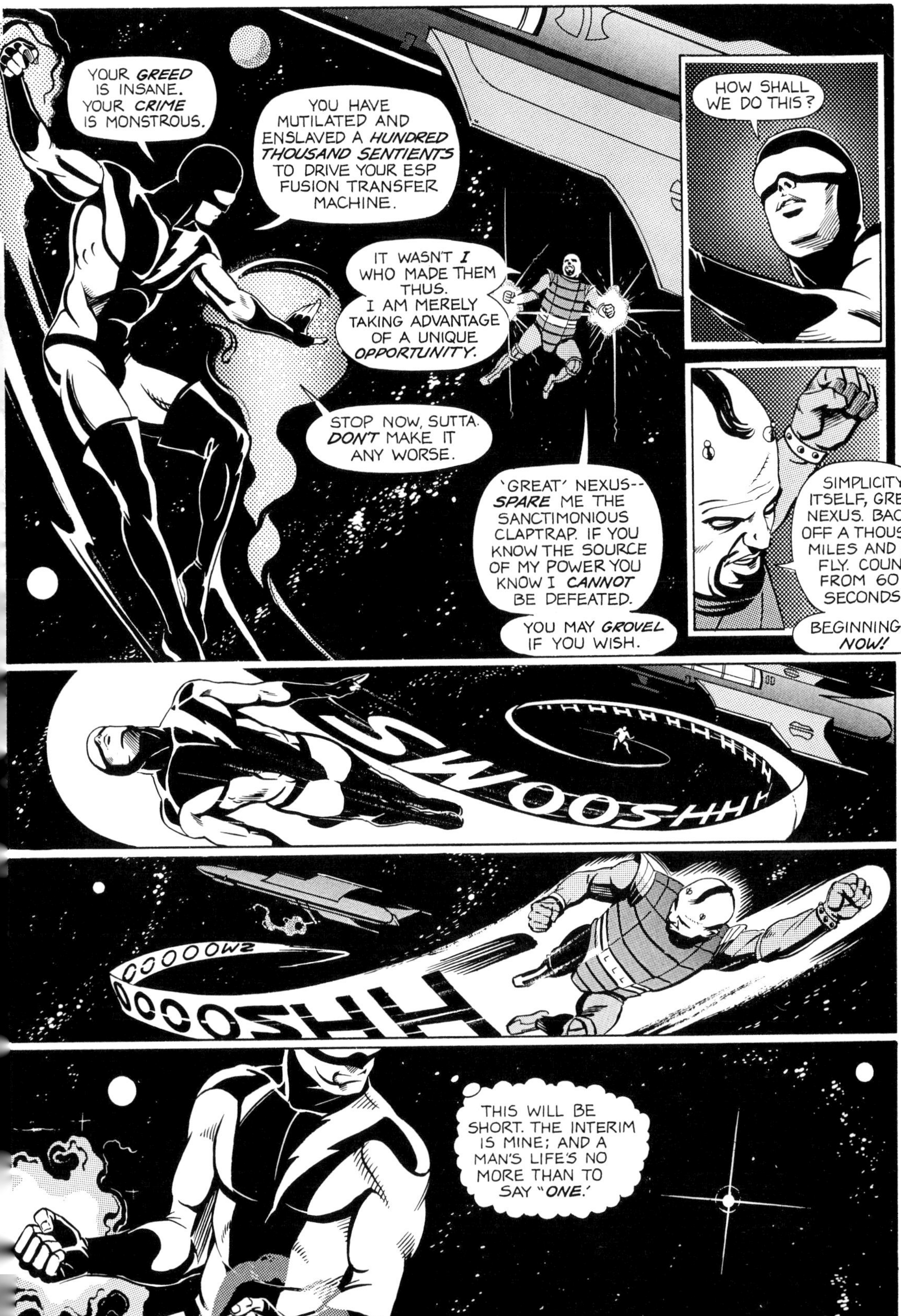

YOUR GREED IS INSANE. YOUR CRIME IS MONSTROUS.
YOU HAVE MUTILATED AND ENSLAVED A HUNDRED THOUSAND SENTIENTS TO DRIVE YOUR ESP FUSION TRANSFER MACHINE.
IT WASN'T I WHO MADE THEM THUS. I AM MERELY TAKING ADVANTAGE OF A UNIQUE OPPORTUNITY.
STOP NOW, SUTTA. DON'T MAKE IT ANY WORSE.
'GREAT' NEXUS-- SPARE ME THE SANCTIMONIOUS CLAPTRAP. IF YOU KNOW THE SOURCE OF MY POWER YOU KNOW I CANNOT BE DEFEATED.
YOU MAY GROVEL IF YOU WISH.
HOW SHALL WE DO THIS?
SIMPLICITY ITSELF, GREAT NEXUS. BACK OFF A THOUSAND MILES AND LET FLY. COUNT FROM 60 SECONDS--
BEGINNING... NOW!
SWOOSHHHHH
THIS WILL BE SHORT. THE INTERIM IS MINE; AND A MAN'S LIFE'S NO MORE THAN TO SAY "ONE.'

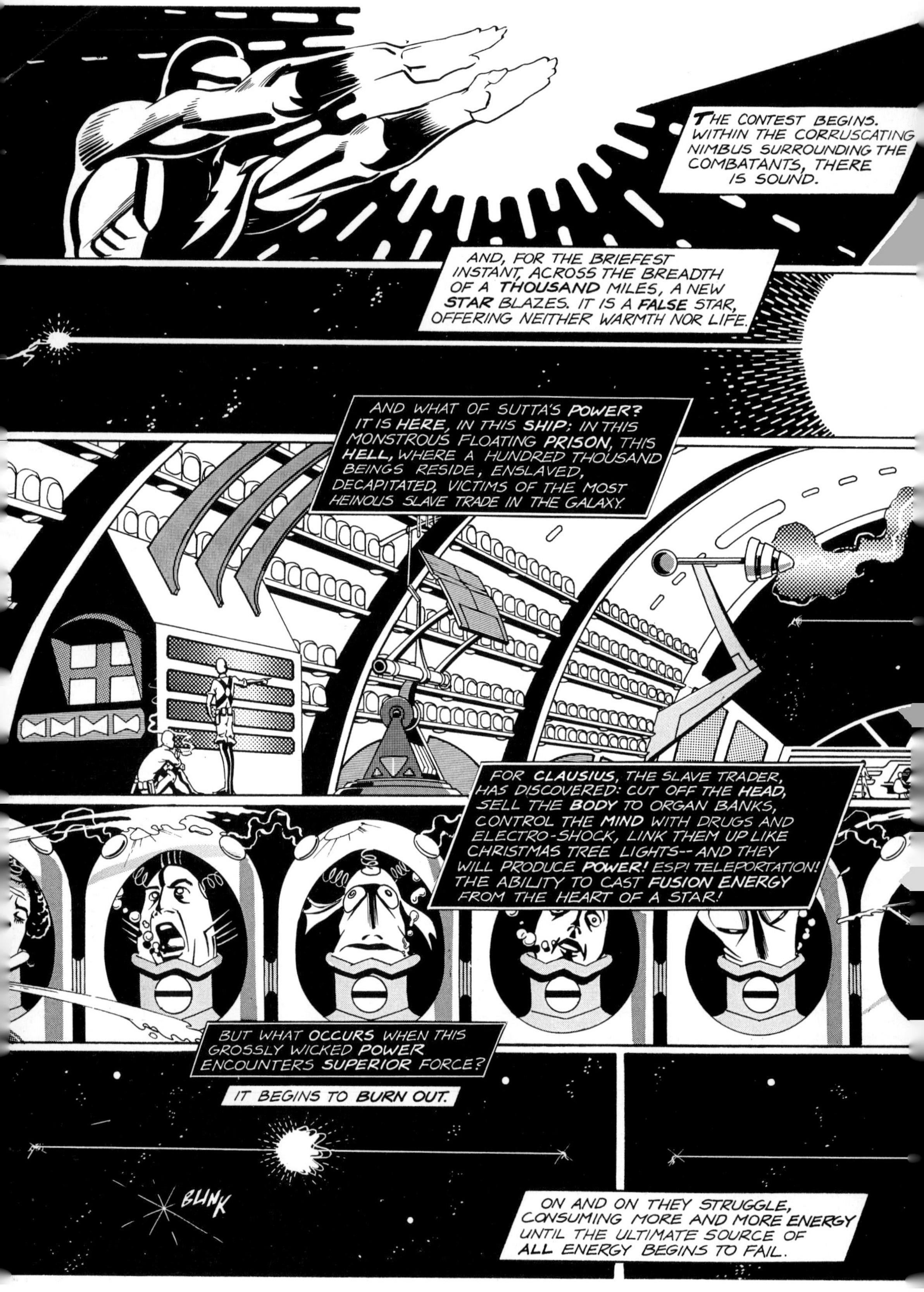

THE CONTEST BEGINS. WITHIN THE CORRUSCATING NIMBUS SURROUNDING THE COMBATANTS, THERE IS SOUND.
AND, FOR THE BRIEFEST INSTANT, ACROSS THE BREADTH OF A THOUSAND MILES, A NEW STAR BLAZES. IT IS A FALSE STAR, OFFERING NEITHER WARMTH NOR LIFE.
AND WHAT OF SUTTA'S POWER? IT IS HERE, IN THIS SHIP: IN THIS MONSTROUS FLOATING PRISON, THIS HELL, WHERE A HUNDRED THOUSAND BEINGS RESIDE, ENSLAVED, DECAPITATED, VICTIMS OF THE MOST HEINOUS SLAVE TRADE IN THE GALAXY.
FOR CLAUSIUS, THE SLAVE TRADER, HAS DISCOVERED: CUT OFF THE HEAD, SELL THE BODY TO ORGAN BANKS, CONTROL THE MIND WITH DRUGS AND ELECTRO-SHOCK, LINK THEM UP LIKE CHRISTMAS TREE LIGHTS-- AND THEY WILL PRODUCE POWER! ESP! TELEPORTATION! THE ABILITY TO CAST FUSION ENERGY FROM THE HEART OF A STAR!
BUT WHAT OCCURS WHEN THIS GROSSLY WICKED POWER ENCOUNTERS SUPERIOR FORCE?
IT BEGINS TO BURN OUT.
BLINK
ON AND ON THEY STRUGGLE, CONSUMING MORE AND MORE ENERGY UNTIL THE ULTIMATE SOURCE OF ALL ENERGY BEGINS TO FAIL.

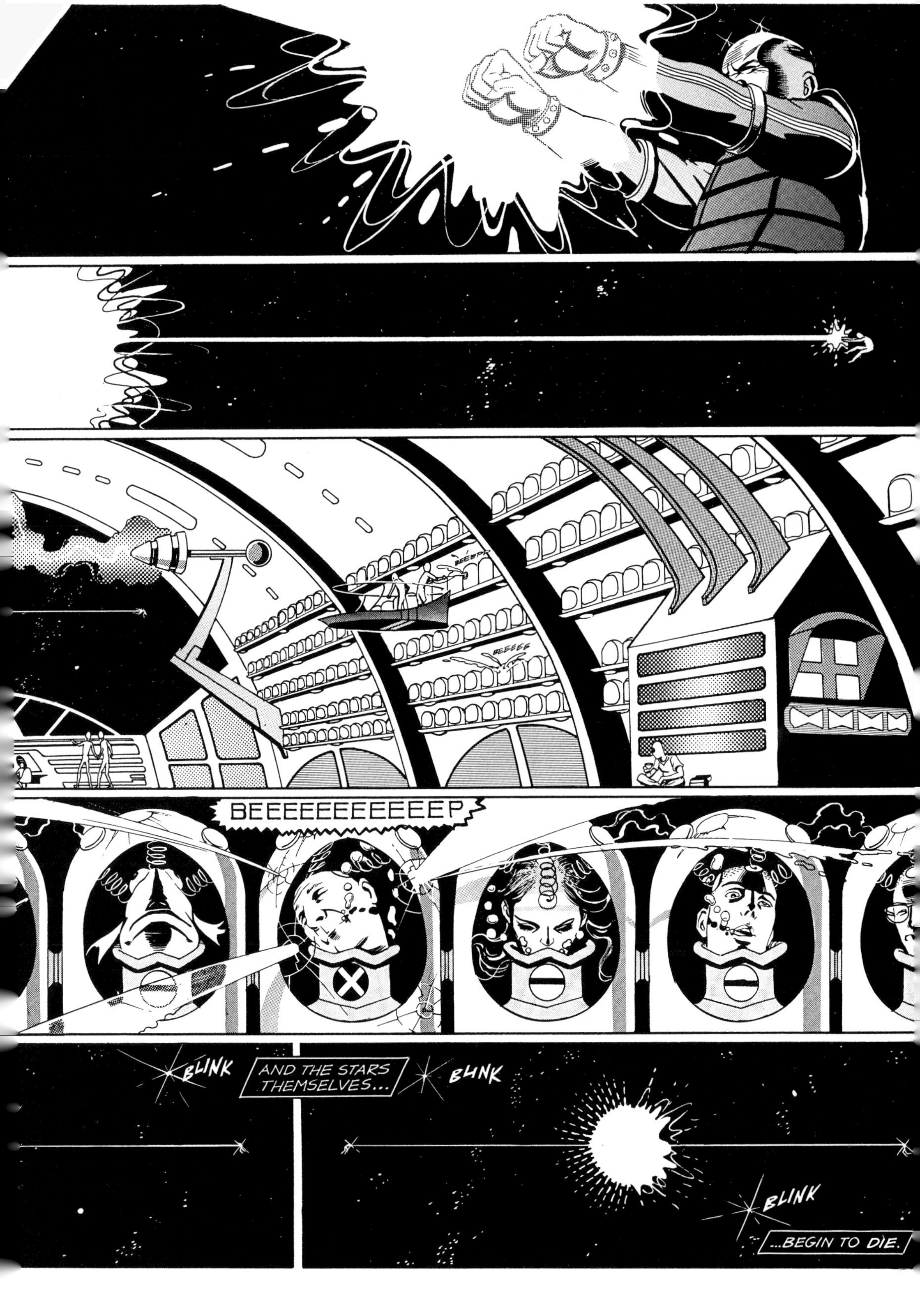
BEEEEEEEEEEEP
BLINK
AND THE STARS THEMSELVES...
BLINK
BLINK
...BEGIN TO DIE.

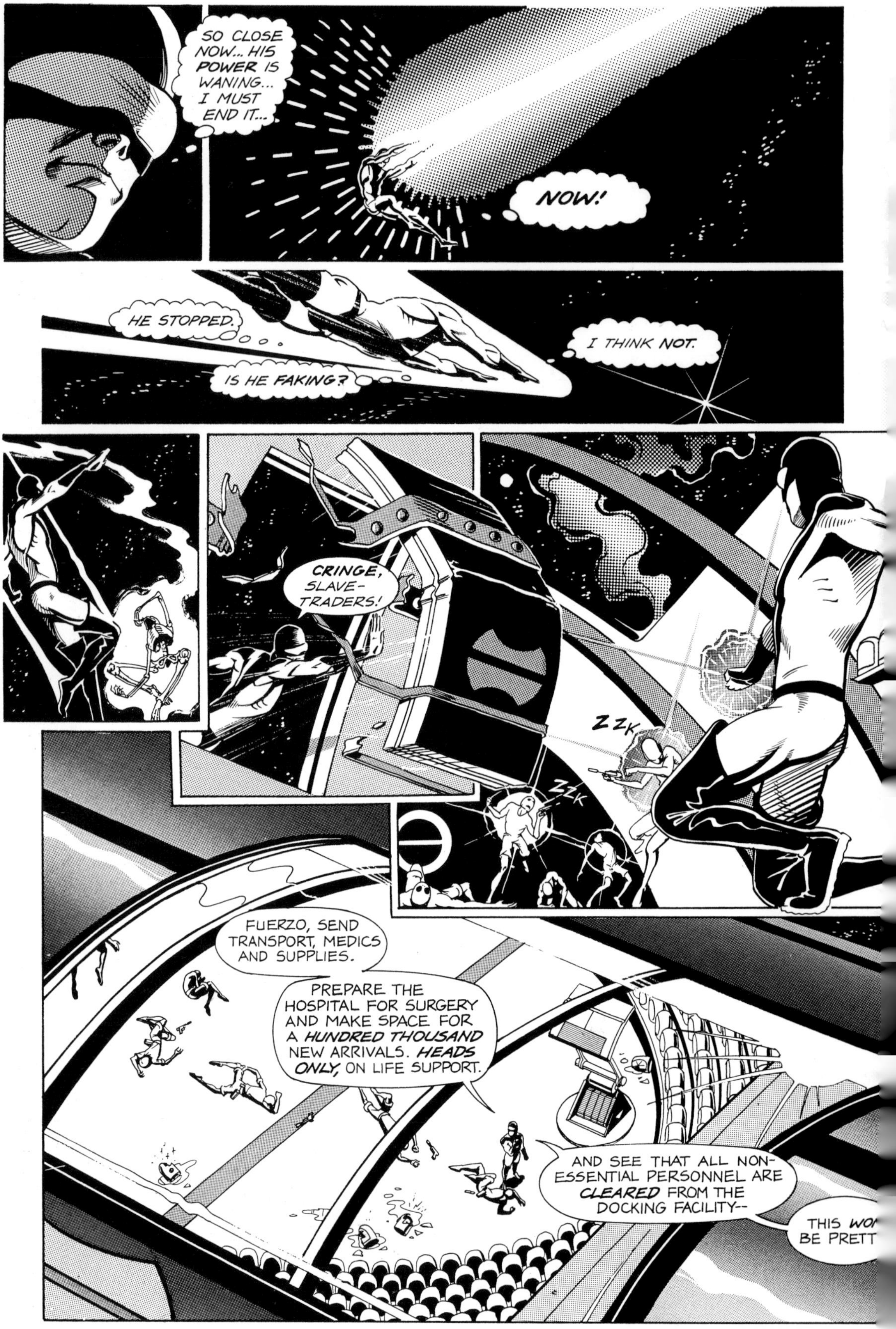
SO CLOSE NOW... HIS POWER IS WANING... I MUST END IT...
NOW!
HE STOPPED.
IS HE FAKING?
I THINK NOT.
CRINGE, SLAVE-TRADERS!
ZZK
ZZK
FUERZO, SEND TRANSPORT, MEDICS AND SUPPLIES.
PREPARE THE HOSPITAL FOR SURGERY AND MAKE SPACE FOR A HUNDRED THOUSAND NEW ARRIVALS. HEADS ONLY, ON LIFE SUPPORT.
AND SEE THAT ALL NON-ESSENTIAL PERSONNEL ARE CLEARED FROM THE DOCKING FACILITY--

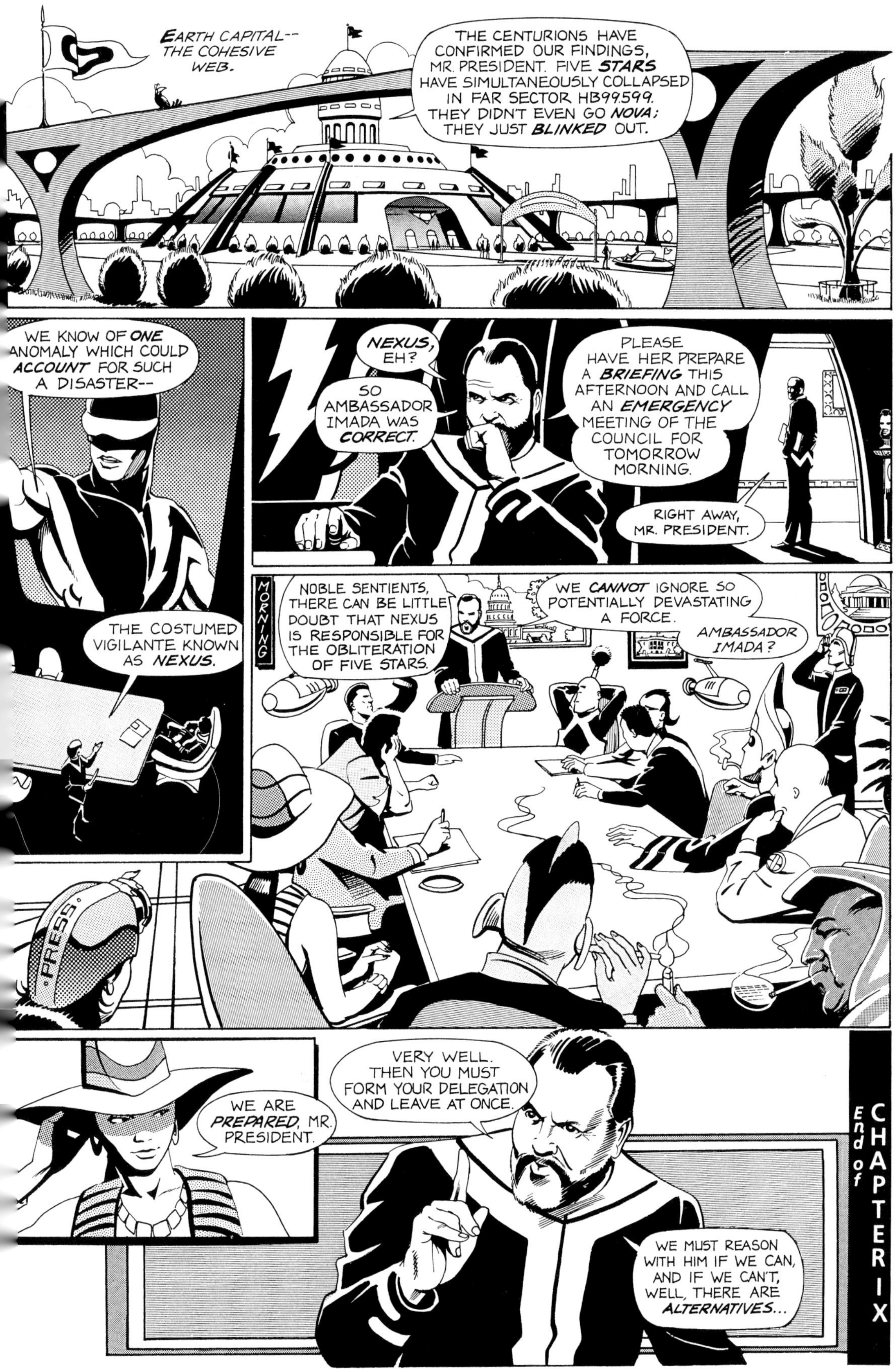
EARTH CAPITAL-- THE COHESIVE WEB.
THE CENTURIONS HAVE CONFIRMED OUR FINDINGS, MR. PRESIDENT. FIVE STARS HAVE SIMULTANEOUSLY COLLAPSED IN FAR SECTOR HB99.599. THEY DIDN'T EVEN GO NOVA; THEY JUST BLINKED OUT.
WE KNOW OF ONE ANOMALY WHICH COULD ACCOUNT FOR SUCH A DISASTER--
THE COSTUMED VIGILANTE KNOWN AS NEXUS.
NEXUS, EH?
SO AMBASSADOR IMADA WAS CORRECT.
PLEASE HAVE HER PREPARE A BRIEFING THIS AFTERNOON AND CALL AN EMERGENCY MEETING OF THE COUNCIL FOR TOMORROW MORNING.
RIGHT AWAY, MR. PRESIDENT.
MORNING
NOBLE SENTIENTS, THERE CAN BE LITTLE DOUBT THAT NEXUS IS RESPONSIBLE FOR THE OBLITERATION OF FIVE STARS.
WE CANNOT IGNORE SO POTENTIALLY DEVASTATING A FORCE.
AMBASSADOR IMADA?
PRESS
WE ARE PREPARED, MR. PRESIDENT.
VERY WELL. THEN YOU MUST FORM YOUR DELEGATION AND LEAVE AT ONCE.
WE MUST REASON WITH HIM IF WE CAN, AND IF WE CAN'T, WELL, THERE ARE ALTERNATIVES...
End of CHAPTER IX

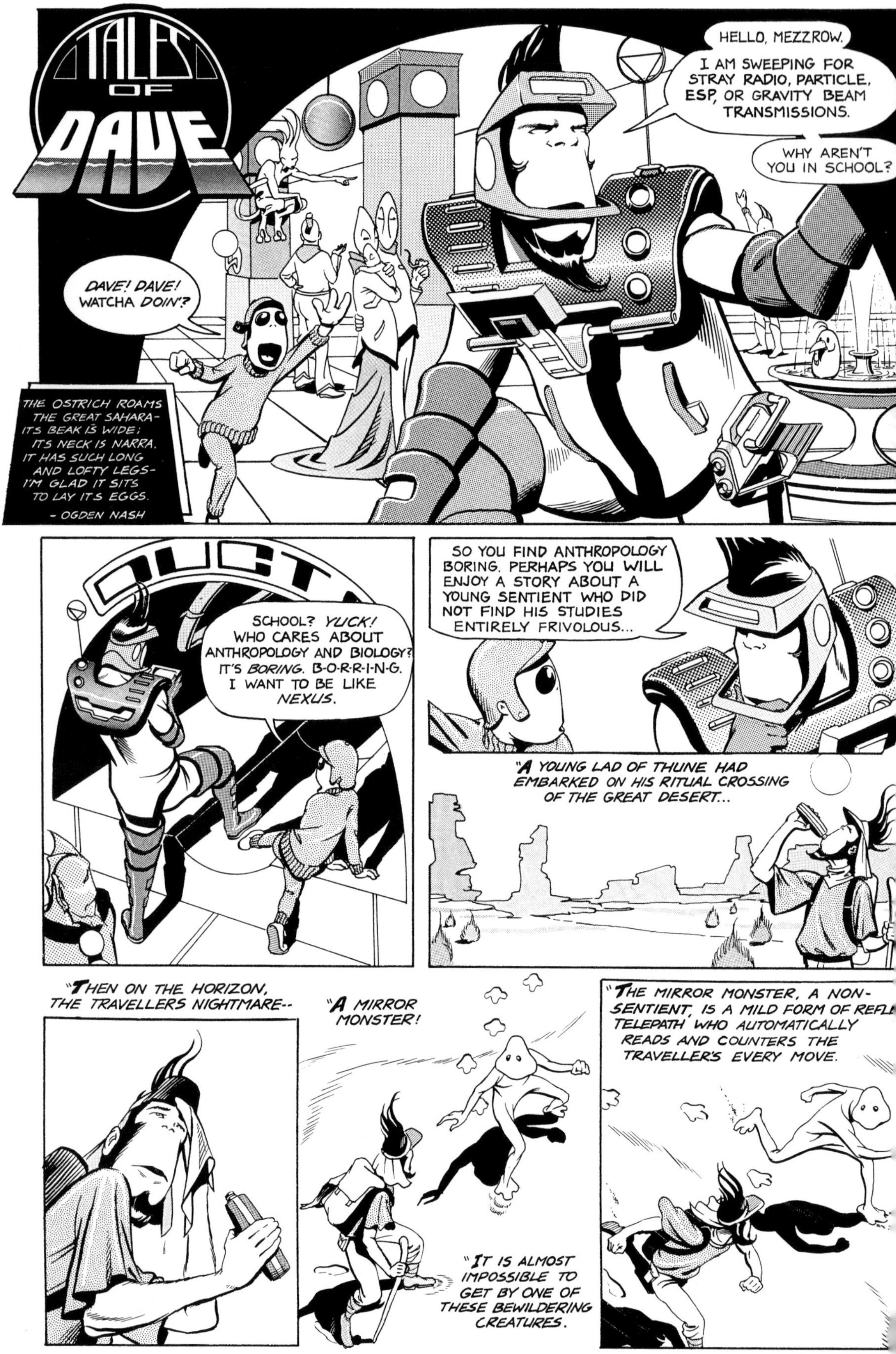
TALES OF DAVE
HELLO, MEZZROW.
I AM SWEEPING FOR STRAY RADIO, PARTICLE, ESP, OR GRAVITY BEAM TRANSMISSIONS.
WHY AREN'T YOU IN SCHOOL?
DAVE! DAVE! WATCHA DOIN'?
THE OSTRICH ROAMS THE GREAT SAHARA- ITS BEAK IS WIDE; ITS NECK IS NARRA. IT HAS SUCH LONG AND LOFTY LEGS- I'M GLAD IT SITS TO LAY ITS EGGS. - OGDEN NASH
SCHOOL? YUCK! WHO CARES ABOUT ANTHROPOLOGY AND BIOLOGY? IT'S BORING. B-O-R-R-I-N-G. I WANT TO BE LIKE NEXUS.
SO YOU FIND ANTHROPOLOGY BORING. PERHAPS YOU WILL ENJOY A STORY ABOUT A YOUNG SENTIENT WHO DID NOT FIND HIS STUDIES ENTIRELY FRIVOLOUS...
"A YOUNG LAD OF THUNE HAD EMBARKED ON HIS RITUAL CROSSING OF THE GREAT DESERT...
"THEN ON THE HORIZON, THE TRAVELLERS NIGHTMARE--
"A MIRROR MONSTER!
"IT IS ALMOST IMPOSSIBLE TO GET BY ONE OF THESE BEWILDERING CREATURES.
"THE MIRROR MONSTER, A NON-SENTIENT, IS A MILD FORM OF REFL TELEPATH WHO AUTOMATICALLY READS AND COUNTERS THE TRAVELLER'S EVERY MOVE.

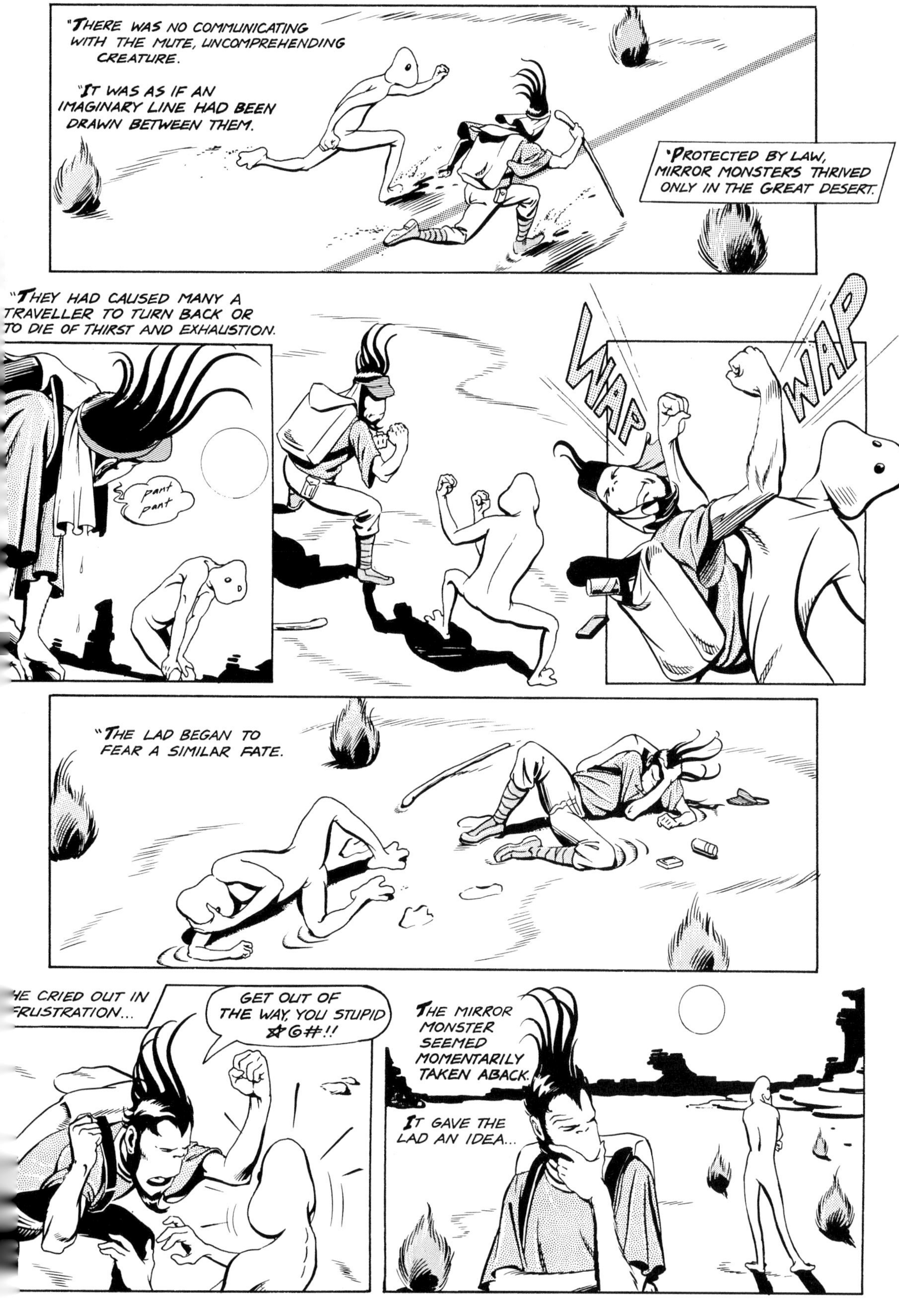
"THERE WAS NO COMMUNICATING WITH THE MUTE, UNCOMPREHENDING CREATURE.
"IT WAS AS IF AN IMAGINARY LINE HAD BEEN DRAWN BETWEEN THEM.
"PROTECTED BY LAW, MIRROR MONSTERS THRIVED ONLY IN THE GREAT DESERT.
"THEY HAD CAUSED MANY A TRAVELLER TO TURN BACK OR TO DIE OF THIRST AND EXHAUSTION.
pant pant
WAP
WAP
"THE LAD BEGAN TO FEAR A SIMILAR FATE.
HE CRIED OUT IN FRUSTRATION...
GET OUT OF THE WAY, YOU STUPID ☆@#!!
THE MIRROR MONSTER SEEMED MOMENTARILY TAKEN ABACK.
IT GAVE THE LAD AN IDEA...

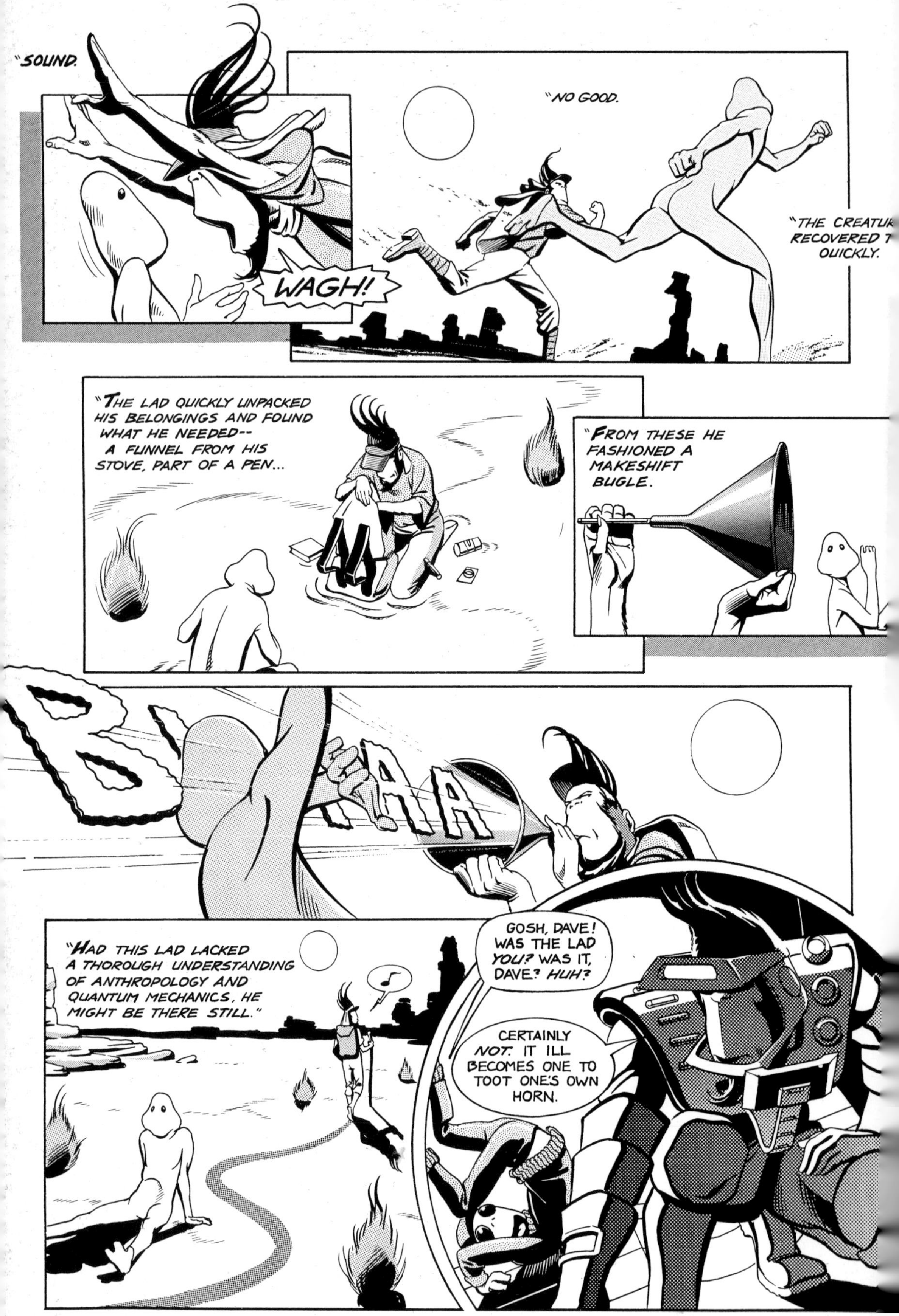
"SOUND.
WAGH!
"NO GOOD.
"THE CREATURE RECOVERED T QUICKLY.
"THE LAD QUICKLY UNPACKED HIS BELONGINGS AND FOUND WHAT HE NEEDED-- A FUNNEL FROM HIS STOVE, PART OF A PEN...
"FROM THESE HE FASHIONED A MAKESHIFT BUGLE.
BAA
"HAD THIS LAD LACKED A THOROUGH UNDERSTANDING OF ANTHROPOLOGY AND QUANTUM MECHANICS, HE MIGHT BE THERE STILL."
GOSH, DAVE! WAS THE LAD YOU? WAS IT, DAVE? HUH?
CERTAINLY NOT. IT ILL BECOMES ONE TO TOOT ONE'S OWN HORN.

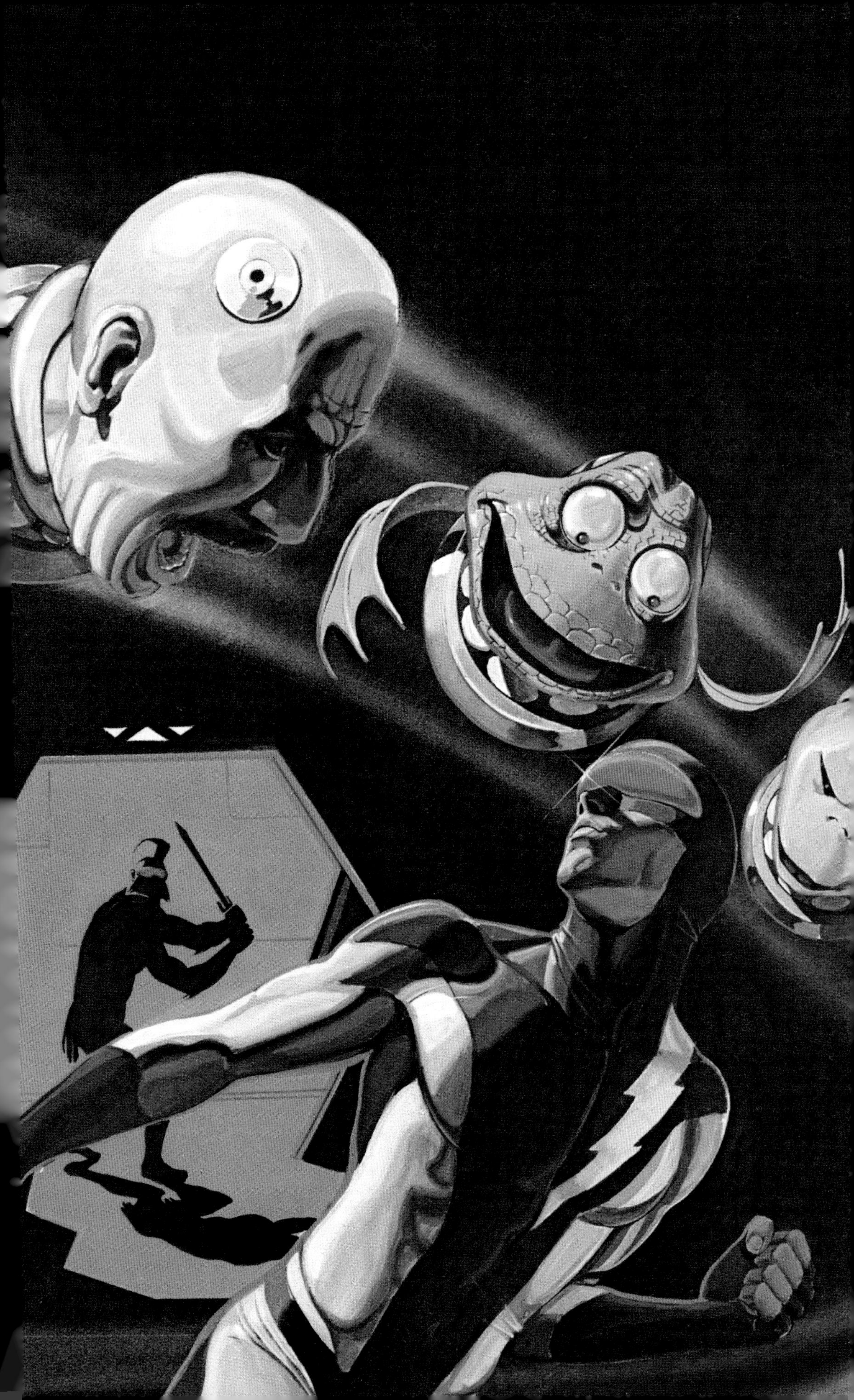

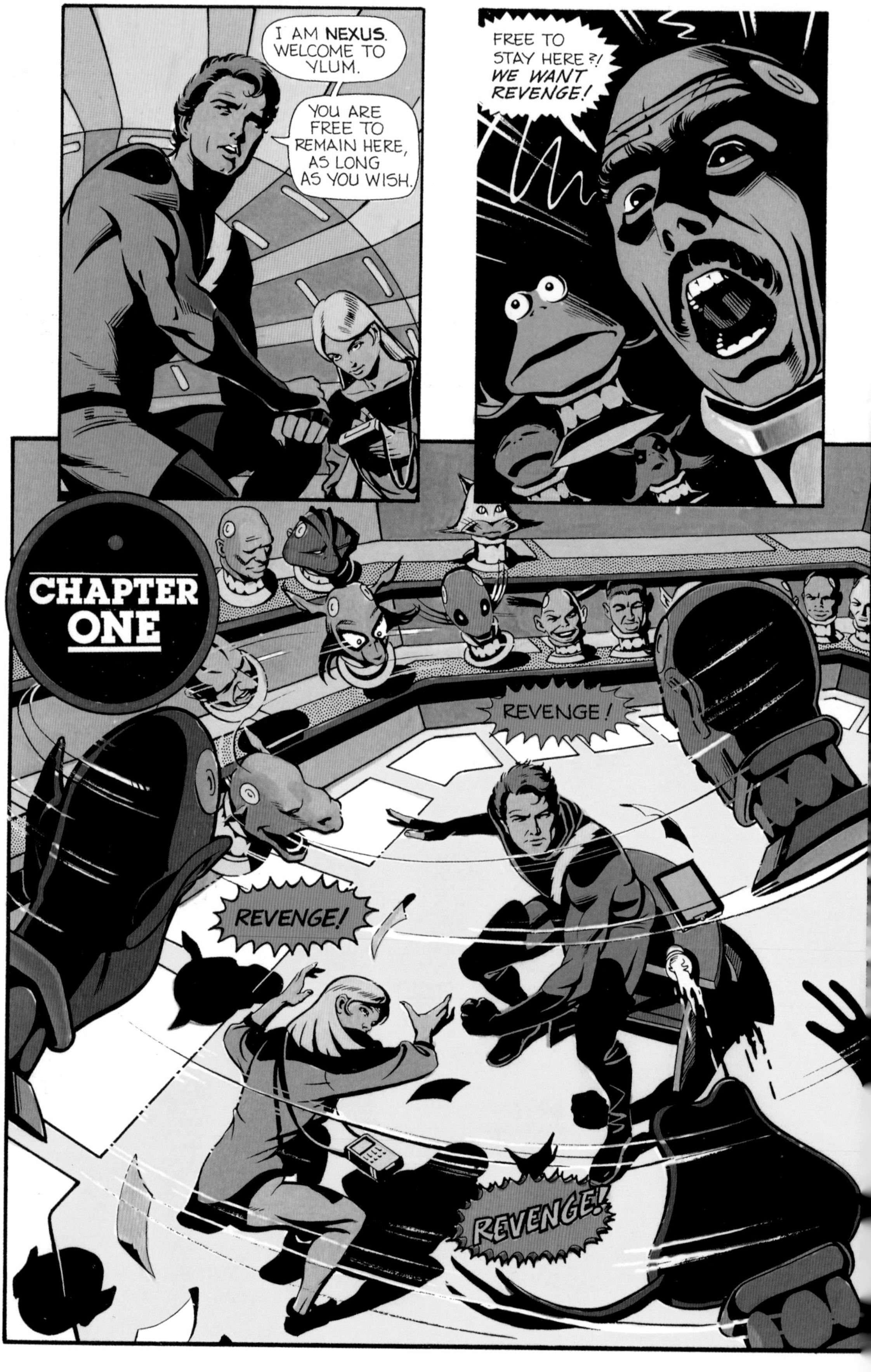
I AM NEXUS. WELCOME TO YLUM.
YOU ARE FREE TO REMAIN HERE, AS LONG AS YOU WISH.
FREE TO STAY HERE?! WE WANT REVENGE!
CHAPTER ONE
REVENGE!
REVENGE!
REVENGE!
2

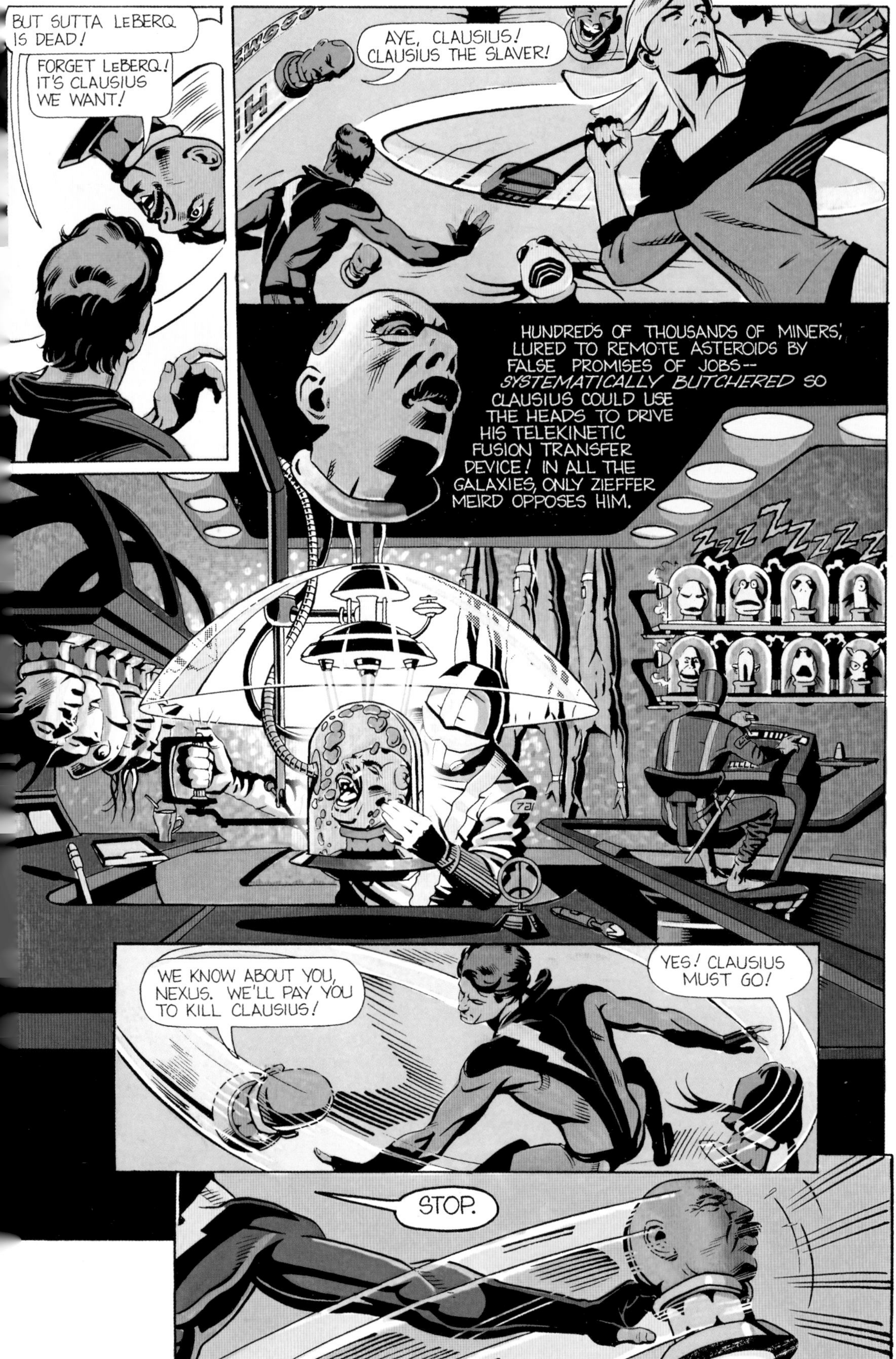
BUT SUTTA LeBERQ IS DEAD!
FORGET LeBERQ! IT'S CLAUSIUS WE WANT!
AYE, CLAUSIUS! CLAUSIUS THE SLAVER!
HUNDREDS OF THOUSANDS OF MINERS, LURED TO REMOTE ASTEROIDS BY FALSE PROMISES OF JOBS-- SYSTEMATICALLY BUTCHERED SO CLAUSIUS COULD USE THE HEADS TO DRIVE HIS TELEKINETIC FUSION TRANSFER DEVICE! IN ALL THE GALAXIES, ONLY ZIEFFER MEIRD OPPOSES HIM.
ZZZZZZZZ
WE KNOW ABOUT YOU, NEXUS. WE'LL PAY YOU TO KILL CLAUSIUS!
YES! CLAUSIUS MUST GO!
STOP.

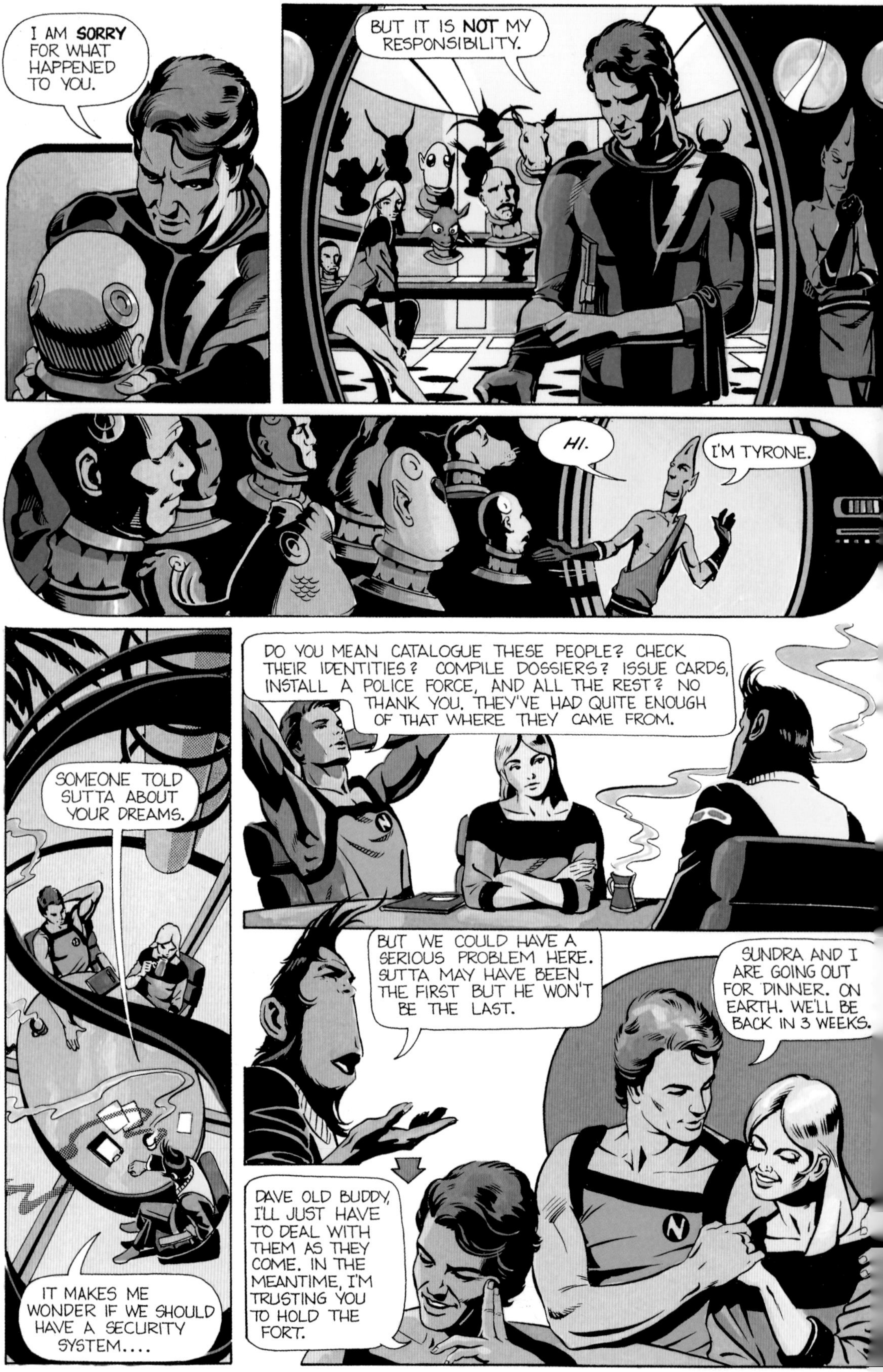

I AM SORRY FOR WHAT HAPPENED TO YOU.
BUT IT IS NOT MY RESPONSIBILITY.
HI.
I'M TYRONE.
SOMEONE TOLD SUTTA ABOUT YOUR DREAMS.
IT MAKES ME WONDER IF WE SHOULD HAVE A SECURITY SYSTEM....
DO YOU MEAN CATALOGUE THESE PEOPLE? CHECK THEIR IDENTITIES? COMPILE DOSSIERS? ISSUE CARDS, INSTALL A POLICE FORCE, AND ALL THE REST? NO THANK YOU. THEY'VE HAD QUITE ENOUGH OF THAT WHERE THEY CAME FROM.
BUT WE COULD HAVE A SERIOUS PROBLEM HERE. SUTTA MAY HAVE BEEN THE FIRST BUT HE WON'T BE THE LAST.
DAVE OLD BUDDY, I'LL JUST HAVE TO DEAL WITH THEM AS THEY COME. IN THE MEANTIME, I'M TRUSTING YOU TO HOLD THE FORT.
SUNDRA AND I ARE GOING OUT FOR DINNER. ON EARTH. WE'LL BE BACK IN 3 WEEKS.

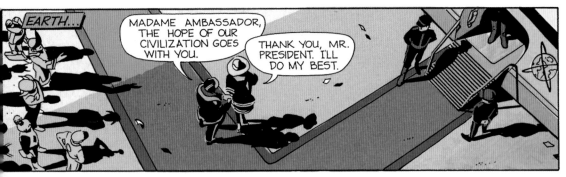

EARTH...
MADAME AMBASSADOR, THE HOPE OF OUR CIVILIZATION GOES WITH YOU.
THANK YOU, MR. PRESIDENT. I'LL DO MY BEST.
AND SO, URSULA X. X. IMADA EMBARKS ON AN HISTORIC MISSION, TO PERSUADE THE VIGILANTE KNOWN AS NEXUS TO EITHER JOIN THE COHESIVE WEB, TO SHARE THE SECRET OF HIS AMAZING POWER, OR, AT THE VERY LEAST, TO CEASE AND DESIST THE DESTRUCTION OF THE STARS....
SCIENTISTS FROM 7 WORLDS HAVE INDEPENDENTLY CONFIRMED WHAT WE HAVE LONG FEARED:
"THAT THE SOURCE OF NEXUS' POWER IS LIVING STARS, AND WHEN HE USES THAT POWER, STARS DIE....
"IF ANYONE CAN PERSUADE NEXUS TO FOLLOW A COURSE COMPATIBLE WITH WEB POLICY, IT IS URSULA X. X. IMADA, FORMER ATTORNEY GENERAL OF THE INNER PLANETS...."
HOLO-VIEW III
HOLO-VIEW III
THANK YOU, ERTEGUN. PLEASE SEE THAT I AM NOT DISTURBED.
NEXUS REMAINS AN ENIGMA. OUR AGENT GAVE US GOOD INFORMATION UNTIL A MONTH AGO - THEN SHE DRIED UP. PERHAPS SHE IS DEAD.
BUT NEXUS IS STILL A MAN... A THING OF FLESH AND BLOOD, OF HOPES AND HUNGERS.
WHICH IS WHY THEY HAVE SENT ME.

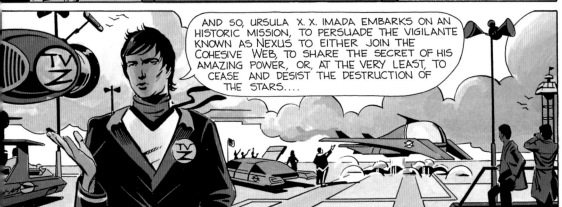

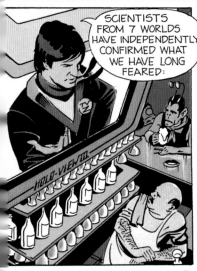

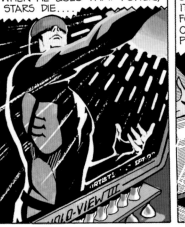

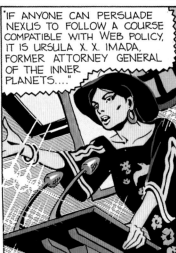

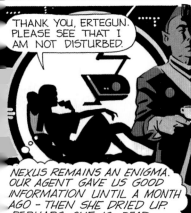

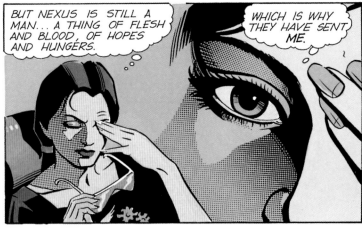

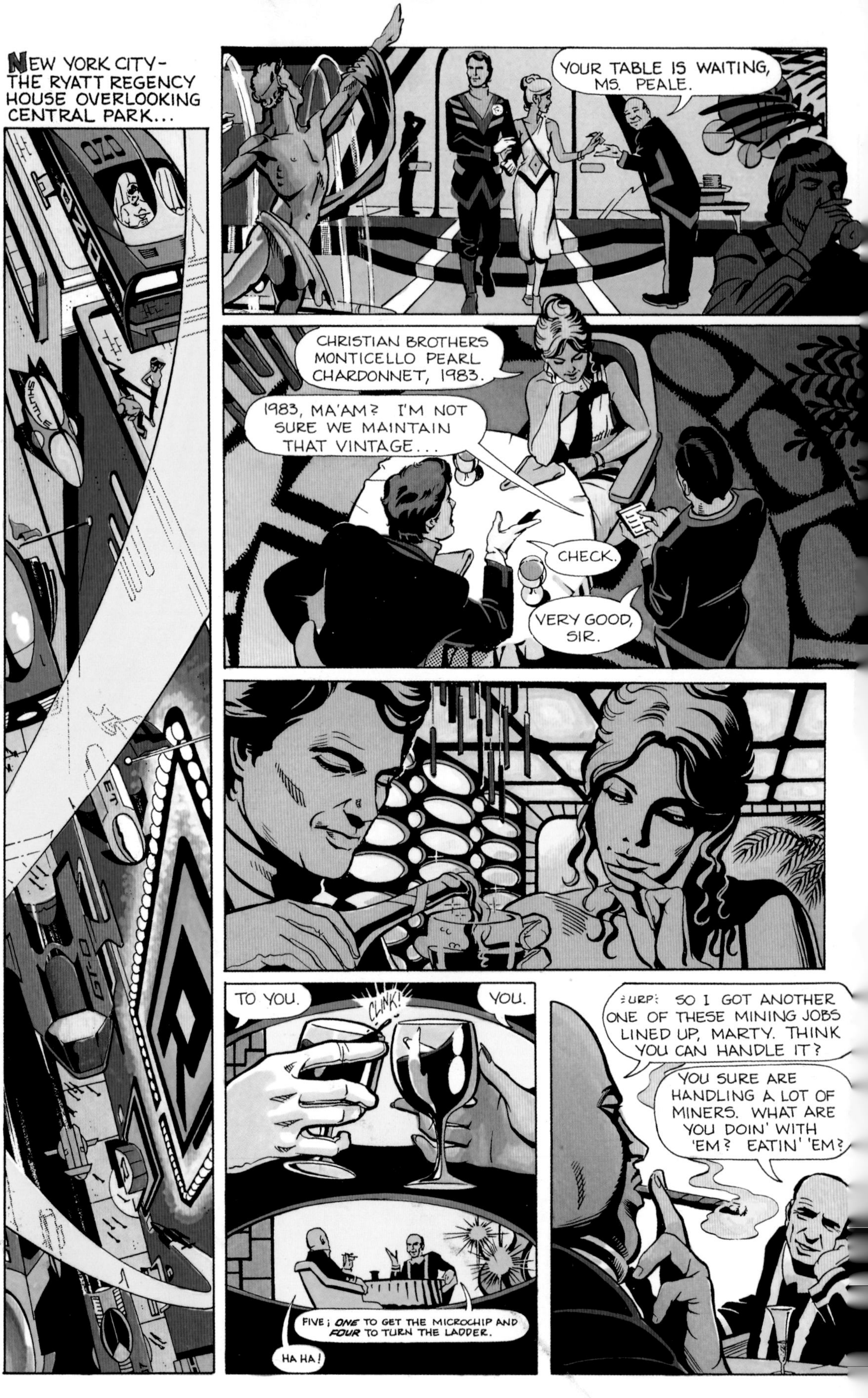
NEW YORK CITY-
THE RYATT REGENCY
HOUSE OVERLOOKING
CENTRAL PARK...
YOUR TABLE IS WAITING, MS. PEALE.
CHRISTIAN BROTHERS MONTICELLO PEARL CHARDONNET, 1983.
1983, MA'AM? I'M NOT SURE WE MAINTAIN THAT VINTAGE...
CHECK.
VERY GOOD, SIR.
TO YOU.
CLINK!
YOU.
FIVE; ONE TO GET THE MICROCHIP AND FOUR TO TURN THE LADDER.
HA HA!
URP SO I GOT ANOTHER ONE OF THESE MINING JOBS LINED UP, MARTY. THINK YOU CAN HANDLE IT?
YOU SURE ARE HANDLING A LOT OF MINERS. WHAT ARE YOU DOIN' WITH 'EM? EATIN' 'EM?

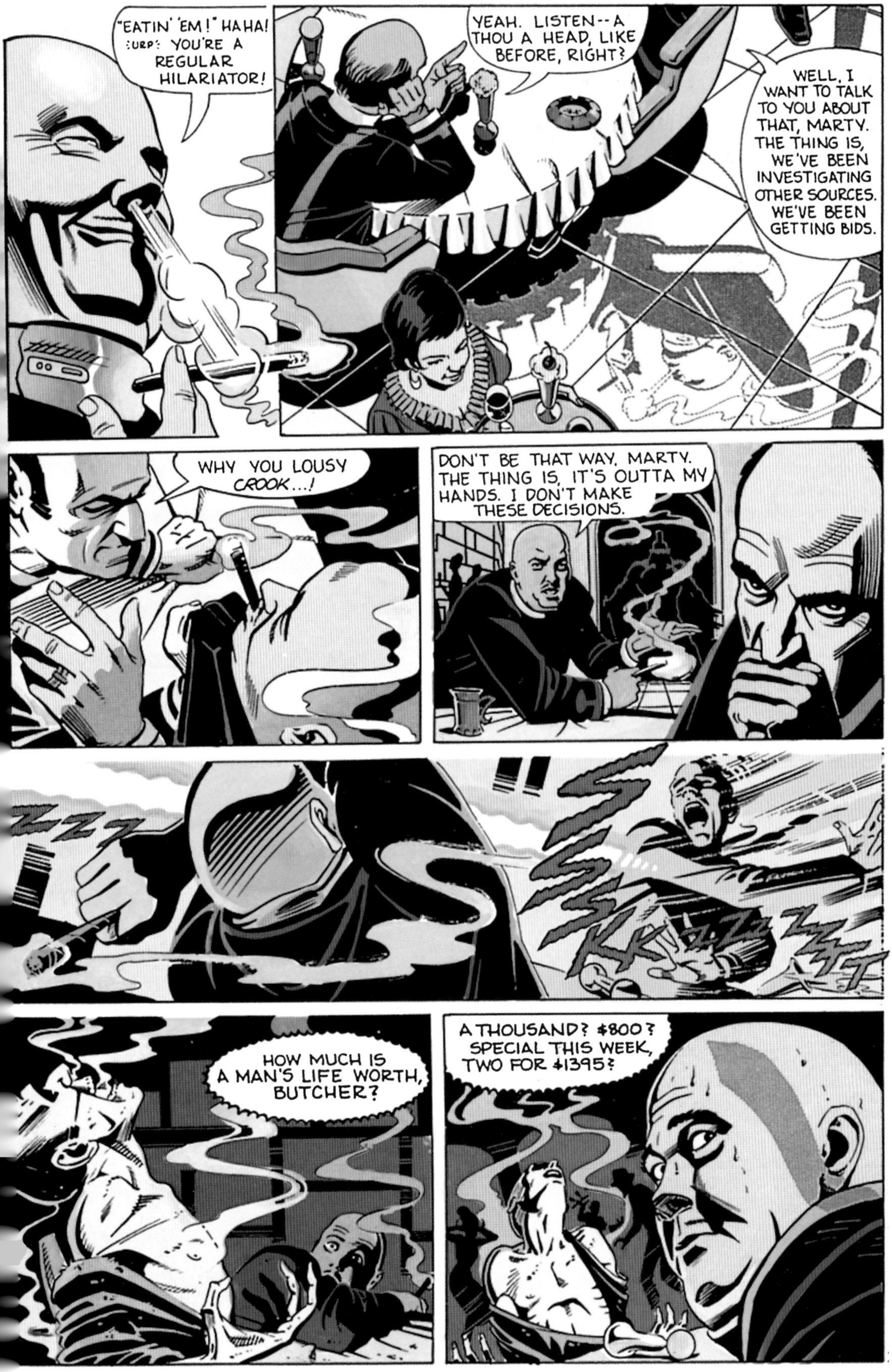
"EATIN' 'EM!" HAHA! :URP: YOU'RE A REGULAR HILARIATOR!
YEAH. LISTEN--A THOU A HEAD, LIKE BEFORE, RIGHT?
WELL, I WANT TO TALK TO YOU ABOUT THAT, MARTY. THE THING IS, WE'VE BEEN INVESTIGATING OTHER SOURCES. WE'VE BEEN GETTING BIDS.
WHY YOU LOUSY CROOK...!
DON'T BE THAT WAY, MARTY. THE THING IS, IT'S OUTTA MY HANDS. I DON'T MAKE THESE DECISIONS.
!!
ZZZ
SSSKK
HOW MUCH IS A MAN'S LIFE WORTH, BUTCHER?
A THOUSAND? $800? SPECIAL THIS WEEK, TWO FOR $1395?

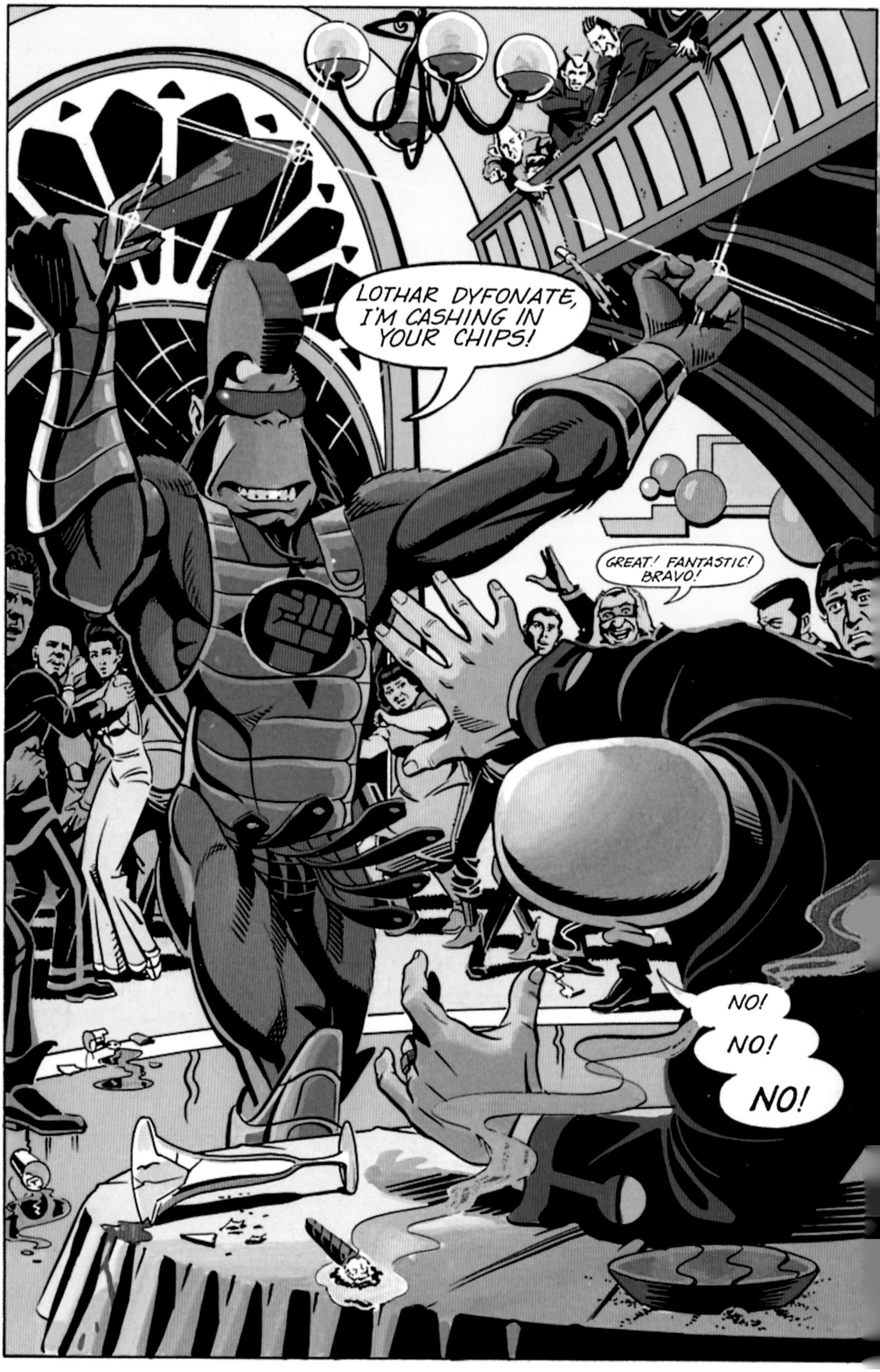
LOTHAR DYFONATE, I'M CASHING IN YOUR CHIPS!
GREAT! FANTASTIC! BRAVO!
NO!
NO!
NO!

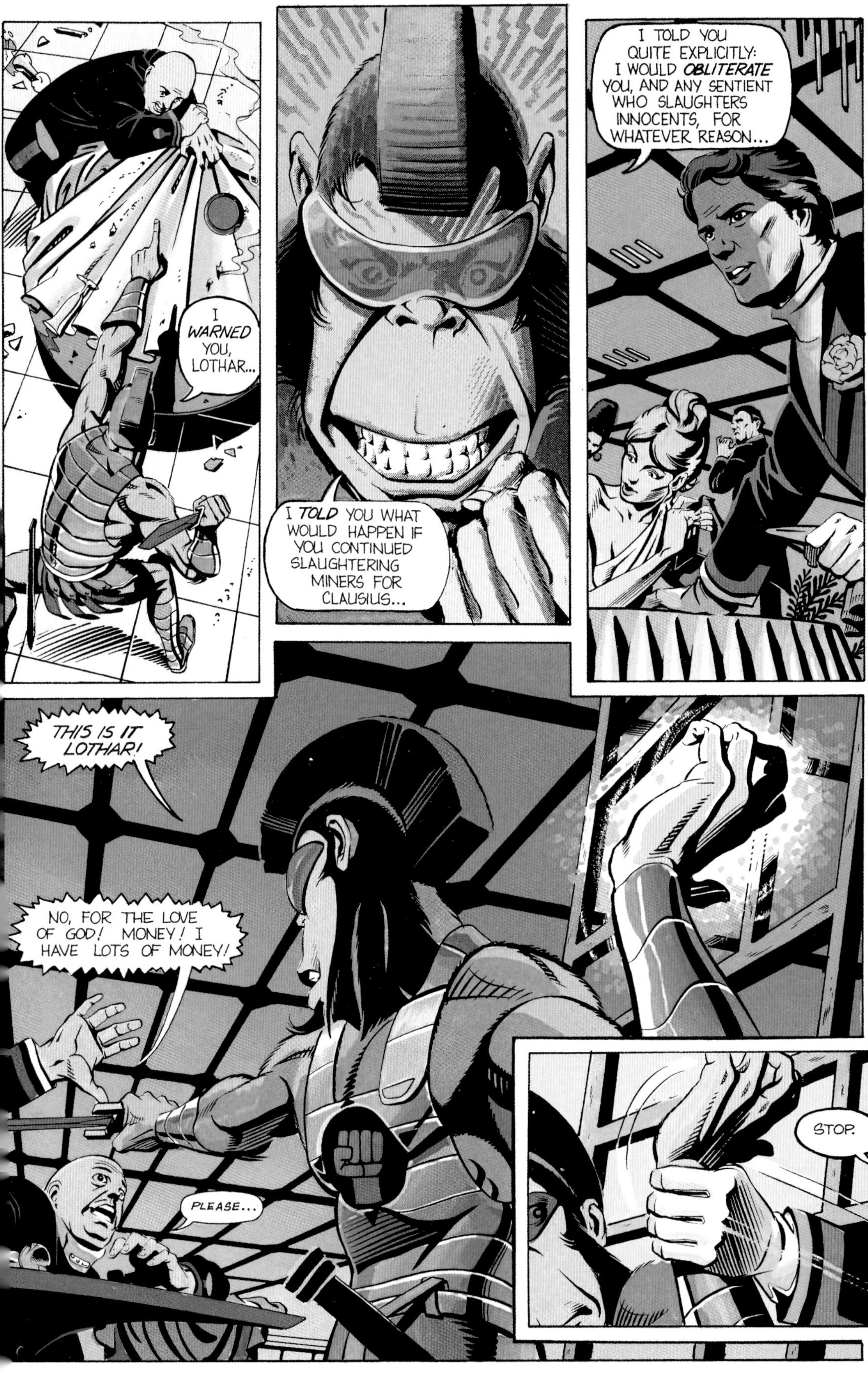
I WARNED YOU, LOTHAR...
I TOLD YOU WHAT WOULD HAPPEN IF YOU CONTINUED SLAUGHTERING MINERS FOR CLAUSIUS...
I TOLD YOU QUITE EXPLICITLY: I WOULD OBLITERATE YOU, AND ANY SENTIENT WHO SLAUGHTERS INNOCENTS, FOR WHATEVER REASON...
THIS IS IT LOTHAR!
NO, FOR THE LOVE OF GOD! MONEY! I HAVE LOTS OF MONEY!
PLEASE...
STOP.

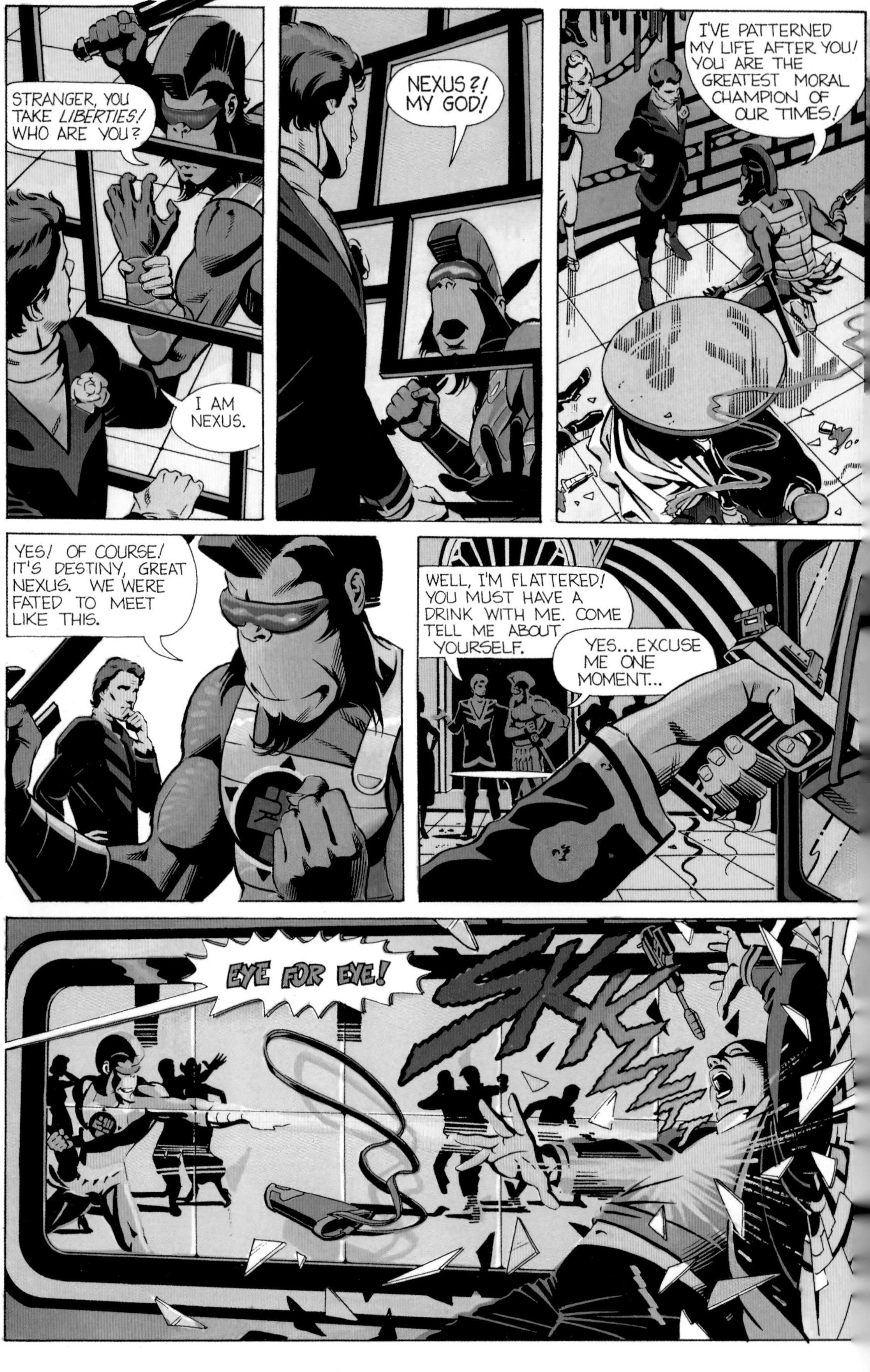

STRANGER, YOU TAKE *LIBERTIES!* WHO ARE YOU?
I AM NEXUS.
NEXUS?! MY GOD!
I'VE PATTERNED MY LIFE AFTER YOU! YOU ARE THE GREATEST MORAL CHAMPION OF OUR TIMES!
YES! OF COURSE! IT'S DESTINY, GREAT NEXUS. WE WERE FATED TO MEET LIKE THIS.
WELL, I'M FLATTERED! YOU MUST HAVE A DRINK WITH ME. COME TELL ME ABOUT YOURSELF.
YES...EXCUSE ME ONE MOMENT...
EYE FOR EYE!
SKZZ

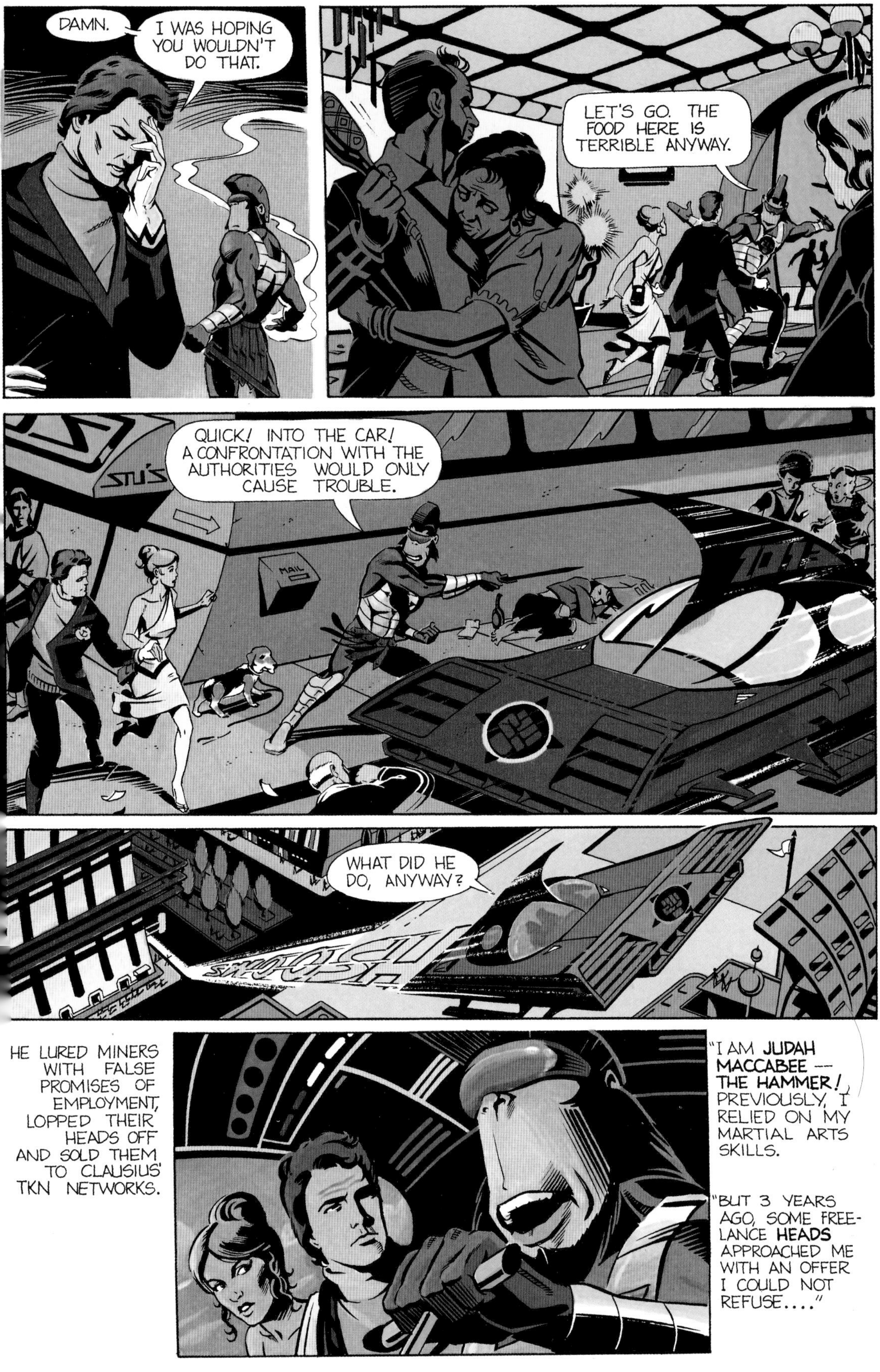
DAMN.
I WAS HOPING YOU WOULDN'T DO THAT.
LET'S GO. THE FOOD HERE IS TERRIBLE ANYWAY.
QUICK! INTO THE CAR! A CONFRONTATION WITH THE AUTHORITIES WOULD ONLY CAUSE TROUBLE.
STU'S
MAIL
WHAT DID HE DO, ANYWAY?
HE LURED MINERS WITH FALSE PROMISES OF EMPLOYMENT, LOPPED THEIR HEADS OFF AND SOLD THEM TO CLAUSIUS' TKN NETWORKS.
"I AM **JUDAH MACCABEE** -- **THE HAMMER!** PREVIOUSLY, I RELIED ON MY MARTIAL ARTS SKILLS.
"BUT 3 YEARS AGO, SOME FREE-LANCE **HEADS** APPROACHED ME WITH AN OFFER I COULD NOT REFUSE...."

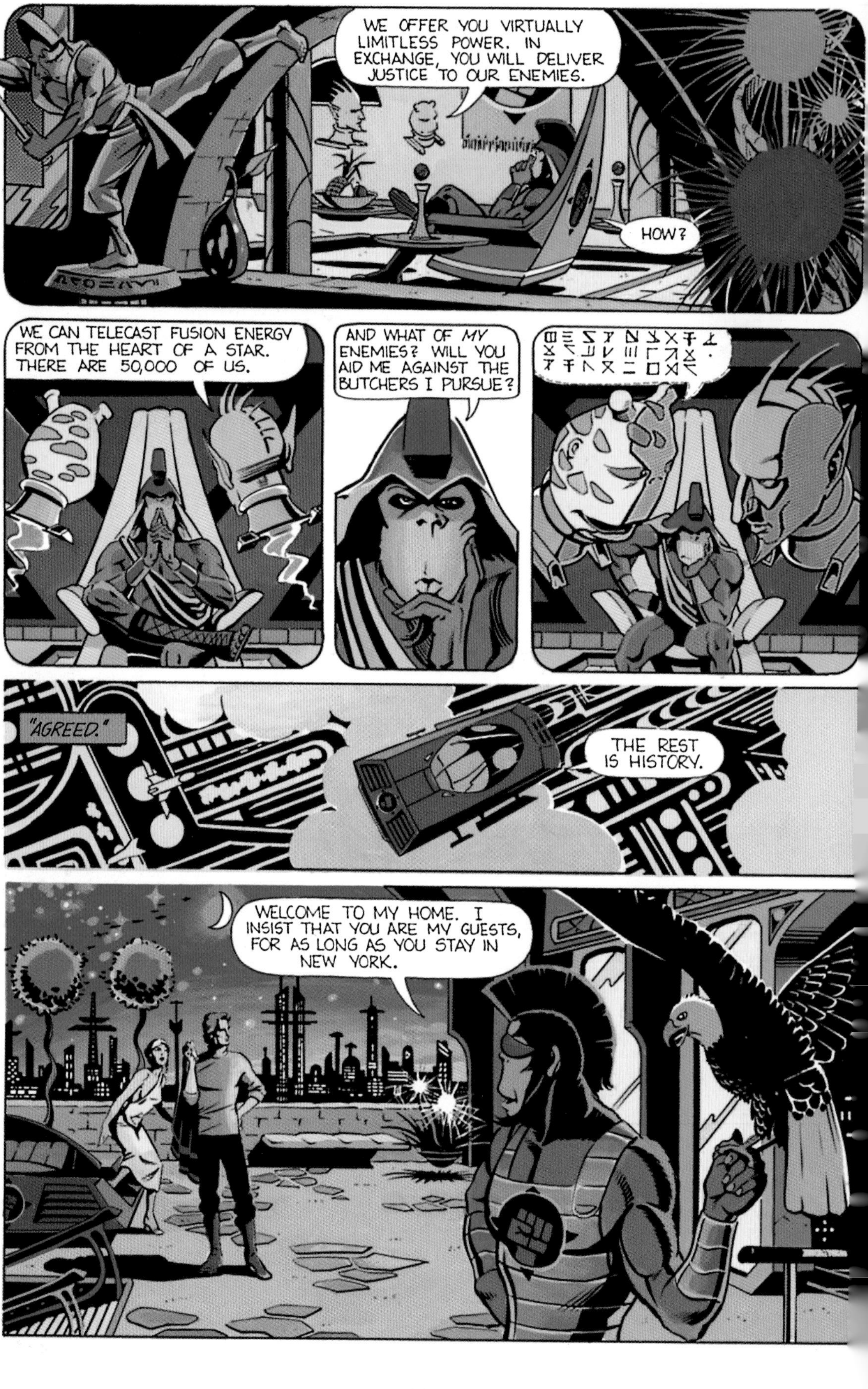
WE OFFER YOU VIRTUALLY LIMITLESS POWER. IN EXCHANGE, YOU WILL DELIVER JUSTICE TO OUR ENEMIES.
HOW?
WE CAN TELECAST FUSION ENERGY FROM THE HEART OF A STAR. THERE ARE 50,000 OF US.
AND WHAT OF *MY* ENEMIES? WILL YOU AID ME AGAINST THE BUTCHERS I PURSUE?
"AGREED."
THE REST IS HISTORY.
WELCOME TO MY HOME. I INSIST THAT YOU ARE MY GUESTS, FOR AS LONG AS YOU STAY IN NEW YORK.

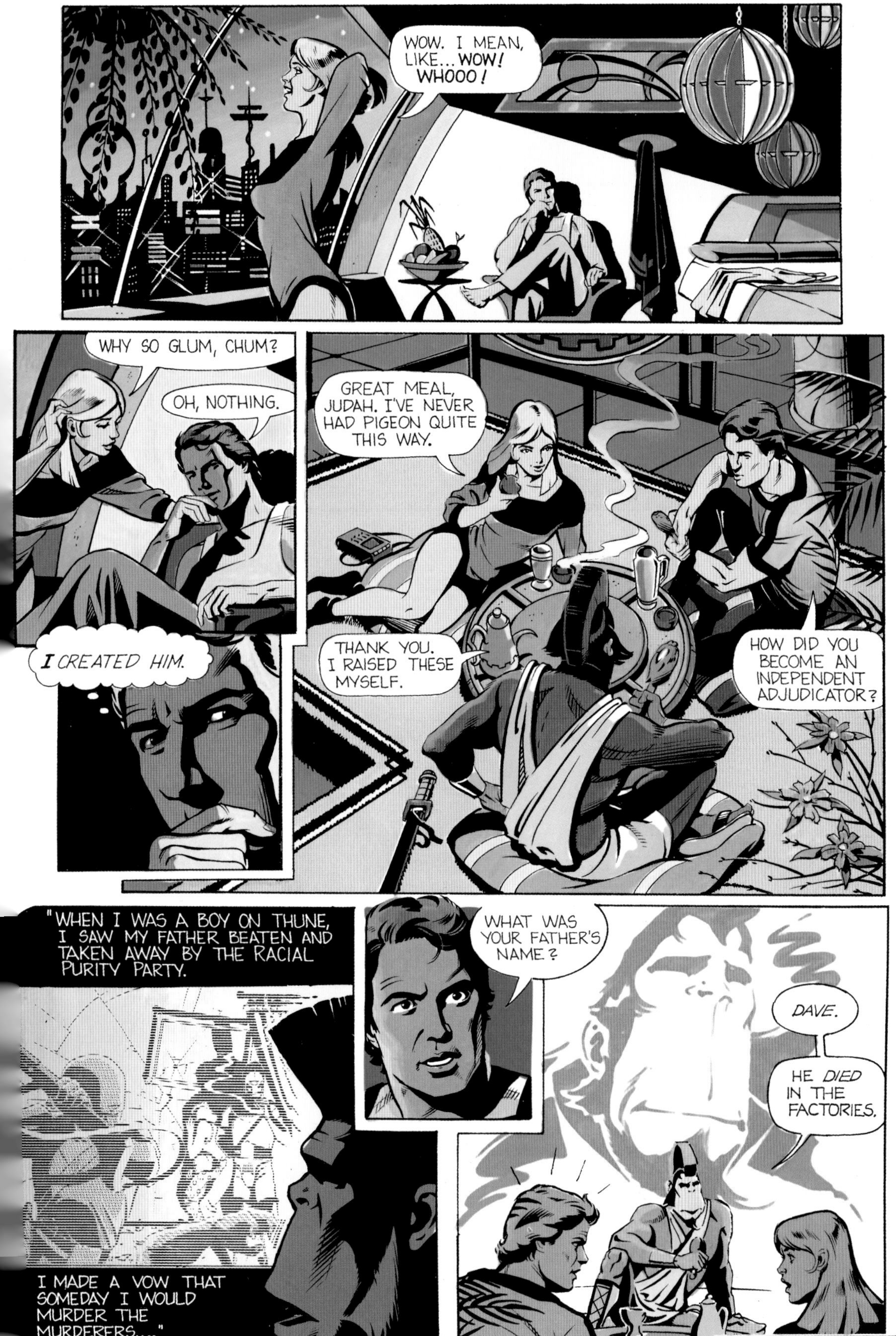
WOW. I MEAN, LIKE... WOW! WHOOO!
WHY SO GLUM, CHUM?
OH, NOTHING.
GREAT MEAL, JUDAH. I'VE NEVER HAD PIGEON QUITE THIS WAY.
I CREATED HIM.
THANK YOU. I RAISED THESE MYSELF.
HOW DID YOU BECOME AN INDEPENDENT ADJUDICATOR?
"WHEN I WAS A BOY ON THUNE, I SAW MY FATHER BEATEN AND TAKEN AWAY BY THE RACIAL PURITY PARTY.
I MADE A VOW THAT SOMEDAY I WOULD MURDER THE MURDERERS..."
WHAT WAS YOUR FATHER'S NAME?
DAVE.
HE DIED IN THE FACTORIES.
End of CHAPTER I

CHAPTER TWO

DAVE.
WHAT IT IS, TYRONE. WHAT IT IS.
WHAT CAN I DO FOR YOU, GENTLE SENTIENTS?
WE WANT ACCESS TO THE DRYDOCK!
WE WANT A WORKING STARSHIP AND WEAPONS!

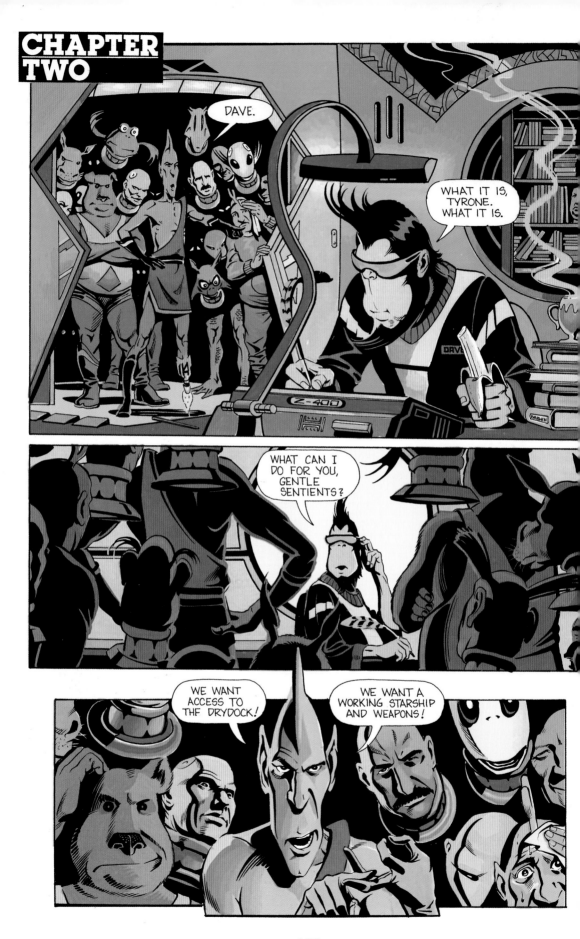

I TOLD YOU, I WOULD TALK TO NEXUS WHEN HE RETURNS FROM EARTH. AS FOR WEAPONS, IT'S OUT OF THE QUESTION.

I'M SORRY. WE CAN'T WAIT FOR NEXUS.

RAUL...?

ZZZZZ

SNATCH!

WITH THIS KEY RING, WE DON'T NEED *ANYONE'S* PERMISSION. COME ON, MEN.

YOU'RE MAKING A MISTAKE, TYRONE.

I DON'T THINK SO.

MEANWHILE...

WE HAVE ARRIVED YLUMSIDE, MADAME AMBASSADOR.

123

ATTENTION YLUM: GREETINGS FROM THE INNER PLANETS. AMBASSADOR URSULA X. X. IMADA OF THE COHESIVE WEB REQUESTS PERMISSION TO LAND.

DAVE! HEY DAVE!

WHEN IT RAINS IT POURS.

MAY I ASK THE PURPOSE OF YOUR VISIT?

WE WISH TO SPEAK TO NEXUS ON A MATTER OF GREAT IMPORTANCE.

NEXUS ISN'T IN RIGHT NOW. CAN I TAKE A MESSAGE?

THAT'S OKAY. WE'LL WAIT.

"OH, VERY WELL. YOU MAY BRING DOWN A PARTY OF FIVE. AFTER WE HAVE ASCERTAINED YOUR PURPOSE AND MOTIVES, AND IF YOU PROVE LEGITIMATE, WE'LL WORK OUT A SCHEDULE TO GIVE EVERYONE A CHANCE TO STRETCH THEIR LEGS."

"THANKYOU."

(HE WAS TOUGH. I ALMOST DIDN'T PULL THAT OFF.)

SHORTLY...

ON BEHALF OF NEXUS, WELCOME TO YLUM, I GUESS.

THANK YOU, MR...

CALL ME DAVE.

THANK YOU, DAVE. THE COHESIVE WEB HAS LONG ANTICIPATED THIS MEETING.

ARE YOU AWARE OF 5 SUNS BURNING OUT IN THIS SECTOR?

YES. ATTRIBUTABLE TO A MADMAN NAMED SUTTA LeBERQ. NEXUS KILLED HIM.

HOW DOES ONE GO ABOUT KILLING SOMEONE WHO CAN DESTROY 5 SUNS?

YOU'LL HAVE TO ASK NEXUS.

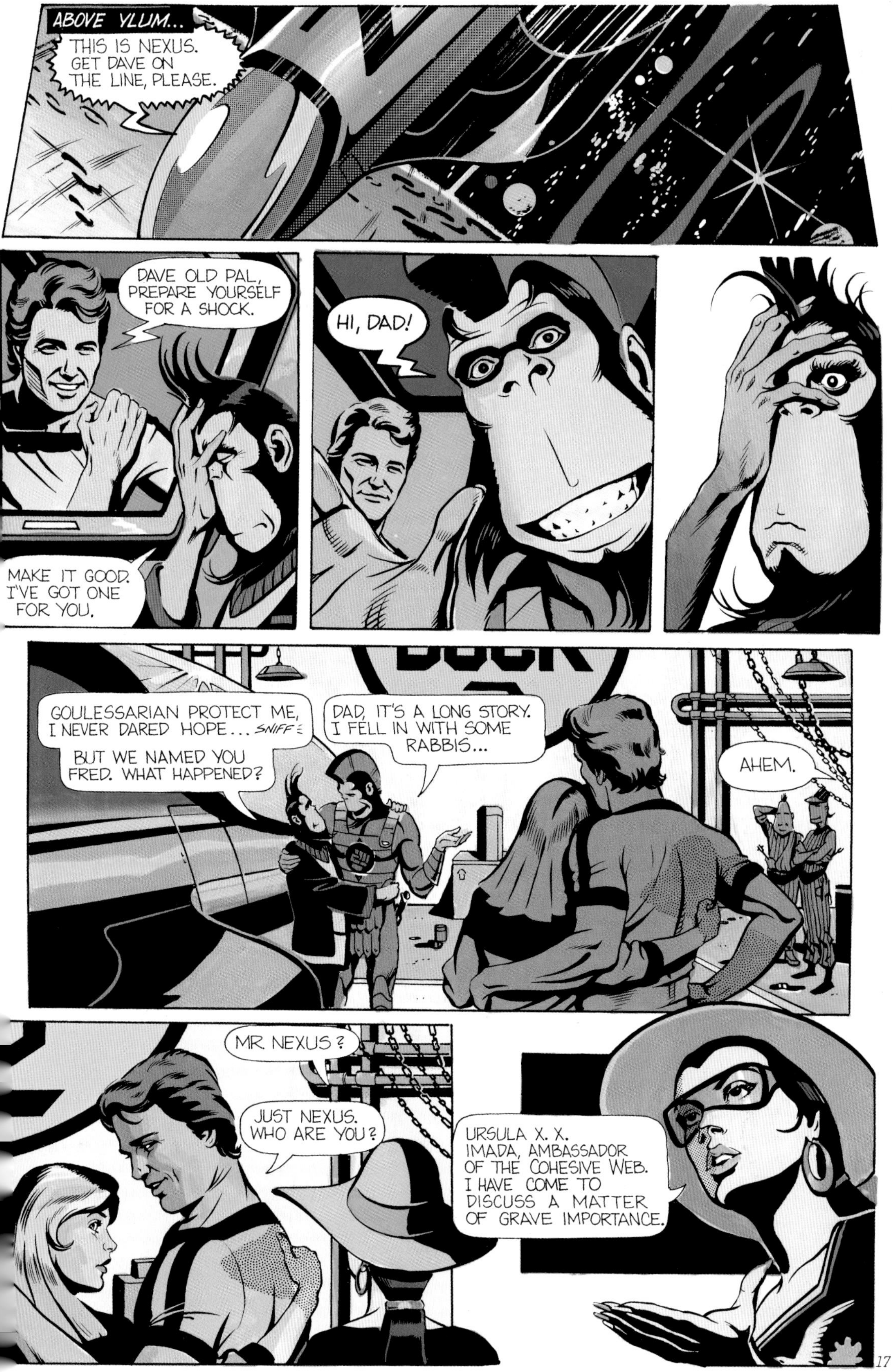
ABOVE YLUM...
THIS IS NEXUS. GET DAVE ON THE LINE, PLEASE.
DAVE OLD PAL, PREPARE YOURSELF FOR A SHOCK.
MAKE IT GOOD. I'VE GOT ONE FOR YOU.
HI, DAD!
GOULESSARIAN PROTECT ME, I NEVER DARED HOPE... SNIFF
BUT WE NAMED YOU FRED. WHAT HAPPENED?
DAD, IT'S A LONG STORY. I FELL IN WITH SOME RABBIS...
AHEM.
MR. NEXUS?
JUST NEXUS. WHO ARE YOU?
URSULA X. X. IMADA, AMBASSADOR OF THE COHESIVE WEB. I HAVE COME TO DISCUSS A MATTER OF GRAVE IMPORTANCE.
17

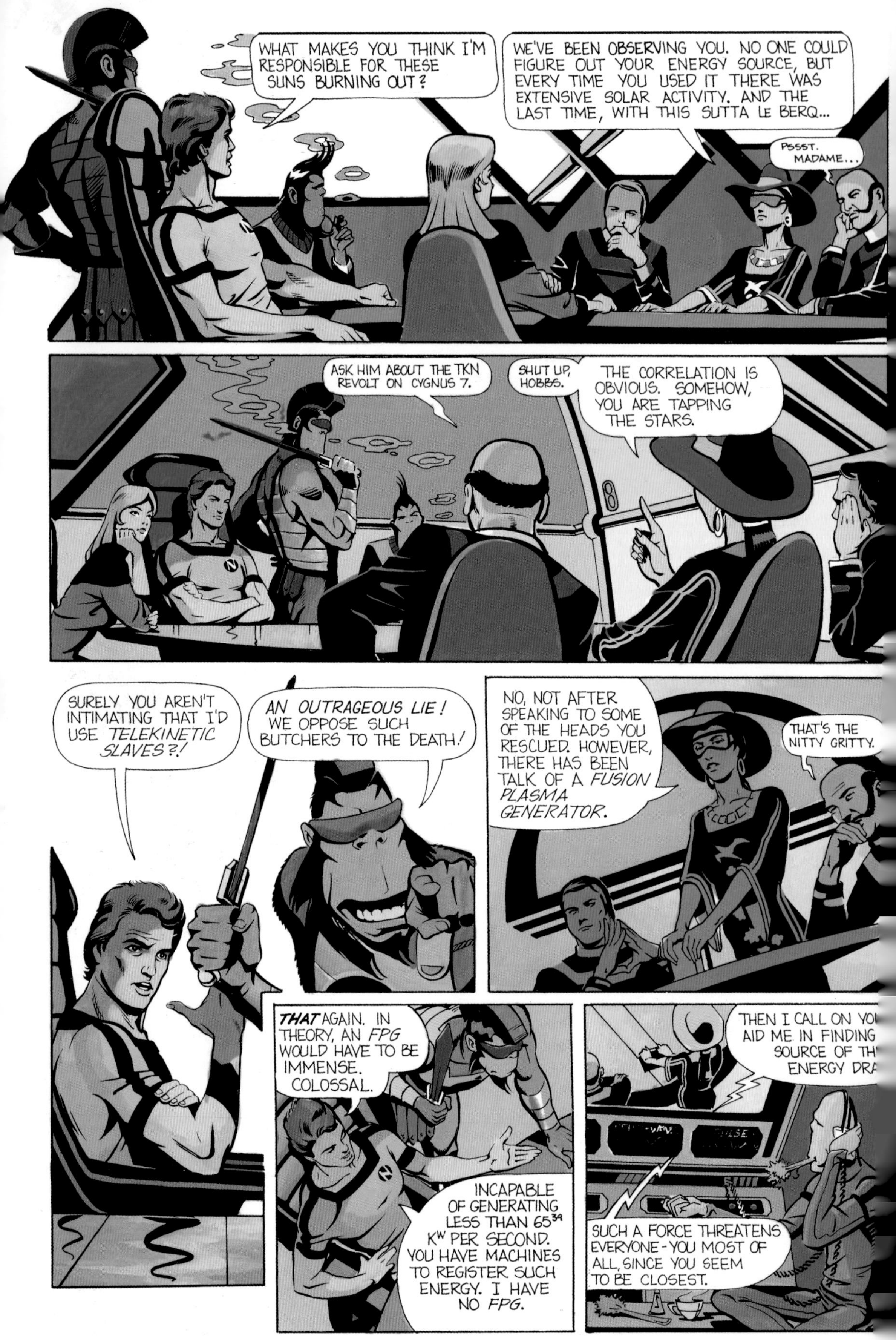
WHAT MAKES YOU THINK I'M RESPONSIBLE FOR THESE SUNS BURNING OUT?
WE'VE BEEN OBSERVING YOU. NO ONE COULD FIGURE OUT YOUR ENERGY SOURCE, BUT EVERY TIME YOU USED IT THERE WAS EXTENSIVE SOLAR ACTIVITY. AND THE LAST TIME, WITH THIS SUTTA LE BERQ...
PSSST. MADAME...
ASK HIM ABOUT THE TKN REVOLT ON CYGNUS 7.
SHUT UP, HOBBS.
THE CORRELATION IS OBVIOUS. SOMEHOW, YOU ARE TAPPING THE STARS.
SURELY YOU AREN'T INTIMATING THAT I'D USE TELEKINETIC SLAVES?!
AN OUTRAGEOUS LIE! WE OPPOSE SUCH BUTCHERS TO THE DEATH!
NO, NOT AFTER SPEAKING TO SOME OF THE HEADS YOU RESCUED. HOWEVER, THERE HAS BEEN TALK OF A FUSION PLASMA GENERATOR.
THAT'S THE NITTY GRITTY.
THAT AGAIN. IN THEORY, AN FPG WOULD HAVE TO BE IMMENSE. COLOSSAL.
INCAPABLE OF GENERATING LESS THAN 65^39 K^W PER SECOND. YOU HAVE MACHINES TO REGISTER SUCH ENERGY. I HAVE NO FPG.
THEN I CALL ON YO AID ME IN FINDING SOURCE OF TH ENERGY DRA
SUCH A FORCE THREATENS EVERYONE - YOU MOST OF ALL, SINCE YOU SEEM TO BE CLOSEST.

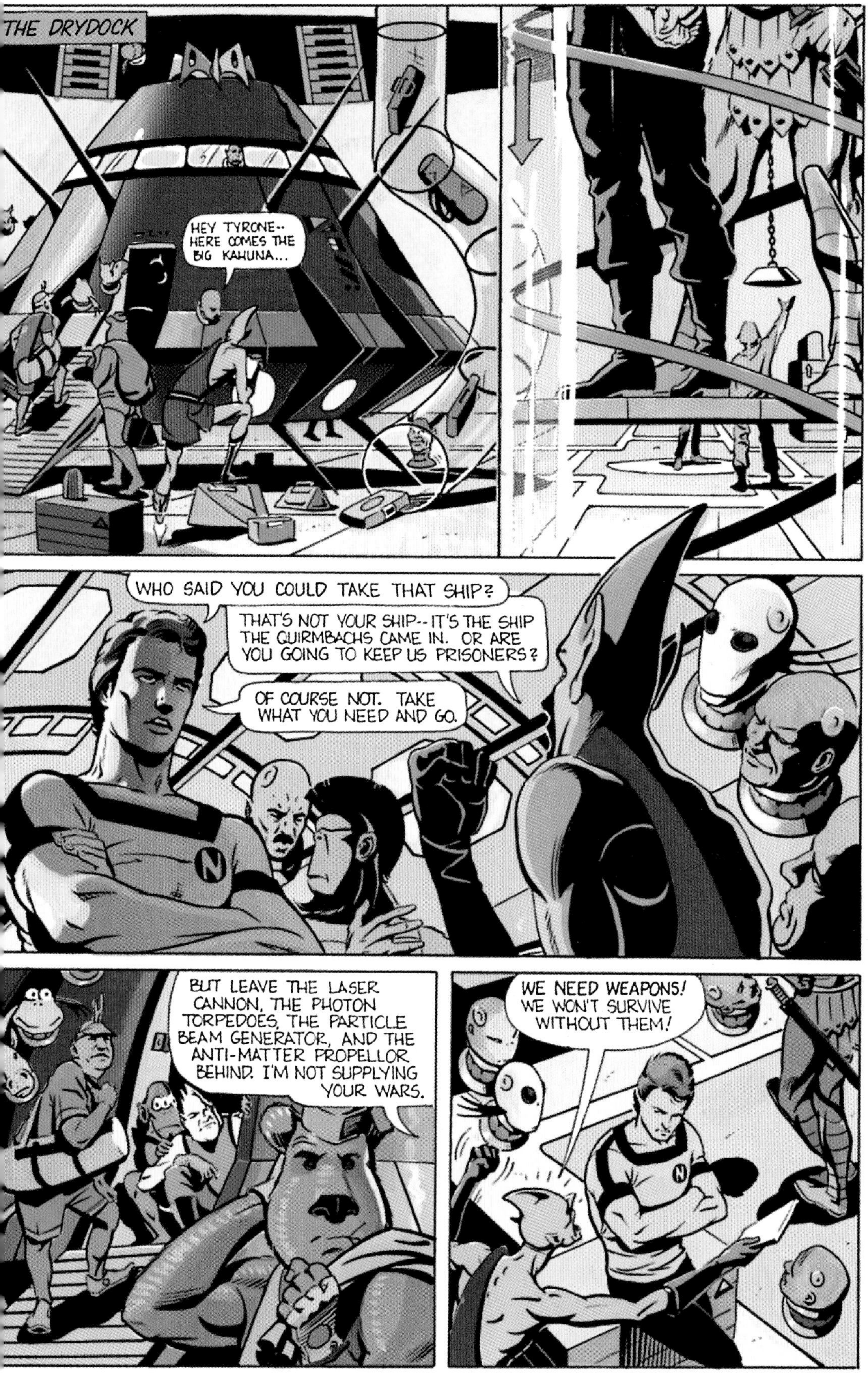
THE DRYDOCK
HEY TYRONE-- HERE COMES THE BIG KAHUNA...
WHO SAID YOU COULD TAKE THAT SHIP?
THAT'S NOT YOUR SHIP-- IT'S THE SHIP THE QUIRMBACHS CAME IN. OR ARE YOU GOING TO KEEP US PRISONERS?
OF COURSE NOT. TAKE WHAT YOU NEED AND GO.
BUT LEAVE THE LASER CANNON, THE PHOTON TORPEDOES, THE PARTICLE BEAM GENERATOR, AND THE ANTI-MATTER PROPELLOR BEHIND. I'M NOT SUPPLYING YOUR WARS.
WE NEED WEAPONS! WE WON'T SURVIVE WITHOUT THEM!

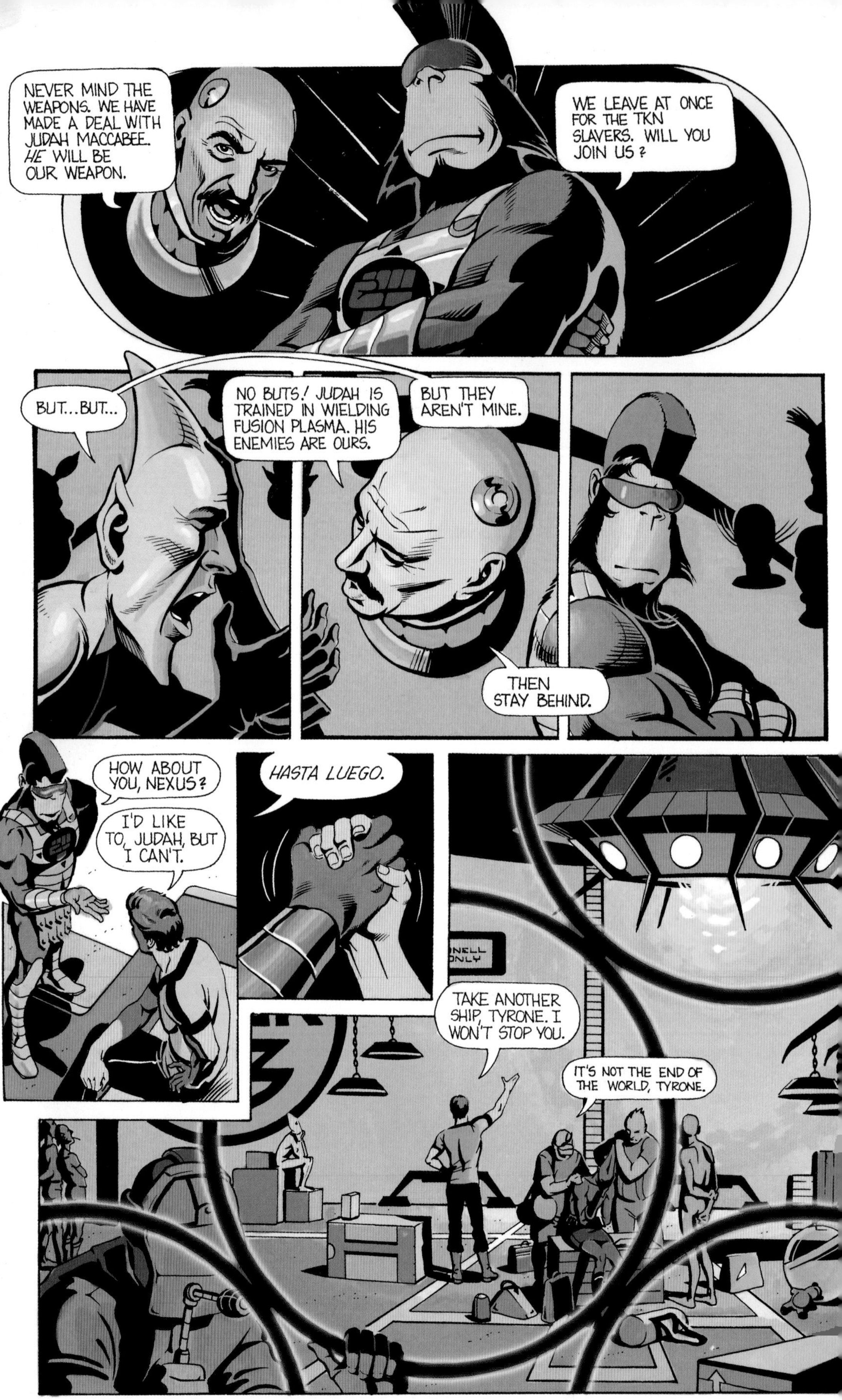
NEVER MIND THE WEAPONS. WE HAVE MADE A DEAL WITH JUDAH MACCABEE. *HE* WILL BE OUR WEAPON.
WE LEAVE AT ONCE FOR THE TKN SLAVERS. WILL YOU JOIN US?
BUT...BUT...
NO BUTS! JUDAH IS TRAINED IN WIELDING FUSION PLASMA. HIS ENEMIES ARE OURS.
BUT THEY AREN'T MINE.
THEN STAY BEHIND.
HOW ABOUT YOU, NEXUS?
I'D LIKE TO, JUDAH, BUT I CAN'T.
HASTA LUEGO.
TAKE ANOTHER SHIP, TYRONE. I WON'T STOP YOU.
IT'S NOT THE END OF THE WORLD, TYRONE.

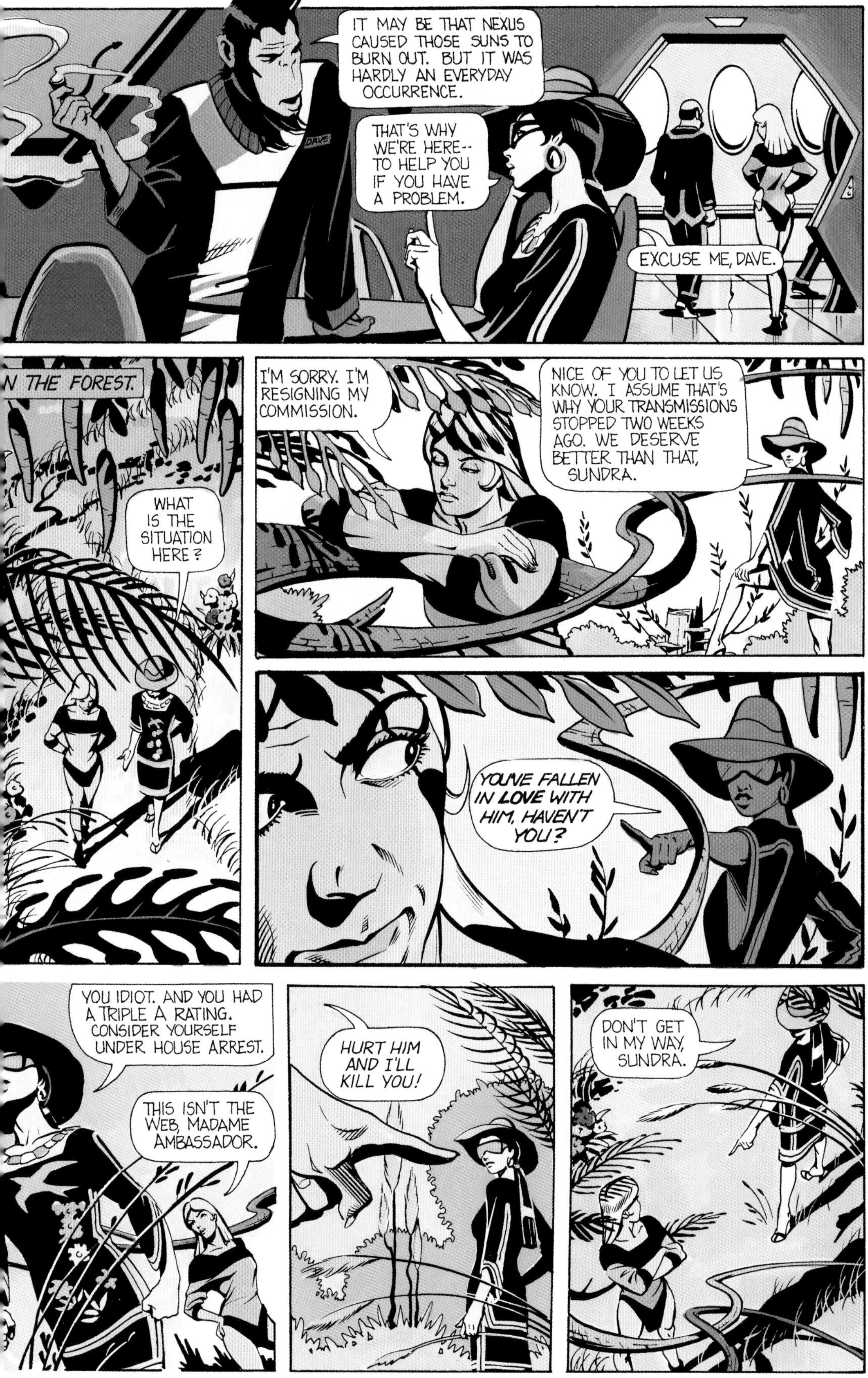
IT MAY BE THAT NEXUS CAUSED THOSE SUNS TO BURN OUT. BUT IT WAS HARDLY AN EVERYDAY OCCURRENCE.
DAVE
THAT'S WHY WE'RE HERE-- TO HELP YOU IF YOU HAVE A PROBLEM.
EXCUSE ME, DAVE.
N THE FOREST.
WHAT IS THE SITUATION HERE?
I'M SORRY. I'M RESIGNING MY COMMISSION.
NICE OF YOU TO LET US KNOW. I ASSUME THAT'S WHY YOUR TRANSMISSIONS STOPPED TWO WEEKS AGO. WE DESERVE BETTER THAN THAT, SUNDRA.
YOU'VE FALLEN IN LOVE WITH HIM, HAVEN'T YOU?
YOU IDIOT. AND YOU HAD A TRIPLE A RATING. CONSIDER YOURSELF UNDER HOUSE ARREST.
THIS ISN'T THE WEB, MADAME AMBASSADOR.
HURT HIM AND I'LL KILL YOU!
DON'T GET IN MY WAY, SUNDRA.

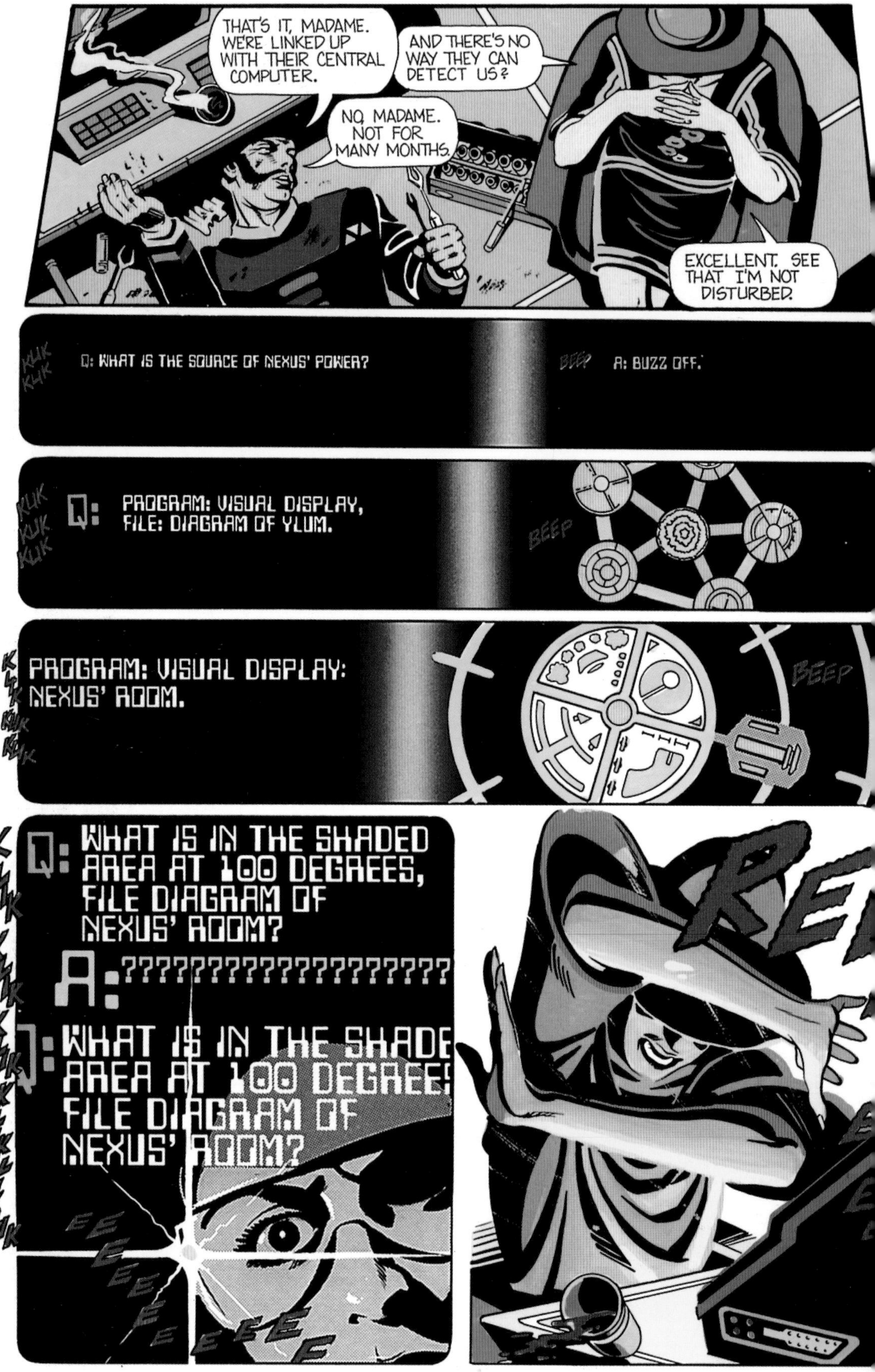
THAT'S IT, MADAME. WE'RE LINKED UP WITH THEIR CENTRAL COMPUTER.
AND THERE'S NO WAY THEY CAN DETECT US?
NO, MADAME. NOT FOR MANY MONTHS.
EXCELLENT. SEE THAT I'M NOT DISTURBED.
KUK KUK
Q: WHAT IS THE SOURCE OF NEXUS' POWER?
BEEP
A: BUZZ OFF.
KUK KUK KUK
Q: PROGRAM: VISUAL DISPLAY, FILE: DIAGRAM OF YLUM.
BEEP
PROGRAM: VISUAL DISPLAY: NEXUS' ROOM.
BEEP
Q: WHAT IS IN THE SHADED AREA AT 100 DEGREES, FILE DIAGRAM OF NEXUS' ROOM?
A: ????????????????????
Q: WHAT IS IN THE SHADE AREA AT 100 DEGREE FILE DIAGRAM OF NEXUS' ROOM?

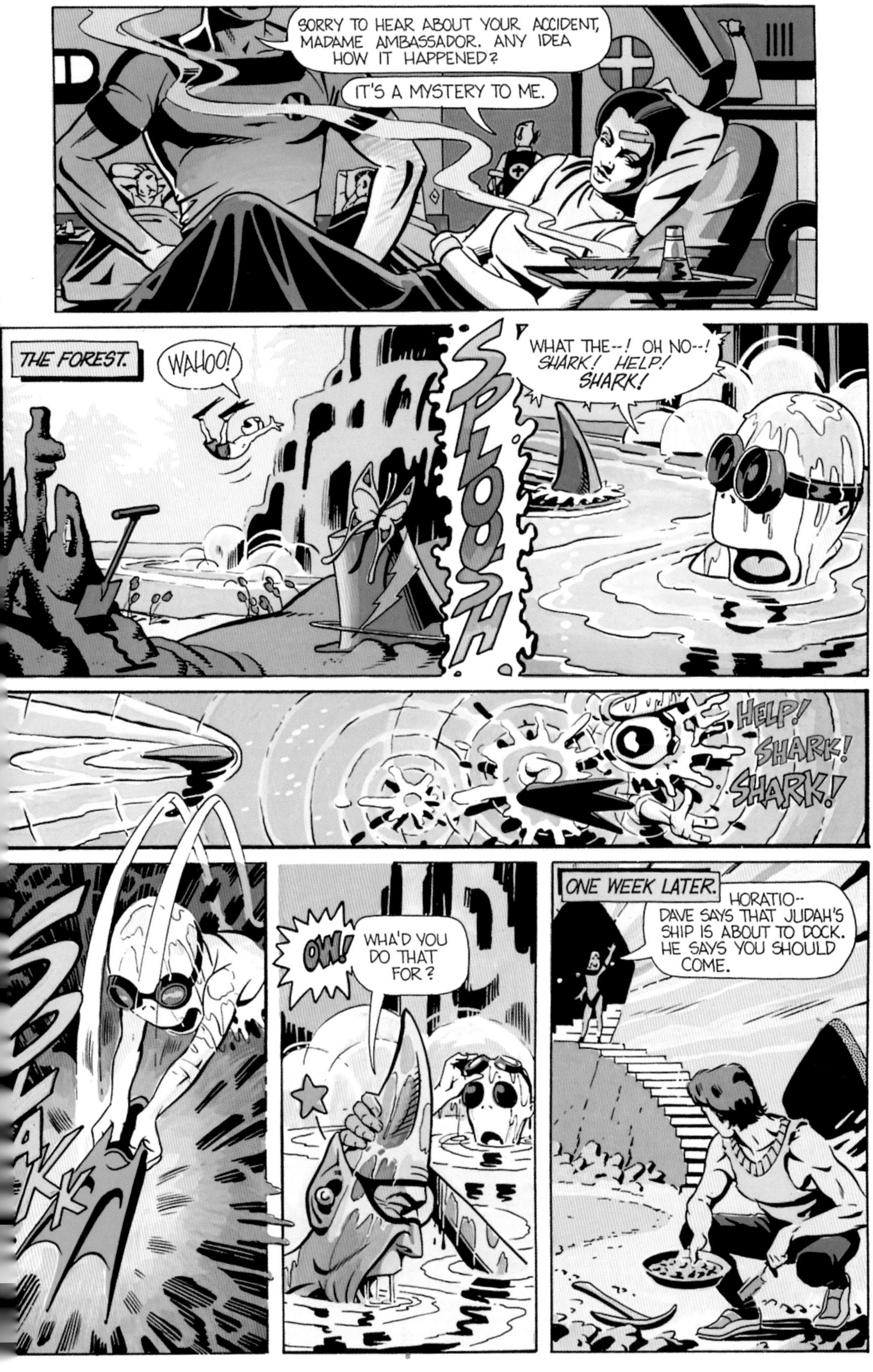
SORRY TO HEAR ABOUT YOUR ACCIDENT, MADAME AMBASSADOR. ANY IDEA HOW IT HAPPENED?
IT'S A MYSTERY TO ME.
THE FOREST.
WAHOO!
SPLOOSH
WHAT THE--! OH NO--! SHARK! HELP! SHARK!
HELP!
SHARK!
SHARK!
OW!
WHA'D YOU DO THAT FOR?
ONE WEEK LATER.
HORATIO-- DAVE SAYS THAT JUDAH'S SHIP IS ABOUT TO DOCK. HE SAYS YOU SHOULD COME.

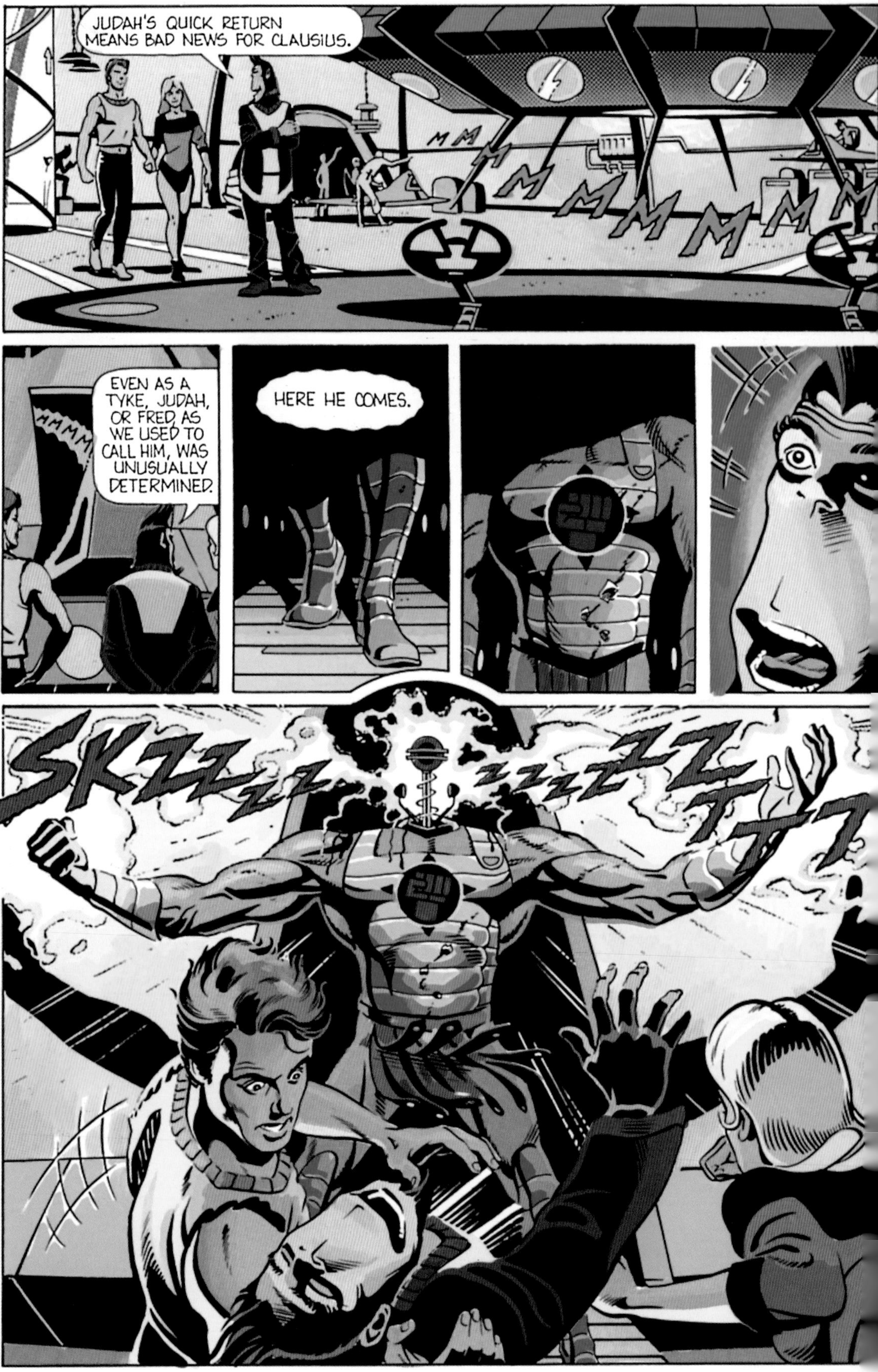
JUDAH'S QUICK RETURN MEANS BAD NEWS FOR CLAUSIUS.
MMMMMMMMMMMMM
EVEN AS A TYKE, JUDAH, OR FRED AS WE USED TO CALL HIM, WAS UNUSUALLY DETERMINED.
HERE HE COMES.
SKZZZzzzzzzzzZZZZT

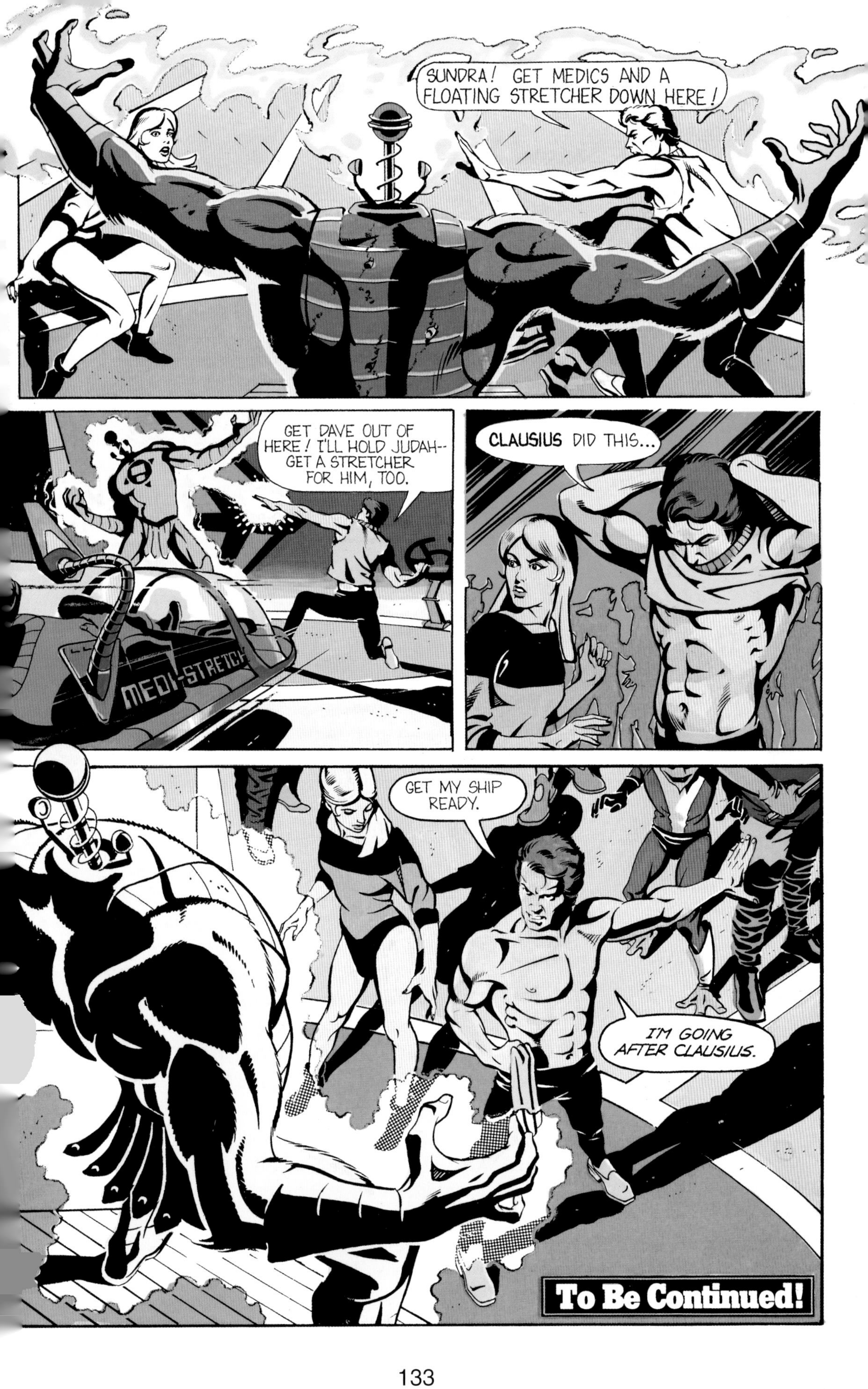
SUNDRA! GET MEDICS AND A FLOATING STRETCHER DOWN HERE!
GET DAVE OUT OF HERE! I'LL HOLD JUDAH-- GET A STRETCHER FOR HIM, TOO.
MEDI-STRETCH
CLAUSIUS DID THIS...
GET MY SHIP READY.
I'M GOING AFTER CLAUSIUS.
To Be Continued!

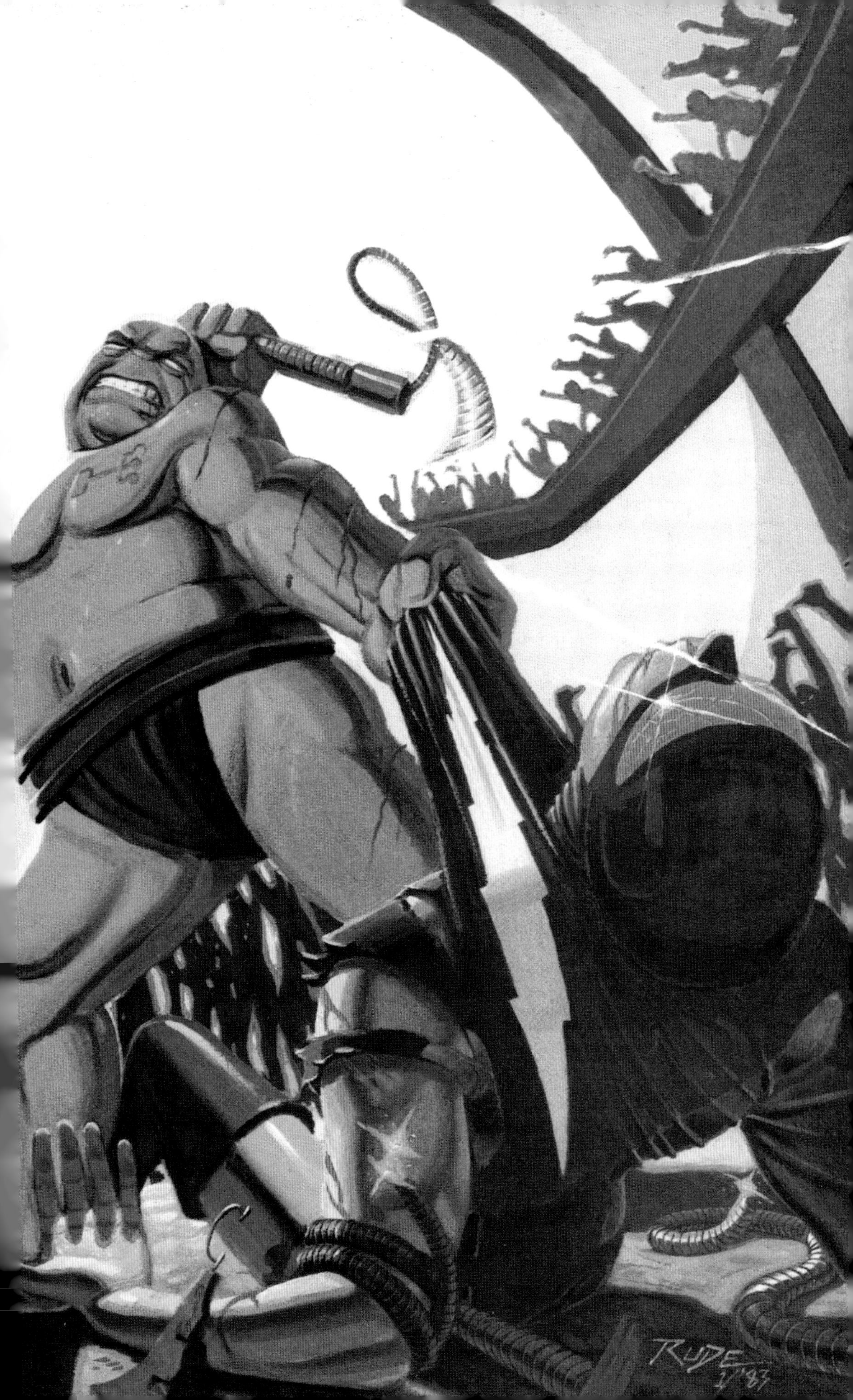
RUDE

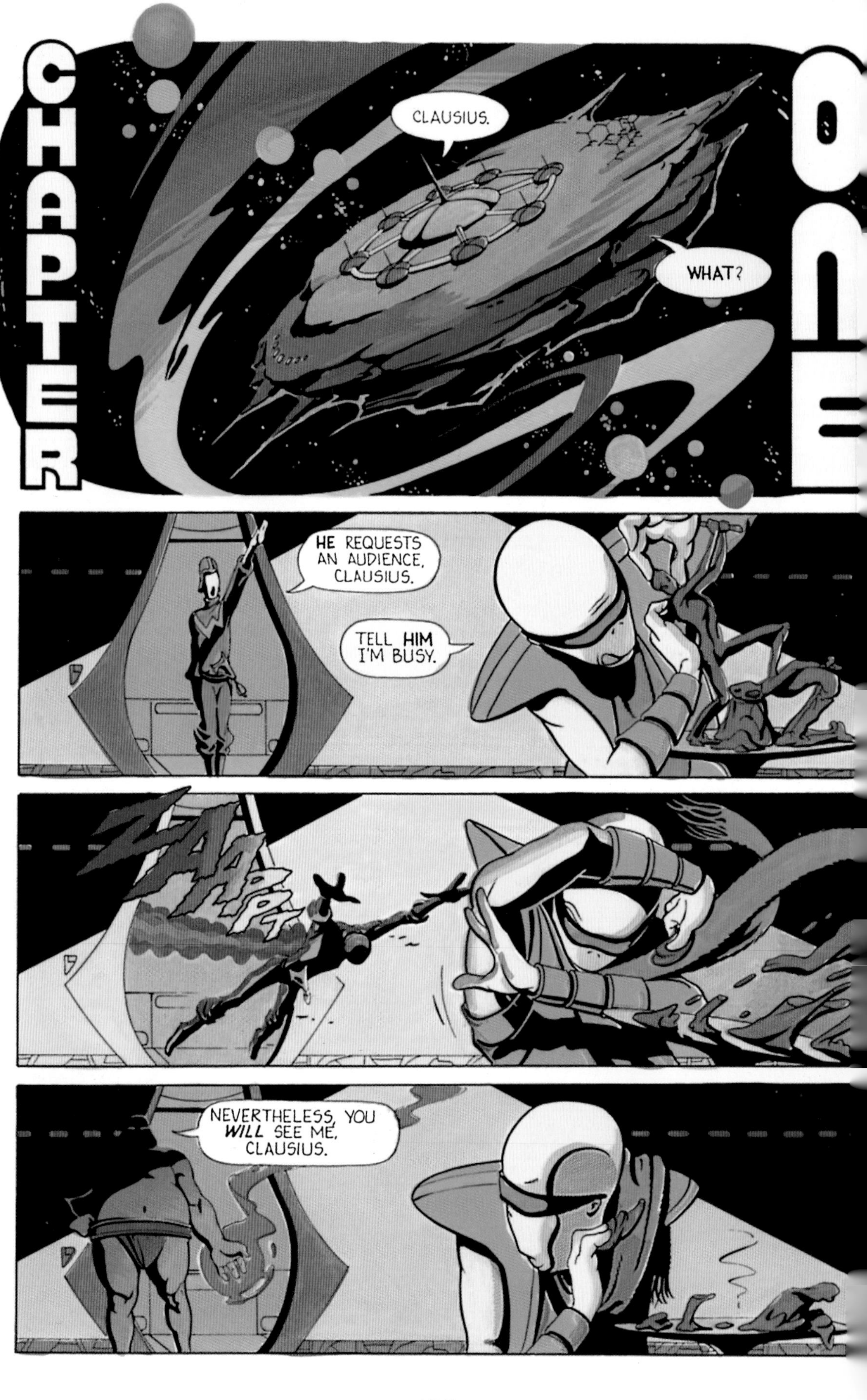
CHAPTER ONE
CLAUSIUS.
WHAT?
HE REQUESTS AN AUDIENCE, CLAUSIUS.
TELL HIM I'M BUSY.
ZAAPPT
NEVERTHELESS, YOU WILL SEE ME, CLAUSIUS.

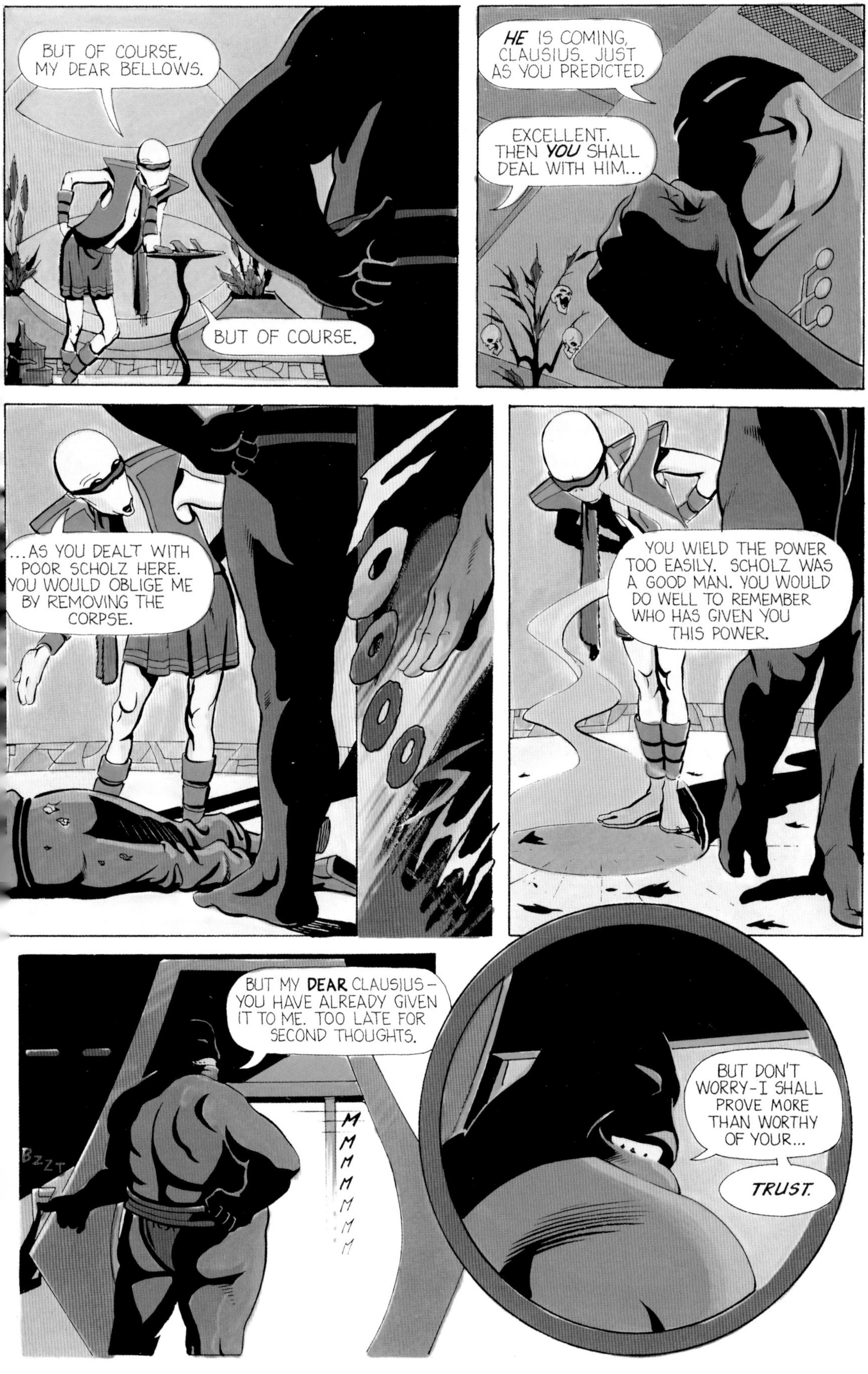
BUT OF COURSE, MY DEAR BELLOWS.
BUT OF COURSE.
HE IS COMING, CLAUSIUS. JUST AS YOU PREDICTED.
EXCELLENT. THEN YOU SHALL DEAL WITH HIM...
...AS YOU DEALT WITH POOR SCHOLZ HERE. YOU WOULD OBLIGE ME BY REMOVING THE CORPSE.
YOU WIELD THE POWER TOO EASILY. SCHOLZ WAS A GOOD MAN. YOU WOULD DO WELL TO REMEMBER WHO HAS GIVEN YOU THIS POWER.
BUT MY DEAR CLAUSIUS– YOU HAVE ALREADY GIVEN IT TO ME. TOO LATE FOR SECOND THOUGHTS.
BZZT
MMMMMMM
BUT DON'T WORRY–I SHALL PROVE MORE THAN WORTHY OF YOUR...
TRUST.

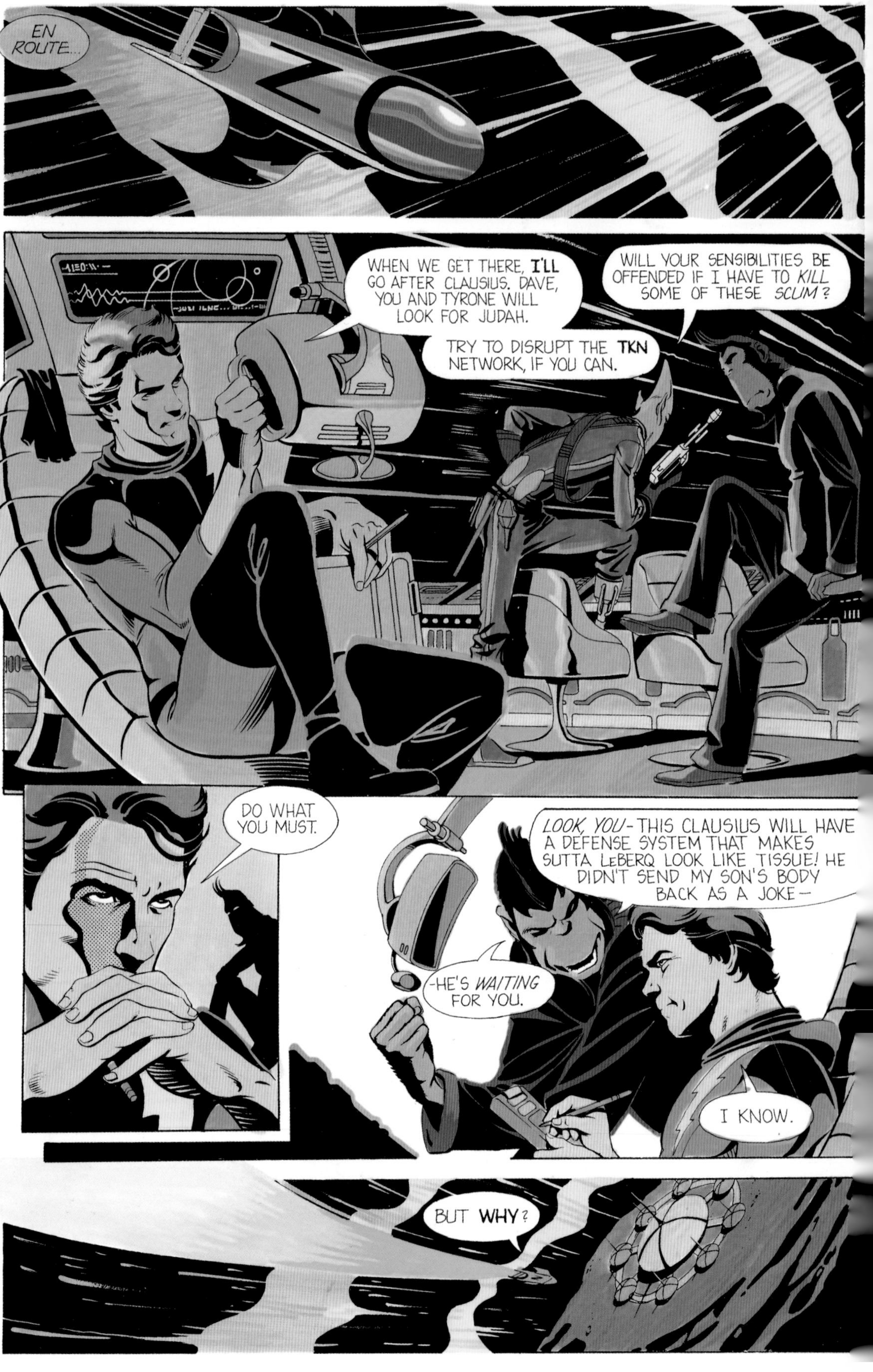
EN ROUTE...
WHEN WE GET THERE, I'LL GO AFTER CLAUSIUS. DAVE, YOU AND TYRONE WILL LOOK FOR JUDAH.
TRY TO DISRUPT THE TKN NETWORK, IF YOU CAN.
WILL YOUR SENSIBILITIES BE OFFENDED IF I HAVE TO KILL SOME OF THESE SCUM?
DO WHAT YOU MUST.
LOOK, YOU- THIS CLAUSIUS WILL HAVE A DEFENSE SYSTEM THAT MAKES SUTTA LeBERQ LOOK LIKE TISSUE! HE DIDN'T SEND MY SON'S BODY BACK AS A JOKE-
-HE'S WAITING FOR YOU.
I KNOW.
BUT WHY?

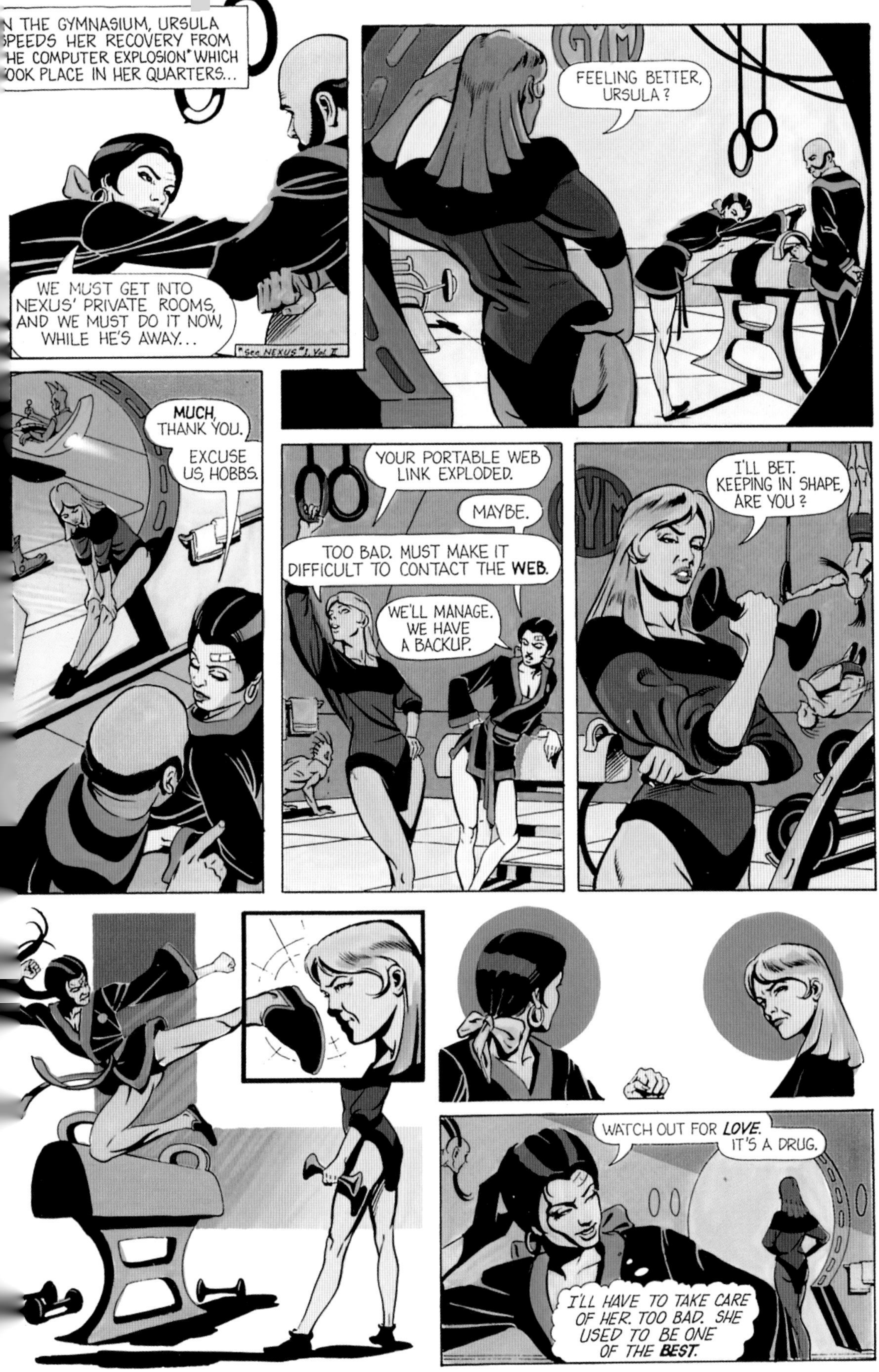
N THE GYMNASIUM, URSULA
SPEEDS HER RECOVERY FROM
HE COMPUTER EXPLOSION* WHICH
OOK PLACE IN HER QUARTERS...
WE MUST GET INTO
NEXUS' PRIVATE ROOMS,
AND WE MUST DO IT NOW,
WHILE HE'S AWAY...
*See NEXUS #1, Vol. I
FEELING BETTER,
URSULA?
MUCH,
THANK YOU.
EXCUSE
US, HOBBS.
YOUR PORTABLE WEB
LINK EXPLODED.
MAYBE.
TOO BAD. MUST MAKE IT
DIFFICULT TO CONTACT THE WEB.
WE'LL MANAGE.
WE HAVE
A BACKUP.
I'LL BET.
KEEPING IN SHAPE,
ARE YOU?
WATCH OUT FOR LOVE.
IT'S A DRUG.
I'LL HAVE TO TAKE CARE
OF HER. TOO BAD. SHE
USED TO BE ONE
OF THE BEST.

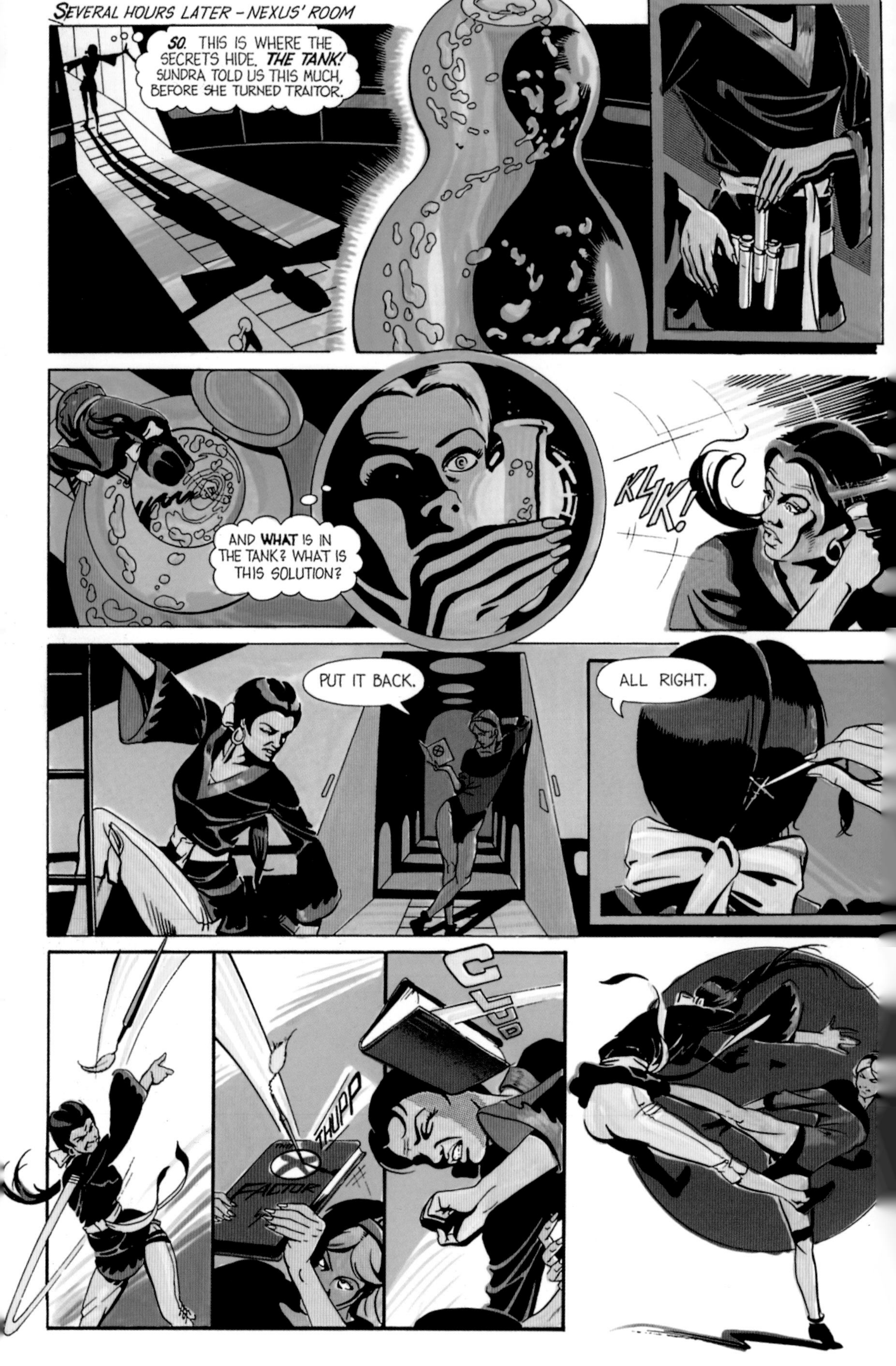
SEVERAL HOURS LATER – NEXUS' ROOM
SO. THIS IS WHERE THE SECRETS HIDE. THE TANK! SUNDRA TOLD US THIS MUCH, BEFORE SHE TURNED TRAITOR.
AND WHAT IS IN THE TANK? WHAT IS THIS SOLUTION?
KLIK!
PUT IT BACK.
ALL RIGHT.
THUPP
FACTOR
CLUD

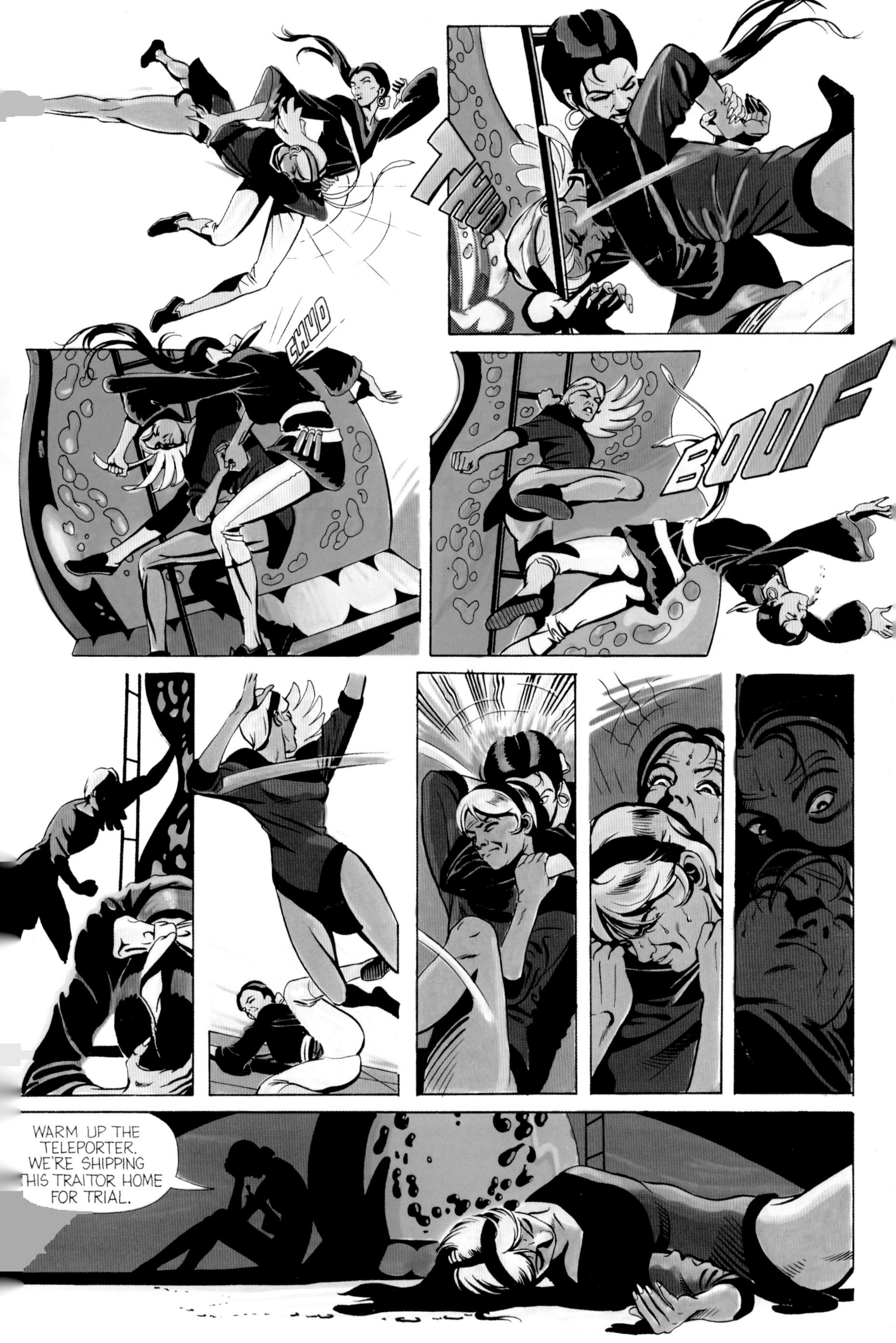
THUD
CHUD
BOOF
WARM UP THE TELEPORTER. WE'RE SHIPPING THIS TRAITOR HOME FOR TRIAL.

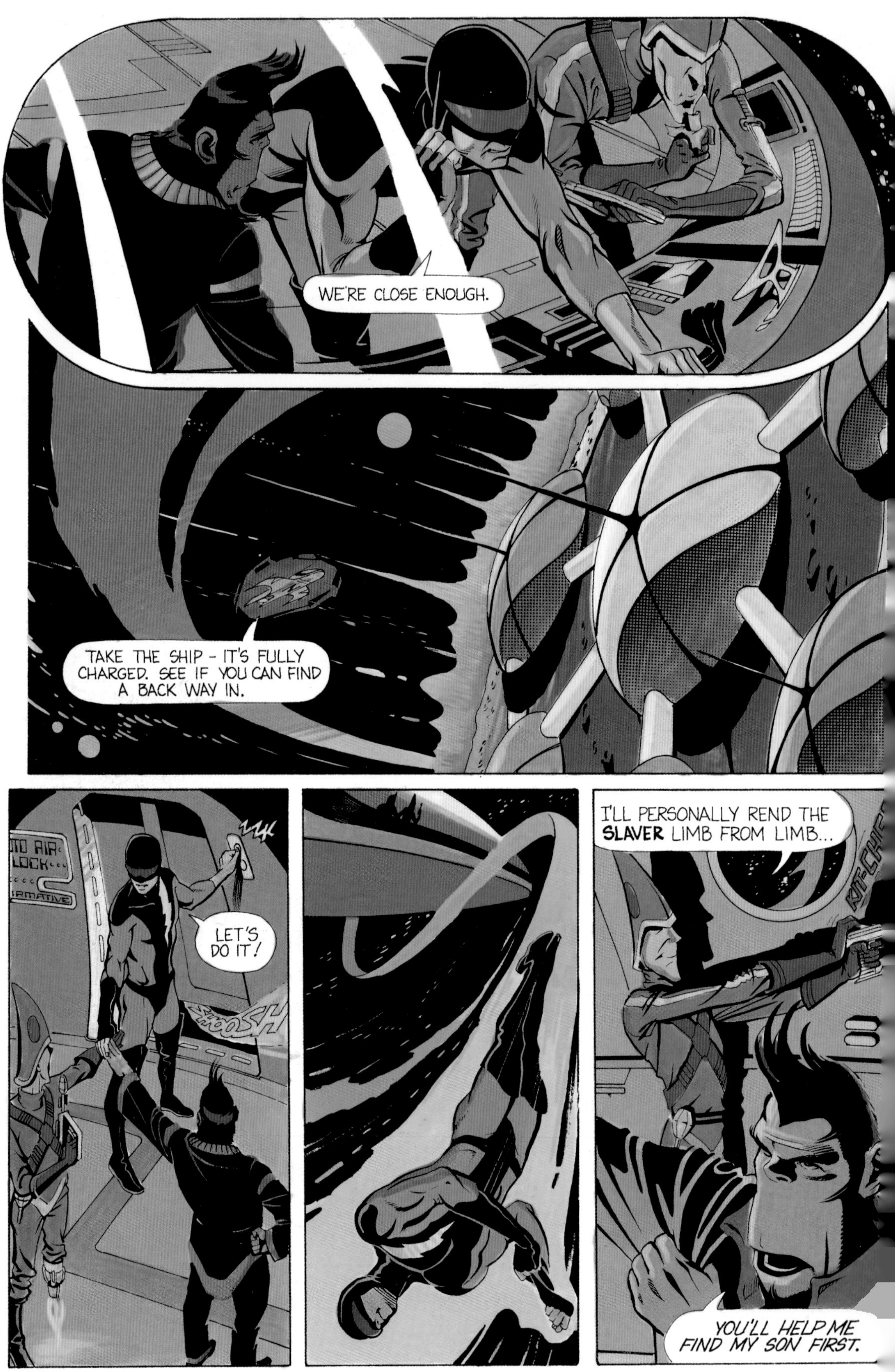
WE'RE CLOSE ENOUGH.
TAKE THE SHIP - IT'S FULLY CHARGED. SEE IF YOU CAN FIND A BACK WAY IN.
LET'S DO IT!
I'LL PERSONALLY REND THE **SLAVER** LIMB FROM LIMB...
YOU'LL HELP ME FIND MY SON FIRST.

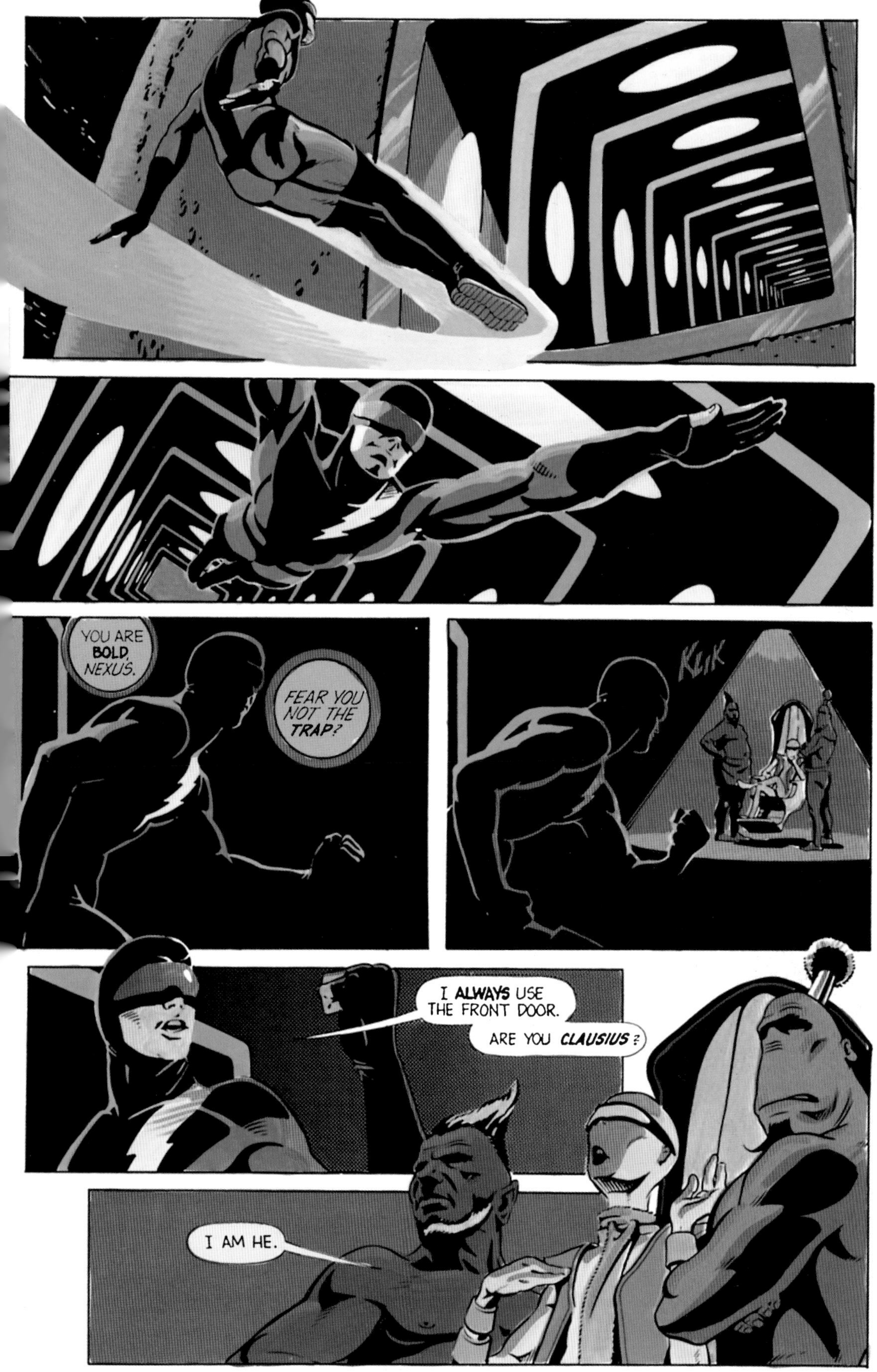

YOU ARE BOLD, NEXUS.
FEAR YOU NOT THE TRAP?
KLIK
I ALWAYS USE THE FRONT DOOR.
ARE YOU CLAUSIUS?
I AM HE.

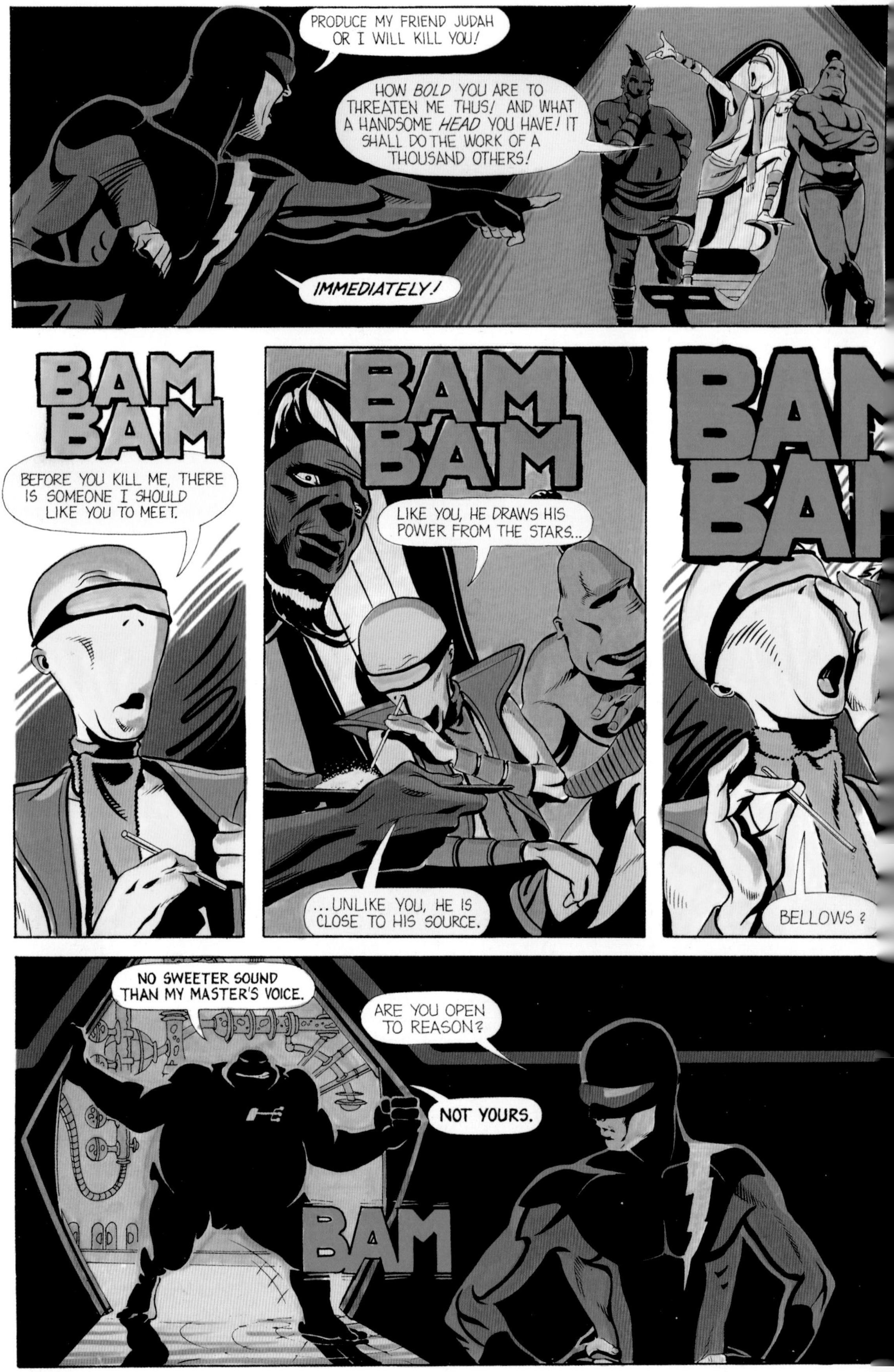
PRODUCE MY FRIEND JUDAH OR I WILL KILL YOU!
HOW BOLD YOU ARE TO THREATEN ME THUS! AND WHAT A HANDSOME HEAD YOU HAVE! IT SHALL DO THE WORK OF A THOUSAND OTHERS!
IMMEDIATELY!
BAM BAM
BEFORE YOU KILL ME, THERE IS SOMEONE I SHOULD LIKE YOU TO MEET.
BAM BAM
LIKE YOU, HE DRAWS HIS POWER FROM THE STARS...
...UNLIKE YOU, HE IS CLOSE TO HIS SOURCE.
BELLOWS?
NO SWEETER SOUND THAN MY MASTER'S VOICE.
ARE YOU OPEN TO REASON?
NOT YOURS.
BAM

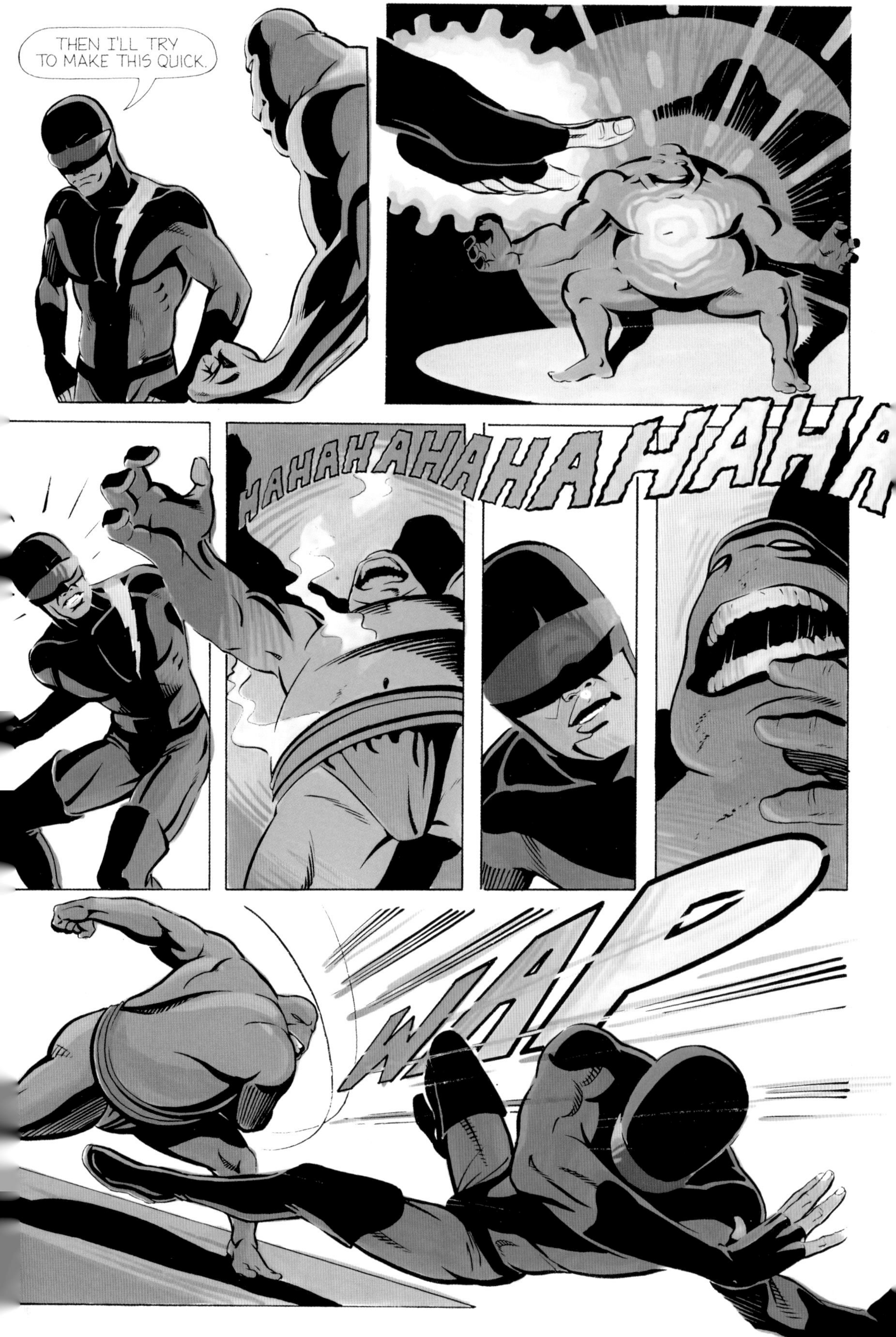
THEN I'LL TRY TO MAKE THIS QUICK.
HAHAHAHAHAHAHAHAHA
WAP

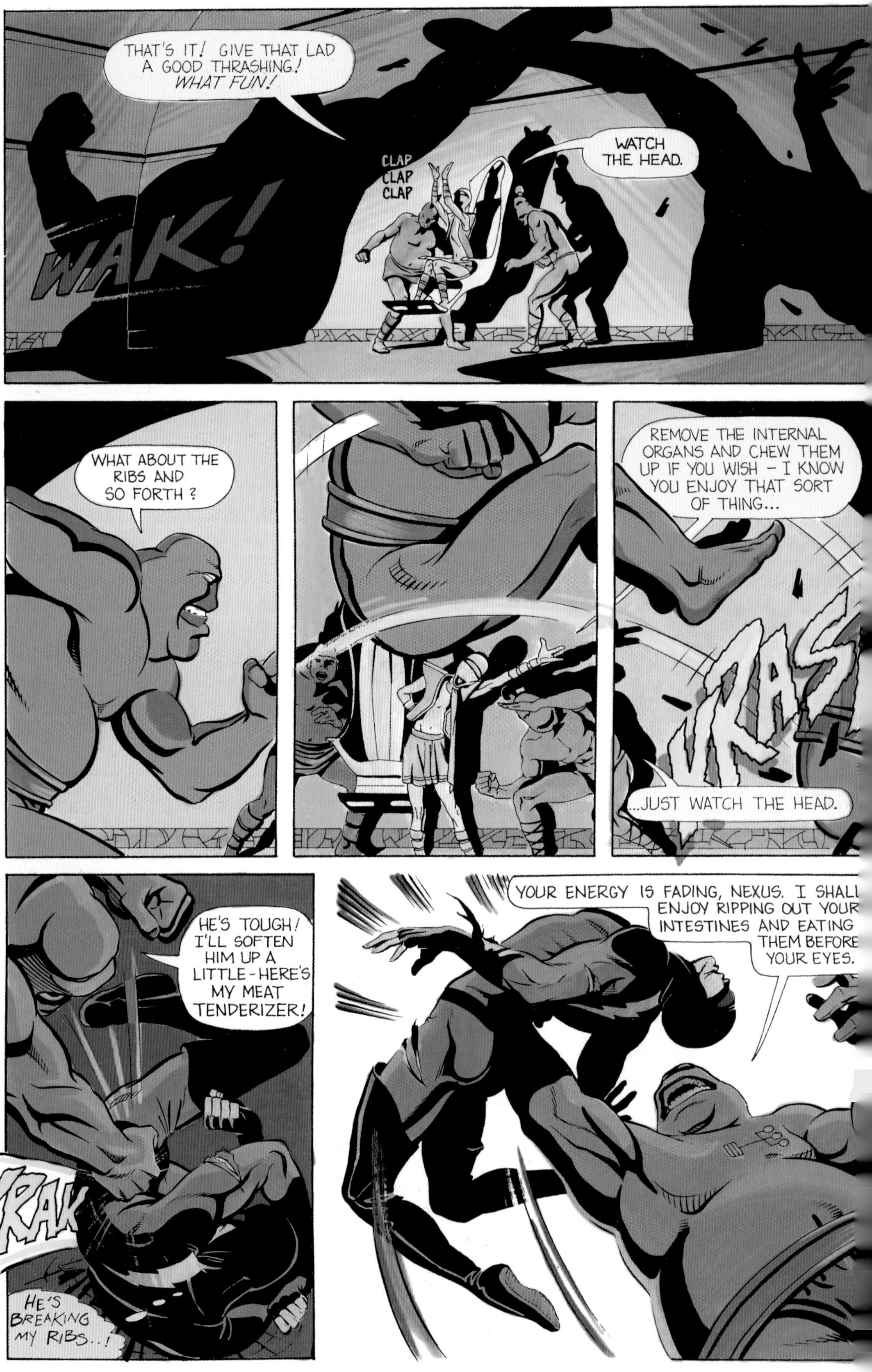
THAT'S IT! GIVE THAT LAD A GOOD THRASHING! WHAT FUN!
CLAP CLAP CLAP
WATCH THE HEAD.
WAK!
WHAT ABOUT THE RIBS AND SO FORTH?
REMOVE THE INTERNAL ORGANS AND CHEW THEM UP IF YOU WISH – I KNOW YOU ENJOY THAT SORT OF THING...
...JUST WATCH THE HEAD.
HE'S TOUGH! I'LL SOFTEN HIM UP A LITTLE–HERE'S MY MEAT TENDERIZER!
HE'S BREAKING MY RIBS...!
YOUR ENERGY IS FADING, NEXUS. I SHALL ENJOY RIPPING OUT YOUR INTESTINES AND EATING THEM BEFORE YOUR EYES.

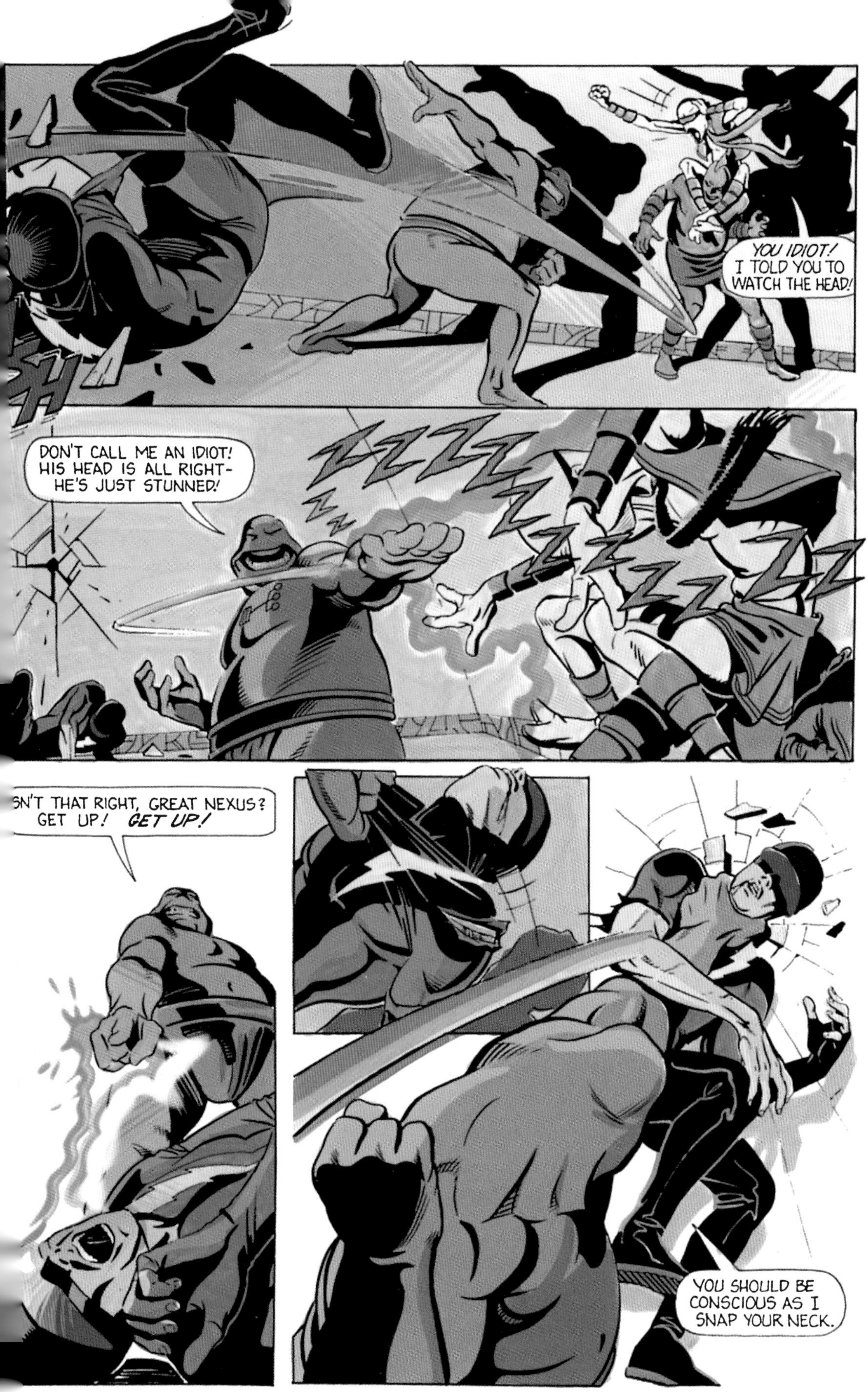
YOU IDIOT! I TOLD YOU TO WATCH THE HEAD!
DON'T CALL ME AN IDIOT! HIS HEAD IS ALL RIGHT- HE'S JUST STUNNED!
SN'T THAT RIGHT, GREAT NEXUS? GET UP! GET UP!
YOU SHOULD BE CONSCIOUS AS I SNAP YOUR NECK.

CHAPTER—TWO

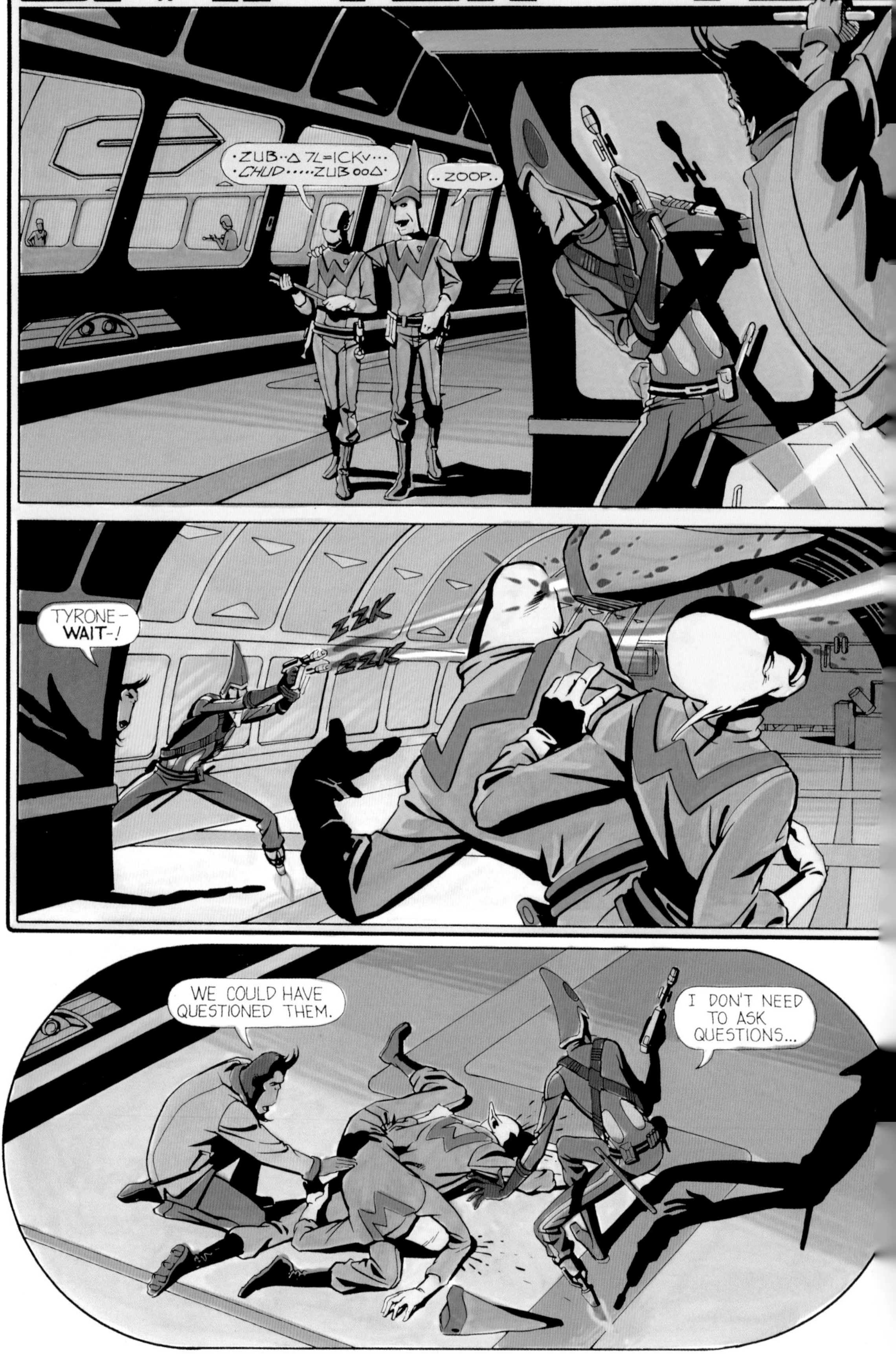

·ZUB··Δ 7L=ICKv···
·CHUD·····ZUBooΔ
..ZOOP..
TYRONE-
WAIT-!
ZZK
ZZK
WE COULD HAVE QUESTIONED THEM.
I DON'T NEED TO ASK QUESTIONS...

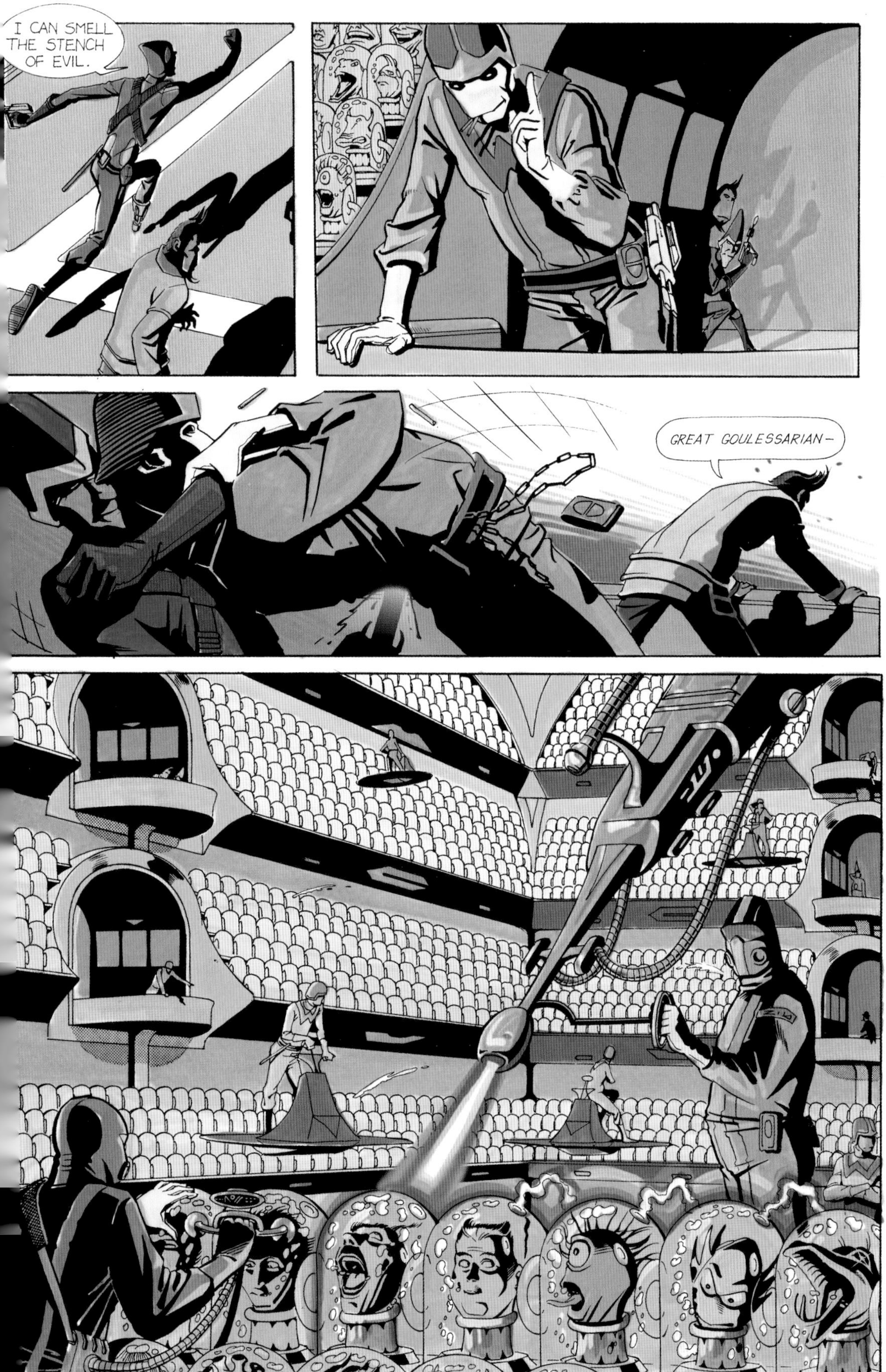
I CAN SMELL THE STENCH OF EVIL.
GREAT GOULESSARIAN—

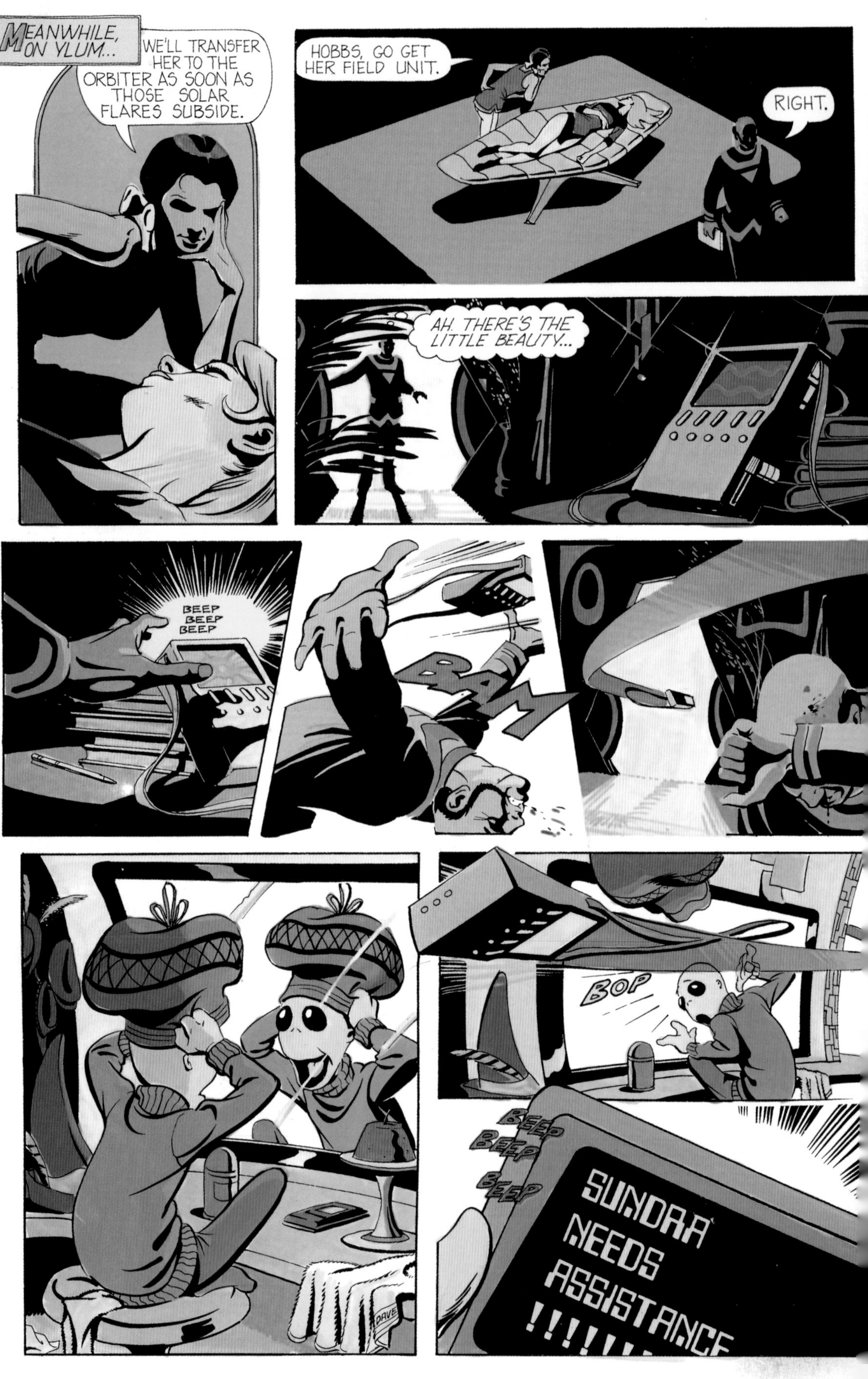
MEANWHILE, ON YLUM...
WE'LL TRANSFER HER TO THE ORBITER AS SOON AS THOSE SOLAR FLARES SUBSIDE.
HOBBS, GO GET HER FIELD UNIT.
RIGHT.
AH. THERE'S THE LITTLE BEAUTY...
BEEP BEEP BEEP
BAM
BOP
BEEP BEEP BEEP
SUNDRA NEEDS ASSISTANCE !!!!!!!
DAVE

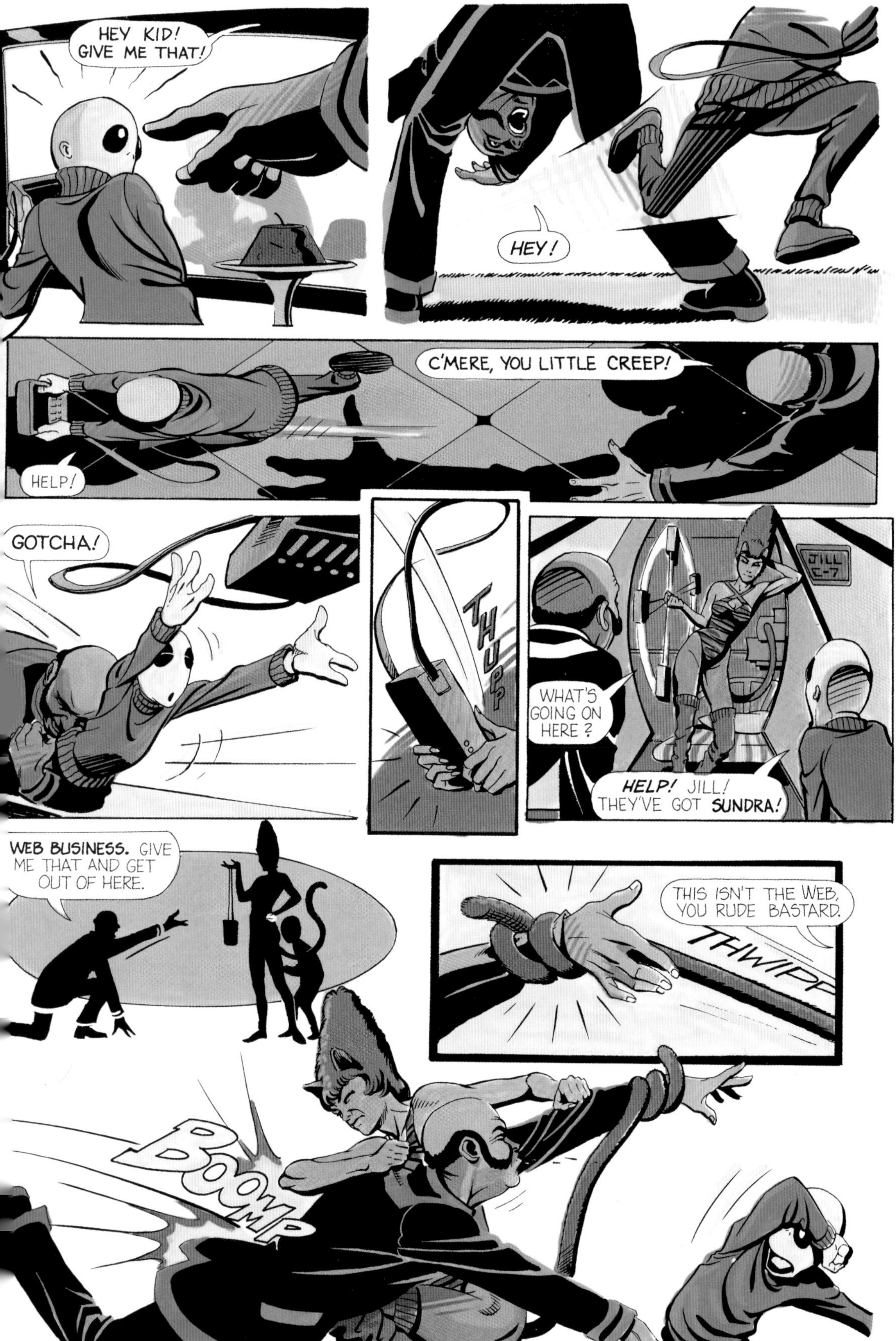
HEY KID! GIVE ME THAT!
HEY!
C'MERE, YOU LITTLE CREEP!
HELP!
GOTCHA!
THUPP
WHAT'S GOING ON HERE?
HELP! JILL! THEY'VE GOT SUNDRA!
JILL C-7
WEB BUSINESS. GIVE ME THAT AND GET OUT OF HERE.
THIS ISN'T THE WEB, YOU RUDE BASTARD.
THWIPP
BOOMP

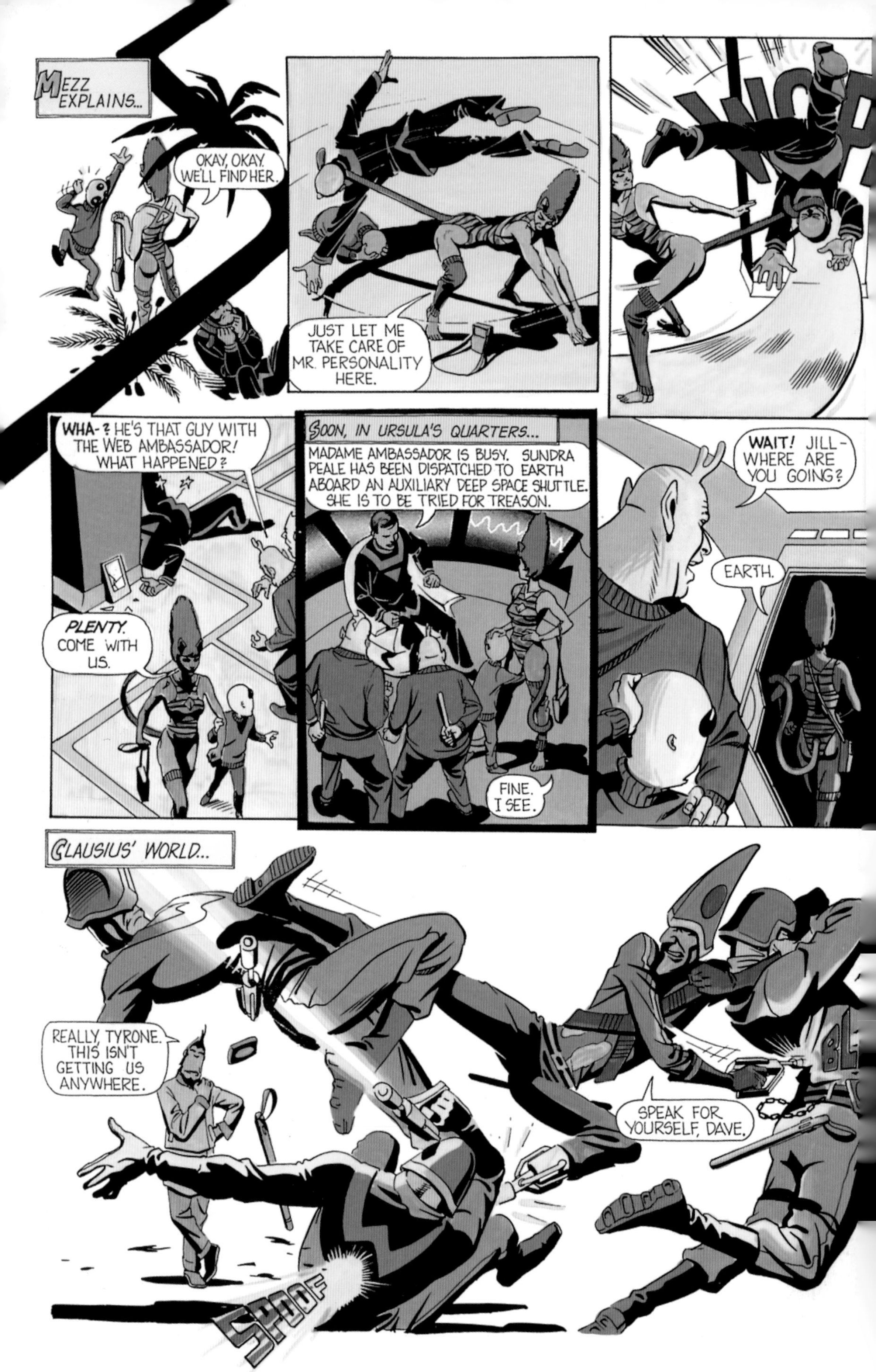
MEZZ EXPLAINS...
OKAY, OKAY. WE'LL FIND HER.
JUST LET ME TAKE CARE OF MR. PERSONALITY HERE.
WHA-? HE'S THAT GUY WITH THE WEB AMBASSADOR! WHAT HAPPENED?
PLENTY. COME WITH US.
SOON, IN URSULA'S QUARTERS...
MADAME AMBASSADOR IS BUSY. SUNDRA PEALE HAS BEEN DISPATCHED TO EARTH ABOARD AN AUXILIARY DEEP SPACE SHUTTLE. SHE IS TO BE TRIED FOR TREASON.
FINE. I SEE.
WAIT! JILL-WHERE ARE YOU GOING?
EARTH.
CLAUSIUS' WORLD...
REALLY, TYRONE. THIS ISN'T GETTING US ANYWHERE.
SPEAK FOR YOURSELF, DAVE.
SPOOF

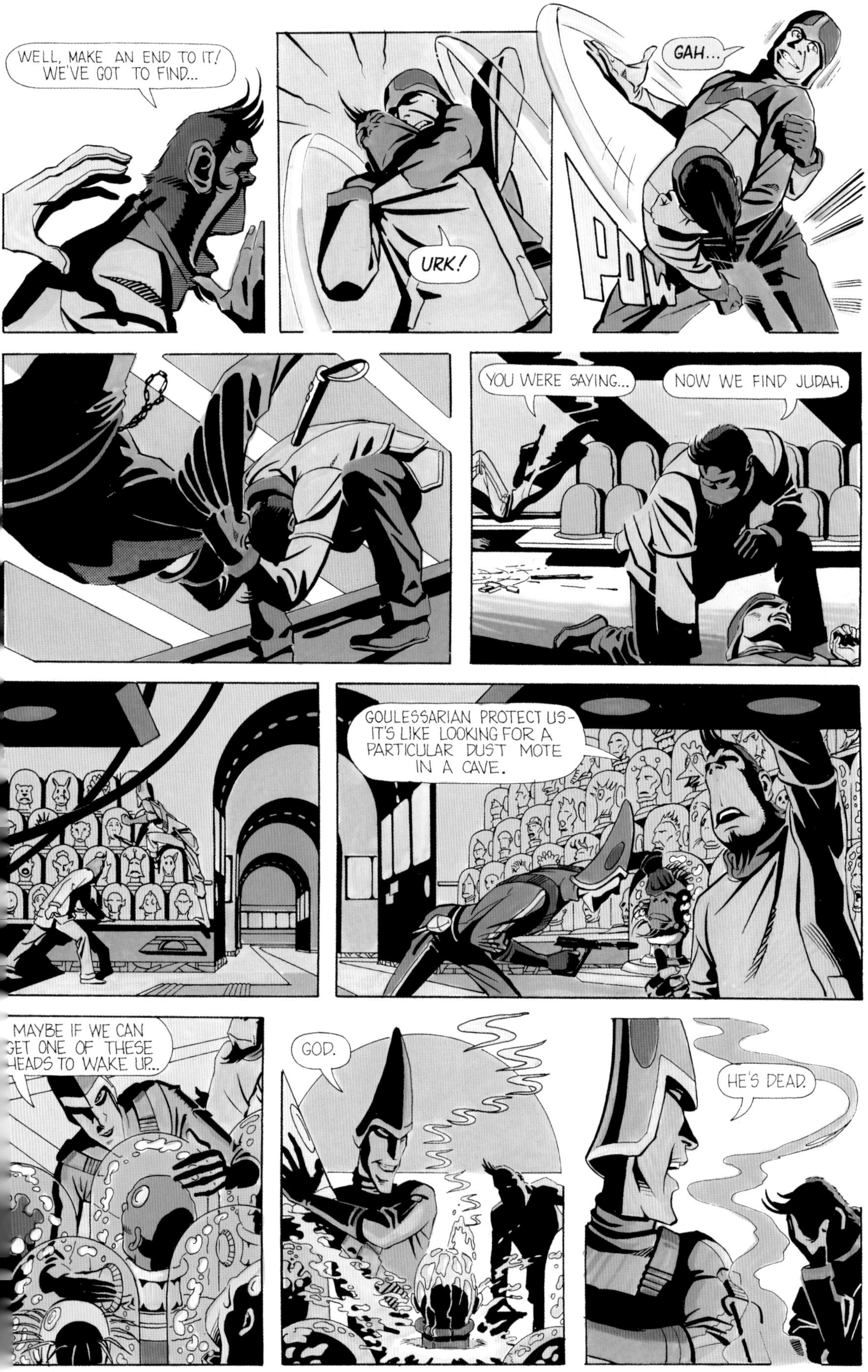
WELL, MAKE AN END TO IT! WE'VE GOT TO FIND...
URK!
GAH...
POW
YOU WERE SAYING...
NOW WE FIND JUDAH.
GOULESSARIAN PROTECT US– IT'S LIKE LOOKING FOR A PARTICULAR DUST MOTE IN A CAVE.
MAYBE IF WE CAN GET ONE OF THESE HEADS TO WAKE UP...
GOD.
HE'S DEAD.

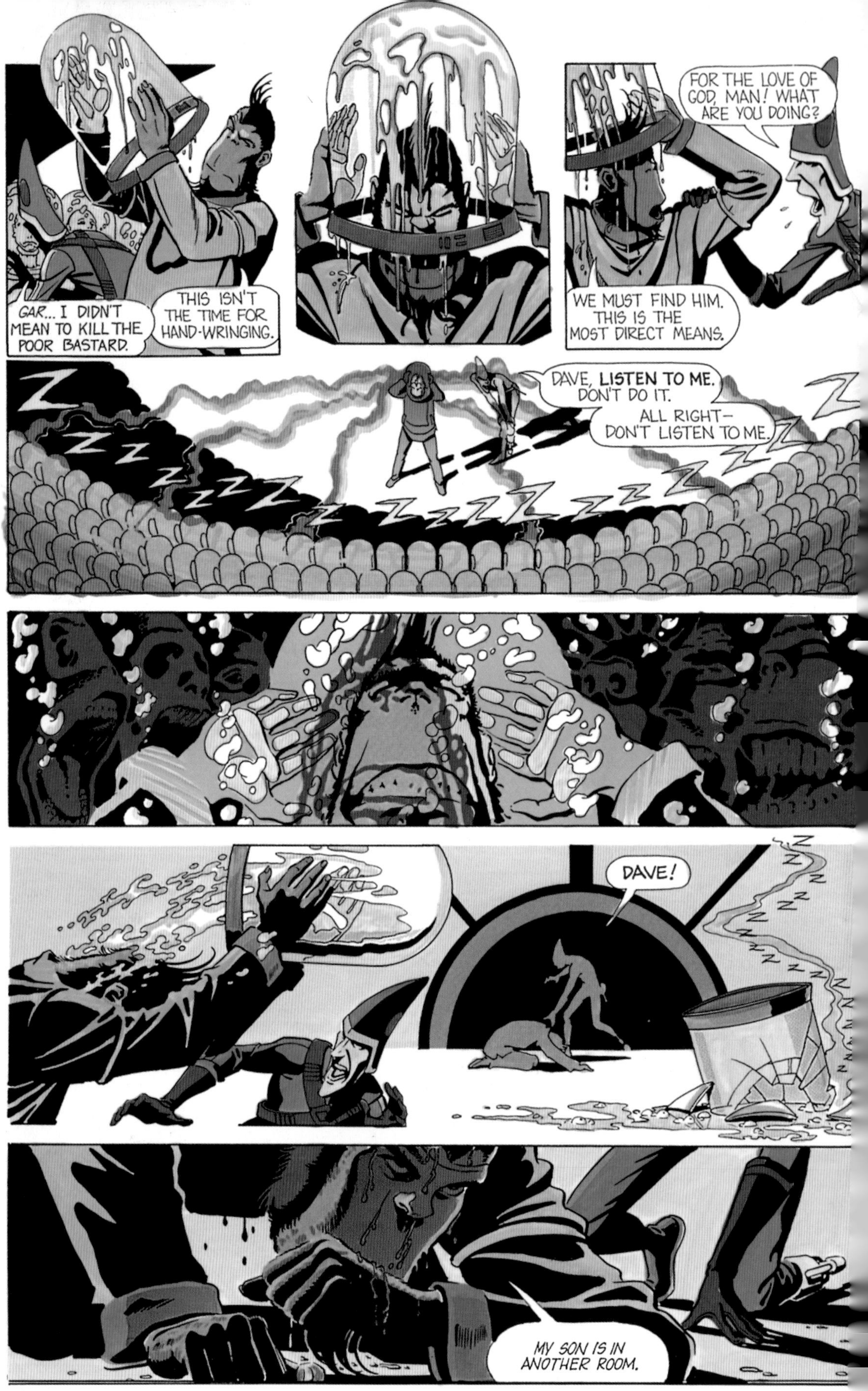
GAR... I DIDN'T MEAN TO KILL THE POOR BASTARD.
THIS ISN'T THE TIME FOR HAND-WRINGING.
FOR THE LOVE OF GOD, MAN! WHAT ARE YOU DOING?
WE MUST FIND HIM. THIS IS THE MOST DIRECT MEANS.
DAVE, **LISTEN TO ME.** DON'T DO IT.
ALL RIGHT— DON'T LISTEN TO ME.
DAVE!
MY SON IS IN ANOTHER ROOM.

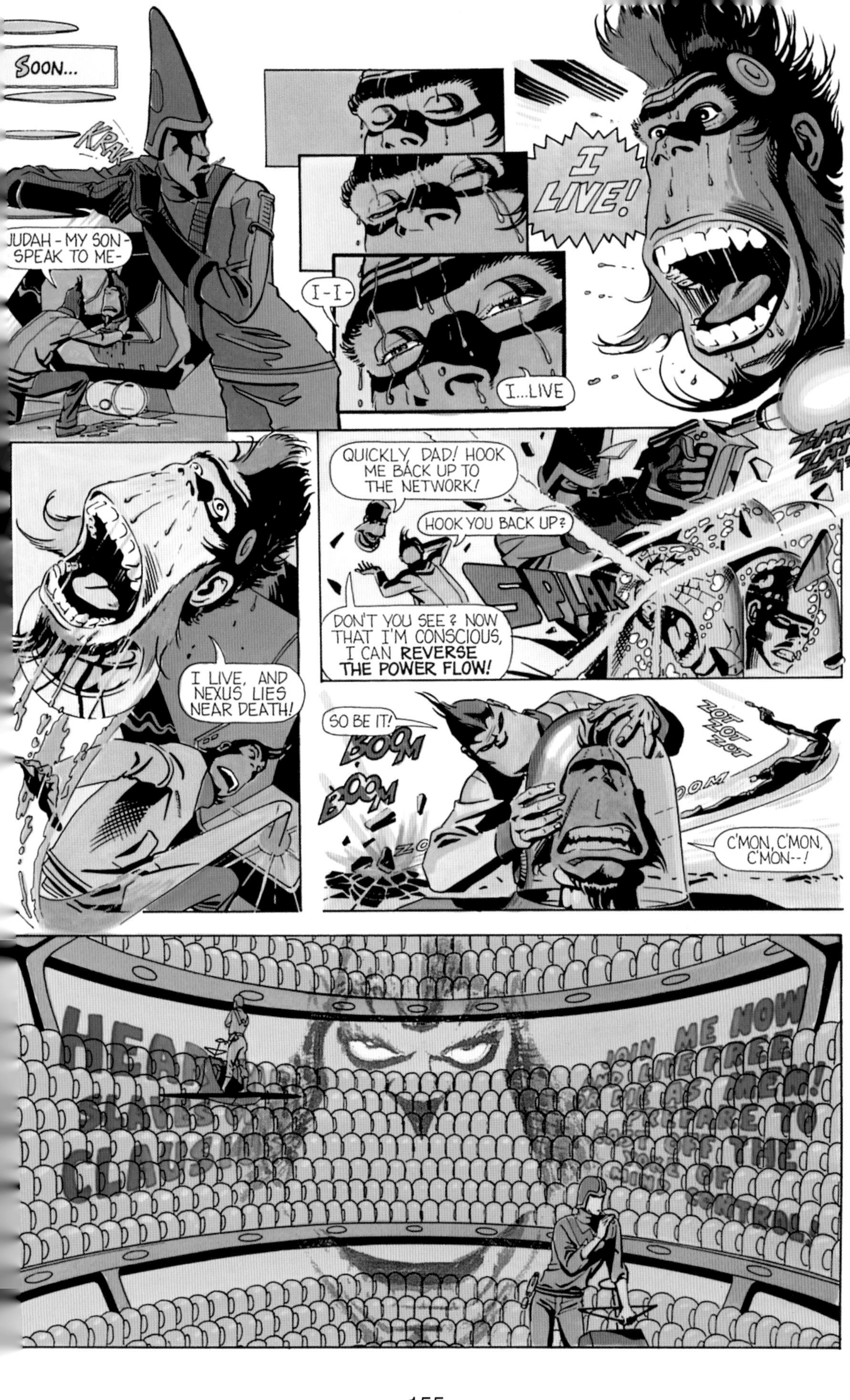
SOON...
KRAK
JUDAH - MY SON - SPEAK TO ME -
I - I -
I...LIVE
I LIVE!
ZLAT ZLAT ZLAT
I LIVE, AND NEXUS LIES NEAR DEATH!
QUICKLY, DAD! HOOK ME BACK UP TO THE NETWORK!
HOOK YOU BACK UP?
DON'T YOU SEE? NOW THAT I'M CONSCIOUS, I CAN REVERSE THE POWER FLOW!
SPLAK
SO BE IT!
BOOM
BOOM
ZOT ZOT ZOT
C'MON, C'MON, C'MON--!
JOIN ME NOW

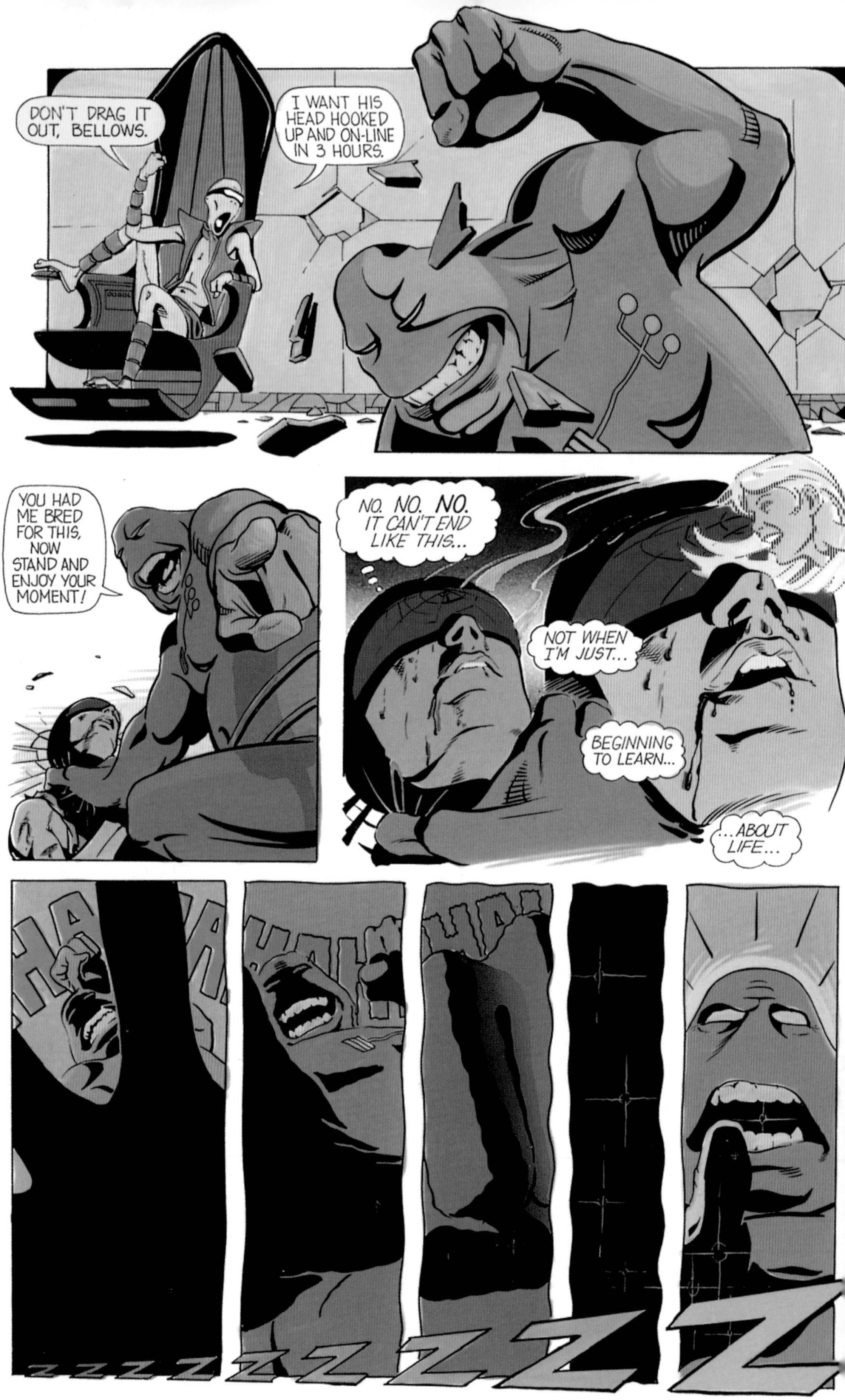
DON'T DRAG IT OUT, BELLOWS.
I WANT HIS HEAD HOOKED UP AND ON-LINE IN 3 HOURS.
YOU HAD ME BRED FOR THIS, NOW STAND AND ENJOY YOUR MOMENT!
NO. NO. NO. IT CAN'T END LIKE THIS...
NOT WHEN I'M JUST...
BEGINNING TO LEARN...
...ABOUT LIFE...

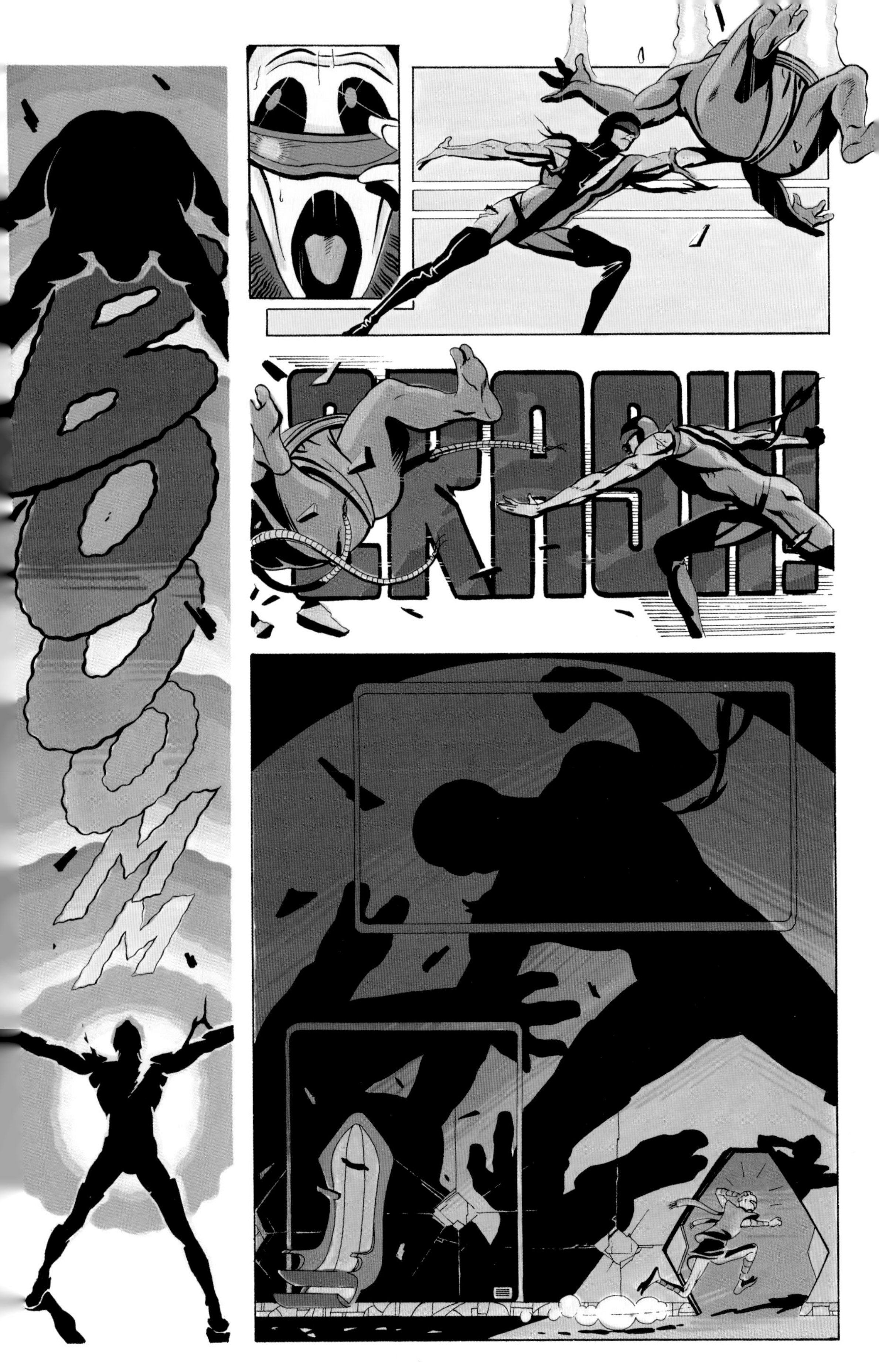
BOOOMM
CRASH!

THIS UNIT IS A WRITE-OFF...

HIT IT, ZUBIN! DON'T WAIT FOR ME TO GET STRAPPED IN!

YES, SIR.

DESTRUCT! DESTRUCT! WHY WON'T THE FURSHLUGGINER THING DESTRUCT?!

KLIK KLIK KLIK

I KNEW THERE HAD TO BE A DESTRUCT PROGRAM.

THIS DEA
SHIP HA
A BRID
WE'LL FI
NEXUS T

YOU SAVED MY LIFE.

AS YOU SAVED MINE.

BUT... A **MILLION** OF THEM! WHAT WILL BECOME OF THEM?

DON'T WORRY ABOUT THE HEADS. FREED OF CLAUSIUS' CONTROL, ARMED WITH THEIR HELLISH GIFT, THEY WILL RECREATE THEIR LIVES HERE.

OR LEAVE, AS THEY WISH.

...OR PERHAPS EVEN JOIN ME IN MY QUEST.

158

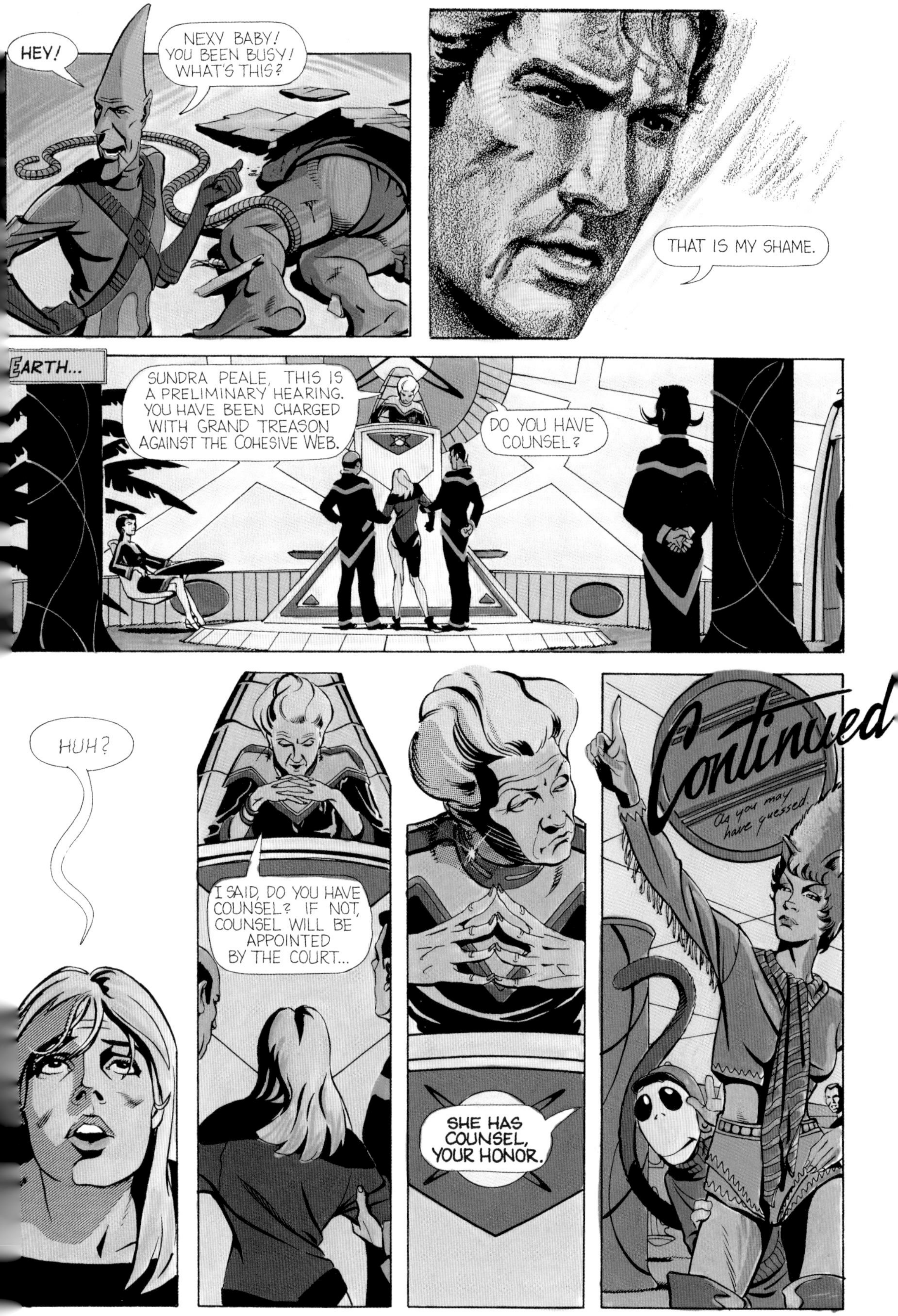
HEY!
NEXY BABY! YOU BEEN BUSY! WHAT'S THIS?
THAT IS MY SHAME.
EARTH...
SUNDRA PEALE, THIS IS A PRELIMINARY HEARING. YOU HAVE BEEN CHARGED WITH GRAND TREASON AGAINST THE COHESIVE WEB.
DO YOU HAVE COUNSEL?
HUH?
I SAID, DO YOU HAVE COUNSEL? IF NOT, COUNSEL WILL BE APPOINTED BY THE COURT...
SHE HAS COUNSEL, YOUR HONOR.
Continued
As you may have guessed.

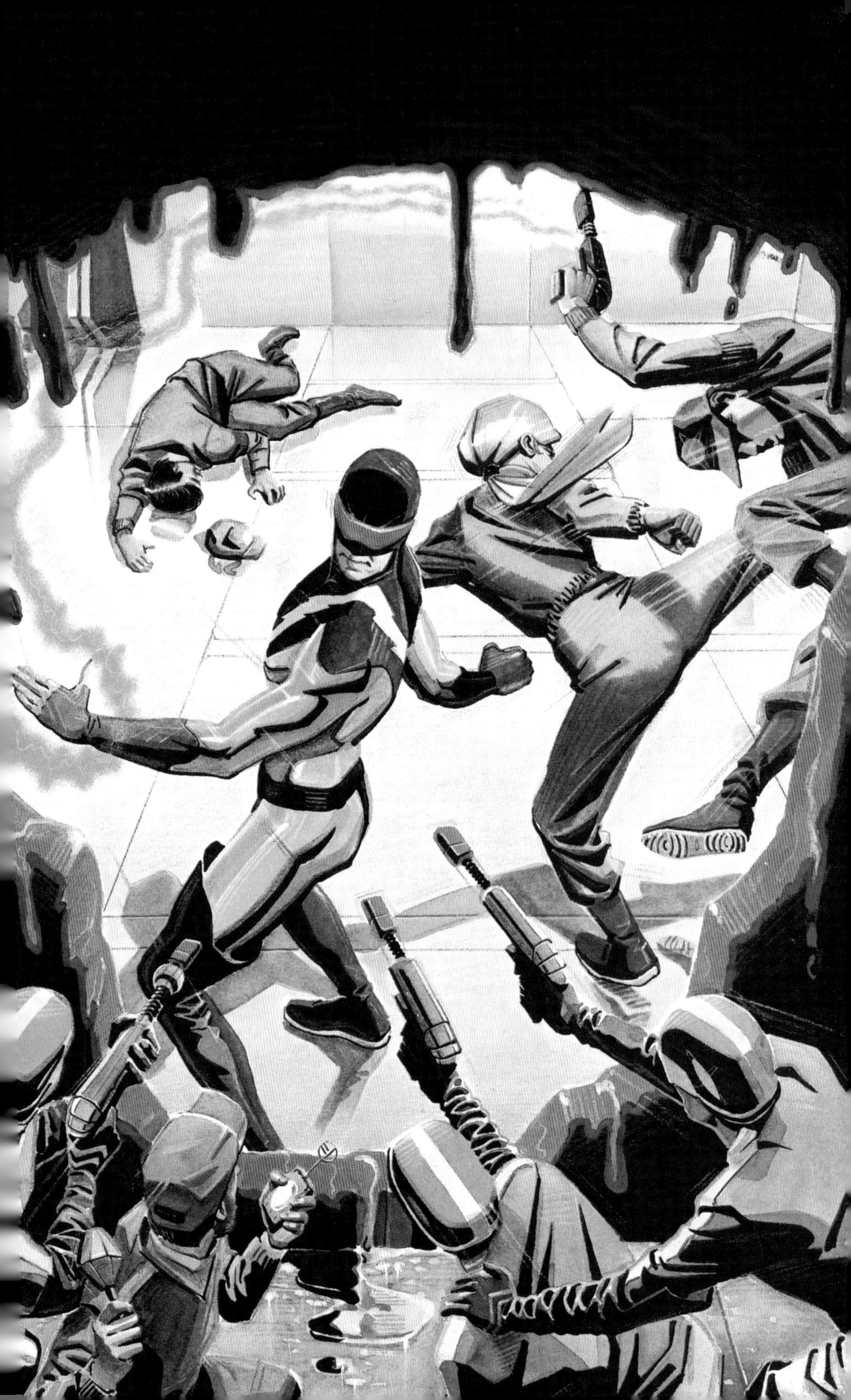

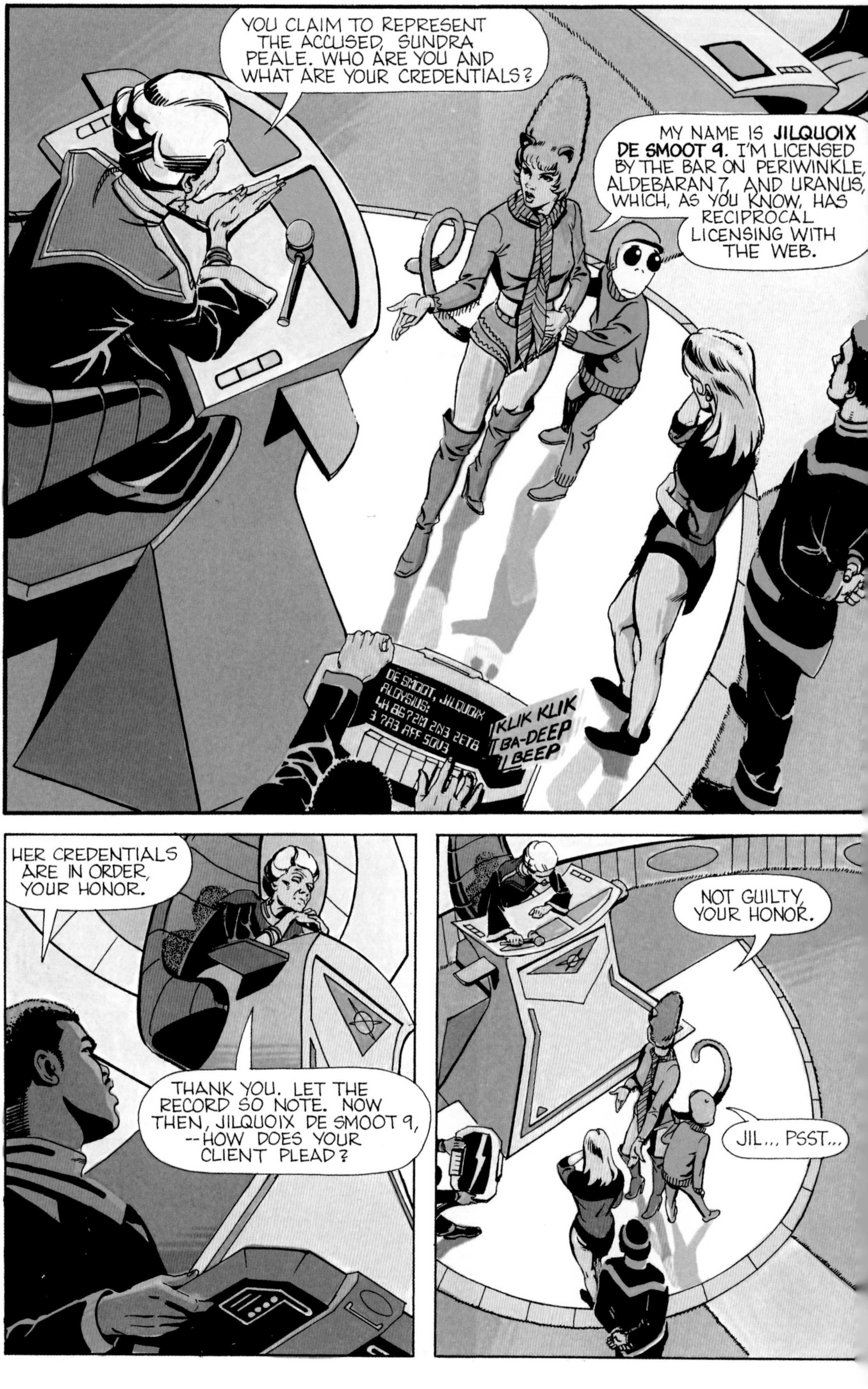
YOU CLAIM TO REPRESENT THE ACCUSED, SUNDRA PEALE. WHO ARE YOU AND WHAT ARE YOUR CREDENTIALS?
MY NAME IS **JILQUOIX DE SMOOT 9**. I'M LICENSED BY THE BAR ON PERIWINKLE, ALDEBARAN 7, AND URANUS, WHICH, AS YOU KNOW, HAS RECIPROCAL LICENSING WITH THE WEB.
DE SMOOT, JILQUOIX ALOYSIUS:
KLIK KLIK BA-DEEP BEEP
HER CREDENTIALS ARE IN ORDER, YOUR HONOR.
THANK YOU. LET THE RECORD SO NOTE. NOW THEN, JILQUOIX DE SMOOT 9, --HOW DOES YOUR CLIENT PLEAD?
NOT GUILTY, YOUR HONOR.
JIL... PSST...

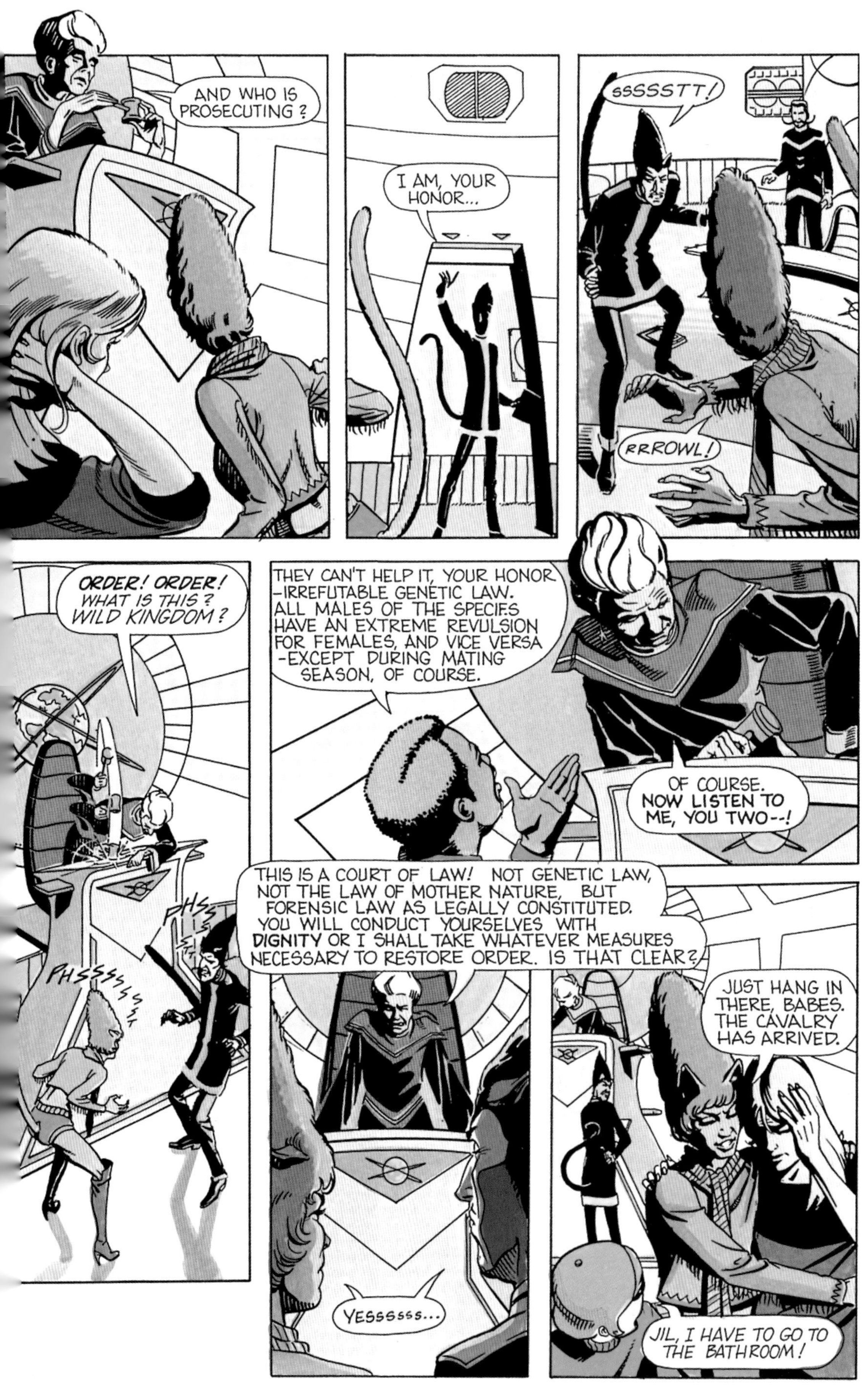
AND WHO IS PROSECUTING ?
I AM, YOUR HONOR...
SSSSSTT!
RRROWL!
ORDER! ORDER! WHAT IS THIS? WILD KINGDOM?
THEY CAN'T HELP IT, YOUR HONOR -IRREFUTABLE GENETIC LAW. ALL MALES OF THE SPECIES HAVE AN EXTREME REVULSION FOR FEMALES, AND VICE VERSA -EXCEPT DURING MATING SEASON, OF COURSE.
OF COURSE. NOW LISTEN TO ME, YOU TWO--!
PHSSS
PHSSSSSSS
THIS IS A COURT OF LAW! NOT GENETIC LAW, NOT THE LAW OF MOTHER NATURE, BUT FORENSIC LAW AS LEGALLY CONSTITUTED. YOU WILL CONDUCT YOURSELVES WITH DIGNITY OR I SHALL TAKE WHATEVER MEASURES NECESSARY TO RESTORE ORDER. IS THAT CLEAR?
YESSSSSS...
JUST HANG IN THERE, BABES. THE CAVALRY HAS ARRIVED.
JIL, I HAVE TO GO TO THE BATHROOM!

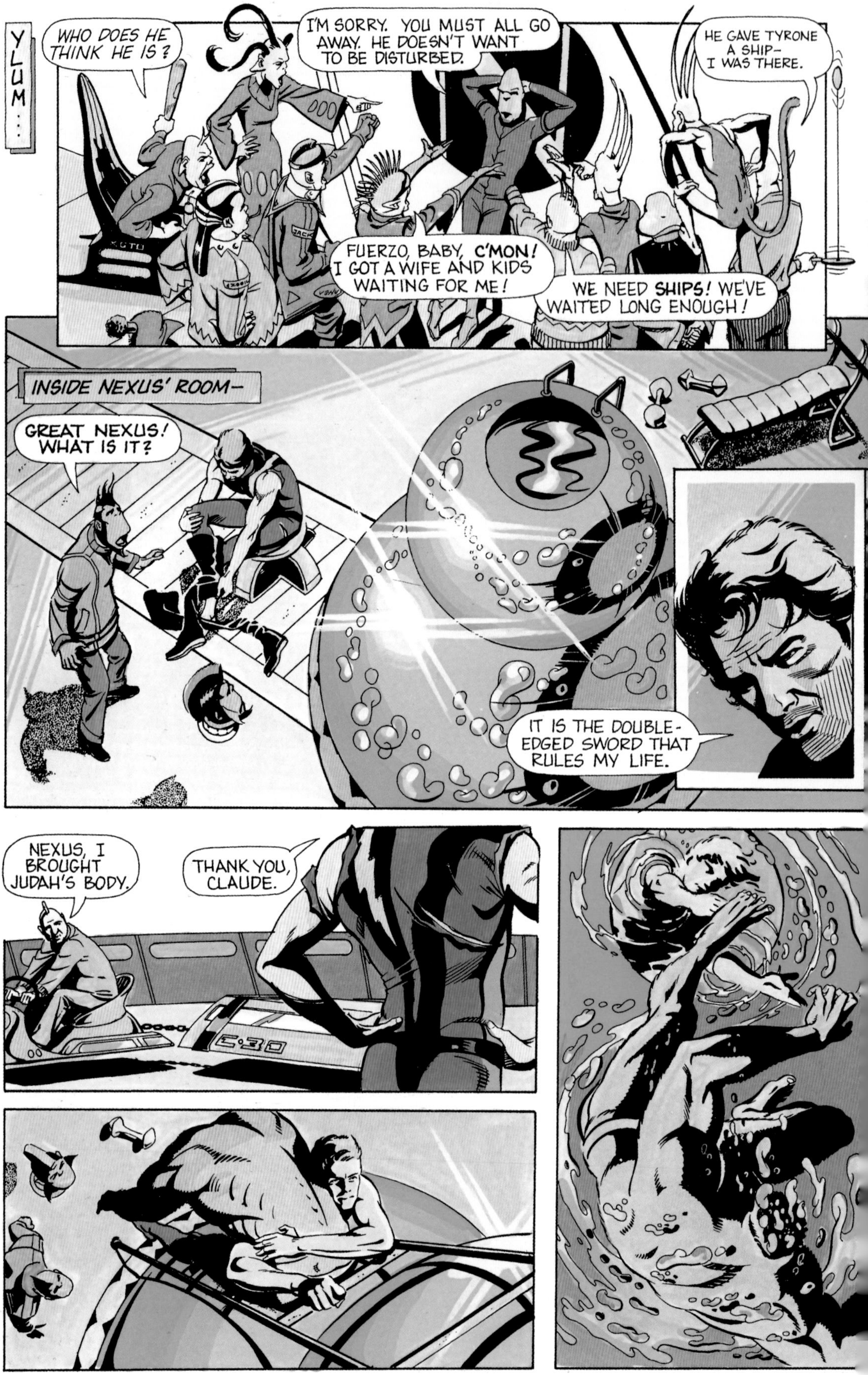
YLUM...
WHO DOES HE THINK HE IS?
I'M SORRY. YOU MUST ALL GO AWAY. HE DOESN'T WANT TO BE DISTURBED.
HE GAVE TYRONE A SHIP-- I WAS THERE.
FUERZO, BABY, C'MON! I GOT A WIFE AND KIDS WAITING FOR ME!
WE NEED SHIPS! WE'VE WAITED LONG ENOUGH!
INSIDE NEXUS' ROOM--
GREAT NEXUS! WHAT IS IT?
IT IS THE DOUBLE-EDGED SWORD THAT RULES MY LIFE.
NEXUS, I BROUGHT JUDAH'S BODY.
THANK YOU, CLAUDE.

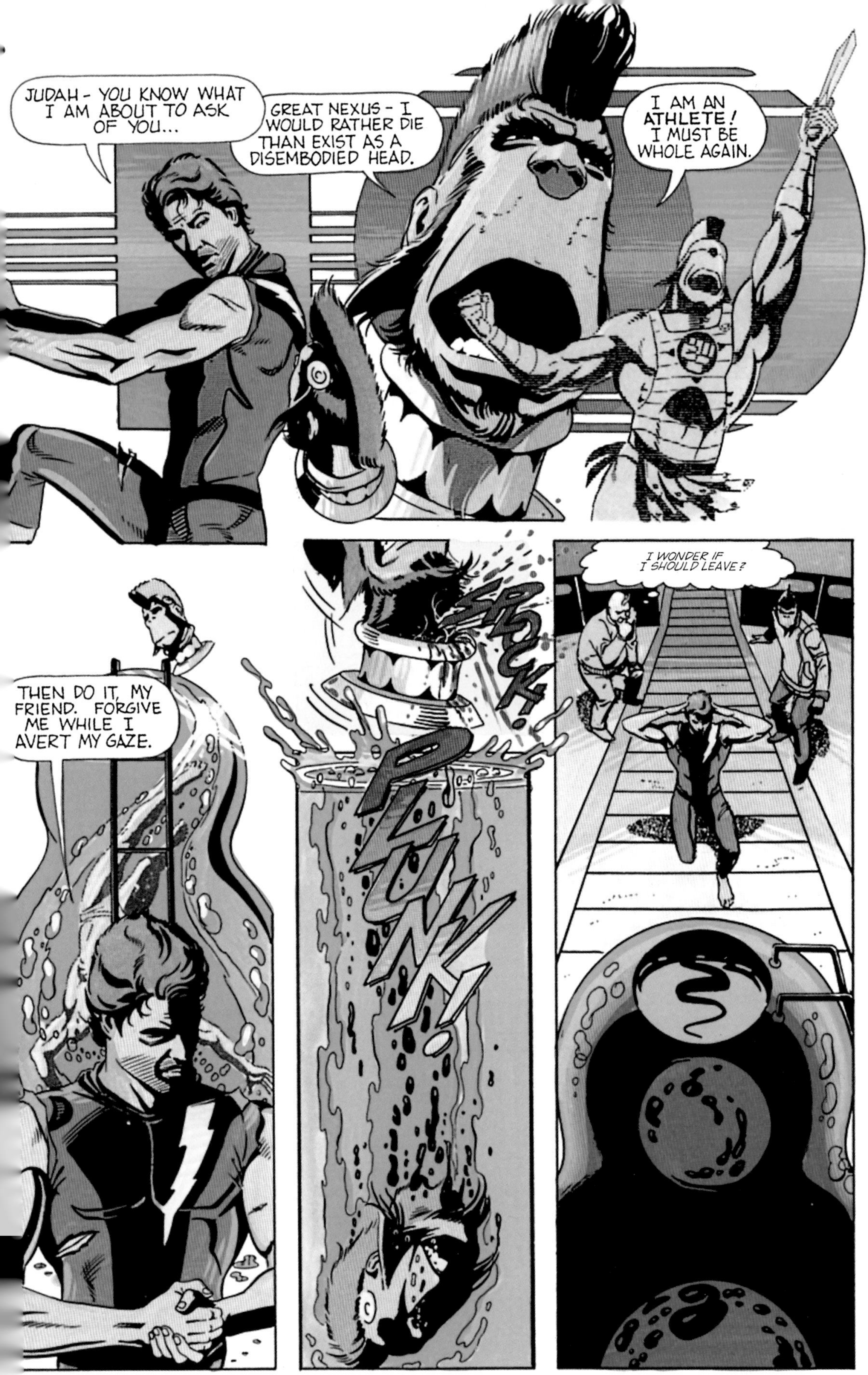
JUDAH - YOU KNOW WHAT I AM ABOUT TO ASK OF YOU...
GREAT NEXUS - I WOULD RATHER DIE THAN EXIST AS A DISEMBODIED HEAD.
I AM AN ATHLETE! I MUST BE WHOLE AGAIN.
THEN DO IT, MY FRIEND. FORGIVE ME WHILE I AVERT MY GAZE.
SPOCK!
PLUNK!
I WONDER IF I SHOULD LEAVE?

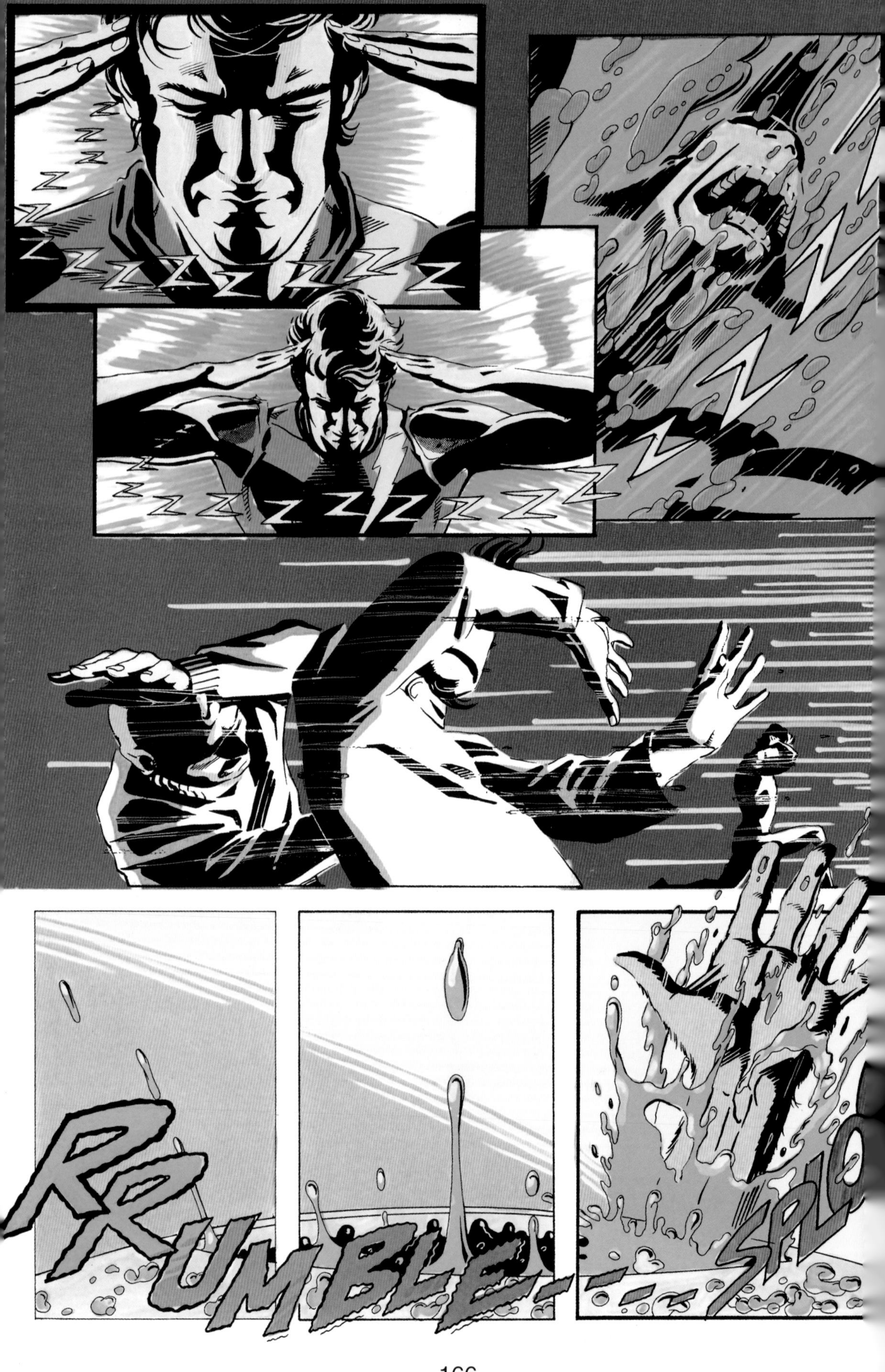
RRUMBLE--SPLO

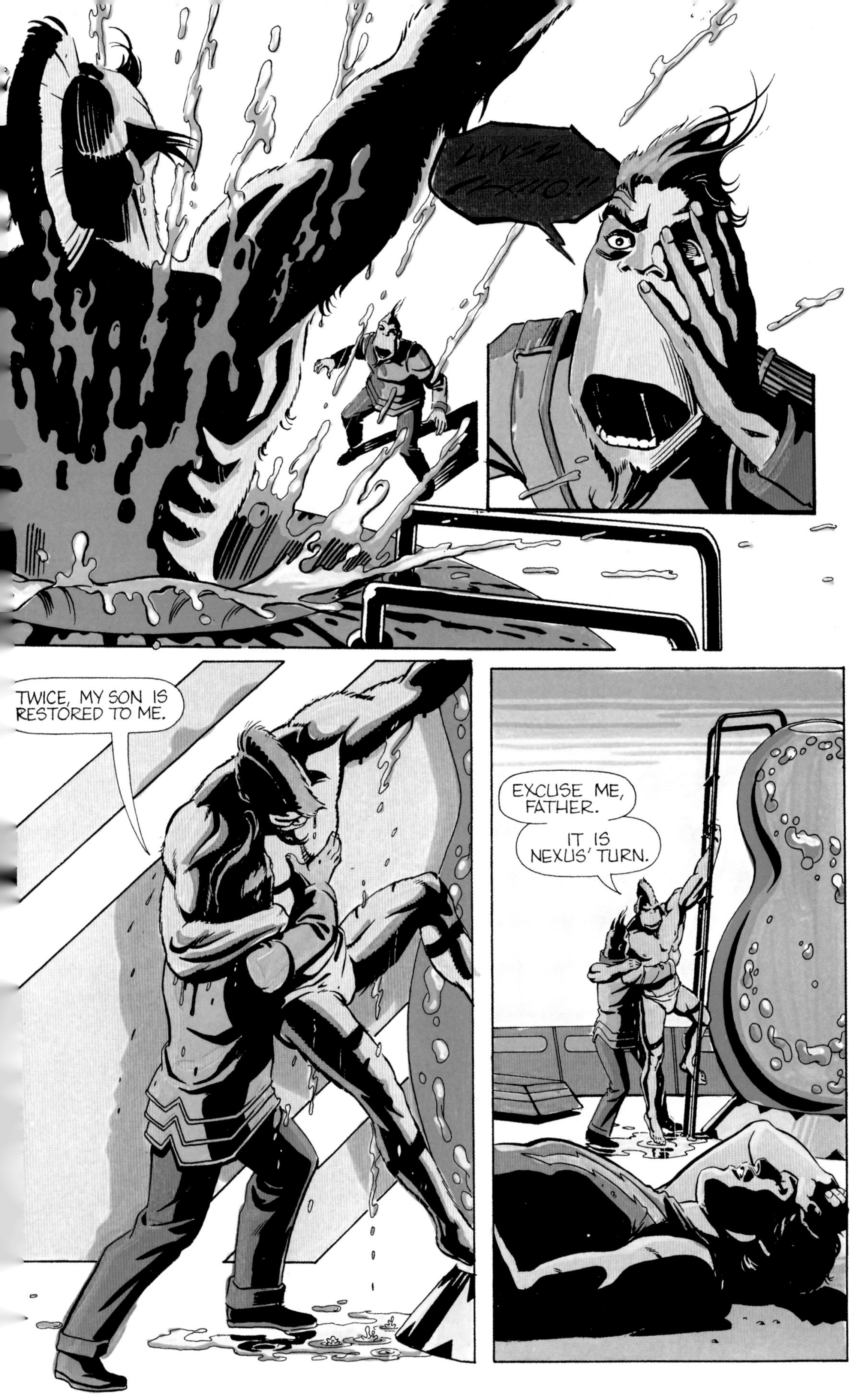
TWICE, MY SON IS RESTORED TO ME.
EXCUSE ME, FATHER.
IT IS NEXUS' TURN.

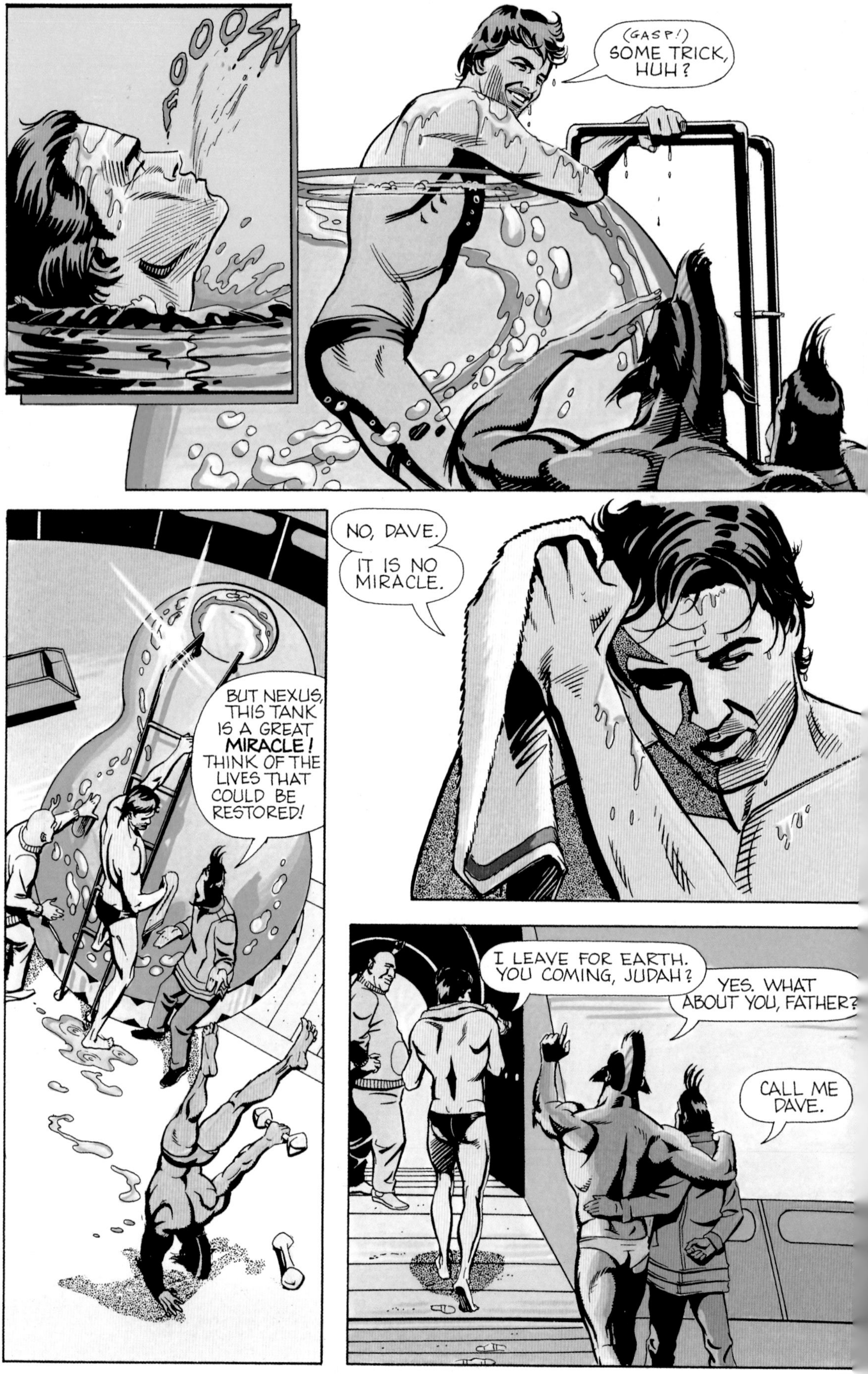
FOOOSH
(GASP!) SOME TRICK, HUH?
NO, DAVE.
IT IS NO MIRACLE.
BUT NEXUS, THIS TANK IS A GREAT **MIRACLE!** THINK OF THE LIVES THAT COULD BE RESTORED!
I LEAVE FOR EARTH. YOU COMING, JUDAH?
YES. WHAT ABOUT YOU, FATHER?
CALL ME DAVE.

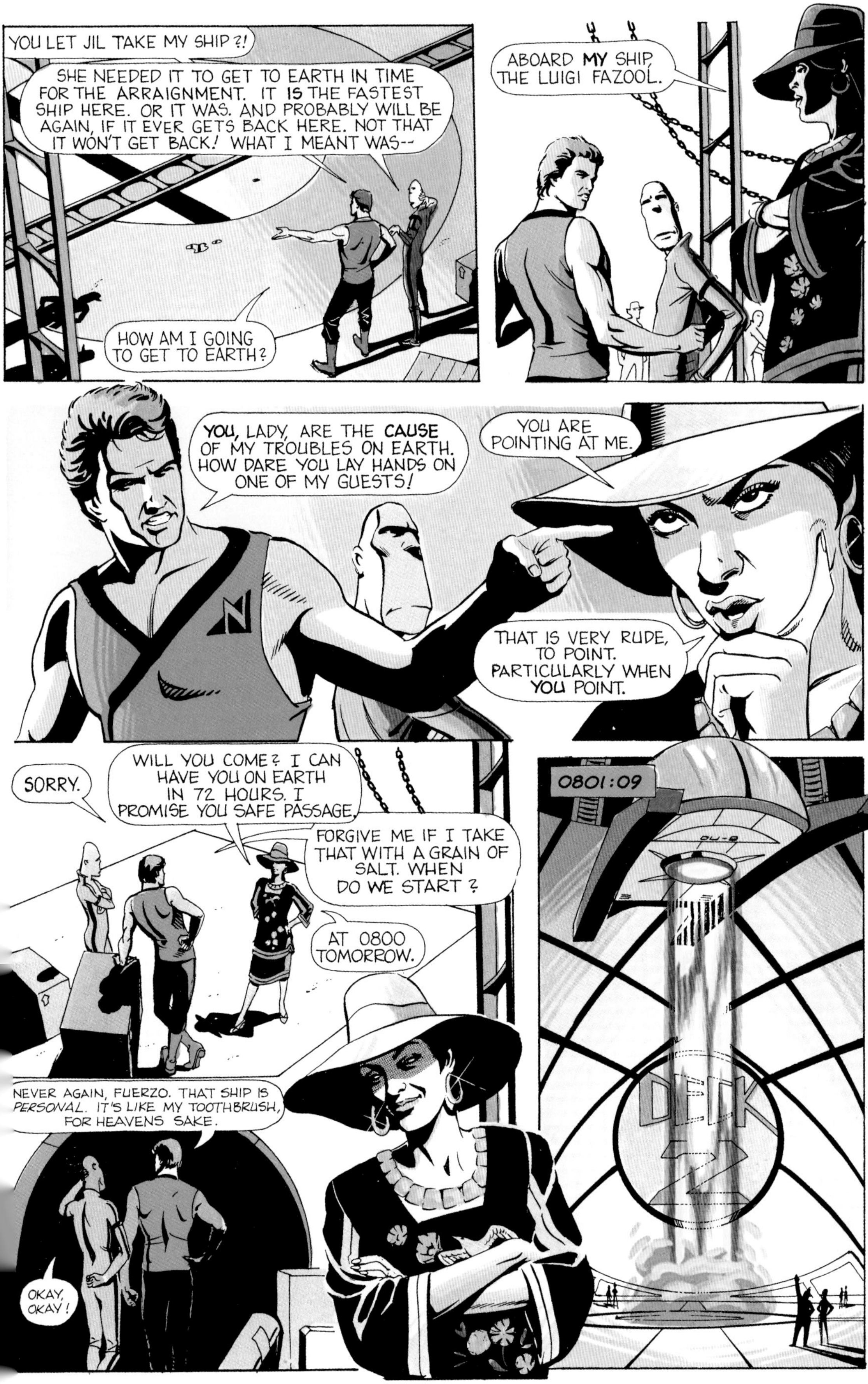
YOU LET JIL TAKE MY SHIP ?!
SHE NEEDED IT TO GET TO EARTH IN TIME FOR THE ARRAIGNMENT. IT IS THE FASTEST SHIP HERE. OR IT WAS. AND PROBABLY WILL BE AGAIN, IF IT EVER GETS BACK HERE. NOT THAT IT WON'T GET BACK! WHAT I MEANT WAS--
HOW AM I GOING TO GET TO EARTH?
ABOARD MY SHIP, THE LUIGI FAZOOL.
YOU, LADY, ARE THE CAUSE OF MY TROUBLES ON EARTH. HOW DARE YOU LAY HANDS ON ONE OF MY GUESTS!
YOU ARE POINTING AT ME.
THAT IS VERY RUDE, TO POINT. PARTICULARLY WHEN YOU POINT.
SORRY.
WILL YOU COME? I CAN HAVE YOU ON EARTH IN 72 HOURS. I PROMISE YOU SAFE PASSAGE.
FORGIVE ME IF I TAKE THAT WITH A GRAIN OF SALT. WHEN DO WE START?
AT 0800 TOMORROW.
NEVER AGAIN, FUERZO. THAT SHIP IS PERSONAL. IT'S LIKE MY TOOTHBRUSH, FOR HEAVENS SAKE.
OKAY, OKAY!
0801:09
DECK

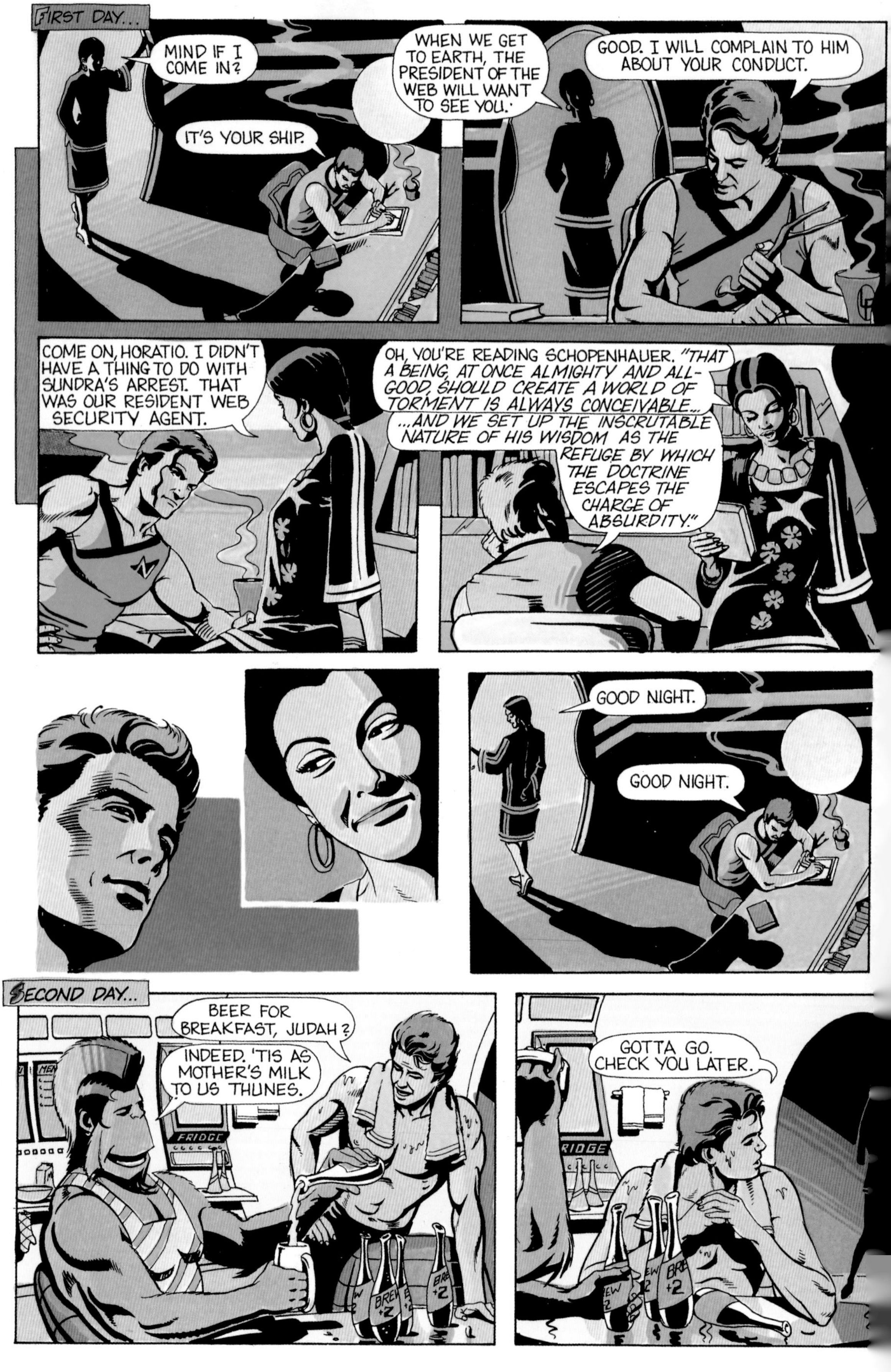
FIRST DAY...
MIND IF I COME IN?
IT'S YOUR SHIP.
WHEN WE GET TO EARTH, THE PRESIDENT OF THE WEB WILL WANT TO SEE YOU.
GOOD. I WILL COMPLAIN TO HIM ABOUT YOUR CONDUCT.
COME ON, HORATIO. I DIDN'T HAVE A THING TO DO WITH SUNDRA'S ARREST. THAT WAS OUR RESIDENT WEB SECURITY AGENT.
OH, YOU'RE READING SCHOPENHAUER. "THAT A BEING, AT ONCE ALMIGHTY AND ALL-GOOD, SHOULD CREATE A WORLD OF TORMENT IS ALWAYS CONCEIVABLE...
...AND WE SET UP THE INSCRUTABLE NATURE OF HIS WISDOM AS THE REFUGE BY WHICH THE DOCTRINE ESCAPES THE CHARGE OF ABSURDITY."
GOOD NIGHT.
GOOD NIGHT.
SECOND DAY...
BEER FOR BREAKFAST, JUDAH?
INDEED. 'TIS AS MOTHER'S MILK TO US THUNES.
GOTTA GO. CHECK YOU LATER.

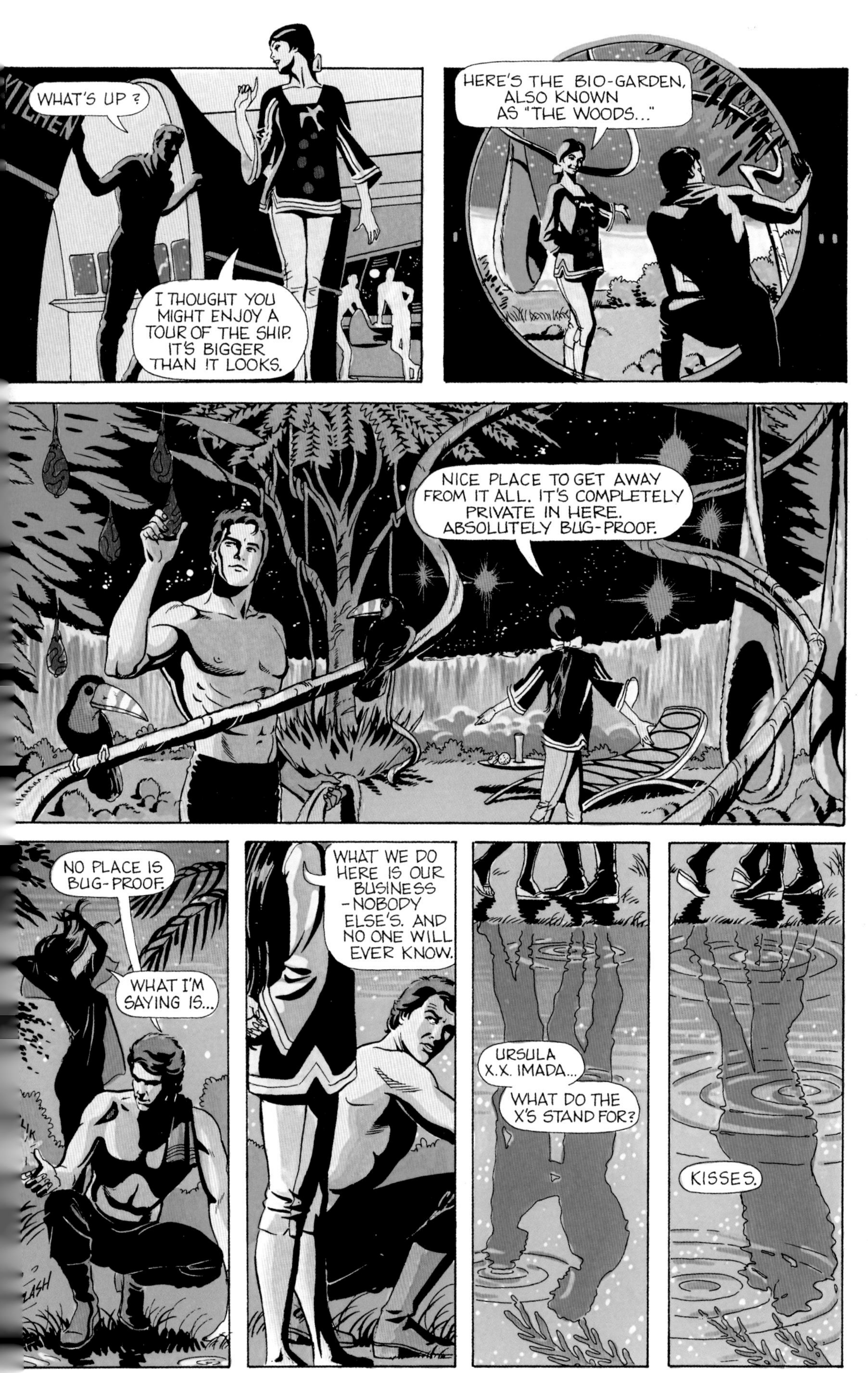
WHAT'S UP?
I THOUGHT YOU MIGHT ENJOY A TOUR OF THE SHIP. IT'S BIGGER THAN IT LOOKS.
HERE'S THE BIO-GARDEN, ALSO KNOWN AS "THE WOODS..."
NICE PLACE TO GET AWAY FROM IT ALL. IT'S COMPLETELY PRIVATE IN HERE. ABSOLUTELY BUG-PROOF.
NO PLACE IS BUG-PROOF.
WHAT I'M SAYING IS...
WHAT WE DO HERE IS OUR BUSINESS -NOBODY ELSE'S. AND NO ONE WILL EVER KNOW.
URSULA X.X. IMADA...
WHAT DO THE X'S STAND FOR?
KISSES.

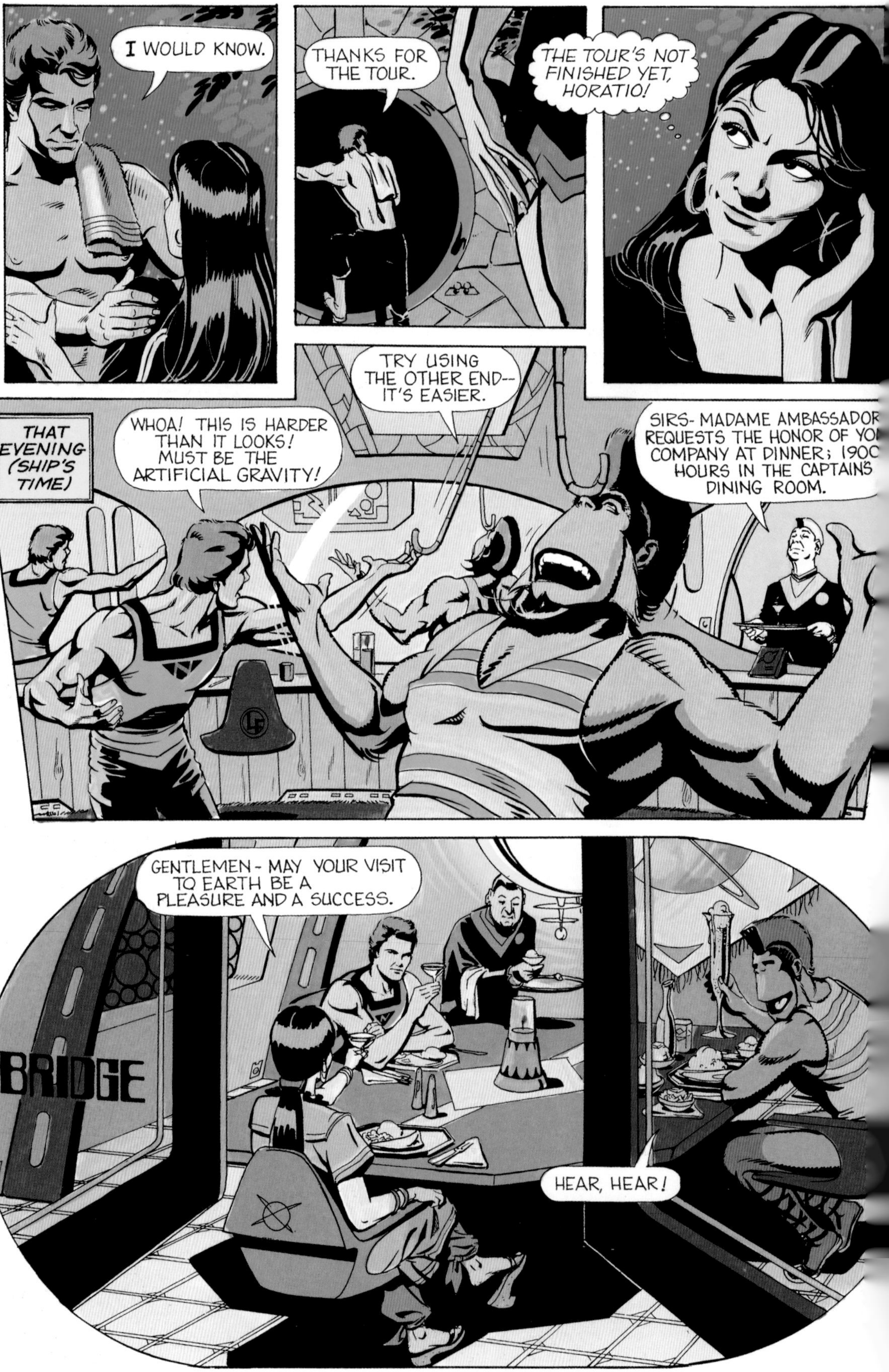
I WOULD KNOW.
THANKS FOR THE TOUR.
THE TOUR'S NOT FINISHED YET, HORATIO!
THAT EVENING (SHIP'S TIME)
WHOA! THIS IS HARDER THAN IT LOOKS! MUST BE THE ARTIFICIAL GRAVITY!
TRY USING THE OTHER END-- IT'S EASIER.
SIRS- MADAME AMBASSADOR REQUESTS THE HONOR OF YO COMPANY AT DINNER; 190C HOURS IN THE CAPTAIN'S DINING ROOM.
GENTLEMEN - MAY YOUR VISIT TO EARTH BE A PLEASURE AND A SUCCESS.
BRIDGE
HEAR, HEAR!

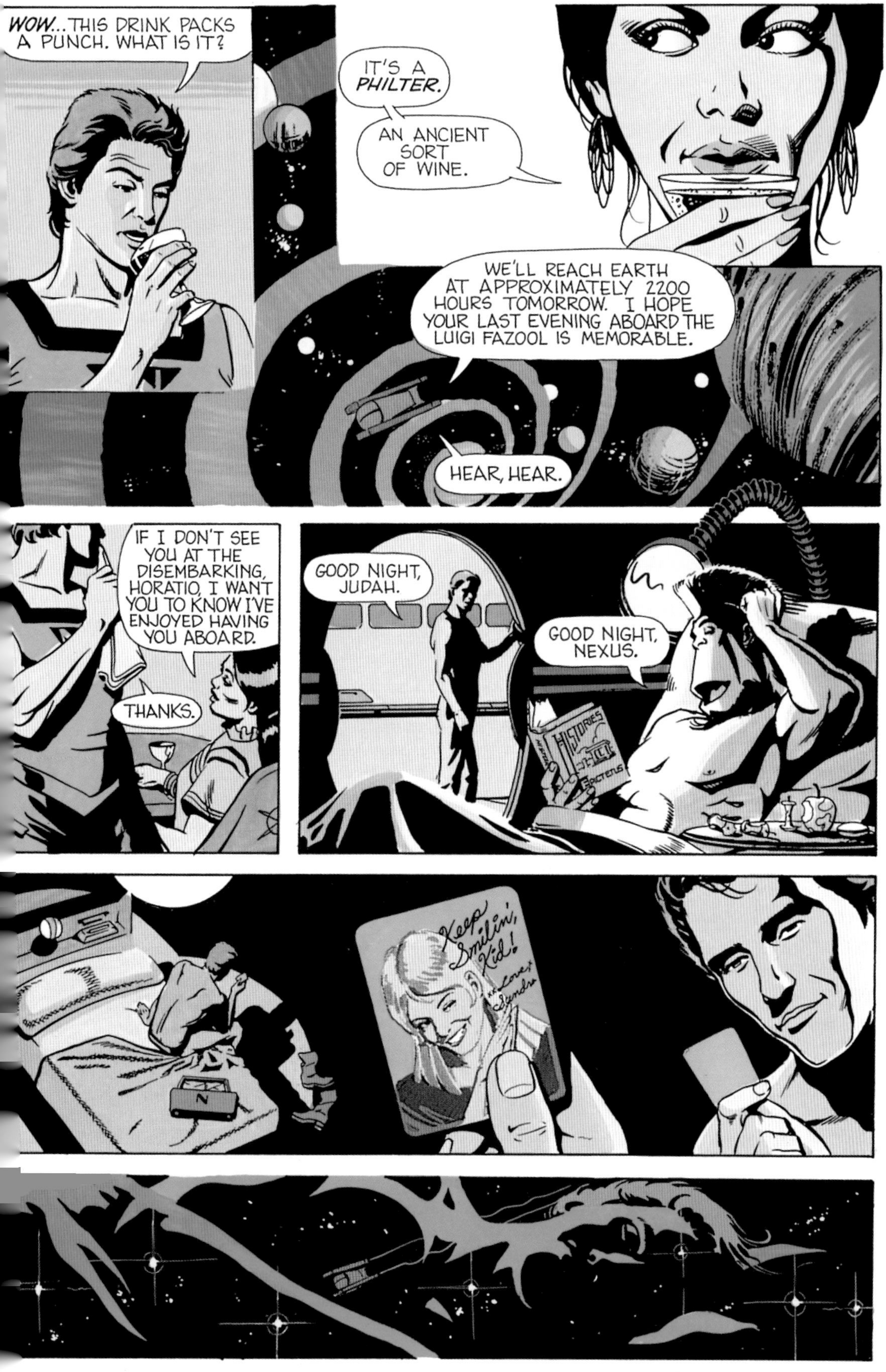
WOW... THIS DRINK PACKS A PUNCH. WHAT IS IT?
IT'S A PHILTER.
AN ANCIENT SORT OF WINE.
WE'LL REACH EARTH AT APPROXIMATELY 2200 HOURS TOMORROW. I HOPE YOUR LAST EVENING ABOARD THE LUIGI FAZOOL IS MEMORABLE.
HEAR, HEAR.
IF I DON'T SEE YOU AT THE DISEMBARKING, HORATIO, I WANT YOU TO KNOW I'VE ENJOYED HAVING YOU ABOARD.
THANKS.
GOOD NIGHT, JUDAH.
GOOD NIGHT, NEXUS.
HISTORIES
EPICTETUS
Keep Smilin', Kid!
Love, Sandra

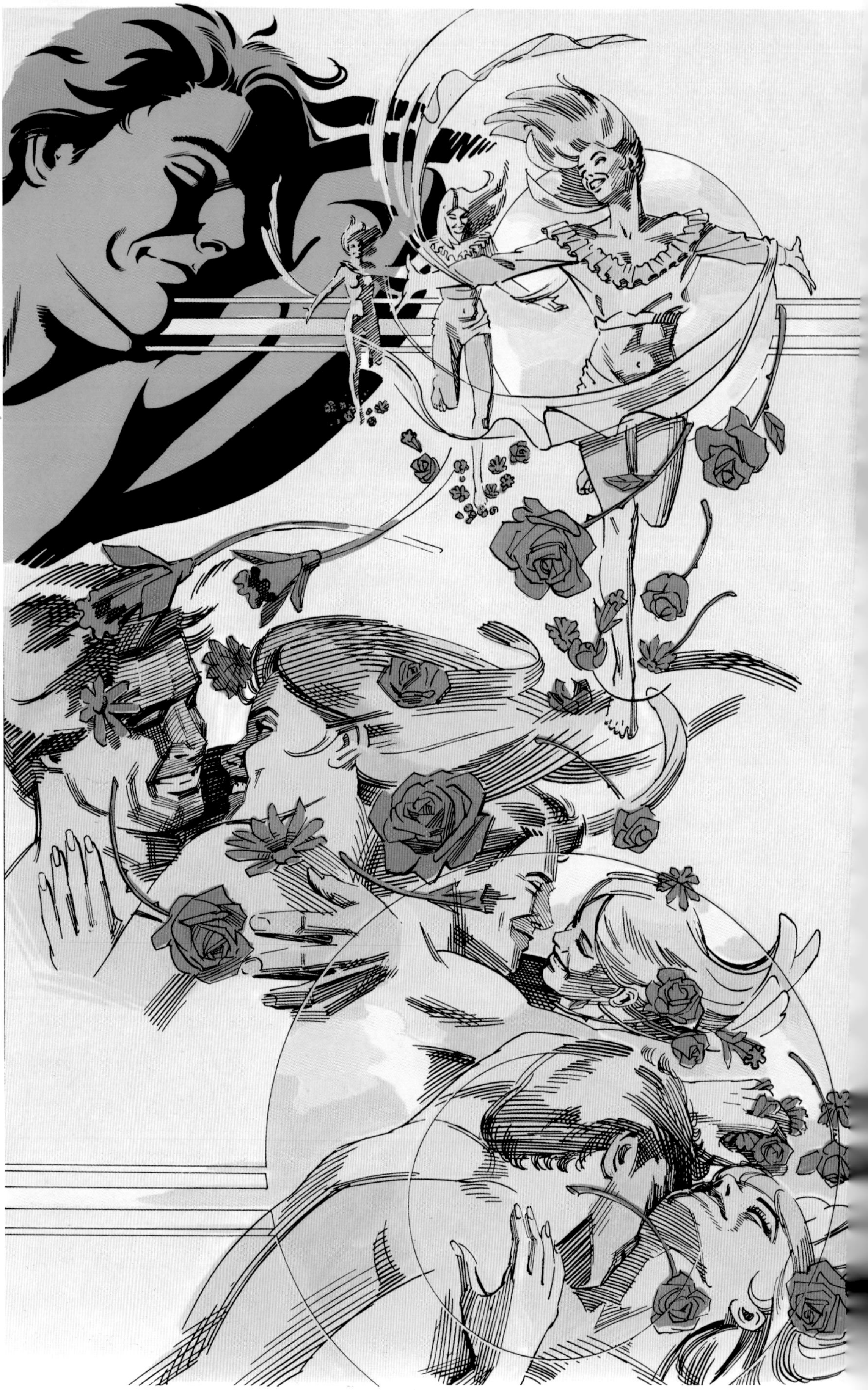

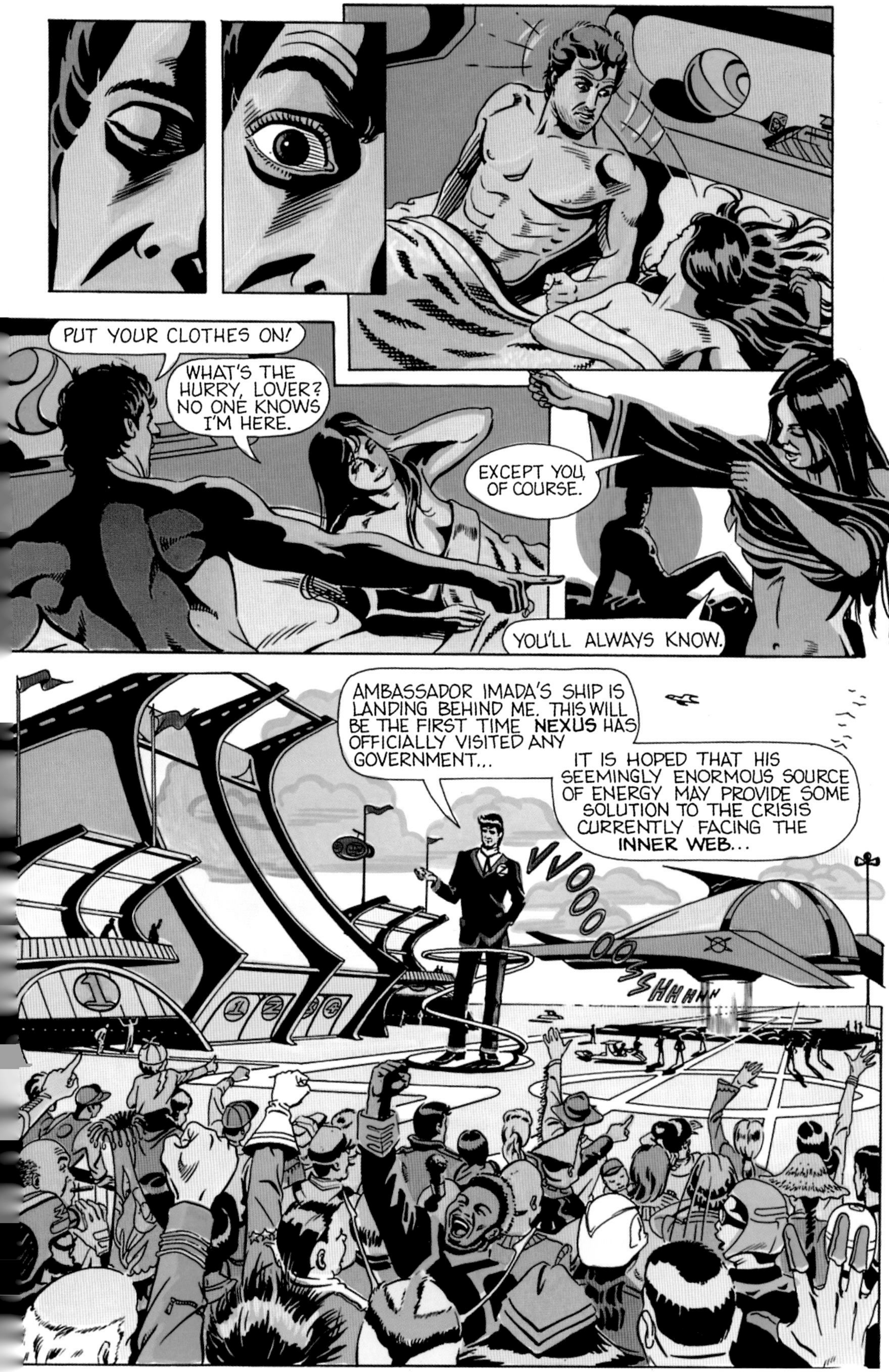
PUT YOUR CLOTHES ON!
WHAT'S THE HURRY, LOVER? NO ONE KNOWS I'M HERE.
EXCEPT YOU, OF COURSE.
YOU'LL ALWAYS KNOW.
AMBASSADOR IMADA'S SHIP IS LANDING BEHIND ME. THIS WILL BE THE FIRST TIME NEXUS HAS OFFICIALLY VISITED ANY GOVERNMENT...
IT IS HOPED THAT HIS SEEMINGLY ENORMOUS SOURCE OF ENERGY MAY PROVIDE SOME SOLUTION TO THE CRISIS CURRENTLY FACING THE INNER WEB...
VVOOOOOSHHHHN

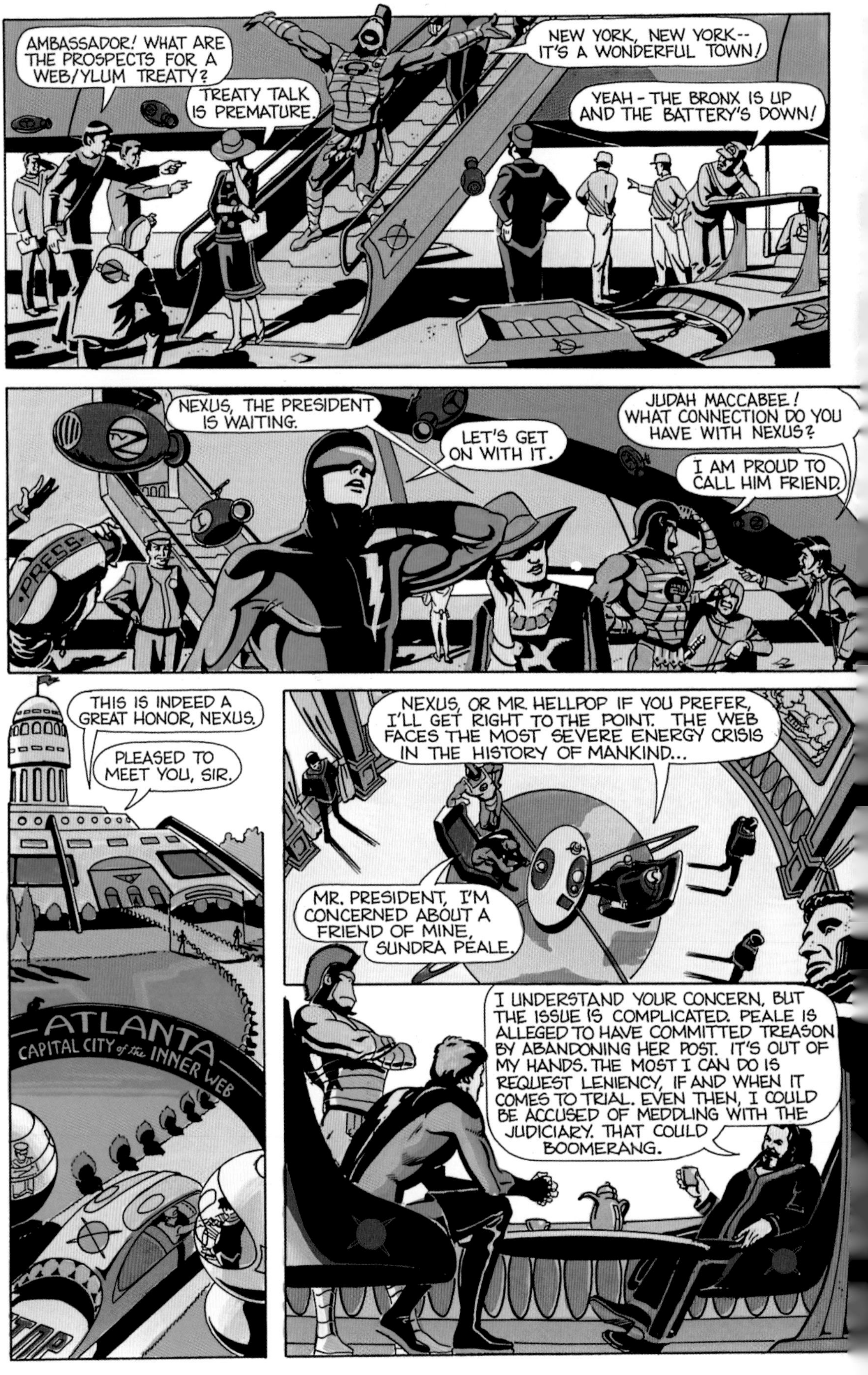
AMBASSADOR! WHAT ARE THE PROSPECTS FOR A WEB/YLUM TREATY?
TREATY TALK IS PREMATURE.
NEW YORK, NEW YORK-- IT'S A WONDERFUL TOWN!
YEAH - THE BRONX IS UP AND THE BATTERY'S DOWN!
NEXUS, THE PRESIDENT IS WAITING.
LET'S GET ON WITH IT.
JUDAH MACCABEE! WHAT CONNECTION DO YOU HAVE WITH NEXUS?
I AM PROUD TO CALL HIM FRIEND.
PRESS
THIS IS INDEED A GREAT HONOR, NEXUS.
PLEASED TO MEET YOU, SIR.
ATLANTA CAPITAL CITY of the INNER WEB
NEXUS, OR MR. HELLPOP IF YOU PREFER, I'LL GET RIGHT TO THE POINT. THE WEB FACES THE MOST SEVERE ENERGY CRISIS IN THE HISTORY OF MANKIND...
MR. PRESIDENT, I'M CONCERNED ABOUT A FRIEND OF MINE, SUNDRA PEALE.
I UNDERSTAND YOUR CONCERN, BUT THE ISSUE IS COMPLICATED. PEALE IS ALLEGED TO HAVE COMMITTED TREASON BY ABANDONING HER POST. IT'S OUT OF MY HANDS. THE MOST I CAN DO IS REQUEST LENIENCY, IF AND WHEN IT COMES TO TRIAL. EVEN THEN, I COULD BE ACCUSED OF MEDDLING WITH THE JUDICIARY. THAT COULD BOOMERANG.

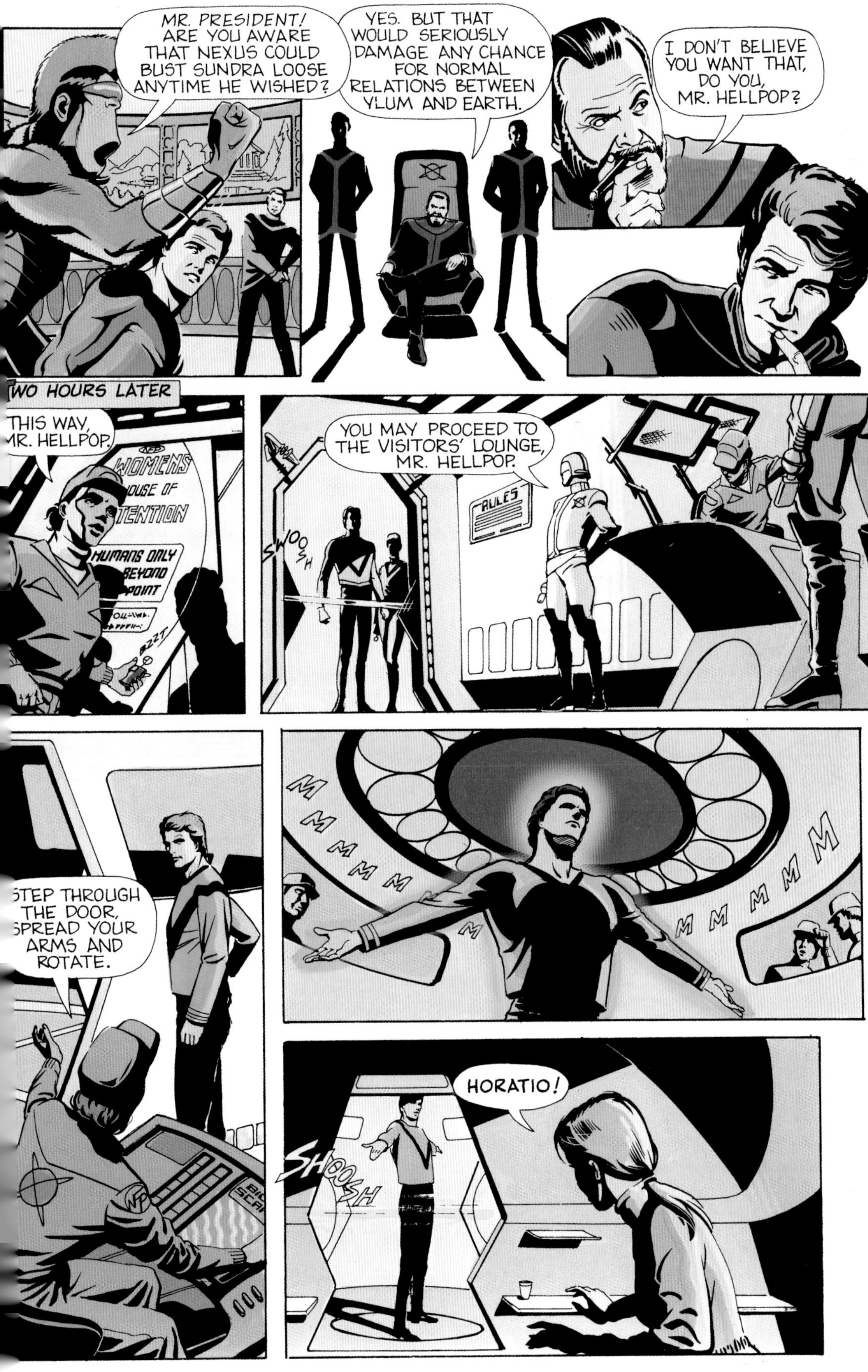
MR. PRESIDENT! ARE YOU AWARE THAT NEXUS COULD BUST SUNDRA LOOSE ANYTIME HE WISHED?
YES. BUT THAT WOULD SERIOUSLY DAMAGE ANY CHANCE FOR NORMAL RELATIONS BETWEEN YLUM AND EARTH.
I DON'T BELIEVE YOU WANT THAT, DO YOU, MR. HELLPOP?
TWO HOURS LATER
THIS WAY, MR. HELLPOP.
WOMENS HOUSE OF DETENTION
HUMANS ONLY BEYOND POINT
BZZT
YOU MAY PROCEED TO THE VISITORS' LOUNGE, MR. HELLPOP.
RULES
SWOOSH
STEP THROUGH THE DOOR, SPREAD YOUR ARMS AND ROTATE.
MMMMMM
MMMMMM
HORATIO!
SHOOOSH

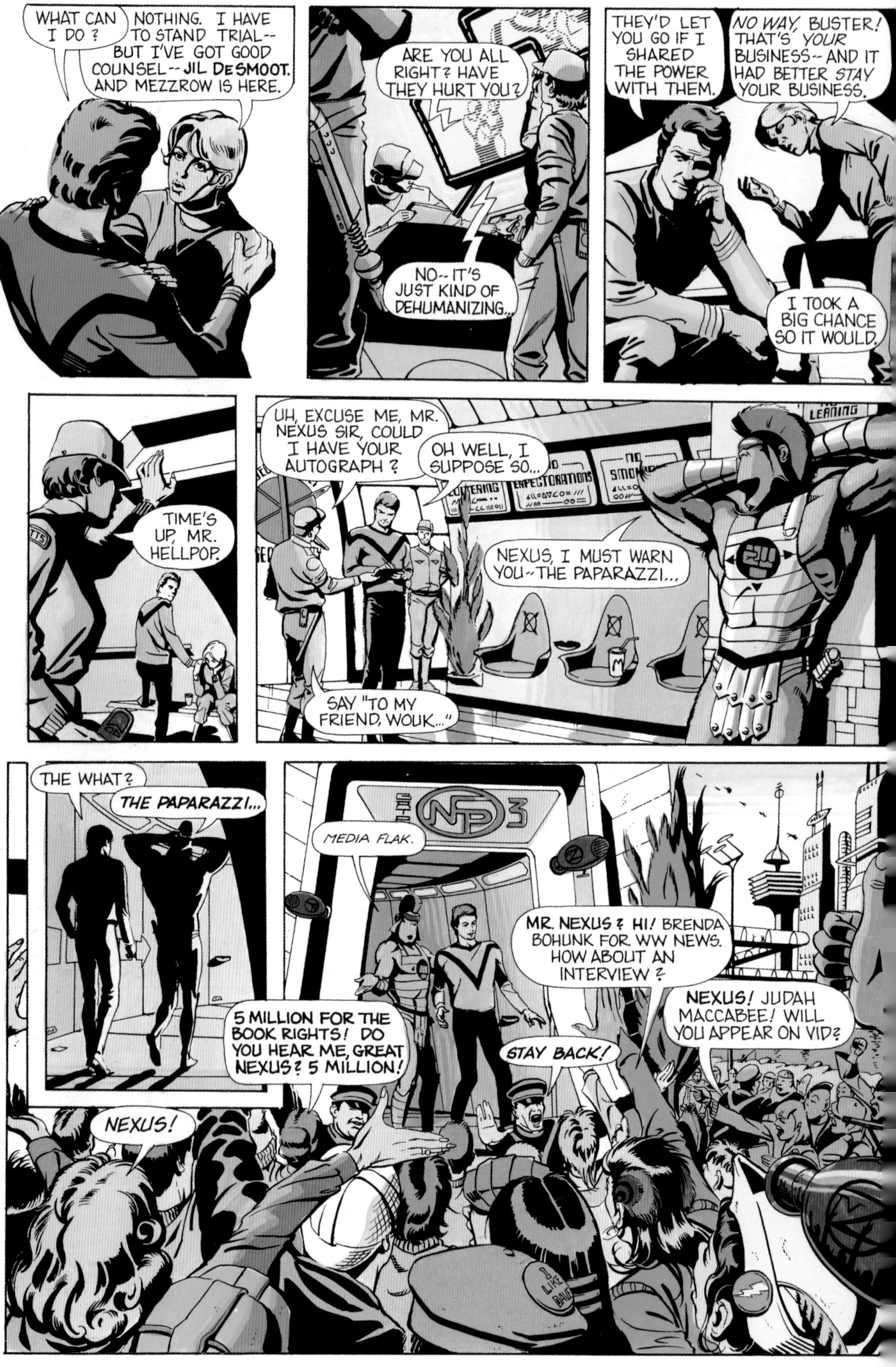
WHAT CAN I DO?
NOTHING. I HAVE TO STAND TRIAL-- BUT I'VE GOT GOOD COUNSEL-- JIL DESMOOT. AND MEZZROW IS HERE.
ARE YOU ALL RIGHT? HAVE THEY HURT YOU?
NO-- IT'S JUST KIND OF DEHUMANIZING...
THEY'D LET YOU GO IF I SHARED THE POWER WITH THEM.
NO WAY, BUSTER! THAT'S YOUR BUSINESS-- AND IT HAD BETTER STAY YOUR BUSINESS.
I TOOK A BIG CHANCE SO IT WOULD.
TIME'S UP, MR. HELLPOP.
UH, EXCUSE ME, MR. NEXUS SIR, COULD I HAVE YOUR AUTOGRAPH?
OH WELL, I SUPPOSE SO...
NEXUS, I MUST WARN YOU-- THE PAPARAZZI...
SAY "TO MY FRIEND, WOUK..."
THE WHAT?
THE PAPARAZZI...
MEDIA FLAK.
MR. NEXUS? HI! BRENDA BOHUNK FOR WW NEWS. HOW ABOUT AN INTERVIEW?
NEXUS! JUDAH MACCABEE! WILL YOU APPEAR ON VID?
5 MILLION FOR THE BOOK RIGHTS! DO YOU HEAR ME, GREAT NEXUS? 5 MILLION!
STAY BACK!
NEXUS!

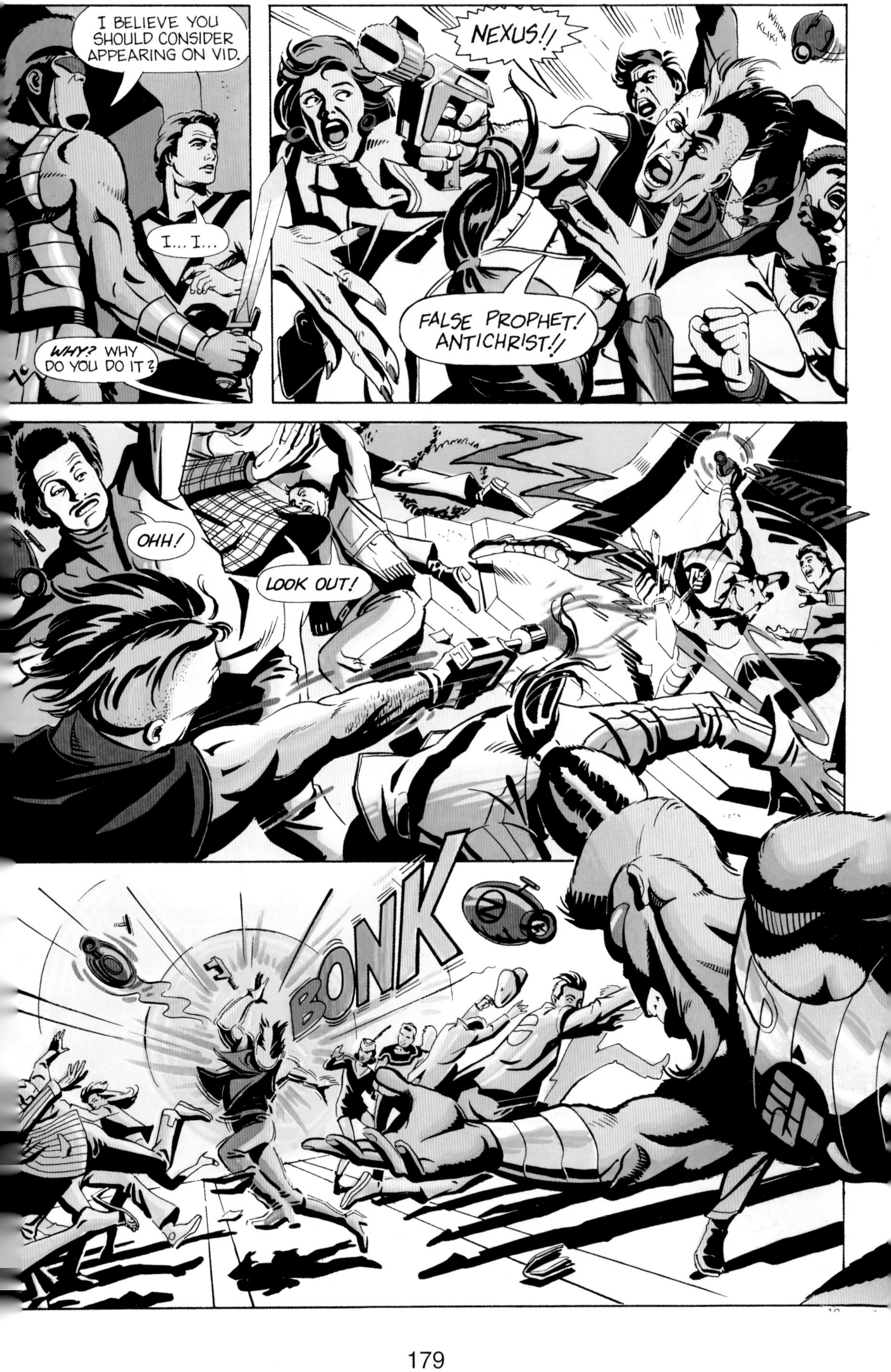
I BELIEVE YOU SHOULD CONSIDER APPEARING ON VID.
I... I...
WHY? WHY DO YOU DO IT?
NEXUS!!
WHIRR KLIK!
FALSE PROPHET! ANTICHRIST!!
OHH!
LOOK OUT!
SNATCH
BONK

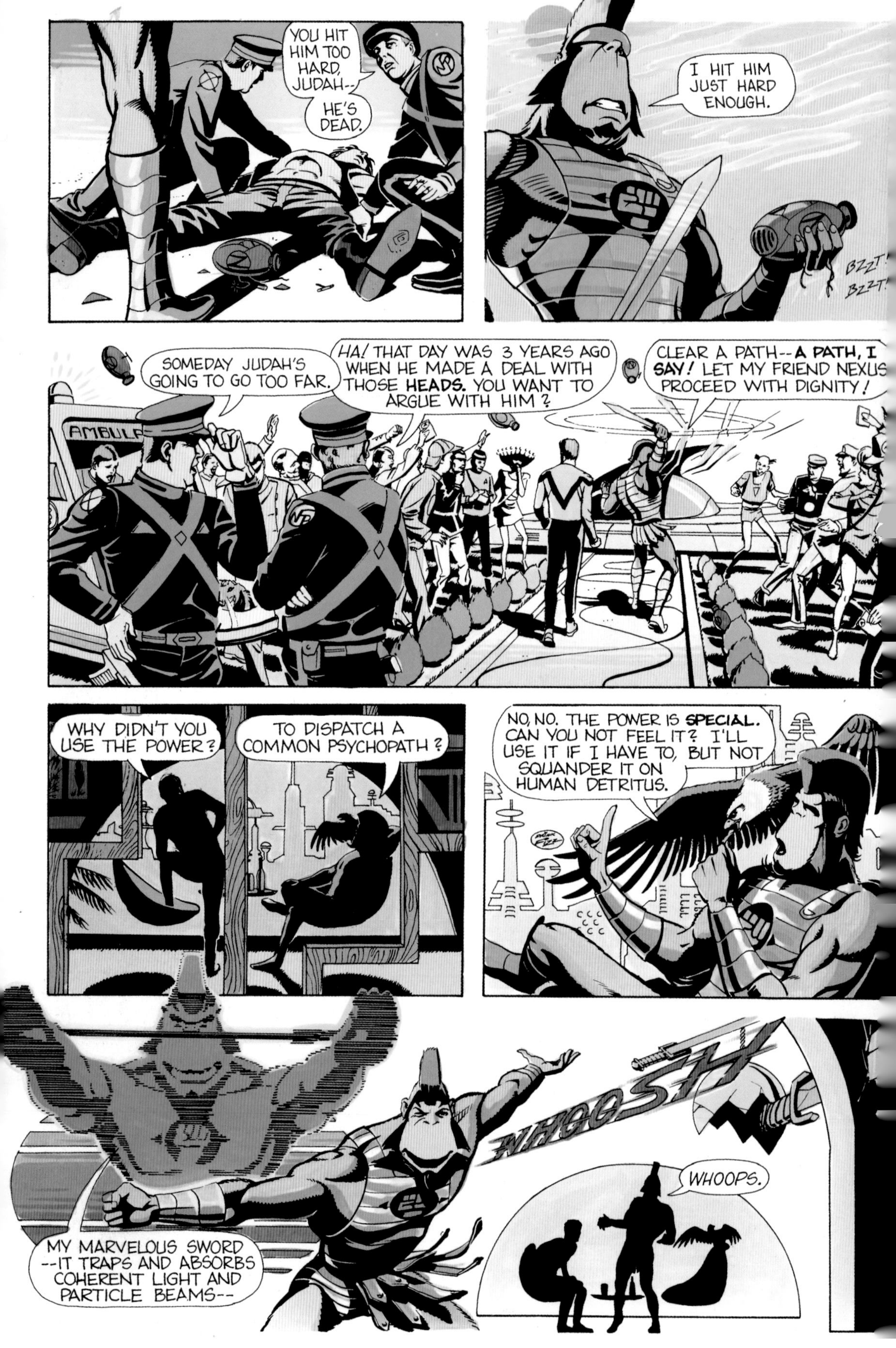

YOU HIT HIM TOO HARD, JUDAH--
HE'S DEAD.
I HIT HIM JUST HARD ENOUGH.
BZZT! BZZT!
SOMEDAY JUDAH'S GOING TO GO TOO FAR.
HA! THAT DAY WAS 3 YEARS AGO WHEN HE MADE A DEAL WITH THOSE **HEADS**. YOU WANT TO ARGUE WITH HIM?
CLEAR A PATH--**A PATH, I SAY!** LET MY FRIEND NEXUS PROCEED WITH DIGNITY!
AMBUL
WHY DIDN'T YOU USE THE POWER?
TO DISPATCH A COMMON PSYCHOPATH?
NO, NO. THE POWER IS **SPECIAL**. CAN YOU NOT FEEL IT? I'LL USE IT IF I HAVE TO, BUT NOT SQUANDER IT ON HUMAN DETRITUS.
MY MARVELOUS SWORD --IT TRAPS AND ABSORBS COHERENT LIGHT AND PARTICLE BEAMS--
WHOOSH
WHOOPS.

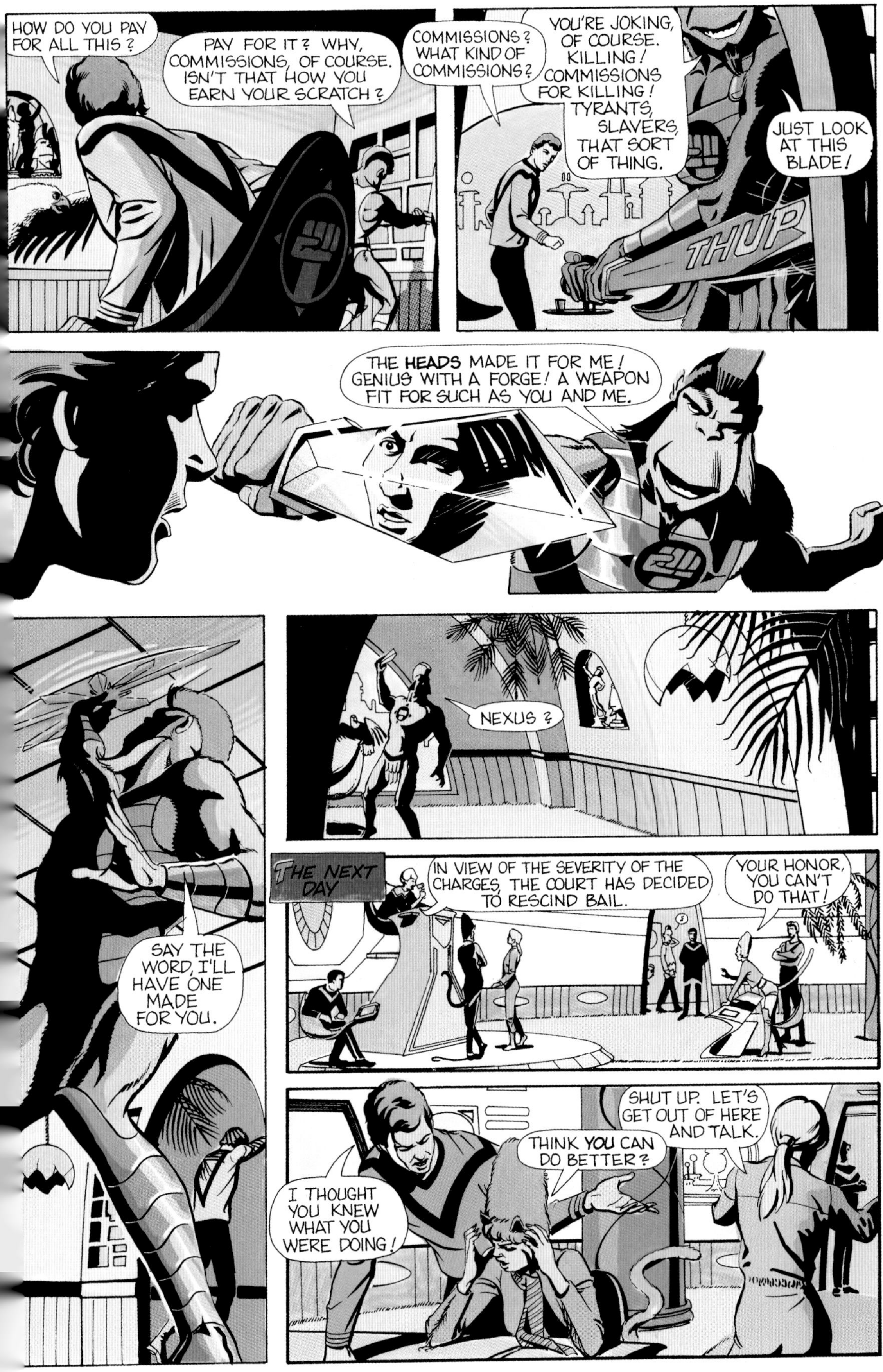
HOW DO YOU PAY FOR ALL THIS ?
PAY FOR IT ? WHY, COMMISSIONS, OF COURSE. ISN'T THAT HOW YOU EARN YOUR SCRATCH ?
COMMISSIONS ? WHAT KIND OF COMMISSIONS ?
YOU'RE JOKING, OF COURSE. KILLING! COMMISSIONS FOR KILLING! TYRANTS, SLAVERS, THAT SORT OF THING.
JUST LOOK AT THIS BLADE!
THUP
THE HEADS MADE IT FOR ME! GENIUS WITH A FORGE! A WEAPON FIT FOR SUCH AS YOU AND ME.
SAY THE WORD, I'LL HAVE ONE MADE FOR YOU.
NEXUS ?
THE NEXT DAY
IN VIEW OF THE SEVERITY OF THE CHARGES, THE COURT HAS DECIDED TO RESCIND BAIL.
YOUR HONOR, YOU CAN'T DO THAT!
I THOUGHT YOU KNEW WHAT YOU WERE DOING!
THINK YOU CAN DO BETTER ?
SHUT UP. LET'S GET OUT OF HERE AND TALK.

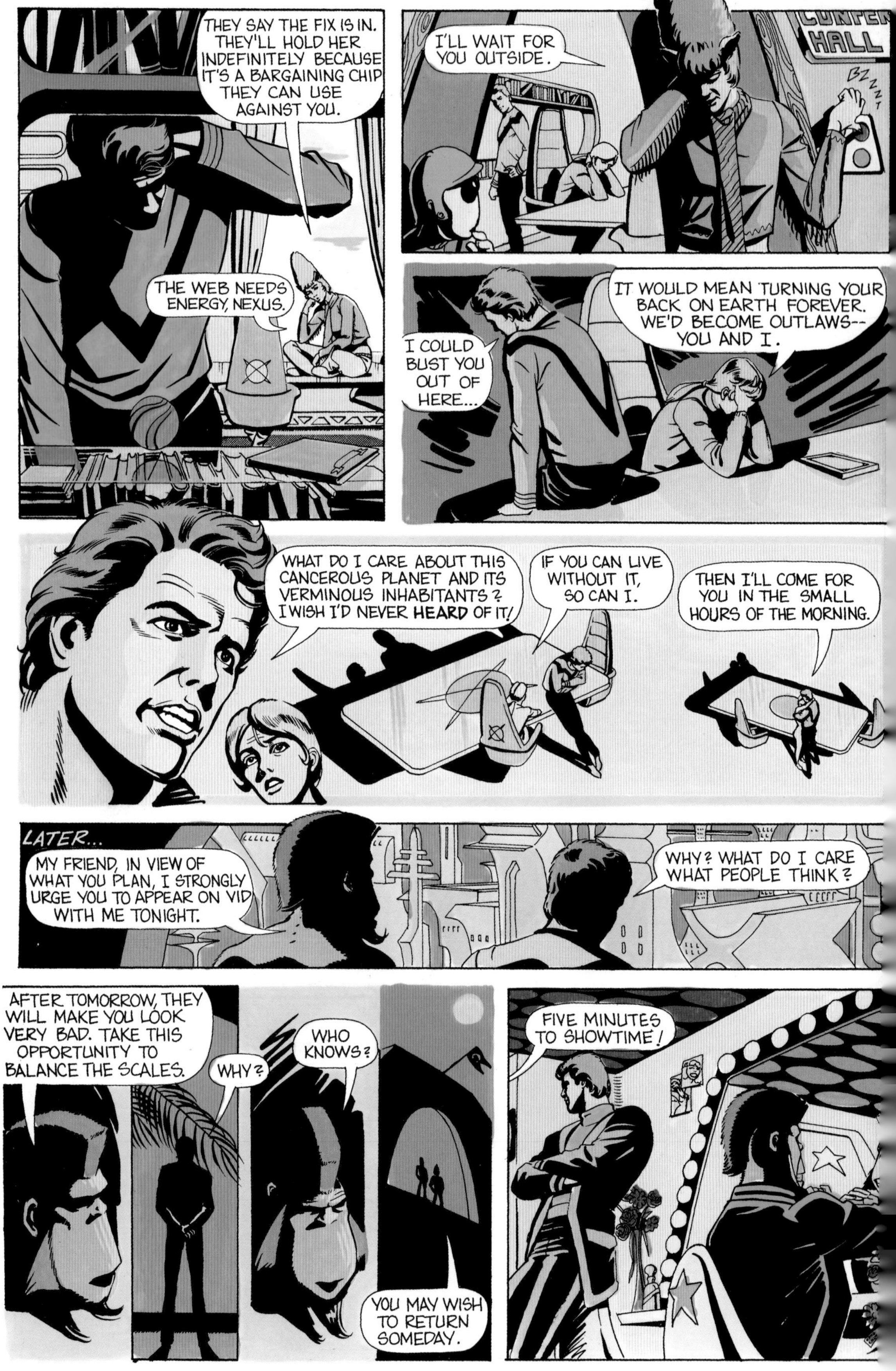
THEY SAY THE FIX IS IN. THEY'LL HOLD HER INDEFINITELY BECAUSE IT'S A BARGAINING CHIP THEY CAN USE AGAINST YOU.
THE WEB NEEDS ENERGY, NEXUS.
I'LL WAIT FOR YOU OUTSIDE.
CONFER HALL
BZZZZ
I COULD BUST YOU OUT OF HERE...
IT WOULD MEAN TURNING YOUR BACK ON EARTH FOREVER. WE'D BECOME OUTLAWS-- YOU AND I.
WHAT DO I CARE ABOUT THIS CANCEROUS PLANET AND ITS VERMINOUS INHABITANTS? I WISH I'D NEVER HEARD OF IT!
IF YOU CAN LIVE WITHOUT IT, SO CAN I.
THEN I'LL COME FOR YOU IN THE SMALL HOURS OF THE MORNING.
LATER...
MY FRIEND, IN VIEW OF WHAT YOU PLAN, I STRONGLY URGE YOU TO APPEAR ON VID WITH ME TONIGHT.
WHY? WHAT DO I CARE WHAT PEOPLE THINK?
AFTER TOMORROW, THEY WILL MAKE YOU LOOK VERY BAD. TAKE THIS OPPORTUNITY TO BALANCE THE SCALES.
WHY?
WHO KNOWS?
YOU MAY WISH TO RETURN SOMEDAY.
FIVE MINUTES TO SHOWTIME!

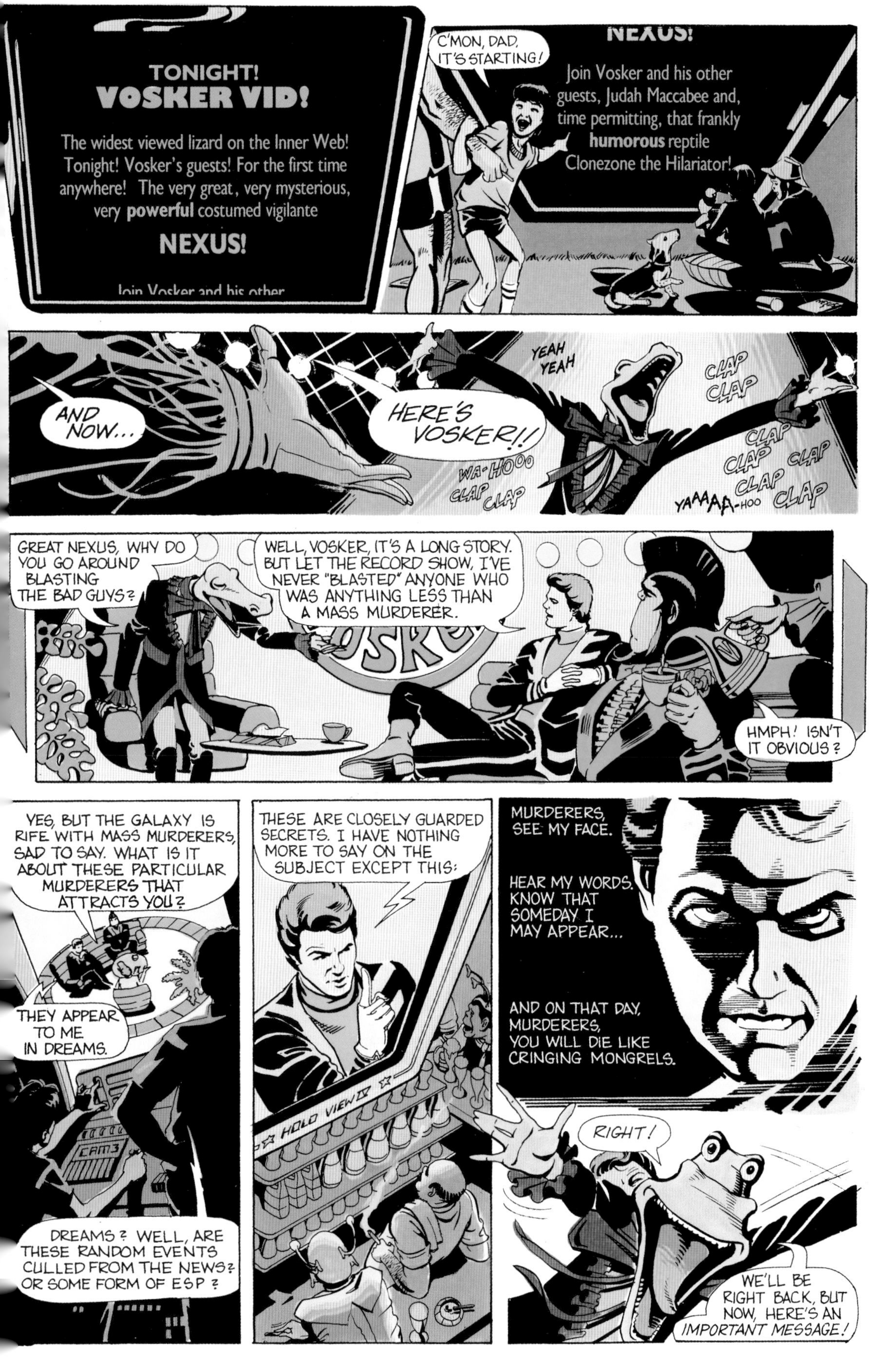
TONIGHT!
VOSKER VID!
The widest viewed lizard on the Inner Web! Tonight! Vosker's guests! For the first time anywhere! The very great, very mysterious, very **powerful** costumed vigilante
NEXUS!
C'MON, DAD, IT'S STARTING!
NEXUS!
Join Vosker and his other guests, Judah Maccabee and, time permitting, that frankly **humorous** reptile Clonezone the Hilariator!
AND NOW...
HERE'S VOSKER!!
YEAH YEAH
CLAP CLAP
WA-HOOO
CLAP CLAP
CLAP CLAP CLAP CLAP CLAP
YAAAAA-HOO
GREAT NEXUS, WHY DO YOU GO AROUND BLASTING THE BAD GUYS?
WELL, VOSKER, IT'S A LONG STORY. BUT LET THE RECORD SHOW, I'VE NEVER "BLASTED" ANYONE WHO WAS ANYTHING LESS THAN A MASS MURDERER.
HMPH! ISN'T IT OBVIOUS?
YES, BUT THE GALAXY IS RIFE WITH MASS MURDERERS, SAD TO SAY. WHAT IS IT ABOUT THESE PARTICULAR MURDERERS THAT ATTRACTS YOU?
THEY APPEAR TO ME IN DREAMS.
CAM3
DREAMS? WELL, ARE THESE RANDOM EVENTS CULLED FROM THE NEWS? OR SOME FORM OF ESP?
THESE ARE CLOSELY GUARDED SECRETS. I HAVE NOTHING MORE TO SAY ON THE SUBJECT EXCEPT THIS:
HOLO VIEW IV
MURDERERS, SEE MY FACE.
HEAR MY WORDS. KNOW THAT SOMEDAY I MAY APPEAR...
AND ON THAT DAY, MURDERERS, YOU WILL DIE LIKE CRINGING MONGRELS.
RIGHT!
WE'LL BE RIGHT BACK, BUT NOW, HERE'S AN IMPORTANT MESSAGE!

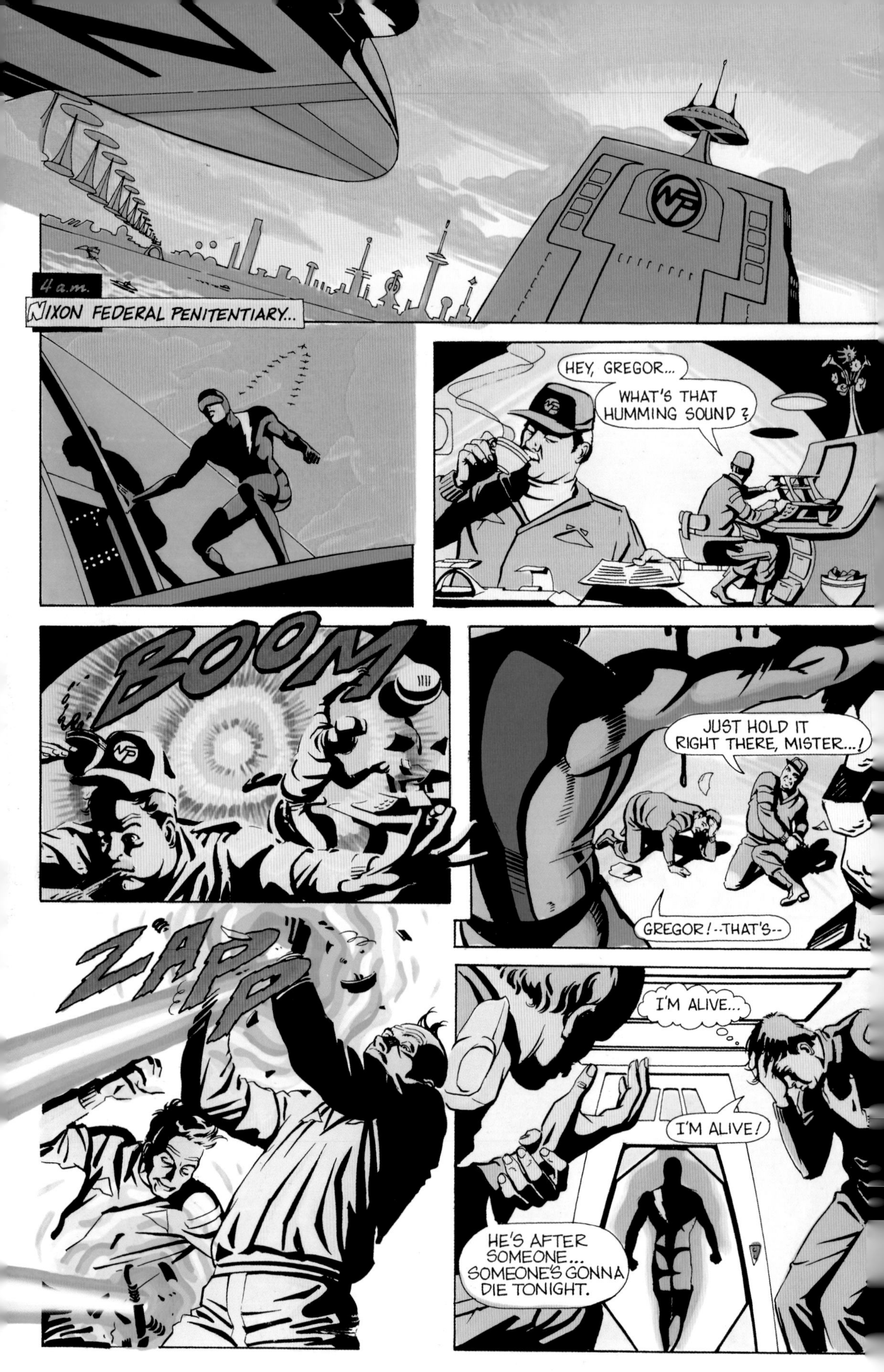
4 a.m.
NIXON FEDERAL PENITENTIARY...
HEY, GREGOR...
WHAT'S THAT HUMMING SOUND?
BOOM
JUST HOLD IT RIGHT THERE, MISTER...!
GREGOR! --THAT'S--
ZAPP
I'M ALIVE...
I'M ALIVE!
HE'S AFTER SOMEONE... SOMEONE'S GONNA DIE TONIGHT.

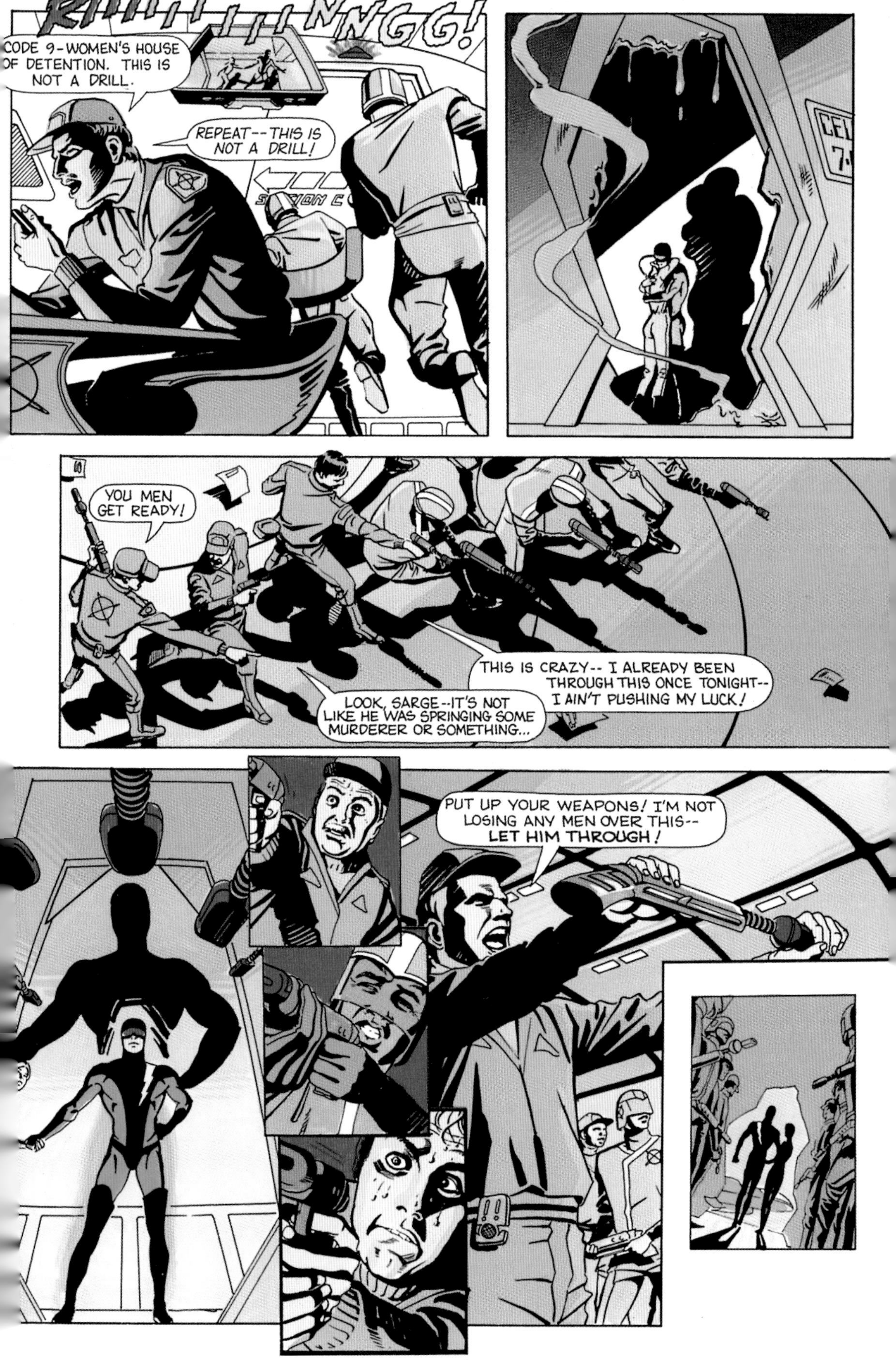
RIIIIIIIIIINNGG!
CODE 9-WOMEN'S HOUSE OF DETENTION. THIS IS NOT A DRILL.
REPEAT--THIS IS NOT A DRILL!
YOU MEN GET READY!
THIS IS CRAZY-- I ALREADY BEEN THROUGH THIS ONCE TONIGHT-- I AIN'T PUSHING MY LUCK!
LOOK, SARGE--IT'S NOT LIKE HE WAS SPRINGING SOME MURDERER OR SOMETHING...
PUT UP YOUR WEAPONS! I'M NOT LOSING ANY MEN OVER THIS-- LET HIM THROUGH!

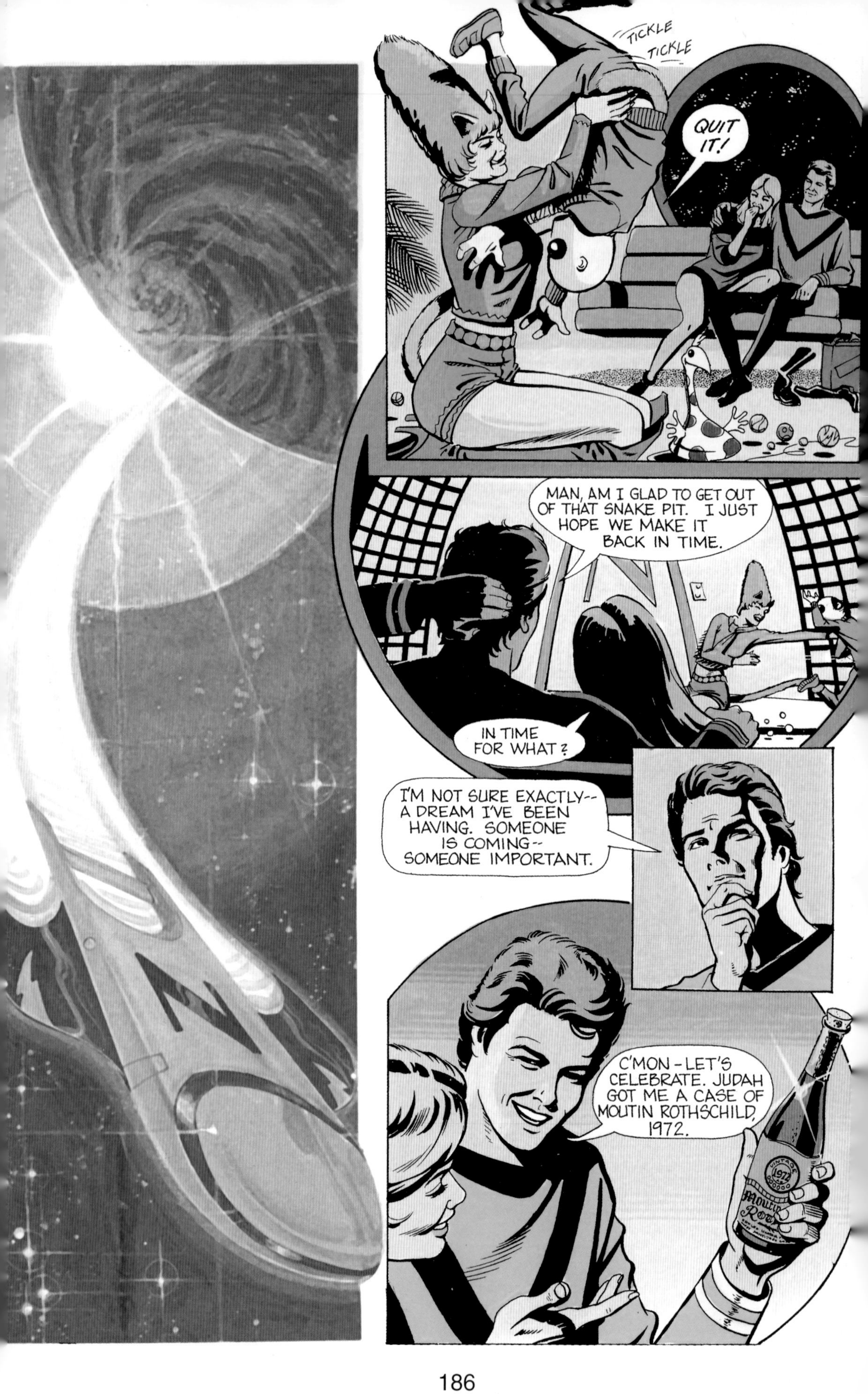
TICKLE
TICKLE
QUIT IT!
MAN, AM I GLAD TO GET OUT OF THAT SNAKE PIT. I JUST HOPE WE MAKE IT BACK IN TIME.
IN TIME FOR WHAT?
I'M NOT SURE EXACTLY-- A DREAM I'VE BEEN HAVING. SOMEONE IS COMING-- SOMEONE IMPORTANT.
C'MON - LET'S CELEBRATE. JUDAH GOT ME A CASE OF MOUTIN ROTHSCHILD, 1972.

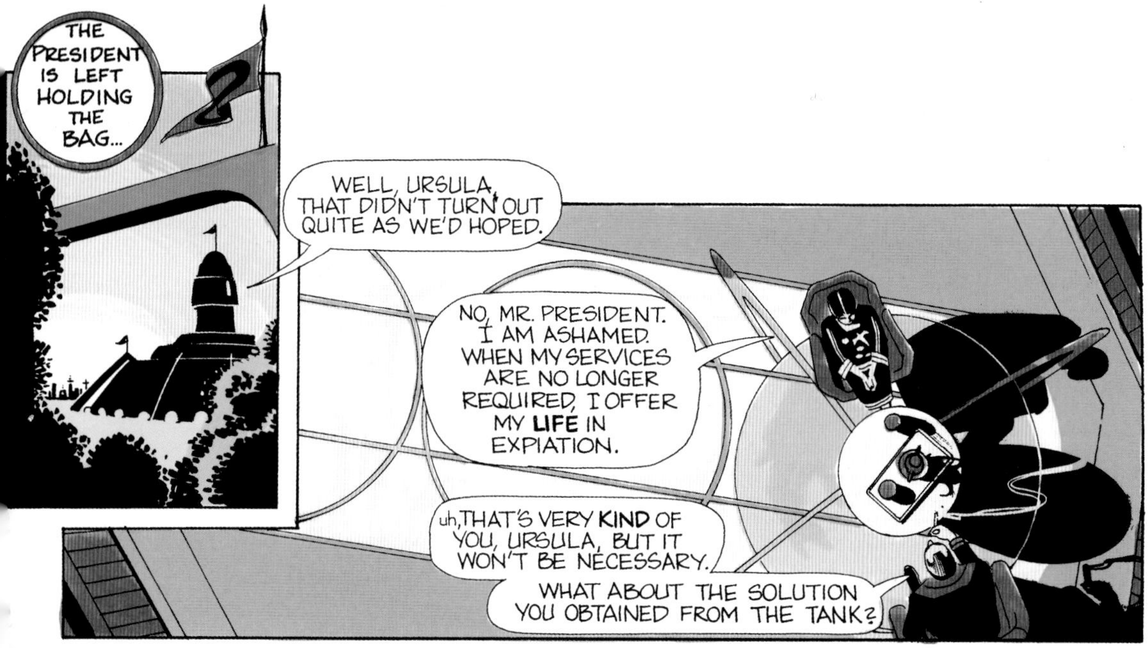
THE PRESIDENT IS LEFT HOLDING THE BAG...
WELL, URSULA, THAT DIDN'T TURN OUT QUITE AS WE'D HOPED.
NO, MR. PRESIDENT. I AM ASHAMED. WHEN MY SERVICES ARE NO LONGER REQUIRED, I OFFER MY **LIFE** IN EXPIATION.
uh, THAT'S VERY **KIND** OF YOU, URSULA, BUT IT WON'T BE NECESSARY.
WHAT ABOUT THE SOLUTION YOU OBTAINED FROM THE TANK?

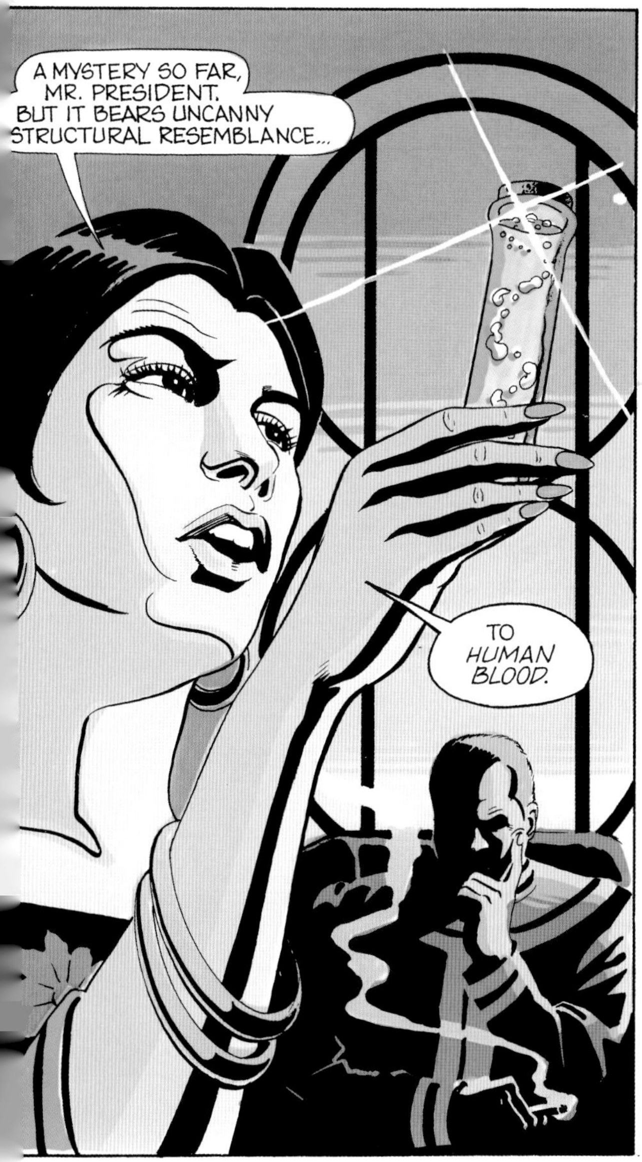
A MYSTERY SO FAR, MR. PRESIDENT. BUT IT BEARS UNCANNY STRUCTURAL RESEMBLANCE...
TO *HUMAN BLOOD.*

NEXT ISSUE

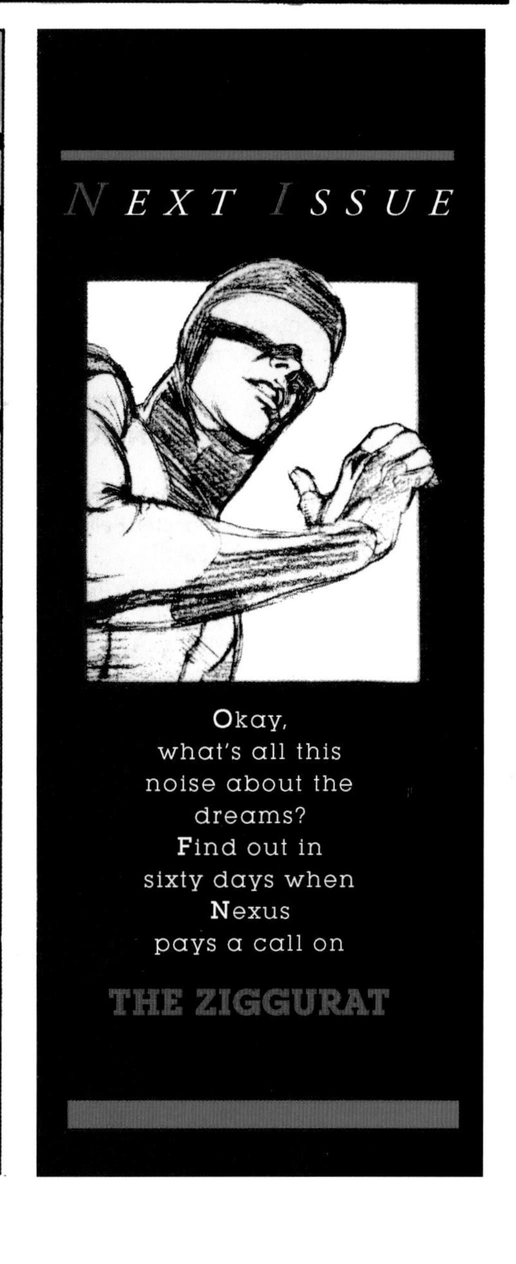

Okay,
what's all this
noise about the
dreams?
Find out in
sixty days when
Nexus
pays a call on

THE ZIGGURAT

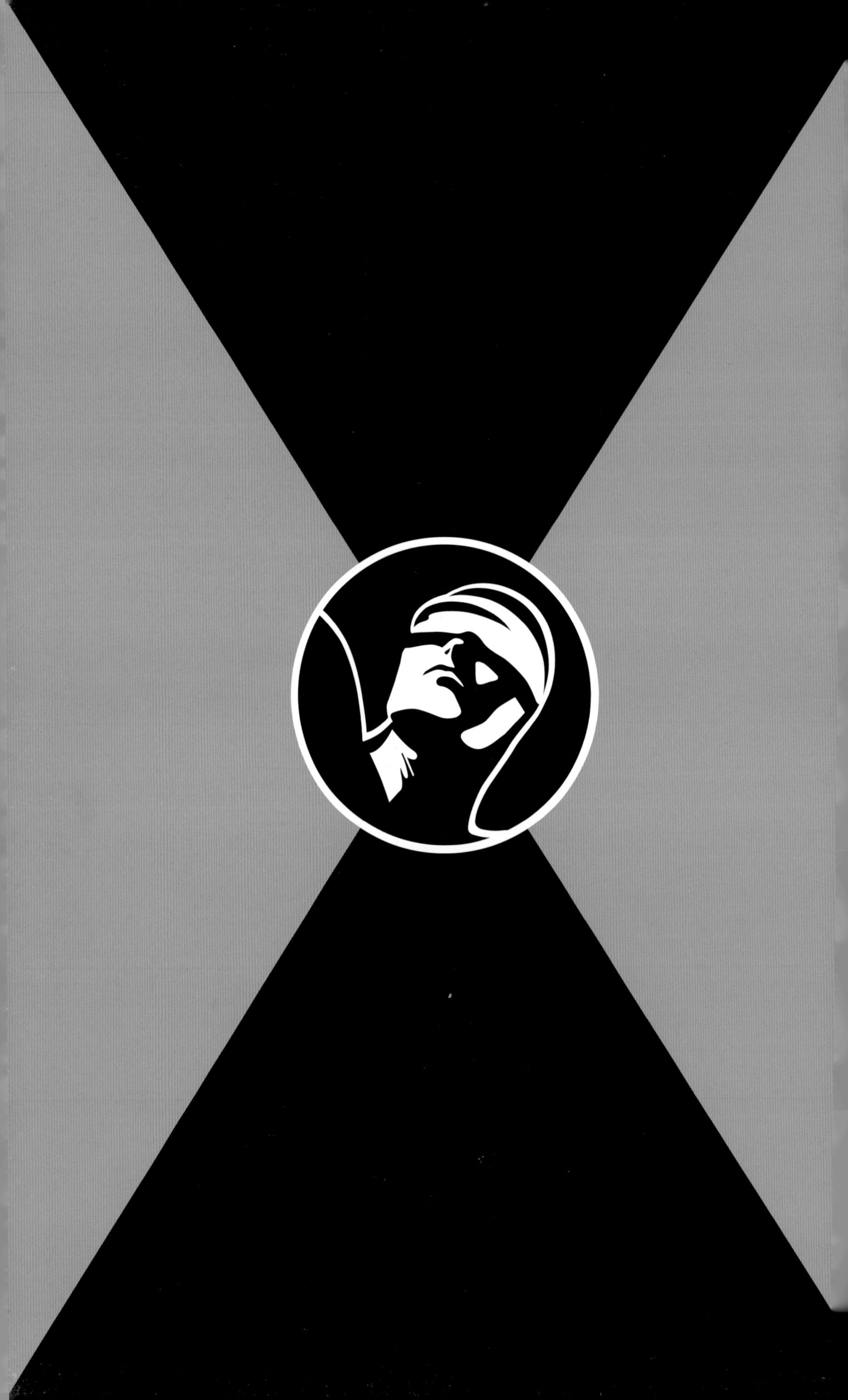

AAAH...

ZOK ZOK ZOK ZOK

KEEKEE-REEKEE

REEEEEK REEEEEK

EEEEEEAHHHH

KYRIEH KYRIASTORAH!

BIZARRE...

MEZZROW! WHAT'S WRONG? WHY ARE YOU CRYING?

I DON'T KNOW!

SNIF

DAVE, WHAT'S GOING ON? WHY ARE THEY BEHAVING LIKE THIS?

THIS HAPPENS SOMETIMES, WHEN THE DREAMS ARE ESPECIALLY ACUTE...

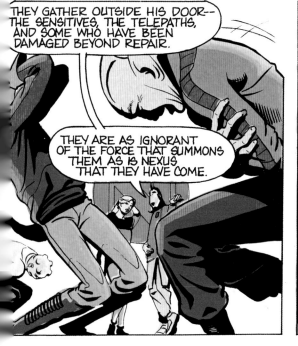

THEY GATHER OUTSIDE HIS DOOR-- THE SENSITIVES, THE TELEPATHS, AND SOME WHO HAVE BEEN DAMAGED BEYOND REPAIR.

THEY ARE AS IGNORANT OF THE FORCE THAT SUMMONS THEM AS IS NEXUS THAT THEY HAVE COME.

YES... I WAS IN THE FOREST WITH JIL WHEN I FELT SOMETHING PULLING ME HERE.

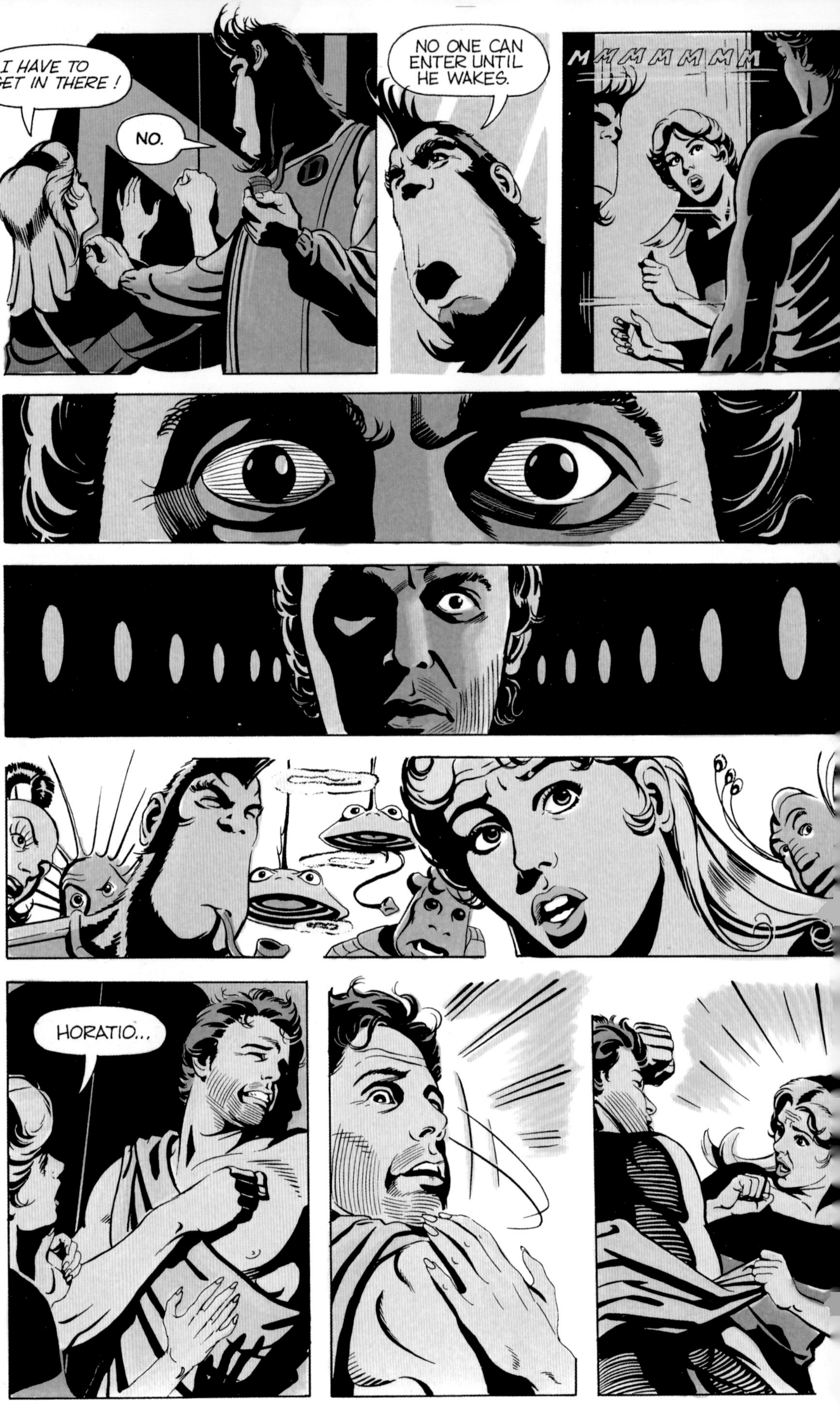
I HAVE TO GET IN THERE!
NO.
NO ONE CAN ENTER UNTIL HE WAKES.
MMMMMMMM
HORATIO...

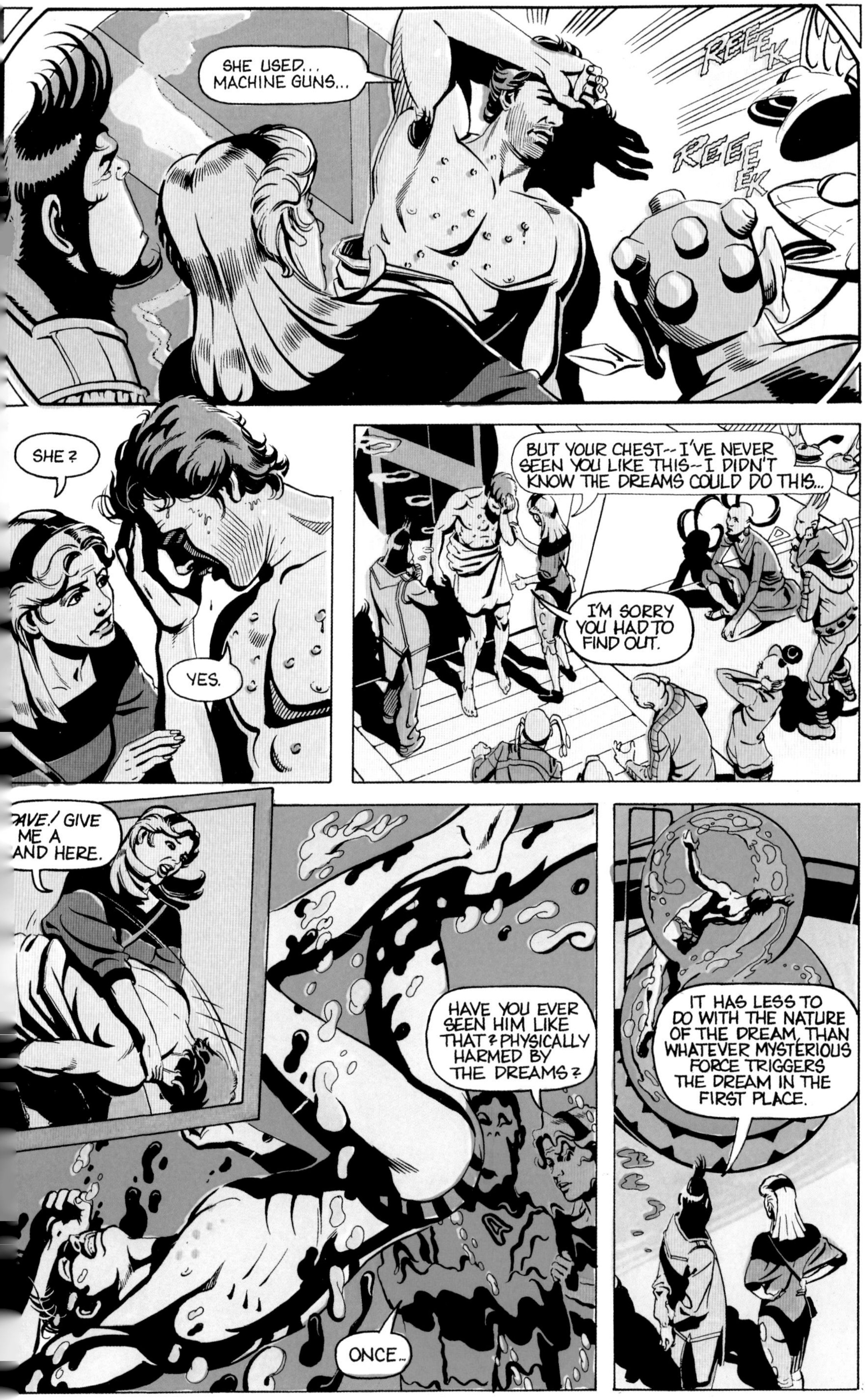
SHE USED... MACHINE GUNS...
REEEK
REEEEK
SHE ?
YES.
BUT YOUR CHEST-- I'VE NEVER SEEN YOU LIKE THIS-- I DIDN'T KNOW THE DREAMS COULD DO THIS...
I'M SORRY YOU HAD TO FIND OUT.
AVE! GIVE ME A AND HERE.
HAVE YOU EVER SEEN HIM LIKE THAT? PHYSICALLY HARMED BY THE DREAMS?
ONCE...
IT HAS LESS TO DO WITH THE NATURE OF THE DREAM, THAN WHATEVER MYSTERIOUS FORCE TRIGGERS THE DREAM IN THE FIRST PLACE.

EVEN TODAY, IN THE 26TH CENTURY, WE DON'T KNOW WHAT CAUSES CERTAIN DISEASES, MIGRAINE HEADACHES, OR THE COMMON COLD, FOR THAT MATTER.

HOW ARE WE TO UNDERSTAND HIS DREAMS?

SORRY, FALSE ALARM.

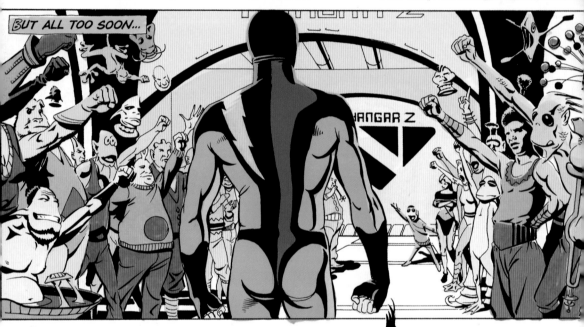

BUT ALL TOO SOON...

KEEP AN EYE OUT FOR SUNDRA, WILL YOU?

YOU BET!

WHATEVER CAUSES THESE DREAMS...

...IT IS MORE CORRUPT THAN ANY CANCER.

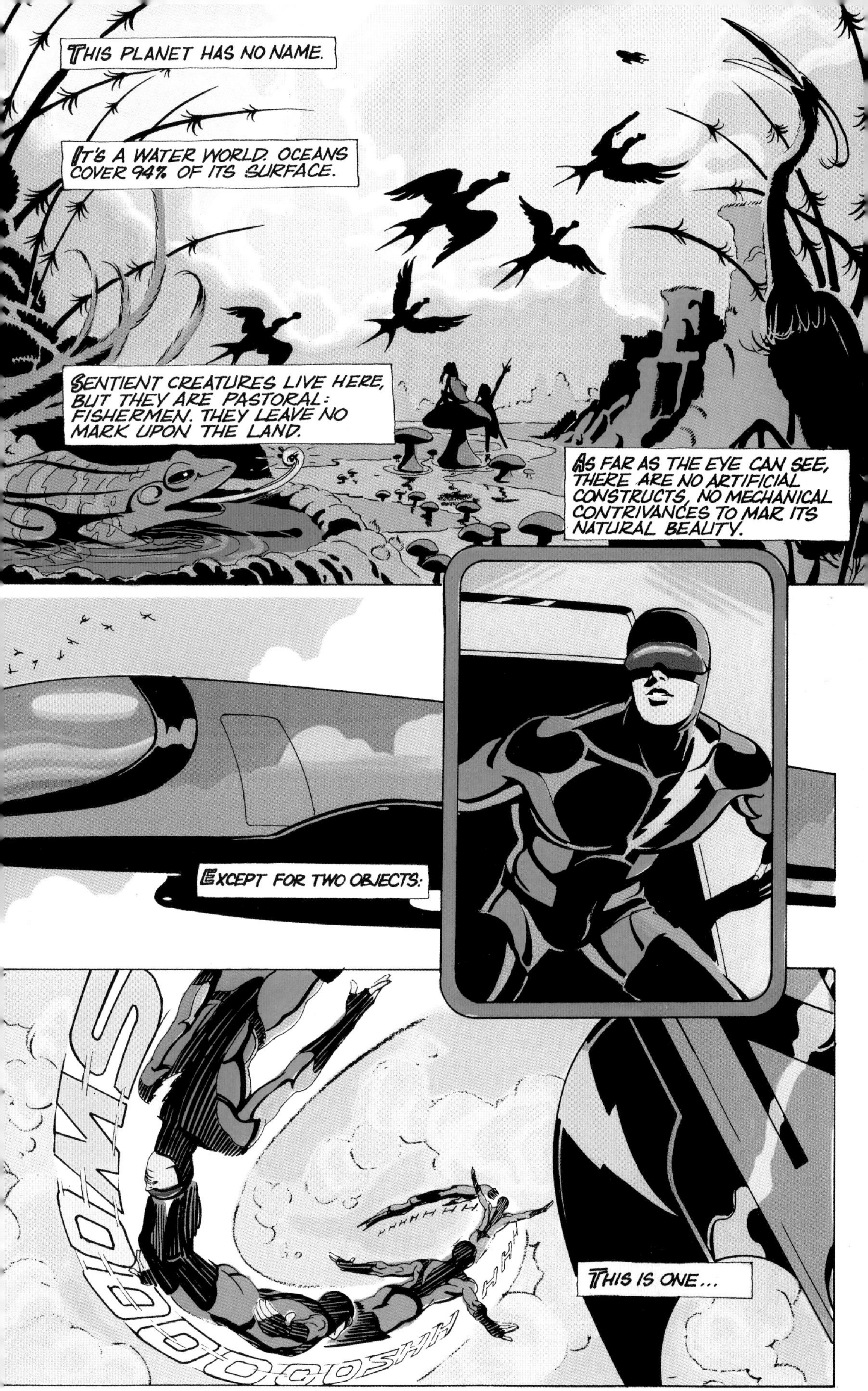
THIS PLANET HAS NO NAME.
IT'S A WATER WORLD. OCEANS COVER 94% OF ITS SURFACE.
SENTIENT CREATURES LIVE HERE, BUT THEY ARE PASTORAL: FISHERMEN. THEY LEAVE NO MARK UPON THE LAND.
AS FAR AS THE EYE CAN SEE, THERE ARE NO ARTIFICIAL CONSTRUCTS, NO MECHANICAL CONTRIVANCES TO MAR ITS NATURAL BEAUTY.
EXCEPT FOR TWO OBJECTS:
THIS IS ONE...

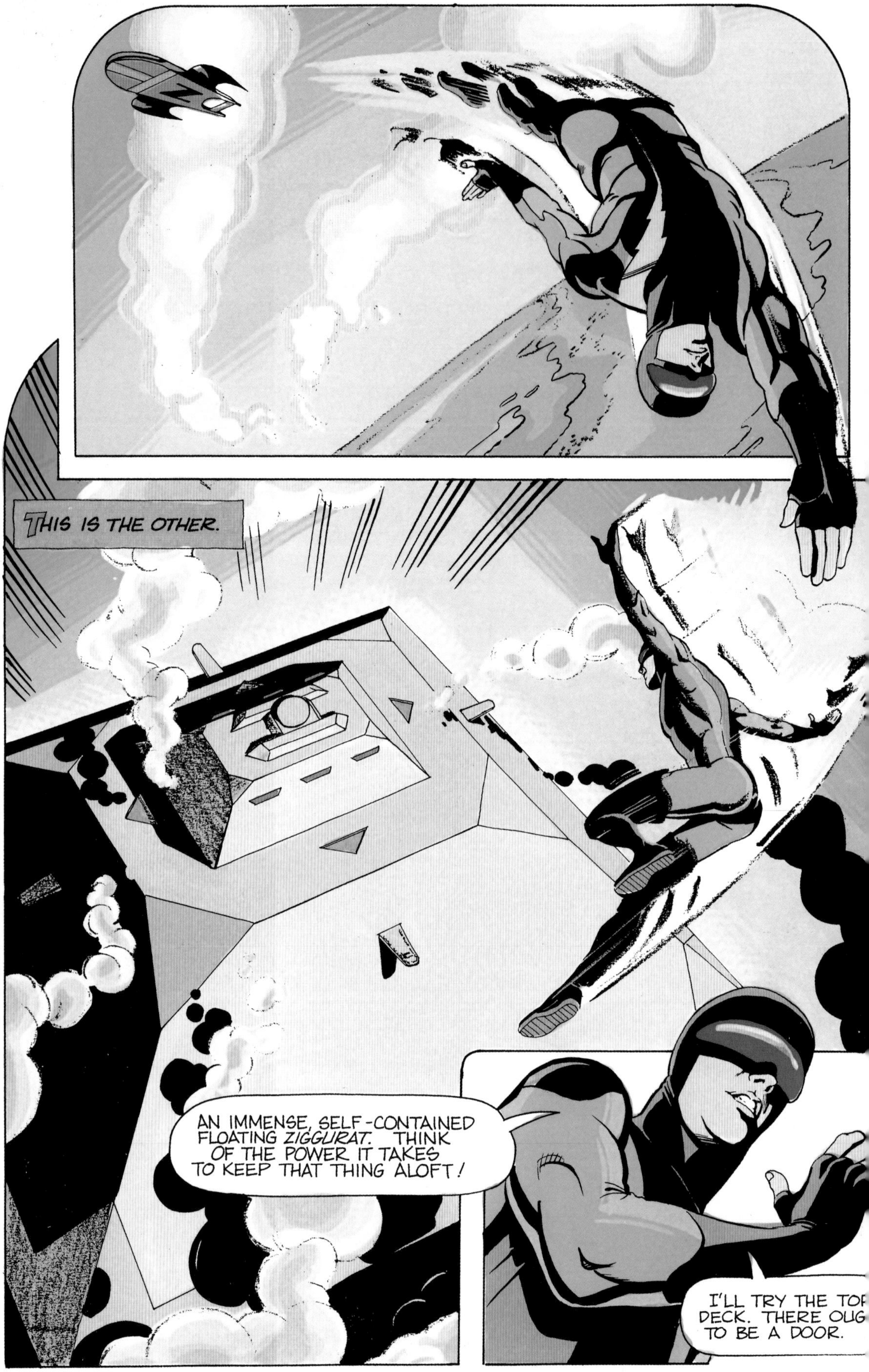
THIS IS THE OTHER.
AN IMMENSE, SELF-CONTAINED FLOATING ZIGGURAT. THINK OF THE POWER IT TAKES TO KEEP THAT THING ALOFT!
I'LL TRY THE TOP DECK. THERE OUG TO BE A DOOR.

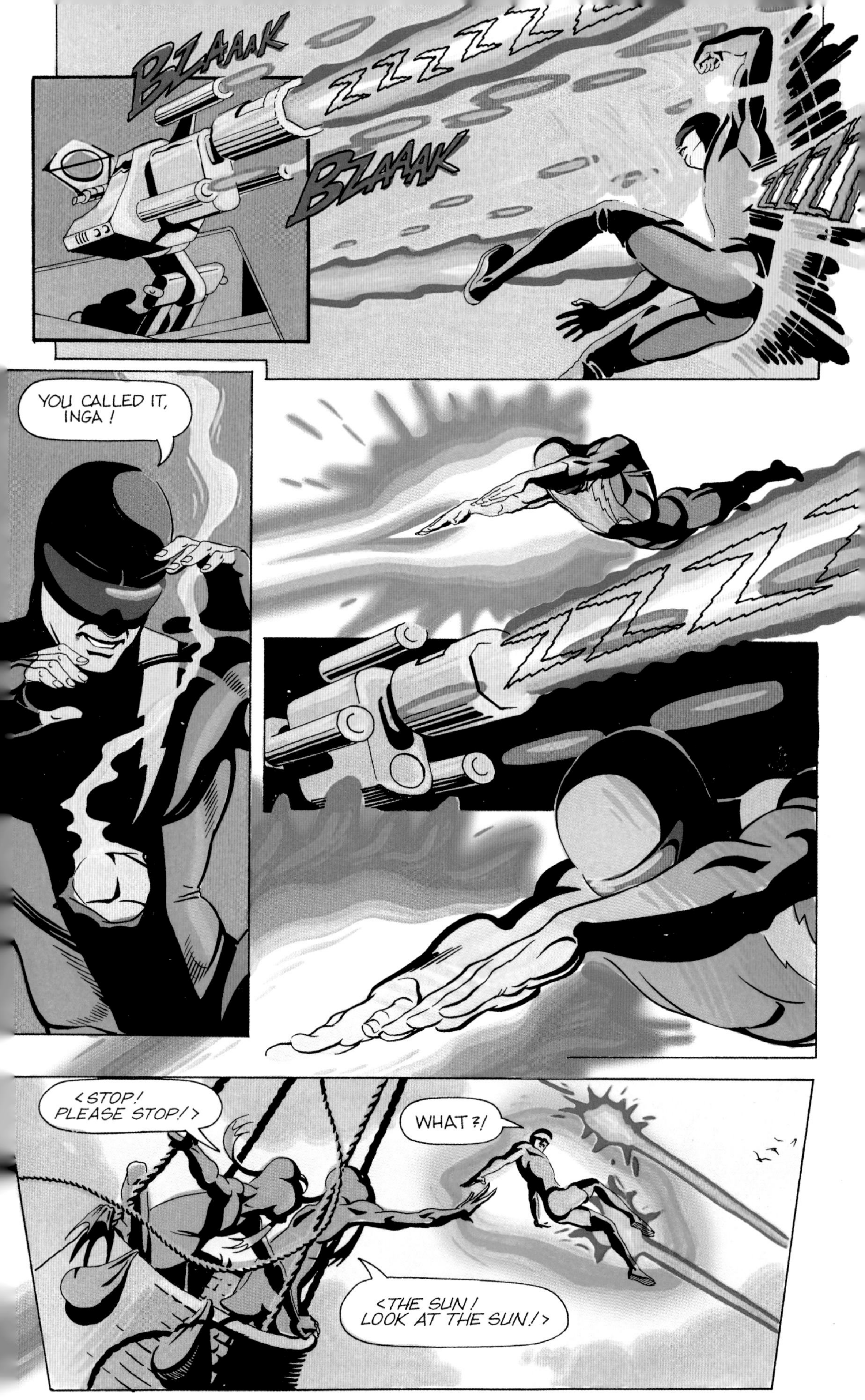
BZAAAK
ZZZZZZ
BZAAAK
YOU CALLED IT, INGA!
<STOP! PLEASE STOP!>
WHAT?!
<THE SUN! LOOK AT THE SUN!>

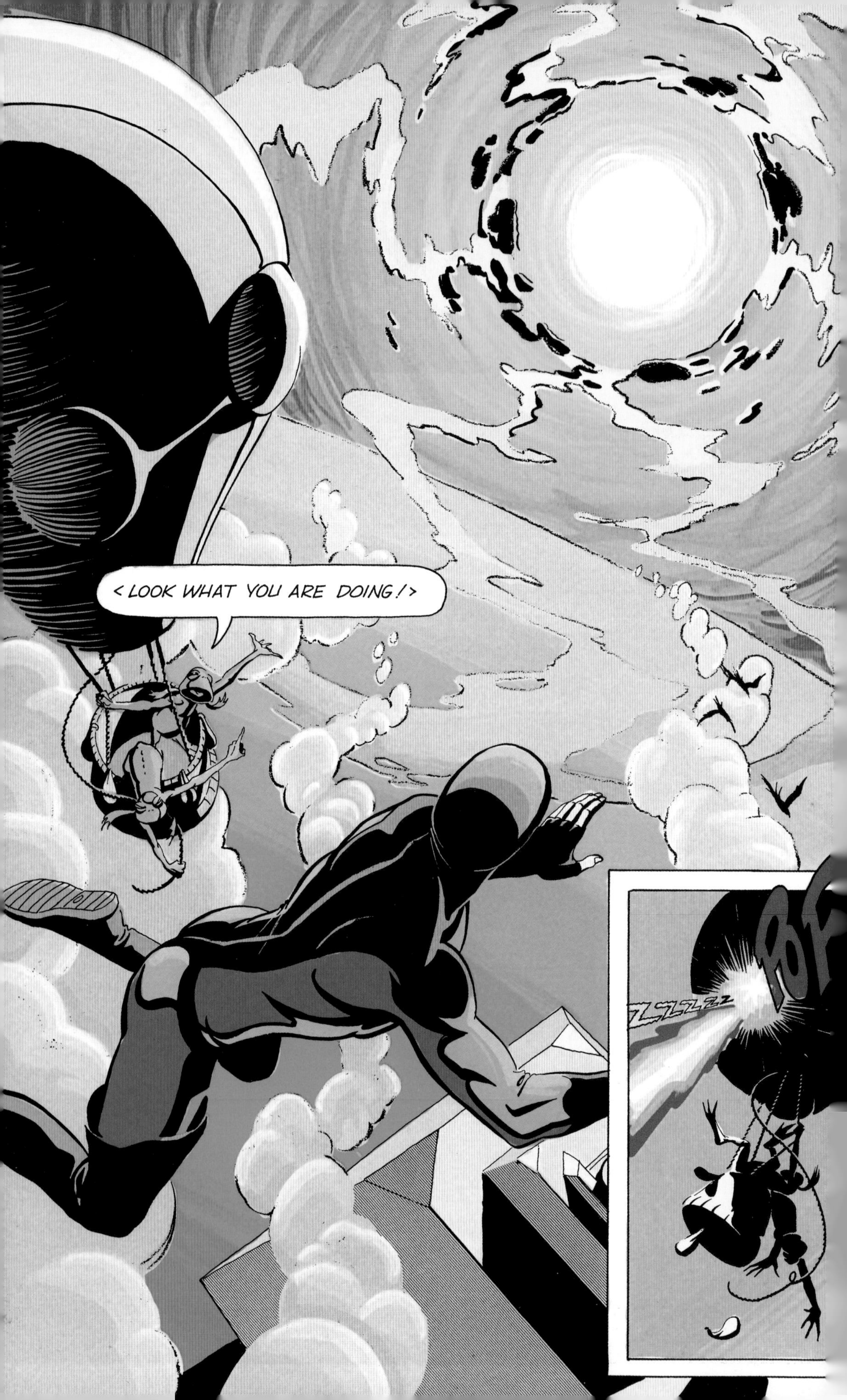
< LOOK WHAT YOU ARE DOING! >
ZZZZZZz

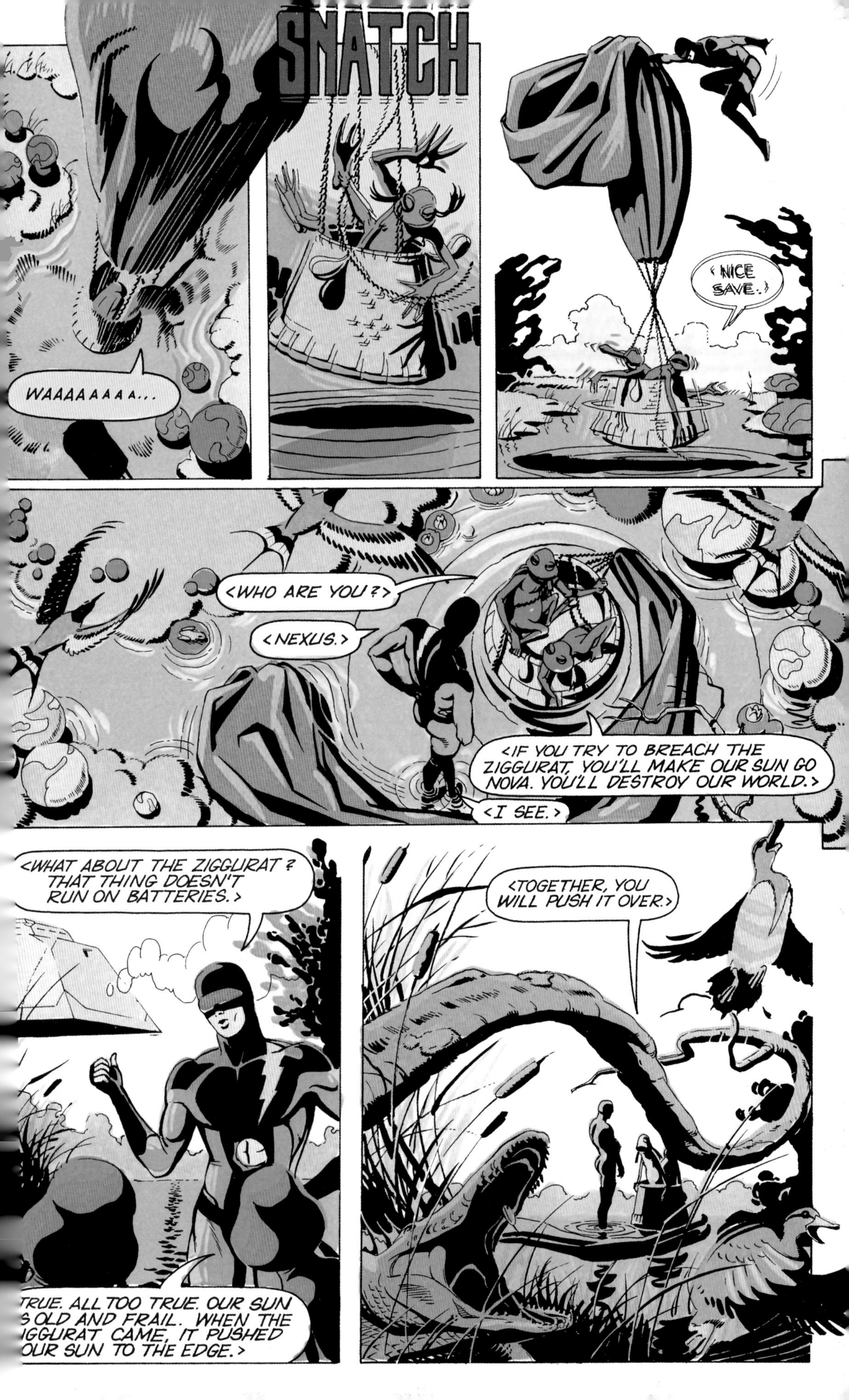
SNATCH
WAAAAAAAA...
‹NICE SAVE.›
<WHO ARE YOU?>
<NEXUS.>
<IF YOU TRY TO BREACH THE ZIGGURAT, YOU'LL MAKE OUR SUN GO NOVA. YOU'LL DESTROY OUR WORLD.>
<I SEE.>
<WHAT ABOUT THE ZIGGURAT? THAT THING DOESN'T RUN ON BATTERIES.>
TRUE. ALL TOO TRUE. OUR SUN S OLD AND FRAIL. WHEN THE IGGURAT CAME, IT PUSHED OUR SUN TO THE EDGE.>
<TOGETHER, YOU WILL PUSH IT OVER.>

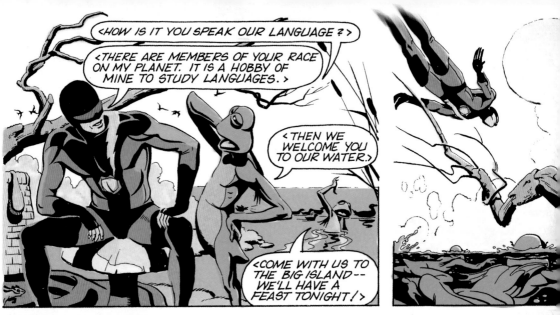

<How is it you speak our language?>

<There are members of your race on my planet. It is a hobby of mine to study languages.>

<Then we welcome you to our water.>

<Come with us to the big island-- we'll have a feast tonight!>

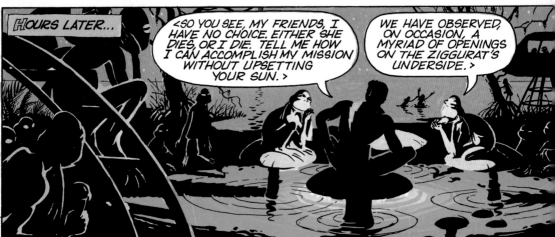

Hours later...

<So you see, my friends, I have no choice. Either she dies, or I die. Tell me how I can accomplish my mission without upsetting your sun.>

We have observed, on occasion, a myriad of openings on the ziggurat's underside.>

<But understand-- many of our world have come to worship the ziggurat- -or whatever is inside-- as a god.

<I know. To prevent my dreams from destroying me, I must destroy the dreams of others.>

< You swim against the current.>

<I fear that many will now seek to worship him.>

<Far better for our world that neither of them had ever come.>

DAWN...

RIBBIT!

I'LL SIMPLY WAIT FOR IT TO PASS OVER. IT WON'T EVEN NOTICE ME DOWN HERE IN THE SHRUBBERY.

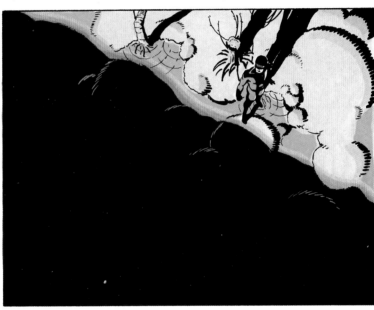

KRAKKK

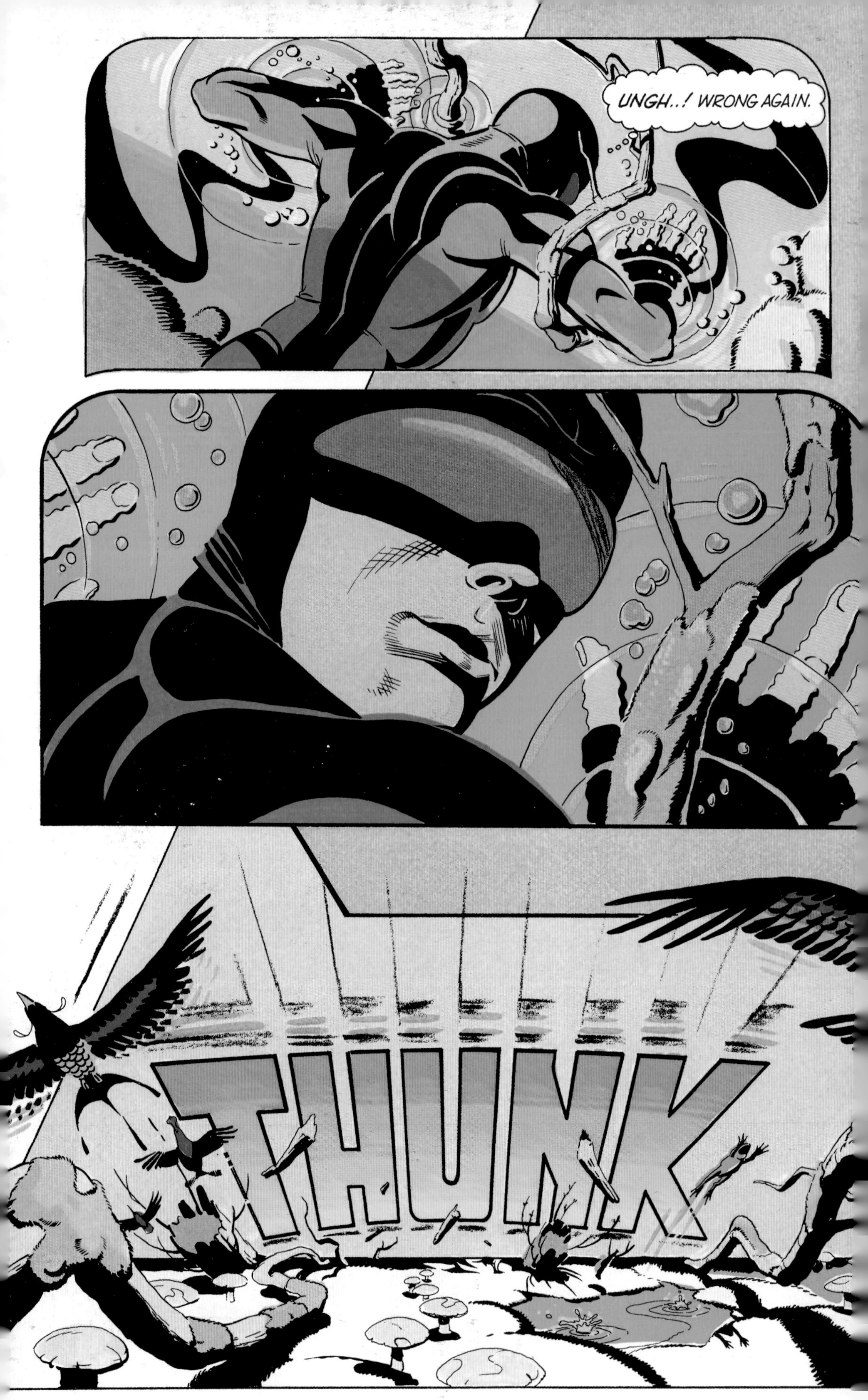
UNGH..! WRONG AGAIN.
THUNK

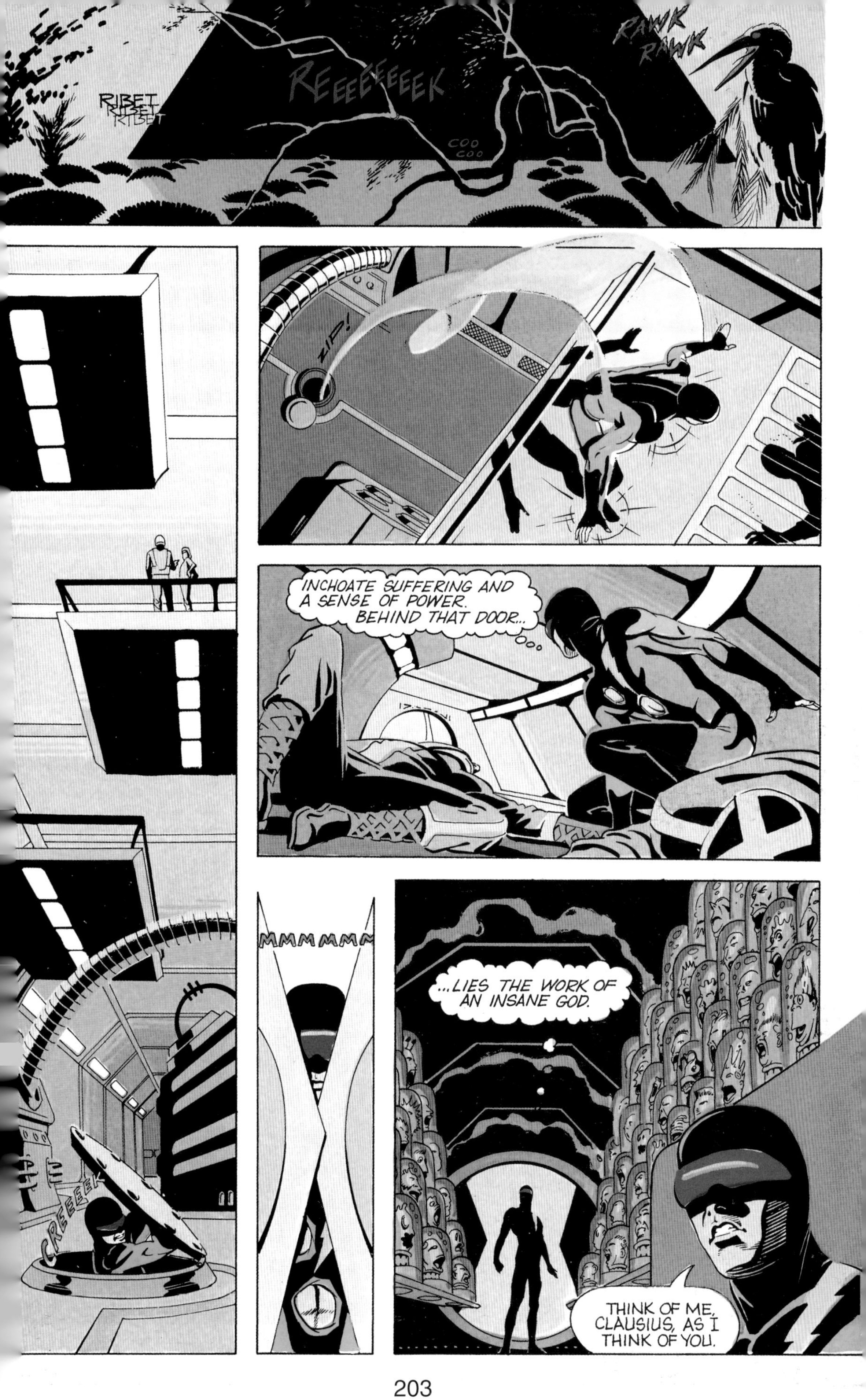
RIBET RIBET RIBET
REEEEEEEEK
COO COO
RAWK RAWK
ZIP!
CREEEEK
INCHOATE SUFFERING AND A SENSE OF POWER. BEHIND THAT DOOR...
MMMMMM
...LIES THE WORK OF AN INSANE GOD.
THINK OF ME, CLAUSIUS, AS I THINK OF YOU.

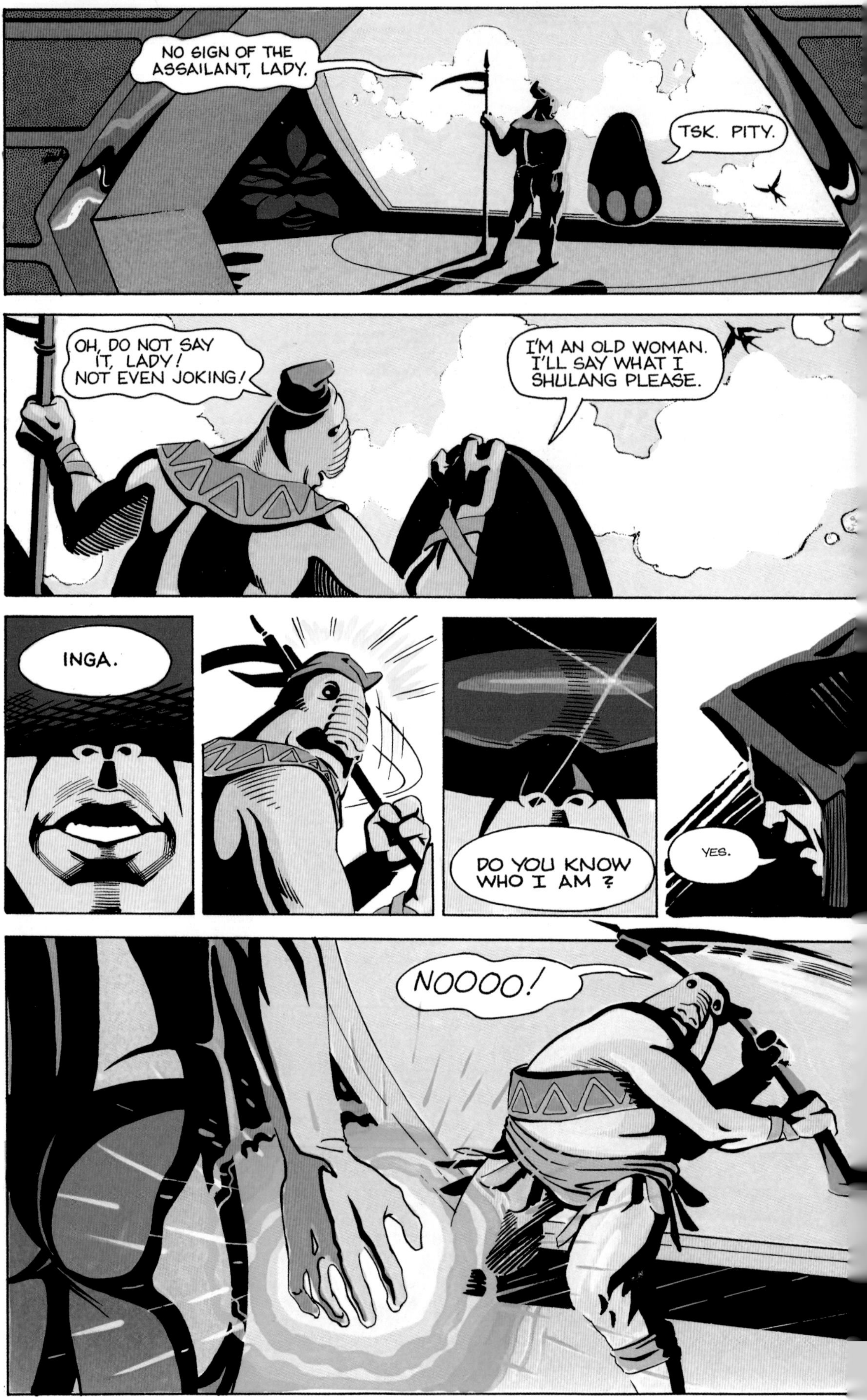
NO SIGN OF THE ASSAILANT, LADY.
TSK. PITY.
OH, DO NOT SAY IT, LADY! NOT EVEN JOKING!
I'M AN OLD WOMAN. I'LL SAY WHAT I SHULANG PLEASE.
INGA.
DO YOU KNOW WHO I AM ?
YES.
NOOOO!

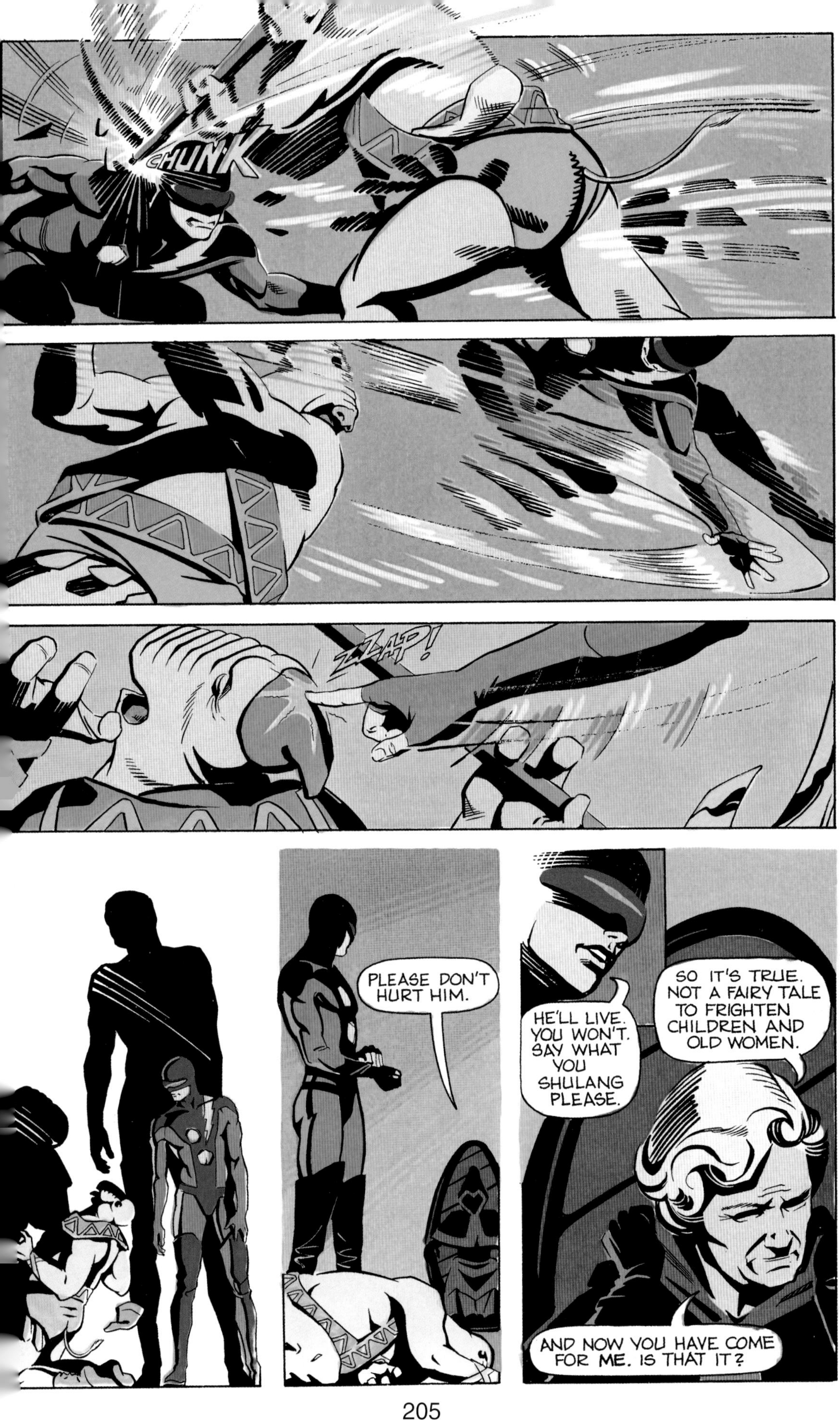
CHUNK
ZZAP!
PLEASE DON'T HURT HIM.
HE'LL LIVE. YOU WON'T. SAY WHAT YOU SHULANG PLEASE.
SO IT'S TRUE. NOT A FAIRY TALE TO FRIGHTEN CHILDREN AND OLD WOMEN.
AND NOW YOU HAVE COME FOR ME. IS THAT IT?

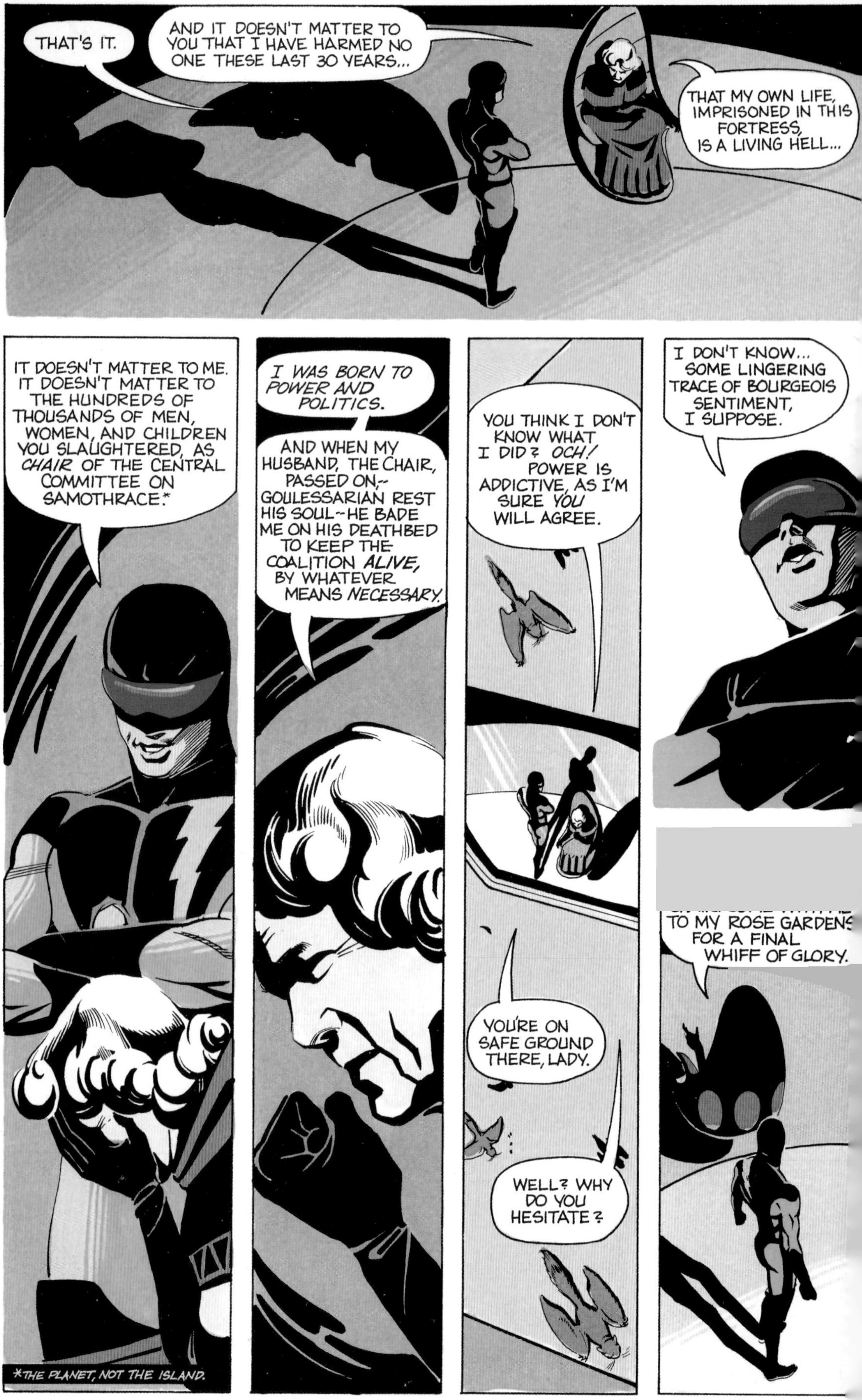
THAT'S IT.
AND IT DOESN'T MATTER TO YOU THAT I HAVE HARMED NO ONE THESE LAST 30 YEARS...
THAT MY OWN LIFE, IMPRISONED IN THIS FORTRESS, IS A LIVING HELL...
IT DOESN'T MATTER TO ME. IT DOESN'T MATTER TO THE HUNDREDS OF THOUSANDS OF MEN, WOMEN, AND CHILDREN YOU SLAUGHTERED, AS CHAIR OF THE CENTRAL COMMITTEE ON SAMOTHRACE.*
*THE PLANET, NOT THE ISLAND.
I WAS BORN TO POWER AND POLITICS.
AND WHEN MY HUSBAND, THE CHAIR, PASSED ON,--GOULESSARIAN REST HIS SOUL--HE BADE ME ON HIS DEATHBED TO KEEP THE COALITION ALIVE, BY WHATEVER MEANS NECESSARY.
YOU THINK I DON'T KNOW WHAT I DID? OCH! POWER IS ADDICTIVE, AS I'M SURE YOU WILL AGREE.
YOU'RE ON SAFE GROUND THERE, LADY.
WELL? WHY DO YOU HESITATE?
I DON'T KNOW... SOME LINGERING TRACE OF BOURGEOIS SENTIMENT, I SUPPOSE.
TO MY ROSE GARDENS FOR A FINAL WHIFF OF GLORY.

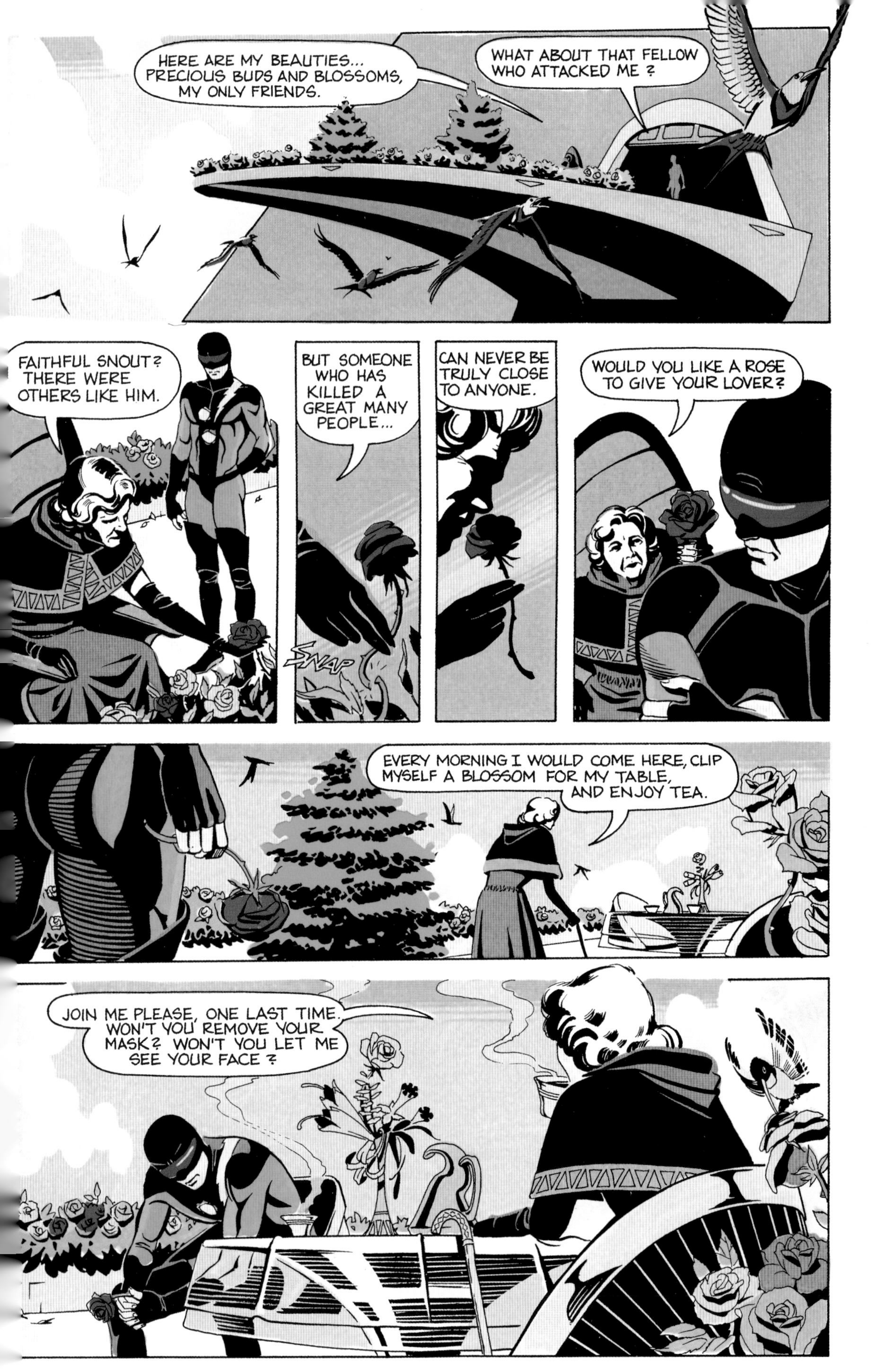
HERE ARE MY BEAUTIES... PRECIOUS BUDS AND BLOSSOMS, MY ONLY FRIENDS.
WHAT ABOUT THAT FELLOW WHO ATTACKED ME ?
FAITHFUL SNOUT? THERE WERE OTHERS LIKE HIM.
BUT SOMEONE WHO HAS KILLED A GREAT MANY PEOPLE...
CAN NEVER BE TRULY CLOSE TO ANYONE.
SNAP
WOULD YOU LIKE A ROSE TO GIVE YOUR LOVER?
EVERY MORNING I WOULD COME HERE, CLIP MYSELF A BLOSSOM FOR MY TABLE, AND ENJOY TEA.
JOIN ME PLEASE, ONE LAST TIME. WON'T YOU REMOVE YOUR MASK? WON'T YOU LET ME SEE YOUR FACE ?

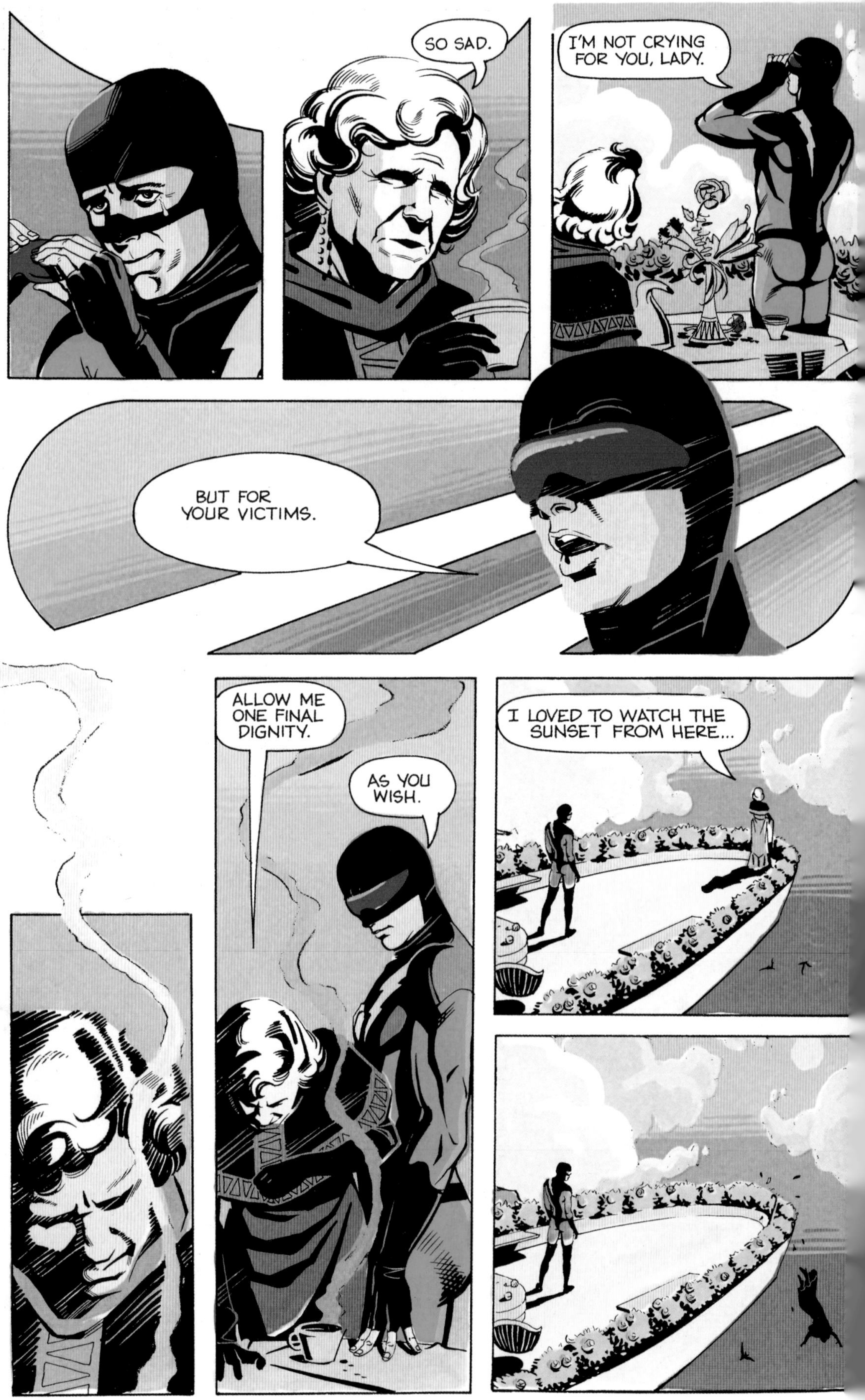
SO SAD.
I'M NOT CRYING FOR YOU, LADY.
BUT FOR YOUR VICTIMS.
ALLOW ME ONE FINAL DIGNITY.
AS YOU WISH.
I LOVED TO WATCH THE SUNSET FROM HERE...

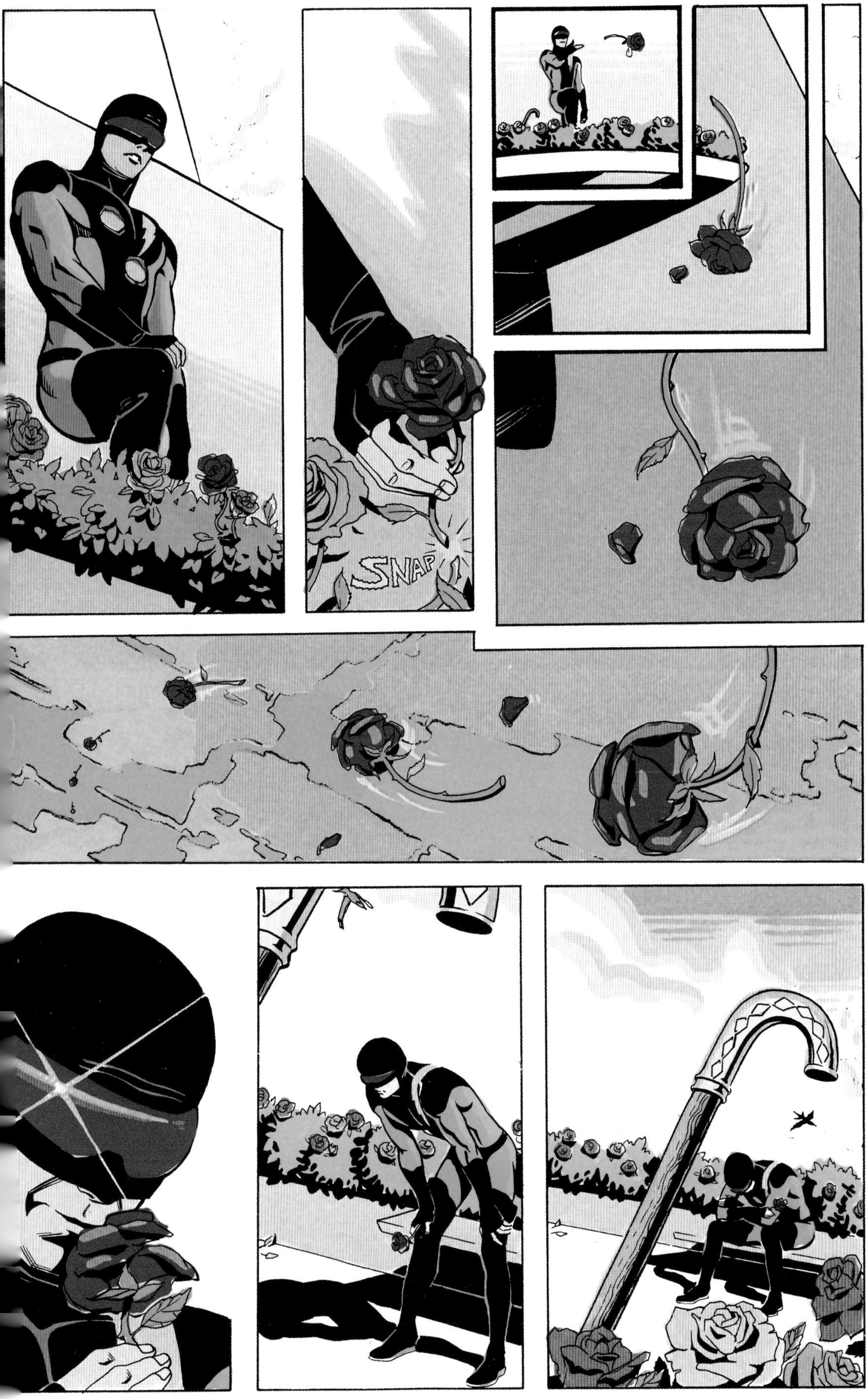
SNAP

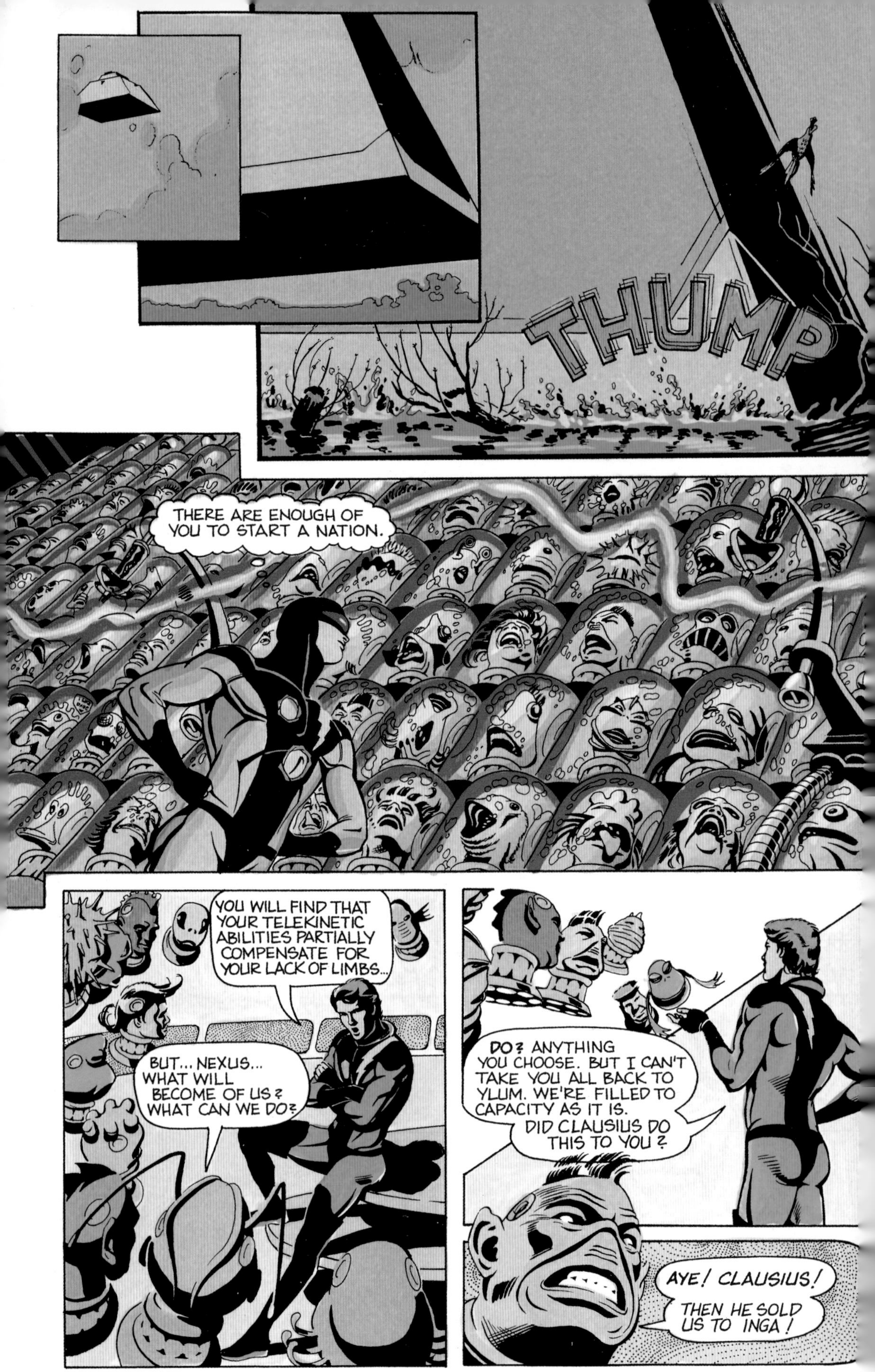
THUMP
THERE ARE ENOUGH OF YOU TO START A NATION.
YOU WILL FIND THAT YOUR TELEKINETIC ABILITIES PARTIALLY COMPENSATE FOR YOUR LACK OF LIMBS...
BUT... NEXUS... WHAT WILL BECOME OF US? WHAT CAN WE DO?
DO? ANYTHING YOU CHOOSE. BUT I CAN'T TAKE YOU ALL BACK TO YLUM. WE'RE FILLED TO CAPACITY AS IT IS.
DID CLAUSIUS DO THIS TO YOU?
AYE! CLAUSIUS!
THEN HE SOLD US TO INGA!

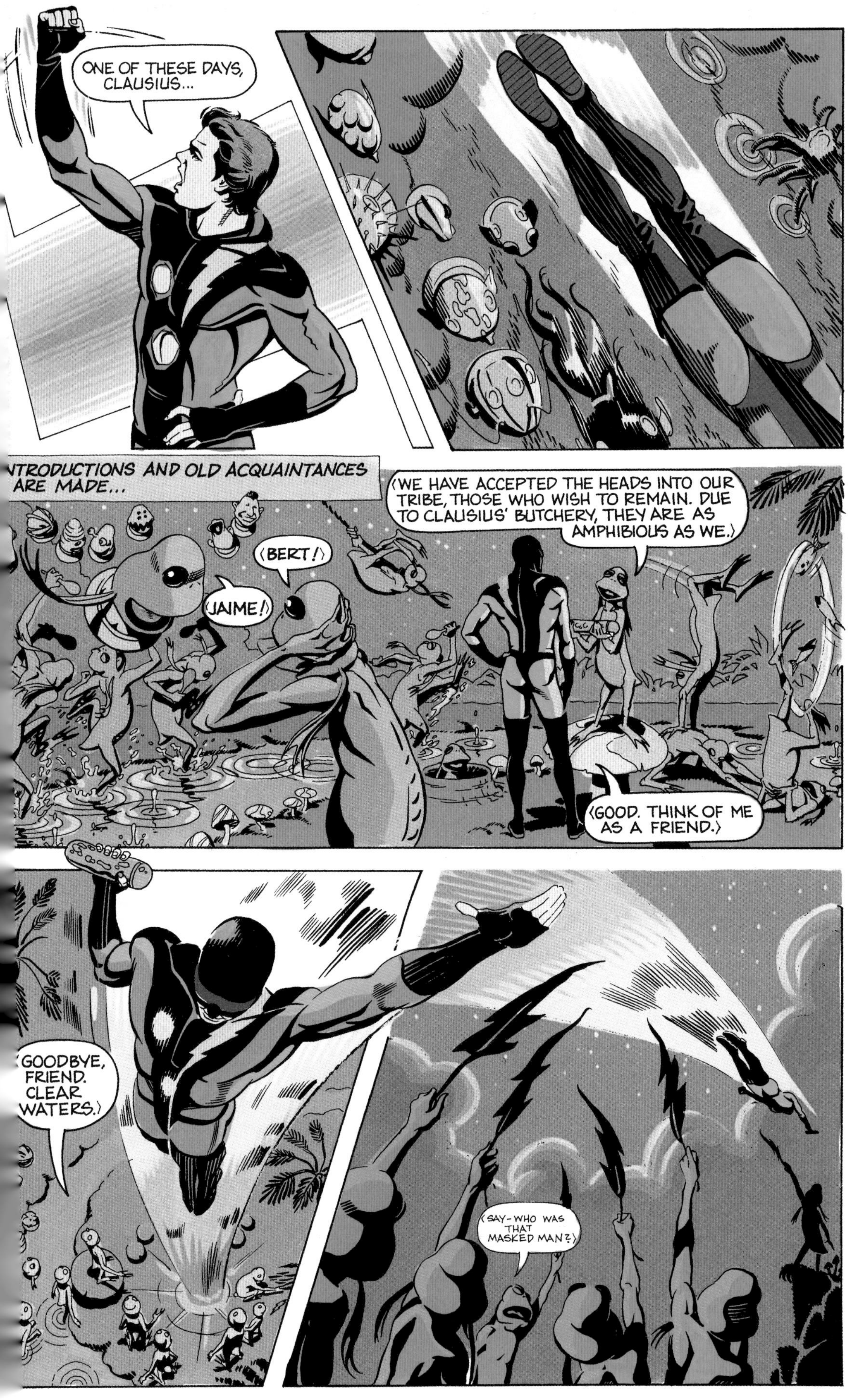
ONE OF THESE DAYS, CLAUSIUS...
NTRODUCTIONS AND OLD ACQUAINTANCES ARE MADE...
⟨WE HAVE ACCEPTED THE HEADS INTO OUR TRIBE, THOSE WHO WISH TO REMAIN. DUE TO CLAUSIUS' BUTCHERY, THEY ARE AS AMPHIBIOUS AS WE.⟩
⟨BERT!⟩
⟨JAIME!⟩
⟨GOOD. THINK OF ME AS A FRIEND.⟩
⟨GOODBYE, FRIEND. CLEAR WATERS.⟩
⟨SAY-WHO WAS THAT MASKED MAN?⟩

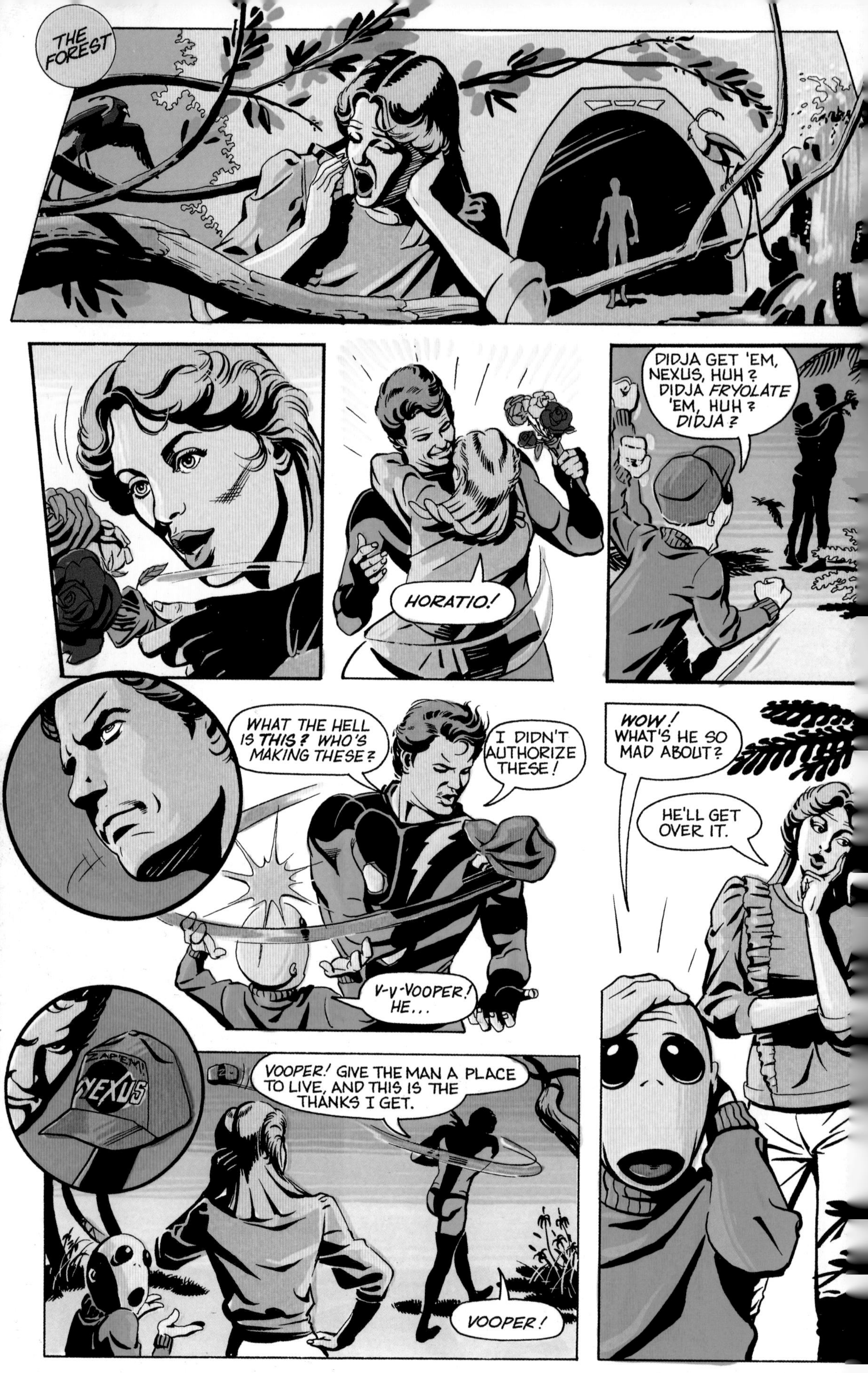
THE FOREST
HORATIO!
DIDJA GET 'EM, NEXUS, HUH? DIDJA FRYOLATE 'EM, HUH? DIDJA?
WHAT THE HELL IS THIS? WHO'S MAKING THESE?
I DIDN'T AUTHORIZE THESE!
V-V-VOOPER! HE...
WOW! WHAT'S HE SO MAD ABOUT?
HE'LL GET OVER IT.
ZAP'EM!
NEXUS
VOOPER! GIVE THE MAN A PLACE TO LIVE, AND THIS IS THE THANKS I GET.
VOOPER!

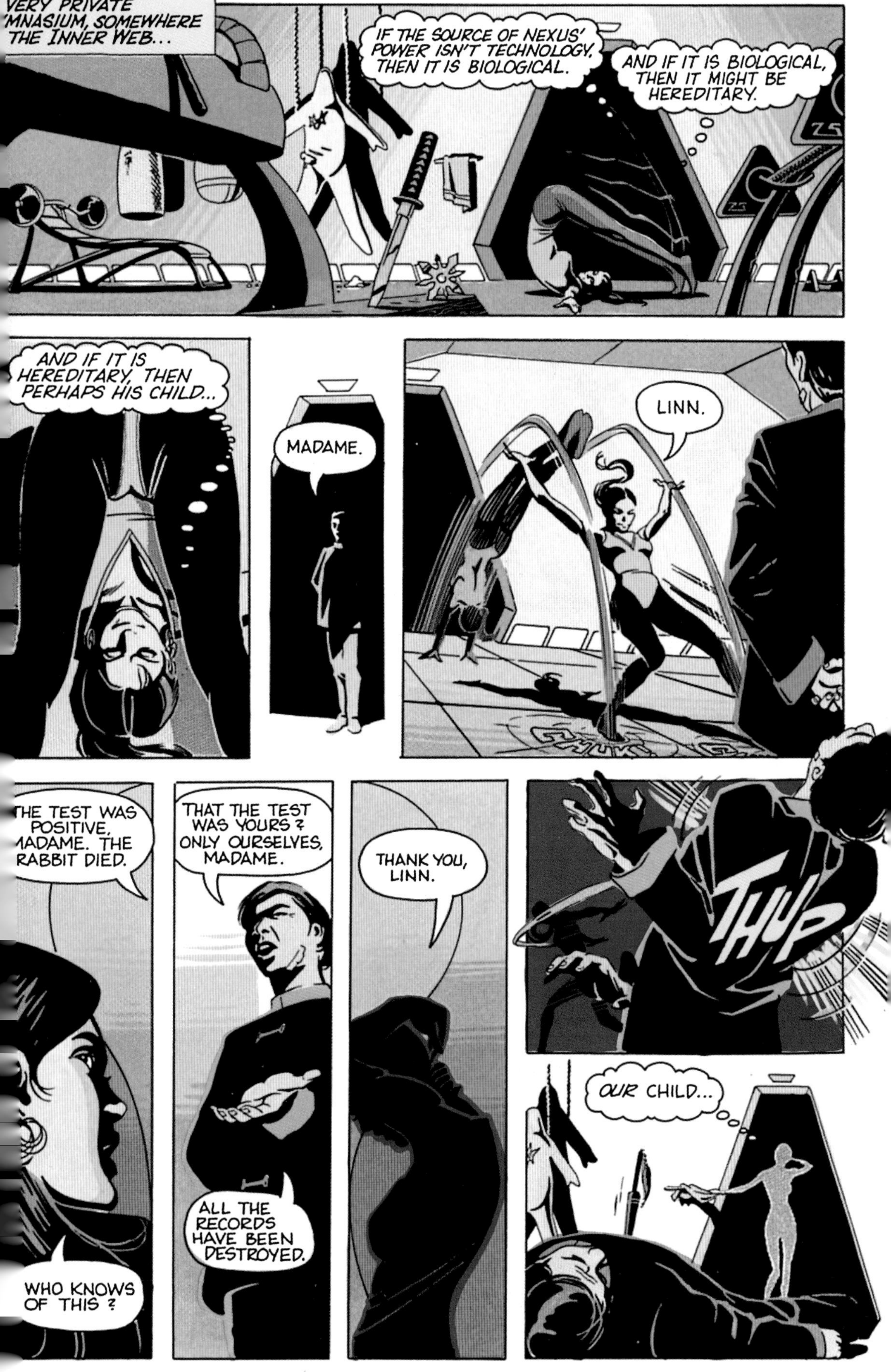
VERY PRIVATE
MNASIUM, SOMEWHERE
THE INNER WEB...
IF THE SOURCE OF NEXUS' POWER ISN'T TECHNOLOGY, THEN IT IS BIOLOGICAL.
AND IF IT IS BIOLOGICAL, THEN IT MIGHT BE HEREDITARY.
AND IF IT IS HEREDITARY, THEN PERHAPS HIS CHILD...
MADAME.
LINN.
HE TEST WAS POSITIVE, ADAME. THE RABBIT DIED.
WHO KNOWS OF THIS ?
THAT THE TEST WAS YOURS ? ONLY OURSELVES, MADAME.
ALL THE RECORDS HAVE BEEN DESTROYED.
THANK YOU, LINN.
THUP
OUR CHILD...

MIKE BARON
by Steve Rude

When I met Mike Baron on the steps of the Memorial Union at the University of Wisconsin in Madison, he was all business. A friend of his from a local newspaper that I had shown some art samples to had advised him to get ahold of me. I wanted to draw comics, Baron wanted to write them. It was in the fall of 1979 and I was in my early twenties, Baron a bit older. That meeting probably lasted no longer than fifteen minutes, but from that brief and unassuming moment, a partnership would begin that would carry us through several decades.

To think back on those early days in Madison is double-edged for me. I was perpetually poor and had to do jobs that weren't exactly my calling in life. If I wanted to meet with Baron and discuss our stories, I had to take a ten-mile bus ride to get there.

I remember one of our early meetings, before Nexus even had a name yet. We were meeting to discuss costume ideas, and Baron already had some specific thoughts, most notably the red visor and his yellow lightning bolt that overlaps his torso. It was winter at the time, and as was the norm back in those winter days, Baron would greet me with twenty layers of long johns and those thermal boot liners everyone in Wisconsin wears. He kept that apartment so cold that as I drew, I swear I could see my breath crystallize.

In spite of the cold, it was a productive evening, and everything was finalized by the end of the night. I had also missed the last bus, and that meant sleeping over in Baron's living room. Instead of turning the thermostat up a couple of degrees, he just threw a mountain of blankets at me and said, "See you in the morning, man!" At least the bus ride home was warm.

Once our exciting new series got underway, Baron would usually hand-deliver the scripts to my place. The procedure rarely varied. With Baron still sitting there, I would read these stories as a fan, laughing over the wacky stuff, and pausing at the traumatic moments that life can deliver to any of us—fictional or otherwise. Then I would go into my annoying "question mode" and begin dissecting the logic of the seemingly impossible feats Nexus was called

upon to do. No matter how seemingly implausible the moment, Mike's answers always made a believer out of me.

I never knew how Baron came up with this crazy stuff, just that he did, story after story, and that I had to illustrate it with the same intensity.

Many people don't know this, but Baron is an excellent chef. While most guys can barely get the directions straight on the back of a frozen meatloaf, Baron excels at the tastiest of dishes. When our character Judah Maccabee—or "Fred" as I call him—started entering cook-offs in our Nexus stories, I knew from where Baron had drawn the obvious reference.

One moment I'll never forget is the day Baron dropped by with a big package in his hands. "For me?" I thought. He said he was always giving his girl friends gifts —why not his guy friends? Inside the package was a sleek and sporty brown leather jacket. I was so touched I could hardly choke a proper thank-you. To this day, I can't recall another moment like that with a male friend.

Interestingly, throughout our entire sixteen-year run, despite its ardent following and having received many top industry awards, Nexus never seemed to translate to higher sales. Another inexplicable but common example of the "art versus commerce" phenomenon.

Entering the new millennium, Mike and I saw many changes take place within our beloved profession, and sadly, some were found wanting. Many of the last decade's most prolific and top creators seemingly fell out of favor with the new editorial preferences that came into play, and hard days fell upon Mike for far too long. Throughout it all, I saw him survive it with dignity.

In my recent conversations with Baron, he's been going full tilt to succeed in his longstanding quest to break into novel writing. That he has the skills for this is the least of my worries. Mike has now reached such a confidence level, through years of toiling the exposition vineyards, that I expect you'll be seeing his name among the Clancys and the Koontzs in short order.

STEVE RUDE
by Mike Baron

Who is this tall drink of water combining the aesthetics of Andrew Loomis, Jack Kirby, and Theodor Geisel, often in the same painting? Steve Rude is a dreamer, a romantic, and a natural-born storyteller—one of those kids who filled the margins of his schoolbooks and notepads with doodles. Dude's doodles always looked more finished than everyone else's. He grew up in thrall to Marvel Comics, Space Ghost, and Bruce Lee, so much so that he named his first son Brandon, after Brandon Lee.

One can't look at his work without comparing it to other great artists of the twentieth century, most notably Loomis and the progenitors of the modern heroic style: N. C. Wyeth, Maxfield Parrish, and Howard Pyle. Throw in Norman Rockwell, J. C. Leyendecker, and James Montgomery Flagg, and you have a synthesis of most of the great illustrators. That effortless glow, the Rembrandt-like lighting, the natural grace of the human figure did not come easily. Steve Rude was born with extraordinary talent and has devoted his life to bringing that talent to fruition. He has studied at the feet of great masters, and although he is a master himself, he has never stopped learning. He still takes painting classes today.

I was working at an insurance company in 1981 when an editor at a newspaper called me: "There's some guy down here trying to sell us drawings and he draws just like you." Obviously, the editor was no fit judge of art. What he meant was, we were both drawing comic-book superheroes, but comparing my work to Steve's was like comparing a Yugo to a Mercedes. I met Steve on the steps of the University of Wisconsin Student Union. One look at his portfolio and I gave up trying to turn myself into an artist. Even then he had a fluidity of line and imagination that beggared most comic-book artists of the time.

When we both lived in Madison, WI, we would go over the layouts for each issue of *Nexus* like Defense Department analysts examine aerial photos of North Korea's nuclear facilities. Dude wanted to know the details of our society down to the manufacturer of the manhole covers. He never faked anything, even though he was drawing a society that existed only in our imaginations. I always told him the past was key to the future. Everything old was new again. He drew inspiration for costume design from the Third Reich, Napoleon's troops, *Star Trek*, you name it. Mostly, he studied the natural form of things. He began keeping his logs in 1976. The logs are huge sketchpads, every page filled with drawings—often in color. Page after page of nothing but the human foot, as seen from all angles. Full-color studies of Degas, Renoir, John Singer Sargent, Alex Toth (lots of Toth), Kirby, Alex Raymond, and Joseph Clement Coll. I believe he's up to log number twenty-five now. When aspiring artists approach me at a convention, I show them Dude's sketchpads. They either shrink to microbe size and vanish, or a flare goes off in their brains and they hustle away to begin drawing. If you would be an artist, carry a sketchpad at all times, and fill it as if you're being paid.

Dude often attends social functions, only to sit in the corner carefully observing and drawing people in the room. This is a cool ploy, as people will eventually wander over to try and catch a glimpse of what's going down. Dude radiates a quiet intensity that acts as a gravitational field.

Steve's a gentle soul who loves animals and has a surprisingly robust sense of humor. Many times he has reduced me to stitches with his impressions. He is also fearless. He met the beautiful Jaynelle hitchhiking. How many people meet their wives hitchhiking? He's the only guy I know (other than myself) who challenges loudmouths in movie theaters. We each have our methods. Mine involve appearing quietly behind them and whispering in their ears. Dude's involve staring them down.

Steve Rude lives in Arizona with his wife, two kids, and a couple of cats.